IDENTITY AND SECESSION IN THE CARIBBEAN

IDENTITY AND SECESSION IN THE CARIBBEAN

Tobago versus Trinidad, 1889–1980

Learie B. Luke

University of the West Indies Press
Jamaica • Barbados • Trinidad and Tobago

University of the West Indies Press
7A Gibraltar Hall Road   Mona
Kingston 7   Jamaica
www.uwipress.com

11 10 09 08 07   5 4 3 2 1

Luke, Learie B.

Identity and secession in the Caribbean: Tobago versus Trinidad, 1889–1980 /
Learie B. Luke

p. cm.

Includes bibliographical references.

ISBN: 978-976-640-199-3

1. Secession – Tobago. 2. Tobago – Autonomy and Independence movements.
3. Tobago – History. 4. Self-determination, National – Tobago. 5. Trinidad and
Tobago – Politics and government. 1. Title.

F2116.L94 2007   927.983

Book and cover design by Robert Kwak.

Set in Spectrum and Minion.

Printed in the United States of America.

To Ivan, Leonora, Sharon and Sharlene Luke

Contents

Tables

Acknowledgements

A number of persons and institutions have contributed to the completion of this book, which is based on my doctoral dissertation. First, thanks to God for wisdom, understanding and good health to complete the project. To my loving, patient wife, Sharon Pierre-Luke, I owe an eternal debt of gratitude for her many years of unwavering support. Thanks to my five-year-old daughter, Sharlene, for helping me keep my priorities straight. My immediate and extended family – especially my mother and father, Leonora and Ivan Luke, my brother, Garry, and sisters, Cathy, Karen and Alicia – assisted me in every way possible. I could always count on their love, support and prayers. I sincerely appreciate the generous hospitality and encouragement from my in-laws, Oswald and Lynette Pierre and their family.

To Dr Selwyn H. H. Carrington, my dissertation supervisor, mentor, father, friend and fellow Tobagonian, I owe a debt of gratitude that I will never be able to repay. Without his guidance, encouragement, support, generosity and goodwill over the last decade, this work would not have made it to the publisher. I am also heavily indebted to the other members of my dissertation committee, Dr Ibrahim K. Sundiata, Dr Edna Greene Medford, Dr Vincent C. Peloso, Dr Emory J. Tolbert and Dr Colin A. Palmer, as well as Dr Joseph P. Reidy for their critique of what is the foundation of this work. Thanks to the University of the West Indies Press management and staff for their patience and guidance. I cannot sufficiently thank Dr Susan Craig-James and Dr Ralph Premdas for allowing me to use their scholarly work and ideas in my dissertation. I treasure the time they took to share their knowledge with me.

I would like to specially thank my many friends, particularly those at the Mary's Hill, Tacarigua, Curepe, Better Living Chapel, Capitol Hill, Metropolitan and Pecan Grove Seventh-Day Adventist churches for their prayers and hospitality over the years. To my very best friends, Clive "Frankie" Smith, Stephen Joseph and Aubrey Thompson, thanks for remaining my friends even when I became too busy with this work or with my professional responsibilities. I also appreciate the time Stephen took to proofread the draft even while he was completing his PhD studies. I must also mention Lloyd, Stephanie, Rhondy, Fiona, Aminah, Rholda, Princess, Lydia, Sylvia, Aunt Rose and Lyndon for their moral and spiritual support as well as loving assistance on innumerable occasions.

I am extremely grateful to Gwen Davis for her hospitality, kindness and friendship to my wife and me throughout my years at Howard University. Special thanks to Glenn Phillips, who was my master's thesis advisor at Morgan State University and he has also been a source of inspiration in many ways. The kindness of my friends in England: the Mendoza family, Jeanette and Martin, as well as Cathy Chance and Brother George, made my research trips to England enjoyable.

I am indeed grateful for the cooperation and assistance of the librarians, archivists and members of staff at the many repositories where I did research: in England, the Public Record Office, the British Newspaper Library, the London School of Economics and Political Science Library; in Trinidad and Tobago, the National Archives, the Main Library of the University of the West Indies, including the West Indiana and Special Collections, the Heritage Library, the Scarborough Regional Library, the Registry Section of CAST; and in the United States, the Library of Congress, Moorland-Spingarn Research Center and Founders Library at Howard University. Thanks also to all the men and women who gave of their valuable time, insight and recollections during oral interviews.

I am very grateful for the financial assistance provided me during my graduate school years from Morgan State University, Howard University, Caribbean Union College (now the University of the Southern

Caribbean), the Caribbean Union Conference of Seventh-Day Adventists, the Sasakawa Young Leaders Fellowship Fund and the Tobago House of Assembly. Without funding from these institutions, I could not acquire the training and conduct the research that has led to this book.

Finally, thanks to President Andrew Hugine and the other administrators at South Carolina State University for authorizing administrative leave for me to work on this project while I carried the responsibility of serving, first, as acting chairman of the Department of Political Science and History and, later, as the interim chairman of the Department of Social Sciences for the last five and a half years. I am especially grateful to the following deans and vice-presidents of academic affairs, who played a direct role in approving my leave requests and supporting my work: Dr John H. Simpson, Dr James Arrington, Dr Rita Teal, Dr Jo-Ann Rolle and Dr Leonard McIntyre.

Chapter 1

Historical and Conceptual Perspectives

The strained and sometimes antagonistic relationship between Tobago and Trinidad can be viewed in the context of identity and autonomy. Identity was the major buttress of Tobago's autonomy movement. This study discusses the significant issues in Tobago's history that led the inhabitants of the island to demand autonomy after Tobago was united with Trinidad in 1889 by British imperial decree. The work covers almost a hundred years of Tobago's history, from the period just before the union to 1980, when Tobago was granted internal self-government.

From its inception the union was problematic. Tobagonians soon became disenchanted over a number of issues and eventually demanded control of their own affairs. Their identity was a unifying force in their quest for autonomy. The ethno-national theory of identity argues that a regional group of people within a state develops a consciousness based on culture, common history and other factors that give it solidarity. Tobagonians' identity was constructed not only on the aspects they shared in common, but also on their view of the "other" – the central government in Trinidad and Trinidadians themselves – and the other's perception of them. Identity, enhanced in "we/they" antipathetic relations, served as the foundation for Tobago's autonomy movement.

Geographical Sketch and Historical Overview

The Caribbean island of Tobago is located approximately one hundred miles off the northern coast of South America and twenty miles northeast of Trinidad. The island borders the Caribbean Sea on its north-western shores and the Atlantic Ocean on its south-eastern coast. Tobago is 116 square miles (301 square kilometres) in area – 26 miles (42 kilometres) long and 7½ miles (12 kilometres) wide – while Trinidad is 1,864 square miles (4,846 square kilometres) in area.[1] Tobago is volcanic in nature, with a central chain of mountains called the Main Ridge extending almost two-thirds of the island's length, from the north-eastern point to the southwest. Its highest point, Pigeon Peak, is 1,804 feet (550 metres) above sea level.[2] The climate is subtropical, with an average daytime temperature of eighty-four degrees Fahrenheit (twenty-nine degrees Celsius). Thus the island was conducive to settlement by a number of groups.

The Carib Indians first inhabited Tobago. These Amerindians subsisted on agriculture, hunting and fishing. Manioc, or cassava, comprised their main diet, but they also cultivated corn and sweet potatoes. They lived in thatched structures called *ajoupas* and slept in cotton-filled hammocks. Their population (exact size unknown) was decimated by the spread of European diseases, wars and enslavement. As a result of their annihilation by the end of the fifteenth century, the Amerindians did not contribute to what later emerged as the Tobagonian identity.

The advent of the Europeans in Tobago – with Christopher Columbus's third voyage to the Americas in 1498 – was a significant juncture in Tobago's experience. Columbus sighted the island on 14 August but never set foot on it; however, from that time Europeans made various attempts to colonize Tobago. It was not until the beginning of the seventeenth century that major colonization efforts took place. The Spaniards never settled in Tobago, probably because of the absence of gold on the island. Later, Britain, France and Holland, and even the Courlanders of the tiny independent Baltic state of Latvia, fought for possession of the island.

One major reason for Tobago's attractiveness to these emerging powers was its strategic location, directly in the path of the trade winds that drove ships across the Atlantic. The island also possessed many safe harbours and watering places, and its land was fertile and had great potential for agricultural development. An intense international rivalry for control of Tobago began in 1626, when the Dutch settled the north-western end of the island, and continued until 1814, when Britain gained final and absolute possession of it by the Treaty of Paris.

British and French colonization was accompanied by plantation agriculture and the introduction of African slavery. Thereafter Tobago's society comprised a tiny minority of white settlers and an overwhelming majority of enslaved peoples of African descent. This ethnic mix has continued to the present time, and it formed the foundation on which Tobagonian identity was built. The English colonizers gave Tobago its British Protestant background, but the African population had the most pronounced effect on Tobagonian identity.

Plantation sugar-cane cultivation was the major economic activity until 1884. In the seventeenth and eighteenth centuries Tobago was an extremely prosperous sugar island; the saying "as rich as a Tobago planter" was then in vogue. But, even before the collapse of the sugar economy in 1884, Tobago lost pride of place, not only in the world market, in which the island became peripheral, but also in the eyes of British Colonial Office personnel. The Colonial Office oversaw the relationship between Britain and its colonies, set colonial policy and made recommendations for appointment of officers in the colonial service. To the British officials Tobago became a "miserable little colony", not worthy of much administrative concern. Notwithstanding, a vibrant peasantry emerged after 1884, comprising the formerly enslaved Africans, who were emancipated in 1838, and their descendants, who possessed land in freehold. The economic activities of this group, including fishing and agriculture, made Tobago self-sufficient in food production and a major exporter of food crops to neighbouring

Trinidad. The two islands were joined in 1889 to form the united colony of Trinidad and Tobago, and up to the 1950s Tobago was known as the bread basket of Trinidad.

Given this background, it is not surprising that Tobago remained an agricultural society. This agrarian factor was a significant component of the way Tobagonians viewed themselves and how others, especially Trinidadians, perceived them. Tobago's union in 1889 with the larger, more prosperous and eventually industrialized Trinidad provided a great boost to Tobagonian identity construction. Tobago entered the British-imposed union with a financially strapped government, a shattered sugar economy and severely reduced political status. Once a separate colony with more than a century of self-government vested in the elected Tobago House of Assembly, at union the island was stripped of its legislature and thus its political and administrative identity.

Tobago's separate identity as a British colony began in 1763, when the Treaty of Paris, which concluded the Seven Years' War between France and England, gave the British sovereignty over the island. By the Order in Council of 7 October 1763, King George III established Tobago as one of several independent, self-governing territories under the Grenada government, along with the Grenadines, Dominica and St Vincent. The governor of Grenada had purview over all the islands, but the General Council – apparently an inter-island body – and a resident lieutenant-governor managed each island directly. The first governor, General Robert Melville, called an assembly in each island. The Assembly shared responsibility for governance with the governor and the General Council.

Tobago was divided into seven parishes in 1763. In September 1767 twenty-eight proprietors petitioned Governor Melville for the formation of a council on the island. Six months later Tobago was granted local government, with the Island Council as its first administrative structure. Initially the Island Council was only an extension of the General Council, but by June 1768 Melville had upgraded it to a bicameral legislature. The upper chamber, called the Legislative Council, consisted of nine members appointed by the governor;

the lower chamber, the Legislative Assembly, was an elected body of thirteen members drawn from the various parishes and the town of Plymouth. The minority white population controlled the political as well as the economic sectors of the island.

In the period up to 1781 the dominant class had developed an identity separate and distinct from that of their peers in the other British colonies. They had their own political institution in the Assembly and, as part of the Windward Islands government, the administration in Tobago reported only to the governor. Through the Assembly, planters in Tobago had the power to make laws that affected their own lives and those of the majority of the population of Africans. These laws were subject only to approval and ratification by the governor and the British Crown. The planters prospered economically and had no reason to feel a sense of dependence on any group in the neighbouring islands, despite their common British ancestry; they were probably dependent only on their creditors in Great Britain. During this initial period of prosperity they could well have felt financially secure and self-possessed while, socially and culturally, they carried on the traditions and values of their homeland, the United Kingdom.

Tobago's administrative structure or identity did not change significantly after the French captured the island in 1781 and held on to it until 1793. The terms of surrender allowed the island's inhabitants to continue their system of government and administration of justice. The French demanded only loyalty to France, which could easily be feigned. When the British recaptured Tobago in 1793 during yet another war with France, Tobago again became a separate, independent government under a governor-in-chief. A council appointed by the Crown and a house of representatives called the General Assembly were re-established. To the dismay of the Tobago planters, however, British rule was short-lived. The Treaty of Amiens, signed on 20 March 1802, once again placed Tobago under French jurisdiction. However, Napoleon Bonaparte was not to lay claim to the planters' insincere loyalty for long. On 10 July 1803 England declared war on France and sent an invasion force to recapture Tobago. The

French surrendered, and the Treaty of Paris in 1814 finally ceded Tobago to Britain.

In the nineteenth century Tobago, along with the other West Indian colonies, experienced an economic decline that affected its independent political and administrative status. The downturn in the West Indian economy was precipitated by the reduced price of sugar on the international market. Given these diminishing fortunes, the British government made a significant retrograde change to the administrative arrangements for many of its colonies. In 1833, five years before the end of slavery, Tobago, Grenada and St Vincent were placed under the authority of the governor of Barbados, who was promoted to the rank of governor-general of a confederation that was an early version of the Windward Islands government. This was done partly because the British wanted to reduce the administrative cost of the colonies. Despite this action, Tobago's bicameral administrative structure was unaffected, and something like a ministerial government came into being with the development of an executive committee whose members were chosen from the legislature.

After emancipation, in 1838, Tobago's economic difficulties continued and were attended by political and administrative troubles. Apathy set in among the members of the Legislative Council, and many of them increasingly absented themselves from meetings. As a result, on the insistence of the Crown, in 1874 the Assembly passed an act amending the constitution, by which the house abolished itself and set up a single-chambered government called the Elected Legislative Council. This body consisted of fourteen members, six nominated by the governor and eight elected by a very limited franchise of white colonists. The planters greeted the first meeting of the Council, on 5 February 1875, with protest, denouncing the new arrangement as a violation of their rights.

The planters' protests changed to fear when the Belmanna Riots broke out in the Windward district in May 1876. The rioters were associated with disgruntled Barbadian immigrants who worked on an estate in Roxborough. By the end of the disturbance one of the rioters, Mary Jane Thomas, had been fatally shot by police officers; Corporal

Belmanna, who was sent to arrest the "incendiaries", had been killed and his body dismembered; the courthouse had been burned and workers from other estates had joined the disturbance. The governor sent a warship from Grenada to restore order.

Threatened by the growing militancy of the black population, the planters called for complete British control of the colony. They sensed growth of the power base of the Tobagonian masses, their own insecurity and inability to protect themselves and their property, and that these circumstances portended their ultimate political demise. Thus, on 6 June 1876 they voted to amend the constitution of the colony, changing the island's governance from a representative system to Crown Colony status, to take effect on 1 January 1877. By so doing, Tobago planters followed the Jamaican example of 1865, when after the Morant Bay Rebellion the planters voted in favour of Crown Colony government.[3] With this system of government the island retained its assembly, but the nominated members, whose loyalty was to the governor – and thus the Crown – became the majority. This enabled implementation of the policies of the Crown without effective resistance from the elected members, who now comprised the minority.

In 1878, two years after the Belmanna Riots, the lieutenant-governor of Tobago, Augustus Frederick Gore, suggested uniting Tobago with Trinidad for the sake of economy; the Tobago government was having difficulties meeting its financial commitments. The Colonial Office did not accept Gore's proposal immediately. However, Tobago's sugar cane–based plantation economy met its final demise in 1884 with the bankruptcy of the London finance house of A. M. Gillespie and Company. This firm had provided credit, marketing and shipping services to many of the island's estates. One year later, by the British Order in Council of 5 March 1885, Tobago, Grenada, St Vincent and St Lucia were merged, forming yet another version of the Windward Islands government. The planter elite was not in favour of this confederation, but the loose union of the islands did not severely affect their separate administrations and identities. In most cases such unions meant only that the islands shared a common governor. However, in 1889 Tobago's political identity had to adjust to a new reality when the island was united with Trinidad to form the colony of Trinidad and Tobago. Under this union Tobago's separate political identity and its autonomy as a self-governing territory were significantly compromised.

Between 1889 and 1899 the island, governed from Trinidad, retained only a financial board with legislative powers limited to local regulations. The board also retained authority over collection and expenditure of the island's very small revenue. Even worse, in 1899 Tobago lost the last vestiges of its semi-autonomous political identity when the island was made a ward, or administrative district, of the united colony of Trinidad and Tobago. The island then became administered as a local government jurisdiction under a senior government official called a warden.

The ward system had been introduced in Trinidad in 1849 to bring a certain measure of local government to the colony.[4] Wards were administrative divisions of a county; for example, at one time St George County in Trinidad had eighteen wards. The wardens were responsible for the general welfare and provision of facilities in their administrative districts. They were empowered to impose rates and taxes that were to be used for the development of their jurisdiction. Extension and maintenance of roads were major aspects of their duties. So was health care and, after 1870, when most schools in Trinidad were either owned or financially assisted by the central government, wardens were also in charge of schools.[5] The wardens became salaried officials in 1854 and their duties expanded, giving them purview over almost every aspect of life in their communities. In the 1860s their function as road officers was transferred to the public works department. "Otherwise, there was no significant cut in their powers until March 1946 when a system of county councils was introduced, each council to look after the whole county rather than have a warden in charge of each ward."[6] Grouping the wards into ward unions, each under a single warden, reduced the number of wardens. When Tobago became a ward, the total number of wards in the colony rose to thirty. "The wardens were virtual governors in their respective wards."[7]

The developments that led to Tobago's becoming a ward placed the island in an unenviable political and economic position. Trinidadian officials treated Tobago as a backward dependant. They also looked down on Tobagonians as inferior, rural people. Tobagonians saw Trinidadians in an equally negative light, as contemptuous and not genuinely interested in their welfare and the economic and social progress of their island. The tense relationship between the two islands over the years and the constant negative comparisons promoted the growth of a distinct Tobagonian identity. Although Tobagonians who viewed themselves as a distinct community made various calls for greater autonomy and even separation, the colony of Trinidad and Tobago became an independent unitary state in 1962 and a republic in 1976. Tobagonians' almost century-long demands for greater autonomy from the central government in Trinidad finally bore fruit in 1980, when the island was granted internal self-government within the republic. A democratically elected Tobago House of Assembly was re-established, and the first chairman and assemblymen took the oath of office in December 1980.

Identity and Autonomy

The words *identity* and *autonomy* are key terms in this study. *Identity* refers to the "growing sense among people that they belong naturally together, that they share common interests, a common history, and a common destiny".[8] It involves a feeling within a group that they share similarities that distinguish them from other groups. Identity is a consciousness among people who possess a sense of belonging to a certain locality, a solidarity or sentiment of loyalty to one another, and a cultural self-awareness based on common experiences and beliefs in certain traditions and values.[9]

Ralph R. Premdas, a scholar of identity and professor of public policy at the University of the West Indies, St Augustine, Trinidad, has developed a conceptual framework of Caribbean identity.[10] He argues that identity is born from collective group consciousness, produces a sense of belonging to a community of common descent and culture, and facilitates the solidarity vital for human existence.

Often this identity is formed in contradistinction to the claims of other groups to a similar sense of uniqueness so that in a real sense identity formation is a relational and comparative phenomenon locked into "we-they" antipathies which may be mildly benign or overtly hostile. To belong is simultaneously to include and exclude, to establish a boundary, even though this line of demarcation may be . . . fluid.[11]

Premdas further argues that while the need to belong is inherent in humans, the "matter" that becomes identity is "malleable and may well for the most part be manufactured in the imagination".[12] As a solidarity structure, identity serves important "instrumental functions" such as satisfying the need for survival. Thus "group membership and individual needs converge as very real and practical events, hardly imaginary".[13] Identity is a functional construct "apprehended in relation to some goal or project" and aimed at meeting instrumental and expressive needs.[14] Since each identity asserts claims and establishes boundaries, it is a potential source of strife.[15] In the Tobago case, identity was used as part of the justification and as a weapon for wresting a greater degree of autonomy from the central government in Trinidad.

The term *autonomy* is multi-dimensional. It can be construed to mean the devolution of central government power of one degree or another to a region within a state. A. N. R. Robinson, leader of the Tobago autonomy movement in the 1970s, argued that devolution is a "constitutional device whereby, in a unitary state, decentralization and participatory democracy can be promoted while maintaining the essentials of national unity".[16] Robinson believed that devolution involved granting "substantial powers" of the central government to a regional group, not merely decentralization through the classic forms of local government. *Autonomy* also refers to the right of a regional group to control its internal affairs. However, it has the larger meaning of the right of a people to self-determination, a definition that includes the right to political independence and statehood through constitutional means or secession. Tobagonians have on many occasions called for secession from Trinidad.

Over the years Tobagonians complained that their island had been neglected and underdeveloped by the central government in Port of

Spain, the capital of Trinidad. These complaints were indicative of the construction of a unique identity in the years after Tobago's union with Trinidad in 1889. Tobagonian identity, strengthened by the tensions between the two islands, played a significant role in the quest for autonomy from the central government. These demands for autonomy resulted in Tobago's being granted internal self-government in 1980. Hence, Tobagonian identity played a key role in Tobago's long-standing autonomy movement.

This work aims to show that identity was the major buttress of the autonomy movement. Second, it demonstrates that the problems about which Tobagonians complained in the 1970s – just prior to the granting of internal self-government – were long-standing, many dating from the time of union. Therefore, characterization of the autonomy movement should not be limited to the period of demands for internal self-government in the 1970s. This study also examines the charges of neglect and underdevelopment made by Tobagonians.

Many factors contribute to identity construction. The shared sense of community is its first factor. This corporate consciousness, which communicates a sense of belonging, is derived from membership in a group bound by various factors such as common descent, race, language, religion, culture and regional origin. Identity construction also involves the we/they dynamic. While humans live and find meaning in ethno-cultural groups to which they experience a sense of belonging through culture, shared values and experiences, "this membership is ineluctably cast in we-they antipathetic relationships with other communities. To belong at once entails to be included in a community and to be separated and differentiated from another or several."[17] The theory is that the human need for belonging can on one level be satisfied only in a "comparative if not appositional relationship of inclusion/exclusion" with other groups. Identity formation and sustenance is relational, often appositional and conflictual. One part of the we/they dynamic is the invention of the other.[18] At times this dynamic may be benign in relation to the other, but, given different circumstances, it may become combative.

There are also primordial bases of identity construction, including the concepts of homeland, historical memory, language, culture and race. Homeland is a major primordial base; colonial legacies contributed to identity formation in the Caribbean by helping to establish "homelands", or territories. The administrative boundaries established by the former colonial powers barely went beyond the shorelines of each island colony. Therefore, during the colonial period the islands had very little interaction with each other in terms of trade but rather dealt directly with Britain, the mother country. This produced strong insular identities and parochialism.[19] The administrative boundaries formed the perimeters of the homelands of the Caribbean peoples, and "these insular spaces, narratives and myths would be infused with memories constructed out of the recent painful past and attached to the land rendering it sacred and historical".[20] As a result, forging common bonds was difficult, even when islands of such close proximity as Tobago and Trinidad were merged. There was no trickle-down effect from administrative union to organic union. The peoples in the united territories saw each other as different groups possessing distinct identities.

Connected with homeland is the concept of historical memory. In a union of unwilling partners, the history of the relationship between two federated entities may be replete with examples of mutual disaffection. Such memories can become the centre of self-definition for one or both of the partners. "How the history is narrated by each side constitutes a self-justifying story constructed in the service of each island's interests."[21]

Language is also a crucial part of identity. In fact, it "constitutes the single most characteristic feature of separate ethnic identity".[22] Tobagonian dialect has never been used overtly as a rallying point of unity and common action; it has in fact been associated with backwardness, lack of education and lack of intelligence. However, it is clear that one of the identifying marks of Tobagonians vis-à-vis Trinidadians is that the former are almost bilingual because of their ability to communicate in a vernacular that is difficult for Trinidadians to understand.[23]

Culture is another aspect of identity construction. A people's customs, music, dance, festivals, food, visual arts, kinship patterns and folklore are configured in a cultural mould to give a unique shape to their identity.[24] And race is yet another aspect of the social analysis of identity. In Tobago, people of African descent comprise the majority of the population. While this demographic dominance forms a basis of unity, it is also featured in identifying the other – namely the multi-ethnic Trinidadian population, made up of Africans, East Indians, Chinese, Lebanese, Syrians, Europeans and a variety of people of mixed heritage.

Grievances form a secondary basis of identity construction. In Tobago these were articulated against a central government that was seen as distant and insensitive. Finally, identity construction theory includes the concept of a "trigger factor".[25] This is an event that leads to mobilization of forces that demand an increased share of public goods and services, devolution of power and, in some instances, secession.

Tobagonian Identity before the Twentieth Century

Over the years Tobagonians have viewed themselves as a distinct people with a unique culture. Their identity – born out of ethnic homogeneity (over 90 per cent of Tobagonians are of African descent), cultural commonality and a strong sense that they and their native island have been disadvantaged in the forced relationship with Trinidad – created a self-consciousness that led them to demand better treatment and greater administrative and political autonomy from the central government. Professor David Niddrie, who conducted a detailed land utilization study of Tobago in 1958 and who later became a keen observer of Tobagonian culture, contends that whatever differences there may be among Tobago's inhabitants are buried beneath "that common pride in being Tobagonian".[26]

In her dissertation, Susan Craig-James, a Tobagonian researcher and sociologist, provides an image of the Tobagonian before the turn of the twentieth century.[27] The vast majority of Tobagonians were formerly enslaved Africans and their descendants. They struggled valiantly for their rights and freedoms against the oppressive and unfair practices of the planter class. Though initially denied access to land, they exhibited a great desire for property and real estate, and by 1900 had acquired them to a significant extent. In the period after emancipation Tobagonians viewed the white ruling class as the enemy, who imposed burdensome taxes and unfair regulations to thwart their aspirations to be truly in charge of their own destiny. They were willing to protest, even riot and strike, against injustice. Tobagonians were energetic, hardworking and resourceful and found creative ways to make a living on and off the estates. They refused to become agro-proletarians, solely dependent on wage labour. By 1900 they had become a thriving peasantry whose produce changed the entire dynamics of the Tobago economy, from one dominated by sugar, molasses and rum to one in which livestock, fruit, wood products, vegetables and ground provisions were predominant. And by 1900 they were exporting the bulk of their produce to Trinidad.

Craig-James further shows that a significant proportion of the adult population was married and that the vast majority of Tobagonians adhered to a Protestant faith. Many members of the labouring class retained African-derived beliefs and practices such as obeah, which were syncretized with European religious systems. Over 40 per cent of the population was literate and, because of the presence and activities of Chief Justice Sir John Gorrie from 1889 to 1892 – he believed that the law should benefit not only the elite – Tobagonians had been exposed positively to the legal system and had become aware of their rights under the law. However, most of them were on the bottom rung of the socio-economic ladder, and some were willing to migrate to Trinidad in search of better economic opportunities for themselves and their families.

Tobagonian identity is closely related to the quest for autonomy. Tobago is a region within a state and within a former colony. Thus Tobagonian identity developed within the context of other groups in the state and asserted itself against the central government in Trinidad. Consequently, Tobagonians exhibit the ethno-national identity type.

Tobago's Identity Type and the Autonomy Continuum

The ethno-national identity type best fits the Tobago case. This identity emerges from sub-state localities with a culture that "imparts a special and unique quality to life".[28] Associated with tightly knit societies "that have mechanisms of closure to outsiders", this parochial identity asserts itself "antagonistically against a central governmental authority. This locality is seen as sacred and pure, a place of freedom and morality, to be protected from the corrupting influence of unwelcome outsiders."[29]

Ethno-national identity is formed in the context of one or more of the following: a large territory, a separate island, remote areas, and populations divided along racial, geographical and cultural lines. Local identity is enmeshed in a web of "interpersonal primary and secondary face-to-face relations in the family, neighbourhood, and community that comprehend and promote the totality of a unified consciousness that is relatively free from internal challenges and dissonances".[30] The Tobagonian collective self is an excellent example of ethno-national identity.

Tobagonian identity and the island's autonomy are inextricably linked. An examination of these issues in Tobago leads one to conceive of an autonomy continuum. Historian Carl Campbell contends that, after union, Trinidadians and Tobagonians perceived the problems of the colony from either an integrationist or a separatist viewpoint.[31] In the context of education in both islands, the integrationists – mainly Trinidadian officials – saw Tobago as an integrated ward of the colony, while Tobagonians viewed their homeland as a separate island. The integrationist viewpoint dominates the historical records between 1898 and 1925. In the education reports for that period, Tobago schools were presented as being as good – or as bad – as schools of "remote rural areas of Trinidad, and as such no alarm was to be raised if they were not as good as the Port-of-Spain schools".[32] In addition, "there had always been a separatist point of view, held almost exclusively by Tobagonians, but not always well articulated".[33]

Campbell's framework is enlightening; however, it presents an integrationist/separatist dichotomy for Trinidad and Tobago. In this work, the opposing perspectives are expanded into a continuum. Thus it is possible to conceive of an autonomy continuum: a fluid line along which the major Tobagonian spokespersons – British, colonial and other officials and groups, as well as rank-and-file commentators – move, but mostly stand, in their articulation and actions concerning the relationship between Tobago and Trinidad. The autonomy continuum allows for shifts in positions from the integrationist perspective, on the right-hand side of the continuum, to the separatist perspective, on the left. The idea of a continuum allows individuals or organizations from England and both islands to be labelled as integrationists or separatists. It also permits a person or entity to change positions, either near one end of the continuum or from one end to the other. Some individuals can also be viewed as centrists, with leanings to one side or the other.

The integrationists saw Tobago and Trinidad as one indissoluble unit. To them, Tobago was just like any other rural region in Trinidad. Integrationists believed that Tobago's isolation was no more of a challenge than that of the remote districts of Trinidad. They trusted the government to take responsibility for the welfare of the minor partner in the union. Integrationists had faith in the trickle-down effect of national development; they believed that economic, political and social development at the centre would expand equitably to the peripheral parts of the union, including Tobago.

The separatists, also referred to as autonomists, occupied several positions on the left-hand side of the continuum. They were not necessarily secessionists, but viewed Tobago as a distinct community with a unique culture. They emphasized the island's physical separation from Trinidad and its attendant inconveniences. They all demanded that the central government make concessions to Tobagonians because of Tobago's isolation from the centre of government and power. However, the separatists did not form a monolithic group. Some simply called for more government services on the island and an increase in Tobago's share of the national economic pie. Others demanded that the government give priority to the economic and social development of the island. Still others requested greater Tobagonian representation in the corridors of power. Separatists who were mid-left of centre demanded significant devolution of government power and a separate administrative structure in Tobago, controlled by Tobagonians. Those on the extreme left of the continuum would be satisfied only with secession and independence from Trinidad. Sometimes the claims of the separatists simultaneously occupied several notches on the continuum. Separatists also demonstrated ambivalence as they moved farther away from the centre of the autonomy continuum.

Chapter 2

Tobagonian Identity Construction

Tobago and Trinidad were united as a result of Britain's desire for administrative economy and control after Tobago's prosperity, like that of the other West Indian colonies, had diminished severely in the latter part of the nineteenth century. The decline in profitability of the sugar colonies resulted from competition on the British market from foreign sugar, especially subsidized European beet sugar, after the passage of the 1846 *Sugar Duties Equalization Act*. This legislation led to the admission of foreign sugar into Britain with increasingly lower tariffs until customs charges for sugar produced in the colonies and for foreign sugar were equalized. The 1884 bankruptcy of the finance house of A. M. Gillespie and Company led to the final demise of the Tobago sugar industry. Thereafter government revenue in Tobago, which depended heavily on customs duties and property taxes, fell to an abysmal level. "The failure of revenue, even at minimal levels of expenditure, led to the abolition of the Tobago Government and the annexation of Tobago to Trinidad."[1]

The union was not organic. Trinidadian legislators viewed Tobago as a financial burden, and the Tobago political elite was sceptical about any economic advantage that might accrue from the union. Before it was finalized, Tobago's legislators unsuccessfully requested that the Crown promise to dissolve the union if it did not prove beneficial to the island. The 1889 union left Tobago with limited autonomy, vested in a financial board that had authority over the collection and expenditure of local revenue. However, complete unification occurred in 1899, when Tobago was made a ward, or administrative district, of the united colony of Trinidad and Tobago; thus the island totally lost its separate political and administrative identity.

Complaints arose almost immediately and continued to bedevil the relationship between Tobagonians and the government seated in Trinidad. It did not help that Tobago was separated from Trinidad by twenty miles (thirty-two kilometres) of ocean. The island's isolation from the centre of government, its depressed economy and its rural character, and the fact that during the first twenty-five years of complete union its local nominated representatives to the Legislative Council did not – or could not – attend council meetings held in Trinidad, did not augur well for Tobago and its people. Their interests and concerns were not well represented in the corridors of power. The unreliability of sea communications between the two islands and the fact that the legislators were not remunerated were disincentives for sacrificing two to three days per week to attend meetings in Port of Spain. At the time of union, Tobago did not even have telegraph communication.[2]

"Why Nearby Tobago Is So Different"

The generally unsympathetic response of government officials to grievances raised by Tobagonians sharpened the distinctions between the two populations and enhanced the we/they antipathies between the people of the twin-island state. Every aspect of cultural difference or uniqueness, every complaint about unfair treatment by the central government, every negative perception of Trinidadians about Tobagonians and vice versa imperceptibly led to the development and entrenchment of a Tobagonian identity vis-à-vis Trinidadians.

Trinidadians saw Tobagonians – as well as people from the other smaller Caribbean territories – as small-islanders, and thus inferior. The late Reverend William H. T. Carrington, an educator and Anglican clergyman, contended that the Trinidadian "feels he is superior" to Tobagonians.[3] The Trinidadians' attitude was based on their perception of Tobago as a largely rural community.[4] The people in Port of Spain believed they were superior to those in Moruga, a rural area in southern Trinidad, but the Morugans felt superior to Tobagonians. This urban/rural dichotomy was not unique to Trinidad and Tobago; up to the 1970s, people in Port of Spain saw everyone living beyond their city limits as rural.[5]

All in all, Trinidadians exhibited an air of superiority vis-à-vis the peoples of other Caribbean territories. Tobago's agrarian nature and stunted development made the island and its inhabitants easy targets for negative stereotyping.

> Until the early 1950s, Tobago was without electricity, limited to one small secondary school, and the way of life was based on the social pattern of a small agrarian community. Exposure to urban life was small, knowledge of events in Trinidad was remote. As migration from Tobago to Trinidad increased, the Tobagonian became caricatured as a dumb, awkward "country bumpkin". Indeed, the relationship between the Tobagonian and the Trinidadian was once so acute that as recently as the 1930s intermarriage was virtually taboo.[6]

Such was the attitude of Trinidadians to Tobago and its people. And other factors contributed to the perception of Tobagonian inferiority as well.

The fact that Tobagonians spoke a vernacular also made Trinidadians feel superior to them.[7] Tobagonians could be unilingual or bilingual, but whether they used formal English or spoke in dialect, all Tobagonians understood the vernacular to some extent. Besides the language factor, Tobagonians were viewed as darker in complexion and their women were seen as "fat" and "ugly". Thus Trinidadians accepted the racial stereotypes that were current even after the mid-twentieth century (not that Tobagonians did not), and they associated Tobago's purer African heritage with being uncivilized, and therefore inferior to Trinidad's more cosmopolitan mixed population.[8] There was also a feeling that

Tobagonians were not qualified or capable of holding high government positions, although "often it [has] proven to be the opposite".[9]

Government officials certainly imbibed the philosophy that Tobago was rural and backward and its people inferior, and they did not want to be associated with the island. Civil servants in Trinidad viewed a transfer to Tobago as a demotion and a form of punishment.

> On the one hand, whenever officers learned of the possibility of a transfer to Tobago, they would develop a high propensity for a variety of illnesses. Of course, many civil servants objected to being transferred for entirely rational reasons, for example, the higher cost of living in Tobago, the problem of schooling, family dislocation and a host of domestic causes. On the other hand, Government met this difficulty in getting officers to Tobago by resorting to sending them there as punishment. Thus working in Tobago acquired an aspect of involuntary exile or "banishment" as it is called among civil servants.[10]

If Trinidadians saw Tobago and its residents as inferior, Tobagonians came to view their neighbours as "Trikkidadians" – cunning and crafty in the negative sense. Such we/they antipathies sharpened as the stereotyping grew. Reverend Carrington articulated the Trikkidadian image: Trinidadians "easily stoop to anything while a Tobagonian will not easily accept what Trinidadians will stoop to". Trinidadians were seen as untrustworthy people. Tobagonians were taught to treat them with suspicion, because one could not always rely on what they told you – "Treat what they tell you with a pinch of salt," declared Carrington.[11] Roger D. Abrahams, a researcher who studied the residents of the village of Plymouth, in north-western Tobago, also noted that Tobagonians held suspect the attitudes and values of Trinidadians, "whom they regard as thieves and, in personal relationships, dangerous and unpredictable".[12]

Despite the fact that the characteristics and culture of Tobagonians have changed over the years, the "rustic, idyllic honesty" found among Tobagonians was not characteristic of Trinidadians. This "rustic naiveté" – their "honest, caring" ways – may be a by-product of their isolation.[13] The "conman/smartman" image associated with Trinidadians was for a long time not found in Tobago, where the people had a reputation for "hard work, dependability and [a] high level of capability – high level in the public service".[14] Tobagonians came to hold Trinidadians suspect and definitely did not trust the central government to act benevolently towards them without prodding. Requests for funding of projects in Tobago tended to be met with the incredulous attitude "How much could Tobago need?" – that is, development needs in Tobago could never be great.[15]

Tobagonian identity should not be viewed only in the clinical, academic sense of something invented or fabricated. Nor should it be characterized as just the product of shrewd politicians whose goal was manipulation of the masses. In interactions between Tobagonians and Trinidadians during the twentieth century, both groups commented on their differences, which were reported in the press as well. Joe Radcliffe, a foreigner who "discovered" Tobago "purely by accident", wrote an article in the *Sunday Mirror* in 1964 cataloguing the virtues of the island and its people.[16] Radcliffe had gone to Tobago on a two-day business trip and was pleasantly surprised by the "riotous exuberance" of the flora and fauna and the "amazing healthiness" of the people. Jeff Cooke, manager of the Arnos Vale Hotel, explained to him that the inhabitants' health was due to the "wholesome air, the sea and the abundance of food".[17] Radcliffe also observed that there were few automobiles to cause pollution, and that Tobagonians rarely used canned foodstuffs.

Radcliffe noted that the people were law-abiding citizens: "crime [was] virtually unknown", to the extent that Neville Miranda, manager of the Della Mira guesthouse, boasted, "Hardly anyone ever bothers to lock his door in Tobago."[18] Concerning the nature of the people, Radcliffe stated,

> Tobago virtually reeks hospitality [and] this unaffected warmth and genuine cordiality is not confined to any particular social level. The rich and the poor, peasant and socialite all possess it. [In comparison] the crude, disgusting waitresses, store clerks and civil servants who serve Trinidadians with a bored "I-am-doing-you-a-favour" attitude, can take an example from their Tobagonian brothers.[19]

Columnist Horace Leighton-Mills, who wrote regularly for the *Express* newspaper, echoed Radcliffe's observations. Leighton-Mills, a Trinidadian, had migrated to "this beautiful Caribbean tourist isle [Tobago, in 1959] from the fast-moving Trinidad where there is no respect for limb or law and where many people ignore the line of demarcation between meum and teum – mine and yours".[20] In a 1976 article he described Tobagonians, "when you get to know them", as "beautiful in their ways as the land of their birth".[21] When he first migrated to Tobago, Leighton-Mills was surprised by the law-abiding nature of Tobagonians:

> A whole family would leave on a Sunday or public holiday to spend a whole day on one of the many picturesque beaches and not only leave their doors unlocked but leave them also sprawling open and return to find everything intact. My comment to a Tobagonian friend who had invited me on my advent here to spend a day by the seaside with his family, that he was forgetting to secure his home elicited the proud reply: "This is Tobago. You are not in thieving Trinidad. Nobody steals here."[22]

Leighton-Mills also pointed out that Tobagonians comprised a very close-knit society: "the stranger would soon learn that everybody in Tobago is related by blood".[23]

A 1972 newspaper article written by columnist Therese Mills also emphasized the long-standing we/they antipathies between Trinidadians and Tobagonians. The article dealt with the issue of making tourism development a priority in Tobago. Mills pointed out that Tobagonians were sceptical of big business because of the threat of foreigners buying land on the island to build hotels and recreational facilities: "Many Tobagonians are fiercely jealous of their land and anxious that it should not fall into the hands of exploiting foreigners. One can easily understand their pride of possession."[24] She argued that Tobagonians were somewhat xenophobic, but her statement revealed more about what Tobagonians thought of Trinidadians than their attitude towards foreigners from distant lands:

> The village people of Tobago do not speak easily to strangers, and everyone is a stranger, especially if they are from Trinidad. Tobagonians think that Trinidadians laugh at them as "country bookies," and as a result they are always on the defensive. Whether as children in school in Trinidad or later in adult life, the born Tobagonian is always on the mark and ready to take on anyone who is critical of his homeland. This attitude is the result of years of sensing the Trinidadian's air of superiority and the patronizing

treatment of the island purely as a "ward" and forgetful of its earlier status. Tobagonians today are, therefore, insisting on strong local government so that they may plan the future of Tobago as they think fit.[25]

Mills's comments also address the issue of mechanisms of closure to outsiders that are found in regions with ethno-national identities such as Tobago. If one was not a Tobagonian one was considered a stranger, not a member of the community.

Similarly, David Niddrie argued that the extremely small proportion of East Indians in Tobago was not only due to the fact that Tobago could not afford East Indian immigration after slavery ended, but also because Tobagonians have treated badly those who migrate from Trinidad. Niddrie explained (inaccurately) that in 1960 there were no East Indians in Tobago and in 1980 there were fewer than twenty families, partly because "the proud independent people of Tobago look upon East Indians as 'strangers' despite the fact that the two islands are one country with a single citizenship, and in several instances have made life so uncomfortable for successful East Indian smallholder vegetable growers and merchants that they have returned to Trinidad".[26] There is a certain contradiction between this view of Tobagonians' apparently negative attitude towards strangers and their reputation for hospitality. If Tobagonians suspect that visitors may have designs on their patrimony, their hospitality can quickly transform into hostility. A 1969 newspaper article described Trinidadian businessmen as "foreigners bleeding Tobago dry".[27] Thus, East Indians who maintained their separate identity were ostracized, but those who integrated as Tobagonians were considered members of the island's community.

Trinidadian political scientist Selwyn Ryan also noted the differences between Trinidad and Tobago and their peoples – those factors that support we/they antipathies and enhance Tobagonian identity vis-à-vis Trinidadians. At the time of his study (1985), Tobago's society was not as stratified as Trinidad's. In both islands wealthy Europeans occupied the top rung of the social ladder. In Tobago, however, below that level there was little social or ethnic differentiation, while Trinidad had (from the nineteenth century) a significant middle class of near-whites and mulattoes and a majority of Africans and

Indians at the bottom of the social pyramid.[28] Ryan pointed out that Tobago is largely a folk (peasant) society made up of a vast majority of Africans, while Trinidad is more cosmopolitan, with East Indian, Chinese, Lebanese and Portuguese inhabitants.

In addition to population differences, the two islands had significantly different religious configurations. From colonial times to the arrival of the French in the late eighteenth century and beyond, Catholicism remained dominant in Trinidad. Ryan's study found that East Indians in Trinidad also practised Hinduism and Islam, both of which were absent from the Tobago religious scene. Protestantism had a strong hold on the population of Tobago, with 90 per cent of the population belonging to one Protestant denomination or another, although Protestant groups in the country as a whole constituted only 35 per cent of the population.[29] Tobagonians viewed themselves as staunchly religious but saw Trinidad as a secular society, and Trinidadians as a people who loved parties and revelling.

Tobagonian Eric Roach wrote a newspaper article in the early 1970s depicting Tobagonian identity and its relation to the demand for autonomy. The article, titled "Why Nearby Tobago Is So Different", provides an insider's analysis. Roach argued that the differences between Tobagonians and Trinidadians lay in Tobago's "history as well as in its culture and character".[30] Unlike Trinidad, Tobago had never undergone Spanish colonization. Furthermore, Tobago had had self-governing institutions since 1763. Trinidad, after it was captured by the British in 1797, was made a Crown Colony controlled directly from Britain. Roach observed that the majority African population of Tobago also set it apart from Trinidad's mixed population: "The island belonged to the black man" and "Tobago lacks almost entirely the creole mixed-blood group so numerous in and around Port-of-Spain – the issue of many races with a wide range of intermediate brown complexions".[31] Tobago was different also because of its economic activities. By the end of the nineteenth century, sugar-cane cultivation had been virtually abandoned on the island while sugar production remained a mainstay of the Trinidadian economy.

The development and persistence of a landed peasantry, whose possessions accorded status and prestige in the community, was a major difference between Tobagonians and Trinidadians. "In the early years of the century, a man owning 25 acres was considered a person of substance. He grew cocoa or coconuts as a staple crop, cultivated vegetable gardens and reared meat animals on tether."[32] Roach further contended that the independent peasantry bred a "civilisation of its own based on the puritan ethic, a few half-remembered African cultural practices, hard work and peasant tenacity". Protestantism was central to Tobago's smaller communities, in which churches and denominational schools served as the hub of village life: "The stolid village life is strongly underpinned by the Puritanism of the Anglican, Methodist and Moravian sects. Each village centres on church and church school where the parson and school-master once had absolute pride of place in the village hierarchy."[33] Tobagonians possessed high moral and ethical values, which they claimed Trinidadians lacked. Bishop's High School, the only secondary school on the island for many decades, "elevated the sons and daughters of the peasant proprietors first into clerkships, later into the universities and professions, and thrust the island's strong peasant conscience and integrity into the Trinidad administration".[34]

Moreover, Tobagonians were different from Trinidadians because the latter displayed a condescending attitude towards the former. "If Trinidadians resent the foreign boss presence, Tobagonians are offended when Trinidadians going there [to Tobago] to work, laud it over them."[35] Roach's comment of the 1970s was based on a long tradition. In 1960 one Tobagonian, "Disenchanted", wrote scathingly of his reaction to Trinidadians' attitude of superiority: "We do, of course welcome Trinidadian visitors. We delight to see them parade through Scarborough in their hot shirts and tight pants, but we are not enamoured of their falsely condescending attitude and arrogant manner."[36] Fitzroy Fraser, writing for the Jamaican newspaper *Gleaner* in February 1961, also noted the "emotional and psychological factors" evident in the uneasy relationship between Tobagonians and Trinidadians. Tobagonians believed "Trinidadians don't like them and always make 'picong' and 'fatigue' at their expense. And now and then, they go on to add that, to tell the truth, they don't like Trinidadians either".[37]

Coupled with Tobagonians' resentment of their neighbours' air of superiority, the former also chafed at the central government's policies on development in Tobago, which were made without their consultation. Roach explained that Tobagonians believed the government's policy of developing tourism in Tobago by allowing construction of "monstrous hotels on the beaches" to be wrong. Tobagonians also disagreed with the position held by Trinidadian tourism officials that tourists prefer foods they are accustomed to, not the local cuisine, and further that tourists do not like to fraternize with "natives". Those assumptions did not apply to Tobago – tourists loved to eat the local food and fraternize with the taxi drivers, "beach boys" and other locals. Tobagonians also resented the fact that hoteliers "put out of their hotels local people whom their guests have invited in for a meal or a drink".[38] In addition they claimed that the tourism policy neglected to foster "(1) the goodwill of Tobagonians towards the industry, and (2) the production of food and the adequate provision of entertainment to meet the two prime needs of the industry".[39] This policy restricted local earnings from tourism. Roach articulated a long-held view of Tobagonians when he argued:

> Tobagonians would like the industry to slant more to homely guest cottages with freer interplay between visitors and the host population. They want their farmers to grow crops and rear meat animals to provide food for the trade. In this way, they claim, the industry would not be regarded as a wart on the island's skin but become integral with the island['s] life.[40]

Its tourism policy clearly demonstrated the government's failure to include Tobagonians in their development planning for the island. On this point Roach noted that a rumour suggesting the Ministry of Education intended to convert Bishop's High School into a junior secondary school was typical of "Trinidadians' arrogance" and "failure to consult with local people". He pointed out that Bishop's High School was to Tobago what prestigious schools such as Queen's Royal College were to

Port of Spain. Most of the island's "foremost" inhabitants were alumni of the school, and the island's "best" people wanted their children to enrol there.

> To be unaware of this fact is not to be a Tobagonian. To think of doing away with or downgrading the school is to ask for an upheaval. This sort of failure to understand, to consult with, to seek out the wishes of Tobagonians is one of the sources of the island's discontent. It sharpens the differences between the two islands and feeds dissent and the extremists['] thoughts of secession.[41]

Roach's article shows the intimate link between Tobagonian identity, as represented in we/they antipathies and grievances, and the desire for autonomy and even secession from Trinidad.

Tobagonians took pride in the legacy of their century-long political and administrative identity that they had prior to union with Trinidad. After the inception of British control in 1763 through the Treaty of Paris, Tobago was granted representative government from 1768 until 1876, when it became a Crown Colony. This long history of self-rule within the British Empire contrasted sharply with Trinidad's experience. Trinidad was captured in 1797, and by the Treaty of Amiens in 1802 it formally became British under Crown Colony government, retaining that status until independence in 1962. "Tobagonians like to look back upon the time when Tobago was on her own, providing for her own Governor, making and passing her own laws, and independent."[42] This rehearsal of stories of past glory also served to strengthen Tobagonian identity.

The cumulative result of rehearsing these and other differences and the grievances that Tobagonians suffered, coupled with continual retelling of stories of Tobago's prosperous and proud past before the union, played a crucial role in the development of Tobagonian identity. The inhabitants of the two islands noticed the differences between them, and the print media helped to make those differences widely known. Grievances with the central government probably did more than most other factors to cement Tobagonian identity – the central government was viewed as the other. Put another way, Tobagonians tended increasingly to collapse the larger, more industrially developed island of Trinidad, the

Identity and Secession in the Caribbean

multiracial people of Trinidad and the apparently unsympathetic and inconsiderate government seated in Trinidad into a Goliath that became increasingly less intimidating.

Primordial Attachments in Tobagonian Identity Formation

Tobagonian identity construction has other premises, and one of these is referred to as "primordial attachments". *Primordial* means "deep-rooted and persistent and not of recent manufacture; primordial categories include territorial homeland, culture and cultural values, and historical memory; however it does not refer to biologically inherent traits".[43]

Tobago is the "homeland" of its proud inhabitants. The vast majority of Tobagonians (more than 90 per cent) are of African descent.[44] Their ancestors came to the island from Africa as captives or indentured servants during and just after the period of transatlantic slave trade. These Africans created a new homeland on the 116-square-mile island that was a separate British colony until 1889. Throughout most of the twentieth century the island was known for its unspoiled scenic beauty and the hospitality of its industrious people, who were devoted to various Protestant religions and in whose community crime was rare. "The idea of homeland assumes a homogenous and uniform familiarity. But it is more than that because it suggests a shared consciousness, a special structure in temporal depth-historical memory, and the veritable mental and emotional environment of the individual."[45] *Homeland* also conjures up the idea of belonging. Association with Tobago's beaches, its famous Nylon Pool and Buccoo Reef, family gardens, family-reared small and large livestock, fishing, flora and fauna, rivers and waterfalls, the historic forts – in other words, attachment to the physical island – fostered Tobagonian identity.

Tobagonians also took pride in the culture and cultural values associated with their homeland. The goat races during the Easter season at Buccoo Point, the native dialect, speech bands at carnival, working in the family garden early on Sunday morning, raising livestock, the "lenhan" (lend-hand) system of village cooperation, folk-songs, folk-tales, folk-dances — all these shaped the Tobagonian collective identity and forged the corporate Tobagonian personality.[46]

Family and kinship ties were deeply rooted aspects of Tobagonian culture as well. In Tobago "one [was] expected to support one's family whatever the area of concern or activity".[47] This cohesiveness of family and community was a fundamentally, though not exclusively, African cultural practice and value. Strong ties with the entrenched extended family and community were partly responsible for the achievements of individual Tobagonians who have held senior government positions. Families pooled their resources to pay the cost of educating their children. This, along with a solid Christian background and involvement of the entire village in raising children, contributed greatly to the success of the young people, who were thereby kept out of trouble. Bonding in the community was forged in children's activities such as boys flying kites together during the Christmas vacation and playing cricket.

The len-han system of village cooperation, also called *guyap* and *day fuh day,* was another cornerstone of Tobagonian culture. It was used a great deal in fishing, in agriculture and in the activities surrounding a death in the village. When cultivating land, villagers worked each other's plots in turn, one day for each owner. "The owner of the land to be worked provides the workers with bakes made of flour and coconut milk, and with as much chocolate tea as they can drink."[48] In addition, "[d]igging songs handed down from their ancestors are sung to the tempo of the digging, jokes are cracked and tales retold".[49] This system also extended to non-agricultural activities such as constructing houses and preparing for funerals. Preparation for a funeral was a village event, with everyone pitching in to help in one way or another with food preparation, building the coffin or digging the grave.[50] As in West Africa, a wake was held for nine nights after the funeral. During the wake numerous hymns were sung and the attendees played card games, drank home-grown coffee and engaged in "the reciting of many long and verbose panegyrics on the deceased".[51]

Other Tobagonian cultural values included respect for adults, good manners, industriousness and hospitality. Respecting one's elders was crucial. Every adult was to be viewed and treated like one's parents; they had the right to discipline unruly children, even those who were not blood relatives. Possessing and displaying good manners, including requesting things in a polite fashion and saying "thank you", in addition to greeting people with the appropriate "good morning" and so on, were also viewed as important aspects of Tobago's cultural values.

Industriousness was another valued cultural trait. Tobagonians prided themselves on being hardworking, and it was a serious insult to be considered lazy. Hospitality was yet another characteristic of Tobagonians. "Hospitality and good cheer are the hall marks of the Tobagonian and good humour and laughter a major part of his life."[52] Consequently Tobagonians resented the fact that, although they treated their Trinidadian friends very generously when they visited Tobago, providing them food and giving them many gifts of foodstuffs and poultry at their departure, when they visited Trinidad they were hardly ever offered a meal.[53] Many Tobagonians reported that, while at the homes of friends in Trinidad during mealtime, each family member would be summoned individually to the kitchen for lunch, and none would be given to them.

Given its rural character, the village was also very important to the island. The villages developed along the coast and in the interior after emancipation. Village loyalties and traditions remained strong: "one knows (as does everyone else) that one's family belongs to a particular village. Those who live in the village but do not belong to it are regarded as 'stranger niggers', a term not often heard in Trinidad."[54] The undying village ethos preserved the features of African collectivism, so unlike the individualism pervasive in Western societies. Industrialization in Trinidad, with its significant petroleum and light manufacturing sectors, produced different socio-economic changes, more in keeping with urbanization. Trinidad also had its villages, but the urban lifestyle was omnipresent, while Tobago's towns were small and the thrust towards urbanization was relatively weak on the island.[55]

As a result of the composition of its population, Tobago's cultural traditions were also unique in that they reflected, to one extent or another, African cultural practices. "It has frequently been remarked that Africanisms are far more persistent in Tobago than in Trinidad, which has been effectively permeated by Western values."[56] Some of these African cultural traits are discussed in "Tobago's Peculiar Culture", a short unpublished monograph describing thirteen cultural elements that distinguish Tobago's culture from that of Trinidad.[57] In that work Tobagonian anthropologist Jacob D. Elder shows that much of Tobago's culture is rooted in African traditions.

One Africa-based cultural trait is patrilineal kinship – descent through the male line. While this is characteristic of families in Tobago, a strong network of interfamilial relationships among the relatives of both parents is also present. Another cultural trait is sensitivity to property and ancestral land – "the heritage from the 'older heads' that is viewed as inalienable". Ancestor cult is the third element. Although traditional religious systems did not survive intact, remnants can be seen in an animist cult that includes a form of ancestor worship. In the cult of the dead, the spirits of departed loved ones are said to respond to invitations to special dances and to assist the living with their problems. At wakes for the deceased, ritual food and music are offered. Those who become possessed by the spirits of ancestors at these ceremonies deliver messages from them and answer questions about the future.

African identity is another facet of Tobagonians' culture.[58] African last names such as Kofi, Quamina and Keorka have been retained, along with some first names. The belief that an infant is a returned ancestor is also found among the peasantry, and ritual burial of the umbilical cord (*nable string* in Tobago) is still performed. The practices of carrying babies on the hip, balancing heavy loads on the head, tying the head or plaiting the hair in corn-rows (*cane-rows*), and cooking with okra (*ochro* in Tobago) are all African cultural retentions.

A modification of endogamy is another African cultural trait found in Tobago.[59] Older Tobagonians insist that their sons should not marry "stranger niggers", that is, persons from outside the local community or, worse, from off the island. This is similar to West African traditions that forbid marriage outside the ethnic group. Many folk-tales tell of misfortune befalling women who marry strangers. Folk-songs also warn men from Tobago's West district ("Low Side") against going to the

Windward district ("Top Side") to court women. Along with endogamy comes the concept of age grades. Age grades have not persisted intact, but Tobago mothers warn their children against playing or associating with others who are not of their age group. "In Tobago there are unwritten rules which lay down that grown adults who were 'playmates' make the best work-partners."[60] Also, in some instances mating or marriage between persons of widely differing ages is frowned upon or socially condemned.

Cooperative work and communal production are crucial aspects of Tobago's culture. Work groups based on real and fictive kin and friends get together to undertake large tasks. These groups are variously called *task-workers, partners, brothers, compares, len-han men* or *fambly* (kinsmen).[61] The most common tasks undertaken by the cooperative labour teams are felling trees to clear virgin forests for agriculture, digging yam holes, picking cocoa, "dancing" cocoa beans to polish them before bagging for export, draining land for planting cocoa seedlings, cutlassing (clearing) lastro (uncultivated) land for corn planting, digging potato banks (mound rows) for planting potatoes, and knitting and "hanging" seines (fishnets). "Throwing-up (also called sou-sou) is the term by which Tobago folk describe the peculiar Tobago cooperative saving scheme by which a group of traders, farmers, artisans or ordinary house-wives save money for purchasing some expernsive [*sic*] article for the home which one person alone may find it difficult to buy."[62] The ethos of mutual trust is what binds these groups together, especially since most of the members are not blood relatives.

Jacob Elder also points to "religiousity [*sic*]" as another principal feature of Tobago's culture. While the ordinary Tobagonian is religious, "this is not a view resting upon attendance at a given church on Sundays (or Saturdays as the Seventh Day-Adventists do). It is seen in attitudes and customs which run deep in the behaviour of folk."[63] In spite of conversion to Christianity by European missionaries, Tobagonians have retained limited aspects of African religious traditions that can be termed ancestor cult, which is widespread in West Africa. The fundamental belief system of the Yoruba Egungun – the divinity for ancestor worship – has been retained in a variety of beliefs and practices among blacks in Tobago. The belief that the dead are interested in the affairs of living relatives is one of these retentions.

Other beliefs have persisted. Some Tobagonians believe that ancestral spirits must be fed ritual food to keep them alive. If the ancestors are treated correctly – through regular rituals involving music, dance, oblations, public respect and supplication – they will manifest themselves and assist living relatives during times of trouble and crisis.[64] Thus, before weddings, boat launchings, laying the foundation of a house, hanging a seine, opening a new business or cutting down forest on newly acquired land, Tobago folk would hold a reel dance to which the ancestors would be invited for their entertainment. At these ceremonies the spirits possess the dancers, who speak in tongues and convey "messages", providing cures for illness and guidance for those facing challenging circumstances.[65] The dance itself is of Scottish origin but it has been syncretized with African rhythms and movement and the use of African drums.[66]

Artistic creativity is another facet of Tobago's culture that is influenced by African traditions. Skilful woodwork, "refabs" made from metal containers, thread work, embroidery, knitting, needlework and shoemaking are evident in the villages of Tobago. Many of these craftsmen and women have declared that they were never trained by master craftsmen, and even though much of their work originated with white missionaries, "many of the crafts are definitely of African style sufficient to identify them as introduced by the African slaves".[67] Among the crafts that can be identified as distinctively African are calabash (gourd) carving, corn-row hairstyling, pads for carrying heavy loads on the head, beadwork, wooden handles for cutlasses and other farming implements that are decorated with zoomorphic designs, vegetable-dyed fabric, musical instruments (banjas, sanzas, flutes, drums, whistles, rattles, shake-shakes, stamping tubes, tambourines, fiddles), and rope-making (from mahoe, sisal, wild cane, big-thatch, cane trash, wild fig leaves and so on). Various objects in the villages are also made from natural materials, such as "mud-walls, mud-ovens, millinery, costume jewelry jewel-boxes decorated with sea shells, flower arrangements with dried leaves, flowers and twigs or grasses, and pins and brooches made from turtle-shell and black coral".[68] Basket weaving is also a significant occupation.

Folk-songs and folk-tales are intrinsic aspects of Tobago's culture. The main theme of Tobago's folk-songs is confrontation between whites and blacks of opposing interests. The songs were preoccupied with escape from the plantations, frustration with white oppression on the estates, and an intuition that the fall of the planter class was imminent – and so was the certainty of freedom.[69] The cultural traits and practices listed in Elder's work all form part of the corporate Tobagonian personality.

Various experiences also contribute to identity construction, for example, "[w]hen the territory is combined with the peculiar historical experiences of a people, this combination of place and memory provides the moral architecture of a deeply embedded identity".[70] Tobagonians' way of life developed during the hardships of slavery and the post-emancipation struggles for independence from the estate and for landownership. The development of a distinct culture also fostered pride and conferred an identity that separates Tobagonians from Trinidadians.

Identity construction developed from at least two histories that offer contrast and self-definition.[71] Both Trinidad and Tobago share a common history of slavery, but the post-emancipation period forged a distinct Tobagonian self. The peasantry in Tobago was not formed until just before the union, and landownership by blacks became a matter of pride.[72] C. E. R. Alford, writing in 1938, described Tobagonians as peaceful property owners: "Another big point in Tobago is that the people are peaceful and cheerful. Most of the coloured people have land of their own, however small it may be, which gives them a stake in the Island."[73] Tied to landownership was home ownership, which was especially important to men. To own a house was a badge of honour and status, and also a sign of manhood. At one when Tobagonian men did not get married until they had built their own house.[74]

So attached were Tobagonians to land and property, after emancipation the only inducement for freed people to return to the estates and work for wages was the threat that they would be deprived of their provision grounds and ejected from their dwellings.[75] Given Tobago's agrarian character, land was significant in many respects. It was

> the place of work, the object of labour, a means of production, a symbol of social
> status, and an avenue to full citizenship, since the franchise was always based on
> the possession of property. Access to land was also a key factor in determin-
> ing the relations of production. Furthermore, land ownership was of immense
> symbolic importance in the culture created by the exslaves. This is reflected in
> the practice of burying the dead on their own property, rather than in public
> burial grounds and churchyards, which persisted to the 1880s. It is seen, too, in
> the custom, common in Tobago and in other parts of the Caribbean, of burying
> a child's umbilical cord on the land of its parents and planting a tree to mark
> the place. These practices symbolized the linking of the continuity of the family
> line with the high value placed on the land.[76]

An agro-proletariat, dependent on wages and completely devoid of access to land, did not develop in Tobago after emancipation; by the mid-nineteenth century, access to land was widespread, whether it was rented or purchased.[77] Major Granville St John Orde Browne, in his report on labour conditions in the West Indies in 1935, spoke highly of the industry of the Tobago peasantry and of the desire of Tobagonians to acquire land.[78]

Tobagonian educator Edrick Gift also addressed the importance Tobagonians attached to land and home ownership.[79] Tobagonians, he says, were serious, honest, hardworking and independent – all character traits of the peasantry. They owned property and land on which they pursued agriculture for a living, and they could survive without salaried work. Further, they did not favour renting; they took pride in owning a house and having no mortgage, which gave them a feeling of security. Landownership gave Tobagonians a sense of self-worth. On the other hand, Trinidadians were comfortable renting houses, and if they bought a house, generally they would not have much land with it. Gift argues that Trinidadians do not associate a positive self-concept with landownership the way that Tobagonians do.

The differences between Trinidadians and Tobagonians are only one facet of the equation of identity and autonomy in Tobago. These differences simply lay claim to the uniqueness of Tobagonians and their culture in contradistinction to the Trinidadians with whom they share citizenship in the Republic of Trinidad and Tobago. Other groups in the country also have a unique identity, but Tobagonian identity has provided a solid foundation for them in uniting behind their leaders, protesting their treatment as second-class citizens, and demanding social and economic development from their government. It has also strengthened their calls for an administration that will allow them to determine their own priorities and chart their own destiny.

The Role of Historical Memory in the Construction of Tobagonian Identity

The history of the relationship between Tobago and Trinidad is at the core of Tobagonian self-definition. Both islands were joined by imperial fiat in 1889. At that time the islands were Crown Colonies and Britain had sovereign power over their destinies. The Trinidad political elite accepted the union unwillingly, and their counterparts in Tobago did so with much suspicion over how they would be treated by the larger partner, especially in light of the fact that Tobago was entering the union as the underdog, its economy shattered and its political stature emasculated. Over the years Tobagonians have expressed much dissatisfaction with the way the government in Port of Spain has treated them and their island. They have also resented the belittling attitude of Trinidadians towards them.

Tobagonians narrated the history of the relationship in a way that justified their claim to a greater share of the national economic pie and greater autonomy and control of their own destiny. At the time of union, and continually thereafter, Trinidadian legislators saw Tobago as a financial burden, a backward appendage. The crucial aspect of Tobagonian antipathy towards Trinidad was that, up to 1956, the colonial government neglected the smaller island; thus a pattern of uneven economic, social and political development set in. Under the administration of the People's National Movement (PNM) government that came to power in 1956, plans were laid to redress these historical wrongs.[80] However, various promises for infrastructure development fell by the wayside. While the PNM government did better than its predecessors, progress was still painfully slow.

Tobagonians also emphasize their separation from the central government by miles of ocean. The central government is viewed as distant, unconcerned and unsympathetic to their special needs and circumstances. The Trinidadian counter-narrative is that initially it was forced into the union and that expenditure on Tobago has been greater than whatever revenue the smaller island generated. The Tobagonian politicians' rejoinder is that Tobago's revenue was not consistently – if at all – disaggregated from that of Trinidad (not a simple task). Most important, the central government has not made economic development in Tobago a major priority so that the island can raise enough revenue to support itself and contribute a surplus to the national coffers. In addition, Tobagonians argue that the administrative arrangements for Tobago have been stifling, in that all policy decisions for the island are made in Trinidad, and Tobagonians are not allowed to determine local development priorities and chart their own destiny.

In the context of the struggle for internal self-government in the late 1970s, therefore, historical memory and narrative were major facets in the campaign that asserted the right of Tobagonians to self-determination. The autonomists of the 1970s, as well as those who came before, boisterously proclaimed the frustrations and disadvantages that were the bitter fruits of the union. The separatists' repertoire was replete with slights, denials and neglect, tales of administrative inconvenience and woe. Tobagonian leaders lamented that the lack of viable opportunities on the island had led many of its young, brilliant sons and daughters to leave the island in search of education and jobs.[81] These and other concerns led to calls for self-determination.

The Right to Self-Determination

Tobagonian separatist parliamentarians, notably A. P. T. James, A. N. R. Robinson and Dr Winston Murray, claimed that Tobago had the right to self-determination.[82] The articulation of this right contributed to enhancement of Tobagonian identity. For James, the Tobago member of the Legislative Council from 1946 to 1961, self-determination meant Tobago's gaining political status as a separate unit in the British West Indies Federation (1958–61) and, probably, secession. Physician Rhodil Norton also called for secession in 1969.

Not as publicly radical as James and Norton, A. N. R. Robinson, a former senior Cabinet member and deputy leader of the PNM, broke with the government in 1970 and later called for internal self-government for Tobago. He demanded a separate administrative and political structure for the island, one that would have the authority to determine policy. Murray, who entered the political scene in the mid-1970s and joined Robinson's new political party, the Democratic Action Congress (DAC), also supported Robinson's ideas for a while. After Murray began demanding secession, he broke with Robinson in 1978. Robinson and the DAC pointed to the right to self-determination enshrined in United Nations documents. These included the 1948 Universal Declaration of Human Rights, the 1960 Declaration on the Granting of Independence to Colonial Countries and Peoples, and the 1976 International Covenant on Economic, Social and Cultural Rights. DAC supporters claimed that islands smaller than Tobago, and sometimes less endowed with economic potential, had already become independent nations.

Tobago politicians' laments over underdevelopment demonized the Trinidad government as the other, perpetrating a deliberate policy of uneven development in Tobago. Tobagonians articulated their displeasure with the ruling PNM party in 1976 by not supporting it in the general elections. After the PNM's defeat in Tobago, the Trinidadian response was caustic and insensitive. Eric Williams, the prime minister and leader of the PNM, snapped, "If you want to go, go. . . . I always suspected that within the ranks of the PNM so-called there has been a solid section surreptitiously supporting the secession."[83] Tobagonians have never forgiven Williams for his attitude; effectively he had told Tobagonians that he did not care about their fate.

The right to self-determination was well articulated by Robinson, the leader of the DAC, which won the two Tobago constituencies in the

1976 general elections. Tobago had been divided into two electoral districts in 1961. On 14 January 1977 Robinson, the parliamentary representative for Tobago East, moved a motion in the House of Representatives for internal self-government for Tobago. He argued that Tobago had been neglected and underdeveloped by both the colonial and national governments. Robinson contended that the case for internal self-government was based on three factors:

> (1) The failure of the colonial solution of amalgamating Tobago with Trinidad under the act of union of 1887. (2) The failure of the post-1956 solution by which, in spite of the PNM's attempts to have a distinct administrative body for Tobago, the top ranking officers of that organization had no real executive power and had to refer decision-making to senior officers in Trinidad. (3) The dismantling of the ministry of Tobago Affairs as a punitive measure after the 1976 general elections, pointed to Tobago's need for a permanent system of administration, independent of the vagaries of party politics.[84]

Robinson also claimed that the government was hiding the fact that there were commercial deposits of petroleum in the seabed offshore the island of Tobago. Most Tobagonians felt that Robinson was genuinely interested in the affairs of Tobago and hailed him as their champion in the parliamentary struggle for autonomy, which lasted three years, from 1977 to 1980. During that period Robinson and the DAC articulated a litany of woes, and those grievances comprise another brick in the structure of Tobagonian identity.

Grievances: The Secondary Basis of Tobagonian Identity

Grievances are the "secondary incendiary force in a secessionist drive for autonomy".[85] The litany of woes, constantly repeated, played a vital role in the construction of Tobagonian identity. The grievances are built around the claims to a distinct homeland and its special culture that make Tobagonians unique. "Grievances are however not secondary in a less powerful sense than primary attachments but, while derivative, are often time the stuff which, in their particularity, impart practical popular meaning"[86] to Tobago's claim of neglect and unfair treatment by the central government.

Tobagonians disliked being submerged within the national identity. Robinson, in *The Mechanics of Independence* (1971), argued that at union Tobago was viewed by Trinidadians as inferior and that this perception became part of both the official and unofficial attitude in the country. A worse development occurred soon after the union. The negative attitude towards Tobago was reflected in the fact that the country was referred to by what became a generic term – Trinidad. This implied that Tobago's identity had been swallowed up by that of the larger island.

> What was to have been a union of equality degenerated into one of patent inequality, one of the superior and the inferior, one of territory and dependency, and Trinidad's feelings seeped into both official and unofficial attitudes toward the smaller island. The nadir of Tobago's decline was its complete elimination from the political map of the Caribbean; citations in official documents and elsewhere referred to Trinidad only, on the assumption that Tobago was simply a part of Trinidad.[87]

Tobagonians resented being cast into the lumpenproletariat of the nation. They took pride in saying that they were from Tobago, not Trinidad.[88] They did not like the fact that on many occasions the country was called simply Trinidad and that foreigners and even Trinidadians did not think it mattered that they were from the island of Tobago.

Similarly, A. P. T. James became perturbed when in the legislature *Tobago* was not used with *Trinidad* when referring to the colony as a whole, especially in the context of the proposed West Indies Federation. He also took umbrage when a stamp was created that had only *Trinidad* on it. Many Tobagonians were annoyed when national sports teams were referred to as originating in Trinidad only, not called the Trinidad and Tobago team – especially when at least one of the athletes was from Tobago. Tobagonians tend to believe that Trinidadians feel Tobago is unimportant in the national sphere.

The negative social relations between Tobagonians and Trinidadians were another underlying factor that added tinder to the autonomy movement. "Stereotypes and prejudices are frequently found in relations of collective social antagonism even though they may not always be evident in every aspect of social intercourse."[89] Tobagonians' demand for greater autonomy has been motivated in part by their perception that Trinidadians see them as rural and thus backward and inferior people. As mentioned above, Trinidadians who live in the major urban centres tend to view all rural communities and people – even in Trinidad, but especially in Tobago – as backward and socially inferior. Sometimes the belittling manner in which Trinidadians treat Tobagonians has made some of the latter ashamed to be known as Tobagonians when they travel to Trinidad.[90] Some Trinidadians have claimed that Tobagonians suffer from an inferiority complex, an accusation that is vehemently rejected by most Tobagonians.[91] Trinidadian legislators contended that Tobago was suitable only for rearing and exporting goats, in comparison to Trinidad's petroleum industry and exports.[92] At its special convention held at the Chaguaramas Convention Centre in November 1970, the PNM moved to take statements that insinuated that idea out of the party's official documents.[93]

The supposed superiority/inferiority complex in the country is based on Trinidadians' vaunted pride in their advanced industrial economy and society. For instance, Trinidadians boasted that Trinidad had petroleum and asphalt and many cinemas and places of entertainment, while Tobago had only one cinema. Trinidadians pointed out that Scarborough, which had limited nightlife, could not in the least detail be compared to Port of Spain's bustling commercial and entertainment district. Even as early as 1947 Tobagonians wrote about the second-class satellite status of their island in the union: "Time was when this balmy isle was considered in the nature of a spare tyre on a motorcar, a handy substitute. But for what? People in Trinidad had grown to think of Tobago as a real Isle of Goats merely fit for gambol and relaxation."[94] These negative views have tended to entrench in Tobagonians a strong sense of a distinct collective self and have served to heighten the we/they antipathies between the two peoples. Even though many Tobagonians have migrated to Trinidad in search of better opportunities and there has been intermarriage between the two groups, the social stigma of Tobagonian inferiority persists to some degree.

The feelings of distrust between the peoples of the two islands tended to magnify the complaints of neglect and inequality. Tobagonians also complained about the inconvenience of having to go to Trinidad (and, in some cases, to pay bribes) to get official documents such as birth certificates and deeds for land titles from government departments. They also contended that their long-standing demands for a deep-water harbour and an international airport, which would provide direct access to the outside world, had fallen on deaf ears for decades, despite promises from the ruling PNM government since 1956.[95] In addition they cited the need for better roads and more convenient sea transportation on the inter-island route.

The spokesmen of the DAC, the party that championed greater autonomy for the island in the 1970s, claimed that the central government had fostered a policy of economic dependence in Tobago. Tobagonian historian Selwyn H. H. Carrington's work supports this view.[96] Tobagonians believed that the government was interested only in development in Tobago that would be complementary to development in Trinidad. For example, the government focused on fostering local tourism, even though it was clear that Tobago had enormous potential for international tourism. They further argued that the government did not encourage development of industries in Tobago,[97] and that it was doing little about the fact that the cost of living on their island was much higher than in Trinidad. These and other claims demonstrated a legitimate pattern of comparison that hinted at the deliberate neglect and marginalization of Tobago, a pattern that played a crucial role in the construction of Tobagonian identity.

The DAC also pummelled the central government for the lack of Tobagonian representation in certain national institutions.[98] Robinson pointed out in 1977 that there were no Tobagonians in the Trinidad and Tobago Senate and, more important, that no legislation made it compulsory. He also argued that no Tobagonian could be a member of the Cabinet, the highest policy-making body of the country, unless that person was a member of the ruling party. Further, gaining such a position depended on the whims and fancies of the prime minister, who selected the Cabinet members.

Winston Murray, the parliamentary member for Tobago West from 1977 to 1982, who won his seat on the DAC ticket but afterwards broke from the party, tended to be more radical in his views than Robinson. Murray argued that Tobagonians were being "gradually dispossessed [by] the way this government was permitting outsiders to come in through their agents in Trinidad to buy up our land, robbing the Tobagonian of his lands and building factories, and we Tobagonians cannot build a single house".[99] He alluded to permission granted to the East Indian Kirpalani business concern to build a department store in Scarborough; Tobagonian entrepreneurs had been denied this opportunity. Murray emphasized the need to preserve the traditional values of collectivism and other cultural traits for which Tobago villagers were well known.[100] Tobagonians were disturbed by the influx of Trinidadian businessmen, especially those of East Indian descent, who soon became an economic force within Tobago's economy. They owned big businesses and bought land in Tobago; the latter activity was particularly irksome to Tobagonians, since they considered the land part of their ancestral cultural heritage.[101] Murray was viewed as a secessionist; he eventually broke with the DAC in 1978 and formed the Fargo House Movement, named for A. P. T. "Fargo" James.

The ruling PNM government was thoroughly against the movement for internal self-government. Its spokesmen argued that the parliamentary representatives for Tobago, Robinson and Murray, desired only power, self-aggrandizement and secession. Overand Padmore, the minister of finance, contended, "[T]he whole motion [for internal self-government] smacks of an attempt to dismember the unitary state of Trinidad and Tobago."[102] The Tobago members were charged with wanting to be lords and kings of Tobago. During his term in office James was similarly charged with aspiring to be the governor of Tobago.

Despite their arguments for devolution of central government power, the autonomists needed an event or activity around which they could galvanize the support of the people. This trigger factor surfaced after the September 1976 general elections.

The Trigger Factor: From Identity to Autonomy

The combination of primordial bases and secondary grievances needed a push to set the movement for autonomy into high gear.

Identity and Secession in the Caribbean

The dismantling of the Ministry for Tobago Affairs was the spark that ignited the movement for internal self-government in Tobago. The unsatisfactory administrative structure of Tobago was a major plank in the autonomists' platform. Tobago's administrative machinery lacked permanence and did not have sufficient executive authority. The autonomists cited the disbanding of the ministry after the PNM lost its Tobago seats in the 1976 elections, and the administrative chaos and inconvenience that ensued, as the green light for a motion for internal self-government in Parliament. The ministry, which had once coordinated all government departments in the island, was broken up, and its respective units were once more placed under supervision of their parent departments and ministries in Trinidad.

The transition was not smooth. Many Tobago workers went without pay for weeks (even months) on end, and decisions affecting Tobago once again had to be referred to officials in Trinidad before anything substantive could be done. The administrative chaos, worker retrenchment and inability to get paid on time caused Tobagonian resentment to peak. In demanding internal self-government, Robinson argued that Tobago needed a long-term administration independent of the vagaries of party politics. He suggested a permanent administrative structure with a political arm made up of elected representatives from the districts of Tobago, who would be responsible to the people. "The main concern of the autonomy movement was to win the right to run its own affairs and the argument centered around the issue of harnessing the economic institutions and resources of Tobago for the benefit and welfare of Tobagonians in particular and the country in general."[103]

The foregoing has presented in broad strokes the parliamentary struggle for internal self-government that is the subject of chapter 11. However, before that can be discussed fully, the factors that led to the union between Tobago and Trinidad must first be considered.

Chapter 3

The Union between Tobago and Trinidad
Precursors and Concerns

Tobago's quest for autonomy in the twentieth century is linked to the island's loss of political and administrative identity as a separate colony of the British Empire in the decade before 1900. By imperial decree in 1889 Tobago was joined to its closest, larger and more prosperous neighbour, Trinidad. The proximity of the islands, therefore, was an important consideration in uniting Tobago and Trinidad. However, the primary factors that led to the union of the two islands as one colony lay in the interplay of forces between the British colonial policy of full control over its West Indian colonies, on the one hand, and the declining economy of Tobago, which was dependent on sugar production, on the other hand.

Economic Woes and British Federation Designs

Tobago's economy, like those of other British West Indian colonies in the post-emancipation era, was in serious decline after the mid-nineteenth century. Caribbean economies based on sugar-cane monoculture had been on the decline since the last quarter of the eighteenth century. Since the revenue of the Tobago government was tied primarily to customs duties, the decline in exports of its major crop seriously affected the island's economy and thus its ability to meet its financial obligations. Table 1 shows that the difference between government revenue and expenditure from 1869 to 1889 tended to be less than £500 sterling, and half the time in a deficit balance.[1] As early as 24 December 1877, the lieutenant-governor of Tobago, Augustus Frederick Gore, told the members of the Legislative Council that "the existing taxation of Tobago is barely adequate to meet the expenses of its Government".[2]

TABLE 1
TOBAGO'S REVENUE AND EXPENDITURE, 1869–89

Year	Revenue (£)	Expenditure (£)	Difference (£)
1869	9,900	9,814	86
1870	12,177	11,655	522
1871	14,270	10,387	3,883
1872	13,395	13,384	11
1873	9,493	11,330	-1,837
1874	9,518	9,578	-60
1875	11,594	11,484	110
1876	11,769	11,653	116
1877	13,310	13,373	-63
1878	14,306	14,596	-290
1879	11,501	11,726	-225
1880	14,003	13,514	489
1881	16,830	14,844	1,986
1882	13,661	13,748	-87
1883	14,175	14,223	-48
1884	11,370	13,481	-2,111
1885	10,825	12,031	-1,206
1886	8,813	9,529	-716
1887	9,386	6,994	2,392
1888	10,489	8,155	2,334
1889	8,809	10,423	-1,614

Source: Compiled from entries on Tobago in the Colonial Office List for the years 1875 to 1889.

Gore's remark was the preamble to recommending various bills to raise additional revenue, and was indicative of the declining state of the economy and the tight financial position of the government. The decline of the British West Indian sugar economies was wrapped up in the late-eighteenth-century movement for free trade in Britain, which culminated in the abandonment of the British mercantile system for the laissez-faire system. The chief accomplishment of the free traders was the British *Sugar Duties Equalization Act* of 1846. This law gradually removed protection from British West Indian sugar, thereby allowing foreign-grown sugar to enter the British market at the same rate of duty as sugar from the colonies. The subsidized production of beet sugar in Europe also added to the competition that colonial sugar faced on the home (British) market. The glut on the British sugar market led to a drastic fall in prices. These and other forces resulted in the inexorable decline of the profitability of British West Indian sugar plantations, and thus the economies of the sugar islands themselves. Without diversification, a huge influx of cheap, reliable labour through immigration, or increased capital investments to upgrade sugar factories, the British colonies suffered a tremendous economic downturn. Besides these factors, Tobago had suffered a devastating hurricane in 1847 that destroyed sugar mills and other estate property, adding to the woes of the sugar producers.[3]

In addition, the post-emancipation period was marked by a slow but successful attempt of the British Colonial Office to erode the executive powers of the colonial assemblies. In 1838 Henry Taylor, chief clerk in the West India Department, argued that West Indian governments could not be trusted to rule after emancipation, since the ascendancy of whites would be replaced by that of blacks and coloureds without changing the problems the British government had with the assemblies. Under the old representative system, the assemblies had considerable power and were constantly wrangling with the home government in order to have their own way, especially with respect to bills aimed at raising revenue. The Colonial Office had had enough of this resistance to both the implementation of British policy and the power of the governors.

Therefore Taylor advocated that all British territories should become Crown Colonies with wholly nominated legislatures like those in Trinidad and St Lucia, where the governors' power was unfettered.[4] In 1865, after the Morant Bay Rebellion in Jamaica, the Assembly there abolished itself and the island became a Crown Colony because of fears that the black majority, now enfranchised and having the qualifications to hold office, would soon control the reins of power. After 1865 the British embarked on a strategy of encouraging the simplification of legislatures in order to achieve Crown rule.[5] Instead of a legislature with executive and legislative branches, a single-chambered legislature with a nominated majority was recommended. This change took place in the Leeward Islands of St Kitts, Nevis, Antigua, Montserrat and Dominica between 1866 and 1869. In the Windward Islands, St Vincent was the first to succumb; by 1867 it had a unicameral legislature with the Crown having the casting vote.[6]

In 1868 the secretary of state for the colonies, the Earl of Buckingham and Chandos, clearly outlined British policy in a circular memorandum. That document reflected the Colonial Office's authoritarian and racist thinking. Crown rule was deemed best to ensure financial and commercial prosperity as well as securing the welfare of inhabitants of the colonies. The Crown was viewed as the best ruler because the whites governed only in their own interests and the "uneducated blacks 'were incapable of contributing to the formation of any intelligent public opinion.'"[7] The memorandum offered imperial grants if "adequate powers" – majority control or a wholly nominated legislature – were given to the Crown. The offer of grants was an extremely tempting inducement to the Tobago planters, who "hoped for economic aid and for greater imperial defence against insurrection from within. In particular, they wanted British support for a central factory for the Leeward District, which would make production and manufacture of sugar more efficient."[8] Those hopes were never realized.

In the mid-1860s the Colonial Office decided that the Leeward and Windward islands should form a single federation,[9] and by 1871 the Leewards were united. In 1869 the new governor of Barbados and the Windward Islands, Sir Rawson William Rawson, was given the task of uniting the islands under his jurisdiction.[10] However, the governor of Trinidad, Sir Arthur Gordon, contended that Tobago should fall under his jurisdiction. At that time the political elite in Tobago did not want the island to be united with Trinidad. The other Windward Islands and Barbados were also reluctant to confederate. The political elite in each island wanted to maintain as much autonomy as possible – they had grown accustomed to their independence. Rawson proposed that the colonies should adopt simple unicameral legislatures and become Crown Colonies first; then attempts would be made to confederate them.

The Tobago political elite opposed any reduction of the political and administrative status of the colony. In order to counter this, Rawson sought the help of the most influential planters to establish a unicameral legislature in the islands. In Tobago he appealed to John McCall to use his power to effect this change.[11] McCall, the leading planter, merchant, attorney and a partner of A. M. Gillespie and Company from the mid-1860s until his death in 1879, cooperated in this venture. While these plans for changing the constitution were being worked out, Lieutenant-Governor Frederick Kortright introduced legislation to increase the franchise and thereby undermine the control of the big planters. The legislation expanded the franchise by reducing the minimum voter qualification to £5 sterling of real property; it came into effect with the elections of 1873 and resulted in increased enfranchisement of coloureds and blacks. Kortright's action, which worked at cross purposes with the desires of the Crown, angered the men in the Colonial Office and led to his speedy transfer.[12] His indiscretion led Chief Clerk Taylor to the conclusion that, given the rising number of blacks in the assemblies and the spectre of the Morant Bay Rebellion, it was possible to tap into the fears of whites and coloureds by urging the change to a single-chambered legislature.[13]

However, by May 1874 McCall had wielded his influence and got the House of Representatives to vote its conversion to a unicameral legislature of six nominated and eight elected legislators. The smaller planters, merchants and other middle-class persons opposed this measure as retrograde, because it lowered the number of elected members from sixteen to eight, effectively eroding their recent political gains.[14] However, this pleased the Colonial Office officials. Two years later their plans were given a fillip when the Belmanna Riots of May 1876 led the plantocracy to vote for conversion to a Crown Colony government. The riots occurred in Roxborough, in the Windward District, where John McCall and his brother James had consolidated their holdings. The "main complaints were low wages, lack of proper medical care, wage stoppages for goods supplied from the estate shop on the truck system, and the high prices of those goods".[15] Fearing the rising black masses, the planter class quickly voted to abolish Tobago's constitution and do away with its independence under the old representative system.[16] Thus the protest action of the labouring class should also be seen as contributing to the move to federate Tobago with other colonies. The abandonment of the old representative system of government was a crucial early juncture in the demise of Tobago's separate political and administrative identity.

The decline of the British West Indian economies provided added incentive for the British government to federate its colonies in order to effect administrative economies of scale. Instead of paying the home salaries of the governors in two different colonies, the Crown made one governor governor-in-chief of two or more colonies.[17] Tobago suffered this fate by being united with Trinidad.

Union with Trinidad: The First Proposal

The first formal recommendation to unify the two colonies came on 1 November 1878 from Lieutenant-Governor Gore, who had been head of the Tobago administration for exactly one year. He wrote to the lieutenant-governor of the Windward Islands, distressed over the worsening financial state of his government. He advocated a union of the two colonies, which would result in savings to the Crown: "I am of the opinion that there is no necessity for maintaining the colony as a separate government. The distance from Trinidad to Tobago is only 18 miles from land to land, and if a good road were made from Port of Spain to Toco and a steam launch were employed, daily communications might be established between Port of Spain and Scarborough. The saving that would be effected by the move would be £3,775."[18]

Thus, proximity and economy were Gore's main considerations. He contended that further savings would follow as soon as the Trinidad government "had a little experience in the wants of Tobago".[19] His conclusions were based on the "small amount of work" needed to be done by officials whose salaries he proposed to abolish, high unemployment and the fact that the "sugar estates [were] in a very depressed condition". He postulated that diversification, with cocoa as the main crop, would result if union took place, because idle land would be bought by Trinidad "speculators" who had capital, especially since the cost of land on the island was cheaper than in Trinidad, and also because wages were lower in Tobago. This was clearly an opening for Trinidadians to exploit Tobago.

Gore raised the issue of "annexation" once again on 26 September 1879 in the Legislative Council; at that time he submitted correspondence on the matter between him and George C. Strahan, the governor-in-chief. At the next meeting of the legislature, almost one month later, James McCall – obviously not in favour of unification – made a motion requesting, *inter alia,* factual data regarding potential benefits that would accrue from the proposed union. McCall wanted statistics on the extent and nature of trade between the colonies for the previous five years, and the revenue derived from it. He asked for the cost of maintaining a steamer service between the islands and of constructing and maintaining a road from Toco (the village in Trinidad nearest to Tobago) to Port of Spain. McCall also inquired concerning personnel to perform the duties of chief justice, attorney general, local magistrates, public prosecutor and inspector of schools, as well as the cost of effecting changes relating to those offices. He further asked whether there would be any compensation for being "subjected" to Trinidad's rate of taxation and being governed by its laws.[20] The issues McCall raised continued to concern the political elite up to the very date of union. McCall's concerns undoubtedly mirrored those of the other unofficial members of the council who represented the planter elite.[21] Gore later admitted that even though his goal was to effect savings, "the scheme of annexation had found little favour amongst the unofficial section of the Council".[22]

The poor financial state of Tobago's treasury remained a grave concern for Gore, who had a passion for "restoring the equilibrium of the finances".[23] As he opened the 1880 session of the Legislative Council he stated that the revenue of the previous year had been £11,890 and the expenditure £11,726.[24] However, he pointed out that the "existing liabilities amount in round numbers to £3,336, not including the loan of £1,000, the payment of which has been postponed to August 1882".[25] Thus, while revenue exceeded expenditure for 1879, Gore insisted that it was his "disagreeable duty" to call attention to "our financial difficulties". Furthermore, it had been declared that year that Gore's own salary, and those of all the lieutenant-governors of the Windward Islands, would no longer be paid by the Crown but would have to be taken from local revenue.[26] Given the increasing financial obligations and the need to shore up revenues, an export tax was once more imposed, despite the bitter objections of the unofficial members.[27]

The responses to James McCall's queries concerning Gore's annexation proposal came in June 1880.[28] They were not encouraging. First, without giving any statistics concerning the nature and extent of the trade between the two islands and the revenue derived from the same, Gore simply stated that the relevant data could be found in the Customs House records. The cost of operating a small steamer between the colonies was approximately £1,200 per annum. However, the cost of constructing a road from Toco to Port of Spain was prohibitive. Gore proposed that visiting officials from Trinidad or elsewhere would carry out the duties of the chief justice and inspector of schools. As to the potential for increased taxation, the governor of Trinidad indicated that it was impossible to govern Tobago at the existing low rate of taxation on the island, which was only fifteen shillings per capita, the lowest rate in the West Indies. Gore was hard-pressed to bolster his proposal for annexation. His responses to James McCall's questions certainly gave the unofficial members of the government added justification to view the proposal for union with Trinidad as unwise.

The plantocracy was not the only entity that exercised influence over the fate of Tobago. The island was part of the British Empire and had become a Crown Colony on 1 January 1877. The imperial government could determine its fate with a simple proclamation, despite loud protests from the planter class. The difficulties facing the island's economy also served to undermine the planters' political clout with the home government. The sugar depression worsened in the 1870s, resulting in an increase in emigration by labourers and a decrease in exports and revenue. The Tobago government borrowed from local merchants and the Grenada government to meet recurrent expenditures. "Increased direct taxes, cuts in expenditure, retrenchment in the Civil Service and combination of posts, all failed to avert the inevitable collapse."[29] The economic state of affairs in Tobago and the other colonies was so bad that in December 1882 a British Royal Commission was appointed to enquire into the public revenues, expenditure, debts and liabilities of the islands of Jamaica, Grenada, St Vincent, St Lucia, the Leeward Islands and Tobago.

The Crossman Commission's Proposal

Commissioner Crossman and his team arrived in Tobago on 7 April 1883. They found a heavy burden of taxation on the masses, little expenditure on infrastructure, and poorly paid government officials because of the impoverished condition of the treasury. Most of the revenue was spent on departments of the civil establishment; the second-largest amounts were spent on roads and bridges, ecclesiastical grants, other government works and buildings, education, hospital and asylum, and other government services.[30] The problematic financial situation and other matters led the commissioners to recommend a federation of St Vincent, St Lucia, Grenada, Tobago and possibly Dominica, with headquarters in Grenada.[31]

The report of the Royal Commission was published in 1884, the same year that the London mercantile firm of A. M. Gillespie and Company went bankrupt. Gillespie held interest in three-quarters of all the estates in Tobago – nineteen in all.[32] The firm provided credit, shipping and marketing services to those estates, and its demise had a domino effect. Significantly also, Gillespie had formed a partnership with John and James McCall, planters with estates in the Windward District, and by 1870 this conglomerate had emerged as the largest planters and merchants.[33] The bankruptcy of Gillespie and Company was the final straw that broke the back of Tobago's sugar industry. Even before Gillespie's bankruptcy the island had suffered not only from depressed sugar prices – referred to by John Young, Gillespie's trustee, as "the Sugar Crisis" – but also from a "succession of severe droughts which . . . exhausted all local capital".[34] The issue of federation was discussed against this gloomy economic backdrop.

The prospect of an imposed union brought out fears and resistance that triggered sentiments conducive to the development of an autonomy movement in Tobago. The Tobago planter and merchant classes feared that the island would become marginalized and treated unfairly. This led them to seek guarantees that would prevent the island from being disadvantaged in the union.

The proposal to make Tobago part of the confederation was bitterly opposed on the island. Sir William Robinson, governor-in-chief of the Windward Islands government (seated in Barbados), was very much aware of this fact and spoke about it at a meeting of the Legislative Council held on 25 February 1885. He noted the "strong expressions of opinion against the scheme" by two of the unofficial members, the press, persons who had attended two public meetings, and people with whom he had spoken privately. Truly "the public opinion of the Colony was clearly adverse to the proposed Confederation".[35]

Edward Keens, one of the unofficial members of the Council, argued that accepting the confederation "would not be conducive to the welfare of the Island, but, to the contrary, would be detrimental to its interests".[36] Keens' views represented those of the majority of inhabitants of the island, who feared that Tobago would be "neglected" if it were united with its "more important neighbours". Keens anticipated that taxation would increase and reminded his fellow legislators that "Crown Colony Government ha[d] not brought with it the blessings [that is, imperial loans] which were promised . . . at the time of its inauguration"[37] – he did not want to be disappointed again. S. B. Isaacs, another unofficial member of the Council, supported Keens. The "idea of confederation was distasteful to the people of the Colony".[38] He insisted that "evils" would result because of the absence of a resident chief justice.

There were other factors that made the confederation distasteful to the political elite of Tobago. With federation came the recommendation for a Grenada Committee to unify the import tariff, excise laws, inland imposts and land tax of the four colonies. It was estimated that uniform customs duties would lead to a loss of revenue of about £650 per year for Tobago.[39] A Tobago committee (most likely chosen by the Council) that closely examined the proposed confederation also took into consideration the proposal to annex Tobago to Trinidad, which it described as a "very desirable union". If the "strong probability" of union with Trinidad became a reality, the committee opined, it would not be wise to change the customs laws for the time being, since they would have to be altered again to suit those of Trinidad. Despite the protests from the Tobago legislature, on 5 March 1885 an Order in Council constituted the office of governor and commander-in-chief of the Windward Islands of Grenada, St Lucia, St Vincent and Tobago.[40] Thus Tobago became a part of the Windward Islands government and remained in that federation for four years, until it was united with Trinidad in 1889.

The federations of islands in the British West Indies tended to be very loose. They were simply administrative unions in which a governor-in-chief became responsible for all the federal units. Lieutenant-governors in each island assisted him, and the relative autonomy and identity of the federal units were rarely affected. This certainly seemed to be the case in the Windward Islands government, which helps to explain why Tobago's political elite was vehement about maintaining as much autonomy as possible in the forthcoming union with Trinidad. However, while the merger with Trinidad seemed a better option to the unofficial members of the Tobago legislature in 1884, eventually it took the island and its people down an entirely different path.

Inevitable Union: Fears and Objections

Discussions about the union between Tobago and Trinidad took place between the officials at the Colonial Office in London and the governors of the Windward Islands federation and Trinidad. As early as 20 August 1886 William Robinson, now governor of Trinidad, wrote to Governor Walter J. Sendall of the Windward Islands federation with suggestions for the proposed union. The Colonial Office had originally wished Tobago to become a dependency of Trinidad. Robinson objected to this idea, suggesting instead that Tobago be "incorporated with Trinidad and thus become part and parcel of this Colony".[41] Robinson further recommended that Tobagonians should be subject to the duties, taxes, laws and regulations of Trinidad. He suggested that a magistrate, a collector of customs, a couple of clerks and a sub-inspector of police with twenty constables should be "sufficient" for executive administration of the island. Further, he believed that two district magistrates and an assize court meeting three times a year – presided over by the chief justice of Trinidad, who would hear serious cases and appeals – could handle the legal administration of the island.

In addition, Robinson proposed that Tobagonians should be "warned" that these changes would take effect around 30 June 1887 and that "Her Majesty" had decided the matter without recourse to appeal. Robinson went on to recommend that Tobagonians should be "invited to transfer themselves and their effects" to Trinidad, with free passage on the Royal Mail steamer paid for by the Tobago treasury. On the authority of the secretary of state, he would offer one acre of Crown land to every individual who settled in Moruga, supposedly "one of the richest districts in this island". He further proposed that each emigrant be given a bounty. These "crude suggestions", he thought, would lead to the "Tobago difficulty [being] easily settled". However, he was willing to hear Governor Sendall's ideas, which he hoped would not include "a separate staff or . . . a different tariff and code of laws from those in force in Trinidad".[42]

Tobagonian sociologist Susan Craig-James described Robinson's attitude as one of "astonishing flippancy".[43] For him, either a skeletal staff or depopulation – those were his only options – could "easily" solve

Tobago's problems. Indeed, those "crude suggestions" were indicative of the attitude that the Trinidad government would adopt towards Tobago after the union. Robinson did not have the development of Tobago in mind. Clearly he did not want to have to preside over an island that would be more trouble than it was worth, with a separate administration and a tariff and laws different to those in Trinidad.

In Tobago formal discussions on the proposed union with Trinidad took place at the meeting of the Legislative Council held in Scarborough on Wednesday, 19 January 1887. Present were Governor-in-Chief Walter J. Sendall, Administrator Robert B. Llewellyn, Acting Attorney-General S. J. Fraser and the three unofficial members of the Council: Edward Keens, Ebenezer Henderson and John McKillop.[44] Over a month had passed since the formal notice of annexation had been published in the *Tobago Gazette* on 2 December 1886. Sendall's remarks were brief because he had previously discussed the matter fully in an informal meeting with the unofficial members. His formal meeting to hear the objections of the Tobagonian representatives had been ordered by Edward Stanhope, secretary of state for the colonies, who warned him "not to carry through any scheme for the union of the two Colonies against the wishes of the inhabitants".[45] Sendall had deduced from the informal meeting that the major objection concerned finances: "The people of Tobago were apprehensive that if they were wholly incorporated with Trinidad the revenue collected here would be absorbed in the general revenue of the united Colony, and would be employed in maintaining a scale of public expenditure altogether too costly for either the needs or the resources of the small Island."[46] The political elite, who also represented the landed plantocracy, did not want to pay the increased taxes that would be necessary for development of the island. The entire economy was in a downturn that had negatively affected their ability to bear additional tax burdens.

Given the concern of the unofficial members,[47] Sendall simply made a resolution in the Legislative Council that he thought would express "the most advantageous manner for such a union to be effected".[48] His resolution had the following major points: (1) the name of the united colony would be Trinidad and Tobago; (2) there would be one governor; (3) the

Identity and Secession in the Caribbean

colony was to be governed under one code of laws; (4) import duties levied on articles imported from abroad into Tobago should be the same as in Trinidad, and traffic between the two islands should be free; (5) the interests of Tobago required that internal taxes (excluding import duties) "should be imposed and adjusted with strict reference to local circumstances, and should not follow the laws of taxation in force in Trinidad except in so far as the local circumstances may admit of it"; (6) all revenue collected in and on account of Tobago should be spent wholly on administration of the island and not be absorbed into the general revenue of the united colony; (7) no part of the public expenditure of either island should be chargeable on the revenue of the other island, except by mutual consent of both islands; (8) the chief executive officer in Tobago should be in charge of a local board called the Financial Board made up of three resident householders – one nominated by the governor, the others elected by the general body of householders. The duty of the Financial Board was to advise the governor on matters relating to internal taxation and expenditure. Finally, no local tax was to be imposed or altered without the Board's consent.[49] Sendall effectively gave the Tobago political elite a guarantee that they had obviously sought, that the island would not suffer unduly as a result of the union.

McKillop, who seconded Sendall's resolution, described the terms of union as "extremely liberal" given the fact that "the people would have a voice in the affairs of Tobago".[50] The issue of representation was obviously important to him, as it continued to be to subsequent Tobagonian political leaders. Keens also viewed the terms of the resolution as liberal, although he thought the matter should be set out in a more detailed fashion. He obviously wanted additional and more specific guarantees that Tobago would not become the disadvantaged partner in the proposed union. Henderson stated that while the majority of the population had expressed support for the union in two public meetings, he opined that they "did not understand the nature of the question before them".[51] Fraser voted in favour of the resolution, but "looked upon the scheme with some degree of apprehension".[52] Llewellyn supported the resolution wholeheartedly because of the aspects dealing with revenue, expenditure and internal taxation. He did not think that the Trinidad government would have treated Tobago so liberally if the latter had initiated the resolution. It was Llewellyn who advocated keeping the revenue and expenditure of the two islands separate. He was sensitive to local preferences because he previously worked on the union between the Turks and Caicos Islands and Jamaica.[53] He also foresaw that Trinidad's capital, Port of Spain, would replace Barbados as Tobago's entrepôt. Up to that time most of Tobago's trade had been carried on with Grenada, Barbados and England.[54]

Ebenezer Henderson and Edward Keens moved another resolution that demonstrated their and, in fact, the Council's most ominous apprehension about the proposed union. Their fears and the need for guarantees in this early period of autonomy development in Tobago were reflected in the final version of the resolution adopted by the Council. Quoted frequently by later autonomists, it stated:

> That inasmuch as the wish of the people of Tobago for union with Trinidad has principally been based on the representations of the Government and the assurances given to the people that material benefit will result to Tobago from such union, the Secretary of State for the Colonies be respectfully asked in the event of such union taking place to afford the people of Tobago a pledge that should it prove disadvantageous to the Colony, or otherwise undesirable to the majority of the inhabitants; this Colony shall on petition have granted back to it the form of self Government which now exists here.[55]

Henderson, a leading merchant, also presented a petition by "certain Mercantile Firms and others" that opposed the proposed union. The merchants of Tobago mounted the greatest opposition to the union. They perceived that the loss of customs revenue that would necessarily result from customs union between the two islands would be a serious problem. "The merchants who operated small sailing ships between Tobago and Barbados realized that they would lose that trade and would be restricted to doing business with Trinidad. That eventuality would stifle the import-export business and made the government officials concerned that Tobago's declining revenue would be further diminished."[56] However, Sir Edward Wingfield, head of the West India section of the Colonial Office, insisted that the union was worth the risk.

The reservations of the Tobago merchants notwithstanding, Sendall went to Trinidad to take up the matter of union with the legislators there. On 23 January 1887 he met with the unofficial members of the Trinidad legislature, informing them of the resolution for union passed by the Tobago Council. After much discussion, all the legislators except G. Townsend Fenwick voted in favour of the union.[57] This does not mean that they welcomed the union; Fenwick's opposition may well have represented the unspoken sentiments of Trinidadian legislators.

Fenwick opposed the proposal for union on several grounds.[58] First, he believed that Tobago's bankrupt state and "no prospect of better times in the near future" would "injuriously" affect Trinidad's ability to receive commercial credit from abroad. Second, he opined that while administrative annexation would reduce expenditure for official salaries in Tobago, such reductions would not be enough to keep Tobago's expenditure within the limits of its diminishing annual revenue. Fenwick also hinted that Tobago's revenue could decrease by 50 per cent if a proposed Trinidad ordinance to repeal certain customs duties came into effect. Third, contemptuously arguing that Tobago could only benefit from the union given the transfer of Trinidad capital there and the "enterprise of Trinidadians", Fenwick contended that Trinidad needed such resources for its own development. Of course, the implication was that union would hinder development in Trinidad to the extent that Trinidad's resources would be expended on the smaller island. Fenwick's fourth objection also centred on expenditure of capital from which he thought Trinidad would not benefit. He claimed that union would necessitate establishing a steamer service between the islands, the cost of which, he contended, Tobago was unable to bear even a part. He further argued that while Trinidad was the closest island to Tobago, given the flow of the ocean currents it was not as convenient for trade as Grenada or Barbados. Fenwick's objections, especially those suggesting that Tobago would become a financial burden on Trinidad, foreshadowed the arguments Trinidadian officials made continuously after the union was effected.

Fenwick's fourth objection to the union was based on the trend of increasing production of ground provisions in Trinidad. Tobago's major export to Trinidad was also ground provisions, and Fenwick argued that with increasing production of the same commodities in Trinidad, the larger island would soon need to export such products rather than import them. (That scenario never became a reality, for even today ground provisions continue to be imported.) He also contended that Tobago's increasing export of small livestock to Trinidad was not an indication of a "prosperous trade" but "merely an indication of the distress to which proprietors, great and small, of that colony are now reduced".[59] Fenwick also objected to using Trinidad's public officers in the Tobago administration. He surmised that if such officials had time to spare to work in Tobago, there was "room for economy" in their various departments. Fenwick's seventh objection was that administrative annexation would inevitably lead to total incorporation or absorption of Tobago by Trinidad as soon as the "futility of the present arrangement is sufficiently demonstrated".[60] On that point he was prophetic, since Tobago was eventually made a ward of the united colony. However, Fenwick's reasoning was faulty; part of the rationale for making Tobago a ward had to do with Trinidadian officials' view of Tobago as too much of an administrative and financial burden to administer as a separate entity.

Fenwick's final objection was based on the grounds that "an overwhelming majority of all classes in Trinidad strongly disapprove[d] of the annexation of Tobago".[61] Governor Robinson later wrote to Sir Henry T. Holland, secretary of state for the colonies, stating that Fenwick was the only one who was opposed to the proposal. He also argued that his contention that the majority of Trinidadians opposed the union was "without the least foundation".[62] The "majority" to which Fenwick referred was limited to people of wealth and standing in the community, not average Trinidadians. There were, in fact, mixed views on this issue. On the one hand, some Trinidadians agreed with Fenwick that Tobago "would drain us of our substance", while others saw Scarborough as an ideal alternative international port.[63] Scarborough was conveniently placed to be a transhipment point for the agricultural produce of Trinidad's north coast, particularly cocoa, which had to be carried by ships plying the perilous waters of the Bocas to Port of Spain or by beasts of burden across the mountains of the northern range.

Shipping the produce to Tobago would greatly reduce shipping time to the international markets.

The Trinidad government officially approved the union, though not wholeheartedly. Fenwick voted against the resolution and Dr A. de Boissiere declined to vote.[64] On 8 March 1887 the Trinidad Legislative Council passed a resolution stating that the Council had "no objection to the administrative annexation of Tobago".[65] In spite of the official vote, Robinson wrote to Holland that the unofficial members believed Trinidad would not benefit from the union, a view with which he did not concur.[66] The unofficials sometimes voted in favour of a measure even though they were against it in principle, because in the Crown Colony system they were outnumbered in the Council. They also supported the governor's proposals because, as nominated members on the Council, they served at his pleasure.

The Trinidad resolution on the union mirrored the one passed by the Tobago Council. However, it stressed the clause that "no pecuniary charge is now or hereafter to be imposed on the Revenue of Trinidad for any service connected with the Island of Tobago".[67] The issue of financial control was the selling point of the resolution for union on both sides. Trinidad's insistence on solely administrative annexation and Tobago's insistence on financial autonomy show that the union was not organic. The officials in both islands regarded each other with suspicion.[68] The governor's comments testify to this: "I believe little is known of Tobago by the inhabitants of Trinidad except that it is supposed to be most unhealthy, very dry, and everything else that is undesirable."[69]

After receiving the resolutions passed by the legislatures of Tobago and Trinidad, Colonial Office officials examined them and objected to two issues.[70] First, Edward Wingfield stated that the Crown, while in favour of the resolution, objected to the composition of the Financial Board. The Crown insisted that the Board should have equal numbers of official and unofficial members, with the chief executive officer having a casting vote. Also, the Crown did not acquiesce to the taxation and expenditure of the island coming under the control of a majority of unofficial members. Second, Wingfield stated that the British government could not accede to the Henderson–Keen pledge because uniting the colonies required an act of the British Parliament, and dissolving it would require the same.

Given those objections, the Tobago Council passed another resolution concerning the union. The first part of this new resolution was that the Financial Board would have an equal number of official and unofficial members, with the chief executive officer having a casting vote. The second stated that, given the Trinidad resolution on union, "it is not now considered necessary to ask from the Secretary of State for the Colonies for any pledge that the Union between the two Islands should ever be annulled".[71] Of course, Keens and Henderson "protested against the withdrawal of the pledge" to annul the union if it proved disadvantageous to Tobago.

The Order to Unite

After passage of the resolutions by the Tobago and Trinidad legislatures, union was inevitable. The British Parliament passed the *Trinidad and Tobago Act* in 1887, authorizing the union under Orders in Council. On 17 November 1888 Queen Victoria proclaimed the Order in Council uniting Tobago and Trinidad as one colony called Trinidad and Tobago from 1 January 1889.[72] The order put an end to Tobago's separate political and administrative identity. The Financial Board was only a shadow of the former Council in status and scope, even though it could enact local regulations. Political power was now concentrated in Port of Spain. The governor in Trinidad became the governor of both islands; any instruction given to him by the Crown applied to Tobago. The governor was authorized to appoint a commissioner of Tobago – the chief executive officer of the Financial Board – as the head of its administration. In the absence of the governor the commissioner had the power of his office, except the authority to appoint and suspend public officers and to pardon criminals. This proviso was never enforced, because in the governor's absence a Trinidadian official always acted in his place. The commissioner was ex officio an official member of the Legislative Council of the colony. In addition, at least one unofficial member of the

Identity and Secession in the Caribbean

legislature was to be a person who ordinarily resided in Tobago. Thus Tobago had only two representatives on the Council to advocate for its interests.

The Order in Council uniting the colonies established the Financial Board of Tobago, which consisted of the commissioner and five other members residing in Tobago. Two members of the Board were to be nominated by the governor and three were to be elected. Qualified candidates had to be a British subject, at least twenty-one years old and resident occupier of a house on the island, who possessed a yearly income of £200 and paid annual direct taxes of not less than £10. Board members could not hold public office and had to be eligible for registration as a voter.

The qualifications for voters included several elements.[73] Voters had to be male British subjects, at least twenty-one years old, without legal incapacity. On 1 January of the election year and in the six months prior to that date they were to be resident occupiers of a house in Tobago. Further, during the preceding year they should have paid either direct taxes or rates of not less than ten shillings, and all taxes and rates due up to 1 January of the election year. A voter was disqualified if he had received relief from public funds within six calendar months preceding 1 January. Voters who had been sentenced to death, penal servitude or imprisonment with hard labour for any term, or without hard labour for a term exceeding twelve months, and did not suffer the punishment to which they were sentenced or other substitute punishment, or were pardoned by the Crown, were not eligible to vote.

The ordinary term of the Financial Board was three years, although the governor could dissolve it at any time. Thus, from the time of union the Tobago political and administrative structure was subject to dissolution by the head of state in Trinidad without consultation with Tobagonians. In 1976, almost a hundred years later, that fact led to demands for self-government. The Financial Board was empowered to make regulations respecting (1) taxation (except customs duties and duties affecting shipping or excise duty on rum or other spirits); (2) collection, receipt, custody and expenditure of public revenue of Tobago; (3) borrowing of money on the credit of the revenue of the island; and (4) markets, cemeteries, public works, granting of licences and matters of a "purely local character", and punishments for contravention of such regulations. The governor's assent to all regulations was required before they became law. The legislature of the united colony had the authority to make laws covering the same subjects over which the Board had purview. Local regulations that were repugnant to the laws of the colony were deemed void. However, it was not lawful for the legislature "to impose, increase, diminish, suspend, or abolish any tax or duty in Tobago other than customs duties and duties on shipping and excise duties on rum and other spirits, or to dispose of or charge any part of the revenue raised in Tobago for any other purpose than for the exclusive public service of Tobago".[74] Nevertheless, the laws of Trinidad became the laws of Tobago.

The revenue, expenditure and debt of Tobago were kept separate from those of Trinidad. The trade between the two islands became a coasting trade; thus customs duties could not be levied on articles imported from either island. However, customs duties levied in Trinidad on articles transferred to Tobago for consumption in Tobago were deemed part of the revenue of Tobago, and vice versa. The same applied to excise duty on rum manufactured on either island but transferred to the other island for consumption.

The Supreme Court of Trinidad acquired jurisdiction over the united colony. Sittings of the court were to be held at least three times a year in Tobago; a single judge could preside over those sessions. Tobagonians had the right to appeal the decisions and judgements of any single judge to the full court in Trinidad. The governor could appoint a commissioner of the Supreme Court in Tobago who would have the power of a Supreme Court judge when none was present in Tobago. The Order in Council also provided for a sub-registrar of the Supreme Court in Tobago. All police magistrates in Tobago became stipendiary justices under the Trinidad law. Loraine Geddes Hay was appointed the first commissioner of Tobago.[75]

Tobago was united with Trinidad with all the necessary imperial, legal and political bonds. However, neither Tobagonians nor Trinidadians genuinely wanted the union. The marriage was prearranged by the Crown

Identity and Secession in the Caribbean

for the sake of administrative convenience because of the economic distress in the smaller island. The parties in the union tried to get along, but there was no honeymoon. During the first ten years the union bore no economic fruit and Tobago remained a satellite of a seemingly distant government. Not many years passed before decisions again had to be made about Tobago's status and identity.

Chapter 4

No Honeymoon
The Impact of Union, 1889–1896

The first few years of union were no honeymoon for Tobago and Trinidad. Almost immediately the islands became embroiled in wrangling over the philosophy and rulings of Chief Justice John Gorrie. His impact on labour relations highlights the problems of class and race in Tobago. Gorrie's insistence that laws should apply equally to all classes provided the labouring class with positive exposure to the legal system.[1] The union also led to some improvement of their economic position. The peasantry had free access to the Trinidad market and was able to increase its standard of living by selling agricultural produce there.

The merger of Tobago and Trinidad also led to the establishment of a customs union. Hence the merchants and planters complained that the union exacerbated the decline in revenue of the Tobago government. As an incipient movement for secession developed, this and other concerns led them to demand separation from Trinidad. During these early years the problems of Tobago were articulated in the context of insufficient representation at the central government level. Demands were made for concessions to Tobago, the disadvantaged partner. Finally, the union highlighted Tobagonian identity. The articulation of this identity, particularly in terms of we/they antipathies, was the most significant development in the early period of union, even though it reflected the bias of the planter-merchant class.

The Impact of Union on the Administration

The Financial Board became the new locus of political power and administrative control in Tobago. Elections to the Board took place on 20 May 1889; one hundred and sixty persons registered to vote and thirty-five were disqualified.[2] The first people to have tenure on the Board were Loraine Geddes Hay, the commissioner, as president; two members nominated by the governor, S. J. Fraser (vice-president) and Dr J. P. Tulloch; and three elected members, William McCall of John McCall and Company of Scarborough, Augustus Briggs of the Lure Estate and the Reverend Canon E. A. Turpin, Rector of St Andrew's Parish Church in Scarborough. In his remarks at the first meeting of the Board, Commissioner Hay advised the members that "the working of all new machinery is liable to friction at first, and that things generally go more smoothly as faults and defects are remedied, and improvements introduced as they may be found requisite".[3] While Hay expected problems, he was also confident that the union would work. To him one of the necessary ingredients for success was frequent and reliable inter-island sea communication. Hay assured the Board that "constant and certain" shipping, which was of paramount importance for the success of the union, was soon to be provided by a contract between the government and the firm of Messrs Turnbull, Stewart and Company.

The administration on both islands had to be established, and in some cases modified, for the new arrangements to function well. One of the immediate, though minor, effects of the union was that changes had to be made in the composition of the former Trinidad legislature to accommodate the new Tobago representatives. The Order in Council that established the union provided for the commissioner of Tobago to serve as an official member of the Legislative Council of the united colony, and for at least one unofficial member to be a person ordinarily residing in Tobago. J. McKillop, an engineer, was chosen to fill the latter position. However, the Order in Council did not increase the total number of unofficials – eight originally – to allow for the additional member from Tobago. As a result, Governor Robinson recommended an amendment to the 19 December 1885 instructions to increase the number of unofficials to "not less than nine".[4] Sir Edward Wingfield of the Colonial Office agreed and the suggestion was implemented. Thus the governor gained discretionary power to appoint more unofficial members, including the Tobago representative. It is significant that the architects of the union saw the necessity for Tobagonian representation in the Legislative Council even when the island still retained limited autonomy through the Financial Board. The issue of representation – the right to have a voice in matters of state, especially those directly affecting Tobago – became a recurrent theme of the autonomists of the twentieth century.

The union had another administrative impact. In Tobago many offices were combined, although this was done mainly to effect economy, given the continual decline of government revenues. For example, Herbert H. Sealy was asked to perform the duties of postmaster, sub-registrar and clerk to the commissioner without any change in his salary of £200 per annum. Robinson's justification was the "necessity of keeping down expenses in Tobago."[5]

Another means by which the union reduced expenditure was in the use of officials from Trinidad to carry out duties in Tobago. This was the case with the Supreme Court justices. With the union, Trinidad's High Court became the colony's Supreme Court. The act of union provided for at least one judge to hold three sessions of the court in Tobago annually. Sir John Gorrie, the chief justice, was a very zealous legal practitioner who embraced Tobago as an extension of his judicial sphere. His actions had a tremendous impact on the labouring class, on planter–labour relations and, tangentially, on the issue of race relations in Tobago.

The Impact of Union on the Legal System, Labour Relations and the Labouring Class

The union had a tremendous impact on the practice of law and, indeed, the entire legal system in Tobago. It gave the lower classes an unprecedented, revolutionary exposure to the legal system in that it emboldened the common man to fight for his rights. This impact was due primarily to the presence, philosophy and personality of Sir John Gorrie.[6] He believed that the legal system should be accessible to all classes, rich and poor. He also insisted that the executive branch of government should not intrude on the judicial branch. These convictions put him at loggerheads with the privileged dominant classes in the colony, especially since his administration of justice was marked by judgements in favour of the labouring class against the planters.

The union of Tobago with Trinidad gave Gorrie an opportunity to expand not only his legal jurisdiction but also the influence of his values as a legal professional. As soon as the union came into effect in January 1889, he insisted on assuming duties as Supreme Court judge in Tobago. Commissioner Hay opposed that plan; he recommended to Governor Robinson that Gorrie postpone his proposed early visit to the island, thus sparing Tobago's treasury the expense. He further reminded the governor that the acting chief justice of St Lucia had held a court session on the island during the previous month.[7] The governor could not persuade Gorrie to change his mind. The unofficial members of the Council protested against the Trinidad treasury's bearing any part of the cost of Gorrie's visit. However, Robinson defied their wishes and proposed to defray two-thirds of the cost from the Trinidad treasury.[8] While Gorrie sympathized with Hay's desire to "press as lightly as possible on the finances of Tobago", he declared, "I do not think that its finances will be improved, or its prosperity promoted, if the people of the Island were not to be stirred out of their lethargy by seeing from the presence of the new officers, executive and judicial, amongst them that the union is complete."[9] Gorrie further argued that it would be unwise to show any sign of delay in implementing the new judicial arrangements. He even offered to accept payment at a later date if the Tobago treasury could not afford to compensate him immediately.

Following Gorrie's visit, Hay reported to the Colonial Office that the cost of visits by officials from Trinidad contributed to the decline of revenue in Tobago. He stressed that the "judicial establishment will cost the island about as much as it did before the annexation", approximately £394 per annum.[10] Hay lamented that "the only result of annexation so far have [sic] been reduced receipts, increased expenditure and general discontent among the people".[11] In response, Wingfield declared that he "never much believed in the annexation leading to economy for Tobago".[12] Another British official contended that the discontent in Tobago was due not to the annexation "but to Sir John Gorrie's mistaken meddling";[13] this discontent concerned industrial action by metayers (sharecroppers) on the Studley Park Estate.

Chief Justice Gorrie came upon the Tobago scene at a time of "economic depression and social disturbance, when traditional agrarian relationships were under challenge", and his presence further exacerbated tensions between the labouring and planter classes.[14] Since the 1840s sugar production in Tobago had been dominated by the metayage (also called metairie or sharecropping) system. Planters provided the land and equipment and metayers provided the labour. Both planters and metayers shared equally in the crop. This system was especially suited to Tobago, whose planters had chronic cash flow problems and therefore found it difficult to pay wages. The sharecropping arrangement, however, was a hotbed for conflict between management and labour. Metayers, who were generally poor, complained of long delays in grinding their cane, which led to loss of income. Harvested canes have to be ground expeditiously because they rapidly lose their sucrose content, producing less sugar when the juice is processed. The metayers also protested against high taxes, especially those imposed on smallholdings and farm animals, "as well as very limited access to land for independent cultivation before the 1880s".[15]

The virtual collapse of the Tobago sugar economy in the 1880s because of the drastic fall in sugar prices on the British market, which was glutted

Identity and Secession in the Caribbean

with subsidized European beet sugar, and the bankruptcy of Gillespie and Company led to a plunge in land values and the abandonment and sale of many estates, resulting in a whole new crop of owners.[16] These owners were soon at loggerheads with their employees. In an attempt to maximize profits, the new owners made planter–labour relations even more volatile by withdrawing "privileges" long enjoyed by resident labourers, "who tried to defend their 'rights' by whatever means were at hand".[17] In 1888 there were work stoppages and the *Tobago News* reported that labourers "ridiculed and defied" their employers.[18]

Within this milieu, Gorrie's favourable rulings for metayer plaintiffs in January 1889 – in cases filed *in forma pauperis* against landowners – only added fuel to the fires of planter–labourer conflicts. "As he had done in Trinidad, he interviewed suitors in his chambers to advise them whether they had good grounds for an action, and, if so, how to draw up their suits and apply for a waiver of court and solicitors' fees."[19] The planters were outraged by the damages awarded to the plaintiffs, who mostly complained that their cane had not been ground at all, or not at the right time. Gorrie's sympathetic attitude to the labourers, his willingness to allow suits against landlords filed *in forma pauperis* and his conviction "that there is no privileged class before the law" made him popular with the labouring class in Tobago.[20] Thus many ordinary Tobagonians were persuaded that they would receive justice when Gorrie presided in court. After the January sitting of the court in Tobago, Gorrie planned to return four months later.

His scheduled return in May 1889 was an event highly anticipated by the labourers, who became emboldened in their relations with the planters. News of this led to foreboding among officials in the Colonial Office: "[T]here is a notion that Sir John Gorrie is going to return in May to inaugurate the millennium, and that all other authorities and powers will then be superseded and put to confusion."[21] Senior official Wingfield's comments reflected the racist attitude of the Colonial Office: "Sir John Gorrie's negrophilism run mad makes him a serious danger and if he goes again to Tobago and lets his tongue run in the usual reckless style there may be bloodshed."[22] It seems, however, that these officials were responding more to Governor Robinson's confidential despatch of 28 February 1889 concerning "a spirit of discontent [that] had made its appearance among the labouring and artizan [sic] classes" in Tobago than to substantiated reports on Gorrie's activities.[23]

After the union, Robinson made his first official visit to Tobago on 9 February 1889. His observations initially led him to conclude that the discontent among the people was due to a demand for higher wages and also to unfair treatment by employers. The labourers' perception was that, since the union, they were "entitled to receive the same wages that are paid in Trinidad, which are considerably higher, and that otherwise they are hardly [that is, harshly] treated by their employers".[24] In Trinidad the law guaranteed male indentured Indians a minimum daily wage of twenty-five cents (about one shilling, or twelve pence); Tobago's average daily wage was eight pence.[25]

During an official reception in the Scarborough Council Chambers on 12 February, the Governor was informed that "several hundred labourers and others in a humble walk of life had filled up the corridors of the building and were clamouring for admittance".[26] Because they were in an "unsettled and excited state" Robinson decided to hear their grievances in the nearby Court House, which had a greater capacity than the Council Chambers. From the grievances aired, Robinson deduced that the general "outcry" was for higher wages and improvement of their sharecropping arrangements. However, he explained to the labourers that the forces of supply and demand set wages, and that although wages were lower in Tobago than in Trinidad, the cost of living in Tobago was also lower. He promised to examine the metayage system with a view to improving it if possible. After listening to Robinson's remarks the labourers appeared as "satisfied as could be expected under the circumstances".[27] While Robinson hoped the "dissatisfaction" among the people had been "dispelled", he was surprised to receive a communication from Commissioner Hay, two or three days after he left Tobago, that trouble was brewing on the island.[28]

Hay declared that the people were in "anything but a quiet state".[29] He recommended the visit of a man-of-war ship to help calm the "unsettled state of the people" and that a puisne judge should preside over the

Identity and Secession in the Caribbean

next session of the Supreme Court in Tobago.[30] The "unsettled state of the people" had its locus on the Studley Park Estate, recently bought by one Mr Date, a Trinidad cattle rancher. On 15 February the labourers "behaved very badly, and were much excited".[31] Newton Browne, the inspector of police, visited the estate and heard the general refrain "We don't want no Governor, we want Gorrie."[32]

The labourers' spokesman, Joseph Prescott, who had also spoken at the courthouse during the governor's recent visit, gave the metayers' side of the story. Date had "declined to grind the canes of his metayers free of charge".[33] Prescott also alluded to other grievances that preceded Date's purchase of the estate. During Prescott's explanation, a young man became very noisy. Date and Browne requested him to leave, to which he retorted, "I will do no such thing. I am as good as you."[34] Date and Browne were trying again to "put out" the man when the labourers charged them with preventing the fellow from speaking because he was "a black man". The charge of racism was denied. Prescott then charged Date and Browne with colluding to trick the workers by representing that they had been sent by the governor to handle the situation. He further declared that Robinson, Hay and Browne were "all one lot who have put their heads together to oppress us. We have no other Governor than Gorrie and he tell us already that he coming back in May. Don't do a dammed thing till he comes and let the canes go to hell!"[35] Those remarks led to a general uproar, with "loud shouts of Gorrie! Gorrie! Damned Tobago Buccras, he cut their tails for them the other day and he will cut their tails again when he comes".[36] Robinson attributed the attitude of the labourers to "some remarks of Sir John Gorrie"[37] and Inspector Browne lamented in a letter to Hay that a "distinct spirit of something worse than discontent has shown itself amongst the lower orders in this Island, and which is by no means confined to the labourers or metayers on Estates; this has manifested itself within the last two months" – the period that coincided with Gorrie's appearance in Tobago.[38]

With a despatch from Governor Robinson that included enclosures from Hay, Browne and the captain of the *Tourmaline,* Mather Byles, whose warship had responded to the distress call, Colonial

Office officials considered the matter. Their comments reflected their disparaging view of the labourers and the chief justice. After pondering the matter, S. Oliver came to believe that Gorrie had told the metayers that the planters "oppress[ed]" them, which he surmised may have been justifiable in fact, though not in policy. He also noted that the "effect of Sir J. Gorrie's words and apparently of his decisions in certain cases, seem to have been to send the Tobagonians off their head[s]".[39] Oliver also cynically referred to Hay's recommendation to send a gunboat to Studley Park as a "panacea for labour troubles" in the West Indies. However, he was concerned about the effect Gorrie's next visit would have on the labouring class. On the one hand he believed that if the Colonial Office paid no attention to Gorrie and allowed him to return to Tobago, the "extravagant hopes" of the people would meet "their implicit disappointment". On the other hand, if Gorrie did not return to Tobago "the negroes will believe that he has been prevented by the Gov't in the interest of the oppressor".[40] In addition, Oliver was apprehensive about the possibility that Gorrie's "windy promises may quicken the seeds of trouble, which I believe must always be present when negroes are working at wages on plantations, and much more so when they work on the wretched Metairie system".[41] Oliver's comments provide evidence of the prejudiced view the Colonial Office held of blacks, and thereby of the Tobagonians.

In letters to Robinson, Hay blamed Gorrie for fostering the "absurd notion" among the labouring class that because of the annexation they should receive an increase in wages corresponding to wages in Trinidad.[42] Robinson joined Hay in strongly recommending that a puisne judge, not Gorrie, should preside at the next session of the Supreme Court in May.[43] Wingfield concurred and contended that if Gorrie defied the request not to return to Tobago, "it may have to be considered whether steps should not be taken for his removal from office".[44] Lord Knutsford, the secretary of state, also agreed that a puisne judge should preside over the next sitting of the court in Tobago, in the "interest of peace & order".[45]

In a letter inviting Captain Mather Byles to patrol the island in the aftermath of the Studley Park incident, Hay argued that "there is, and has been for some time past, a feeling of insecurity among the more respectable portion of the community".[46] The Tobago police force was only fifteen men strong, and Hay wanted a show of force to "awe those who were induced to be lawless and to assure the timid". Even though he admitted that he was not expecting any riots, "it was always best to take early steps to avert what might prove serious trouble".[47] Hay also wanted the man-of-war because he was concerned that Tobago's isolation, "being out of telegraphic communication with the outer world", left the island, especially its white inhabitants, "in a very perilous condition",[48] as in the case of the Belmanna Riots thirteen years earlier.

The newspaper *Public Opinion*, citing the *Tobago News* of 16 February 1889, erroneously represented the conflict between the planters and labourers as having "suddenly sprung up, as if by magic, a class-antagonism that seriously imperils the peaceful relations between employers and employees".[49] Conflicts between labour and management had been long-standing in Tobago. The paper charged that "[t]he advent of Sir John Gorrie gave rise to the strange rumour that he had come to order the proprietors and planters to pay two shillings and two shillings and sixpence per day to their labourers, and that the advent of Sir William Robinson occasioned another rumour, that Sir John Gorrie had sent Sir William to confirm this increase in the rate of wages".[50]

Gorrie vehemently denied that he had led Tobagonian labourers to expect an increase in wages. He described Hay's charges in his letter to Captain Byles as "false and reckless".[51] The rumour concerning increased wages had been spread by Tobagonians living in Trinidad, who told their countrymen that "annexation means one and the same rate of wages for labourers in both countries and that they must not work for less".[52] Gorrie, who apparently had initially agreed not to return to Tobago, changed his mind after he heard of the Studley Park incident.[53] He then described the governor's request for him not to return to Tobago in May as "unheard of". He insisted that the Studley Park affair was a legal matter that demanded his immediate attention. He offered to sail to Tobago in order to hold a special session of the court, as soon as the governor provided him with transportation. He was confident that "the storm in a tea-cup, which Mr Hay has been busy with, will be allayed in five minutes so soon as my arrival is known".[54] Gorrie warned the governor that if he delayed in sending him to Tobago, "the feelings of the people [would] get exasperated by seeing their canes spoilt after all their labour, I, at least, will know where to place the responsibility".[55] Governor Robinson took umbrage at Gorrie's "dictatorial and offensive tone" and asked the secretary of state to take note of it.[56] Not surprisingly, Robinson refused to allow Gorrie to return to Tobago.

In response to Robinson's letter to the secretary of state and to a petition signed by thirty-one inhabitants of Tobago that Gorrie not hold the May court session, Lord Knutsford advised that an ordinance should be passed that the future session of the Supreme Court in Tobago be held by puisne judges "on the [fallacious] ground of saving expense".[57] The petitioners were merchants, planters and estate managers, many of whom had had judgements against them in suits brought by labourers. In a confidential letter Knutsford warned Robinson not to promote the idea that the ordinance was designed to keep Gorrie out of Tobago. However, it was impossible to conceal this fact. Ordinance 7 of 1889 "immediately became known as the 'Gorrie Exclusion Bill'".[58]

Gorrie, like everyone else in the colony, realized that the bill represented a personal vendetta against him. "To remove the pretext of economy, he offered to forgo the difference between his own salary and that of a puisne judge for his visits to Tobago."[59] Recognizing the negative impact the legislation would have on his position as chief justice and the potential curtailment of his influence on matters in Tobago, he travelled to London to present his case for disallowance of the ordinance. In May he met with Secretary of State Lord Knutsford. Despite the opinions of other officials in the Colonial Office, Knutsford acquiesced to Gorrie's wish to have the ordinance disallowed. This victory allowed him to return to Tobago in February 1890 to hold another session of the Supreme Court.

Because of John Gorrie's activities, the union had inadvertently exacerbated industrial and racial tensions in Tobago. It may have entrenched the labourers' view that the planters were oppressors. As shown in chapter 2, this view lived on through folk-songs into the twentieth century. Thus Tobagonians may have passed on to their descendants the attitude that they should be wary of the managerial class.[60] In addition, the Studley Park metayers' declaration that there was probable collusion between Date, Browne and the governor could also have led the peasantry to believe that officials from Trinidad were deceitful and could not be trusted. Both Date and the governor would have been seen as Trinidadians, and the governor represented the Trinidad government. Although Gorrie was also a Trinidadian official, he may have been viewed as an exception. In the call to strike and let the "canes go to hell", Gorrie was not classified with the "buccras" but was seen as the antithesis to them.

Through Gorrie's intervention the labouring class was also exposed to the legal system in a way that empowered them. The metayers at Studley Park saw the court as possessing a higher authority than the planters and even the governor. They must have understood that while the legal system had been used against them during the days of slavery, it could now be used against their oppressors if an impartial judge presided in the court. Their vision of a future society must have necessarily expanded to the inevitable day – depicted in their folk-songs – when the planter class would fall and they would be truly free.

The union also had a positive impact on the material standing of the labouring class. Many of them were engaged in independent agricultural pursuits on freeholds or on metayer grounds; they also raised small livestock and poultry. The union opened the Trinidad market to them. "Free trade with Trinidad, the monthly Royal Mail Packet, and the introduction in 1889 of steamers connecting the joint colony with New York, all combined to give Tobago greater access to other markets."[61] By working for wages and trading their produce in Trinidad, some of them gained wealth and moved up the socio-economic ladder to become storekeepers.[62]

While the fortunes of the labouring class improved, the administration had no cause for celebration. The union failed to arrest the decline in revenue, and this led local groups and colonial and London officials once again to examine the status of Tobago.

The Impact of Union on Tobago's Revenue

Besides leading to wrangling over the jurisdiction of legal profession-als and inflaming "class antagonism", the union also led to conflicts between Tobago civil servants and their counterparts in Trinidad over the loss of revenue allegedly resulting from the customs union and abolition of the 4 per cent *ad valorem* duties on foodstuffs. There was no immediate economic improvement on the island as a result of the union; on the contrary, revenue and exports continued to decline. The decline in revenue led to acrimonious debates about the loss of customs duties and resulted in calls for "customs autonomy" and even separa-tion from Trinidad.

Before the union, a significant portion of Tobago's revenue was derived from customs duties, house and land taxes and various licences. The general decline in revenue continued after 1889. With the union, the trade between Tobago and Trinidad became a coasting trade, and therefore goods from one island entered the other duty free, reduc-ing any customs revenue Tobago had formerly received from trade with Trinidad, and vice versa. In addition, Trinidad's lower customs tariff became the rate for duties charged in Tobago. On the surface this too had the potential to reduce Tobago's revenue base. The Financial Board had no purview over customs and excise duties on the island. Thus, except through the commissioner and the unofficial member from Tobago, who were on the Legislative Council, the island's political elite had no power to counteract the changes in customs laws that they insisted were at the root of steadily declining revenue.

By March 1889 the governor was painfully aware of how laws affect-ing customs duties could have a negative impact on Tobago. In January Lord Knutsford sent a despatch to Governor Robinson confirming and allowing Customs Duties Ordinance No. 21 of 1888. The purpose of the ordinance was to abolish the general *ad valorem* duty on foodstuffs. Abol-ishing *ad valorem* taxes was "considered an act of enlightened policy to do away with duties on foodstuffs, and indeed so lower the tariffs as to allow the general community to be supplied with the necessaries of life at as cheap a rate as possible".[63] While the loss to the Trinidad treasury caused

Identity and Secession in the Caribbean

by this measure was expected to be "comparatively trivial" — estimated at £4,500 — Robinson predicted that the effect on Tobago's revenue, "already seriously diminished by the operation of the Trinidad tariff[,] . . . will be . . . disastrous".[64] Given this prospect, Robinson thought it wise to consider the views of Commissioner Hay on the subject before implementing the measure.

Hay's predictions were ominous. He first intimated that Tobago's revenue was already negatively affected to the tune of £1,600 simply from adopting the Trinidad customs tariff and abolishing shipping dues, as required by the Order in Council that united the two islands.[65] He proposed to offset that loss by increasing the house and land tax by 2½ per cent, an amount that would not totally cover the loss. The abolition of the *ad valorem* tax would result in an additional deficit of £520. Hay also pointed out that while the black population of Tobago did not mind "moderately high customs duties" because they did not view it as a tax, direct taxation was "distasteful" to them, and any attempt to increase it was "invariably met by an outburst of indignation against the Government".[66]

After receiving Hay's comments, Edward Wingfield seems to have become very despondent over the Tobago situation: "I am afraid we must do this [abolish the *ad valorem* duty] — so far the annexation seems to have done no good to Tobago and to be a hindrance to sound fiscal legislation in Trinidad. I wish we had a man like Mr Llewellyn in Tobago."[67] Llewellyn, the first administrator of Tobago, had done a good job of extricating the government from financial problems some years before. In 1890 the revenue collected was £8,656, or £1,063 less than the estimated amount. The auditor was convinced that

> the deficiency is chiefly to be found under the head of imports, which returned £793 short of the sum expected. This result may be accounted for from diminished importations, owing to the fact that a large majority of the people now seek their supplies from Port of Spain instead of purchasing locally, and also to a short crop of sugar, which consequently reduced the circulation of money as compared with the previous year.[68]

The expenditure for 1890 was £9,256, resulting in a deficit of £600. Revenue for 1891 was £8,729 and expenditure was £8,783, producing a deficit of £54. The financial situation was becoming a major cause of concern for both local and Trinidadian officials.

By August 1892 Tobago's fiscal situation was so bleak that, according to a Trinidad newspaper report, Tobago officials had not been paid at the end of July. This news so shocked the new governor, F. Napier Broome, that he made an emergency visit to Tobago on 1 September and remained there for a week trying to come to terms with the problems facing the Tobago administration. A few days after his visit Broome wrote to the secretary of state, the Marquis of Ripon: "Tobago is at the present moment bankrupt, and cannot pay its way, much less its debts."[69] Only £63 remained in the treasury and the island owed the Crown agents £1,300. It also owed Trinidad £5,000 advanced for construction of buildings and roads and £500 as a subsidy for steamer service for 1892. In addition, Tobago owed Barbados £41 for remittances on postal money orders.

Governor Broome explained how the island's administration functioned financially: "The Tobago Government has been partly living of late on the proceeds of postal money orders issued in other countries in the Island, instead of remitting the money to meet the orders."[70] To this revelation a Colonial Office clerk noted in the margin of Broome's despatch, "this is very bad". Broome also found out that many property owners were unable to pay the land and house tax due at the end of September, and thus the Financial Board had passed a regulation extending the deadline to 1 December 1892.

Broome ordered that no payments were to be made from the Tobago treasury without his written consent. However, half of the salaries of government employees were to be paid each month and legal contracts were also to be honoured, as well as expenses needed "to save life, enforce the law, and preserve order".[71] Broome also ordered that funds received for postal money orders were to be kept separate and remitted either by the mail conveying the money orders or by the next mail. No supplies were to be ordered from England without his approval, and half of the funds in the treasury were to be remitted to the Crown agents at each mail towards liquidation of the debt with the agency.

Tobago's financial woes led Broome to an ominous contention: "If Tobago, as is too much to be feared, cannot pay its way under its present circumstances, and with its present establishment, changes must be made. Either the island must be completely annexed to Trinidad, and governed as a ward" or several positions in the civil establishment would have to be merged.[72] He suggested combining the commissionership and the police magistracy, that a sergeant should replace the inspector of police, and that the Windward magistracy be abolished, with its functions to be carried out by the district surgeon and other justices of the peace. Other minor abolitions and amalgamations of offices were suggested as well.

British officials construed Tobago's economic problems as solely an administrative dilemma. In reality, Tobago's sugar crisis, and that of the other British West Indian territories, was on many levels an effect of Britain's colonial policy. First, Britain developed the islands solely as producers of primary products for the benefit of the home market. Second, when Adam Smith's philosophy of laissez-faire took hold in Europe in the late eighteenth century, Britain removed protective tariffs against foreign-grown sugar, deliberately abandoning the colonies to the forces of the world market. Although the *Sugar Duties Equalization Act* took effect gradually from 1846 to 1854, the colonies were virtually left to fend for themselves. In addition, since the mid-nineteenth century Britain had been following a policy of gaining more control over the colonies by converting them into Crown Colonies, but at the same time the Crown was not taking increasing responsibility for their welfare. The Crown did not provide loans for diversification or promote any other means to help the colonies cope with the changing world economic environment. In the eyes of British officials the colonies had outgrown their usefulness and reached a point of diminishing returns. Amalgamating and federating them were simply attempts to reduce their administrative cost to Britain, not measures aimed at ameliorating or solving structural problems in their economies. The proposal to reduce Tobago to the status of a ward is a classic example of the failure of British colonial policy.

Officials at the Colonial Office received Broome's despatch on the Tobago situation on 5 October 1892 and wrote lengthy minutes. One official stated that Governor Broome's claim that the financial crisis was due to problems with the money orders was "not supported" and probably exaggerated, although "we have had to pull Tobago up before in the same direction".[73] This official also pointed out that Tobago "has been liable to ups & downs" and that, given previous proposals for drastic reductions in the civil establishment, the wisest policy would be to exercise caution and not be too "alarm[ed]".

Edward Wingfield blamed the financial problems on Hay's neglect and misadministration. Commissioner Hay had been left in charge too long after he had suffered burnout and succumbed to alcoholism, which had rendered him unfit for office.[74] These problems led the Tobago administration to be "entirely neglected" and resulted in the governor's having no information about Tobago, since Hay simply did not respond to his letters. Wingfield deemed it a mistake to condemn Tobago as being incapable of "paying its way" without sweeping retrenchment in the administration, since the island had been in a worse condition in 1886, and Administrator Llewellyn had been able to turn things around by careful governance. Wingfield was convinced that an "efficient" commissioner would soon be able to steer Tobago back onto the path of financial stability, and he warned that making Tobago a ward would be going against the wishes of the legislators in both islands, who at union had insisted on keeping the finances of both islands separate. Wingfield characterized Broome as "apt to be impetuous" and quite likely to change his mind after a short time.[75] He further urged that the Colonial Office await a report from the interim commissioner of Tobago on the financial state of the island.

In 1892 Hay was forced to resign and Broome appointed D. B. Horsford, the acting auditor-general of the colony, as acting commissioner. Horsford's first assignment was a "thorough investigation" of Tobago's finances. His report of 20 September 1892 revealed a depressing picture.[76] The treasury contained only £201 and the government owed the Crown agents £1,263, most of which was for money orders, the receipts for which had been used locally.

No contribution had been made towards the steamer service for 1891 through June 1892 (Trinidad must have paid Tobago's share of £750), land taxes were in arrears and the island had a deficit of £5,636. In addition, revenue for 1891 was £960 less than projected. Revenue for 1892 had also declined, partly because

> formerly every importation was taxed, since the union with Trinidad the labouring population and others have found a profitable market there for sale of stock and provisions and with the moneys thus obtained large purchases of dry goods and other supplies are obtained there, and as no means exists of making such articles pay Customs Duty to Tobago, Trinidad gets the benefit of the trade and Tobago loses it.[77]

The problems surrounding Tobago's lack of financial buoyancy eventually led to demands for greater autonomy and to the autonomists invoking identity. The alleged loss of revenue to Tobago caused by the customs union became a major point of contention between the two islands. It led Tobago merchants, who were losing business to Trinidad merchants, "to cry out for separation from Trinidad and for their right to levy taxes as in former years".[78] Thus the autonomy movement first reared its head over the issue of loss of revenue, not so much by the Tobago government as by the merchants of Tobago. However, the loss of customs revenue became a major preoccupation of the colonial government during the early years of the union.

On 28 December 1892, William Low, recently appointed commissioner of Tobago, wrote to the colonial secretary concerning the matter. Low accepted the view that the customs union was the primary cause of the steady decline in revenue. He observed that the Order in Council uniting the islands required that the revenue from items brought into Trinidad but used in Tobago should be credited to Tobago. However, the commissioner found that Tobago was not being credited for duties on certain items purchased by Tobagonians in Trinidad and carried to Tobago.[79] Some of these items were not recorded on the ships' manifests before they left Trinidad. In other cases passengers carried various items in their luggage, such as tobacco, that were undetectable by customs officials, and thus no duty was collected. Low proposed two remedies. One was to restrict the landing of goods and luggage to the Scarborough jetty – a measure that was already in force. The other strategy involved having customs officers search all luggage to identify and record dutiable items and have the passengers sign a declaration before the customs officials. The records of items that had escaped duty would be sent to Trinidad on a quarterly basis and the relevant duty credited to Tobago. Low contended that the island was losing at least £1,000 a year because of unpaid duty.

After comparing statistics from 1889 to 1892 in the areas of imports, customs and excise fees, wharf dues and duties on spirits and tobacco, Low alleged that the island had lost £1,231 per annum as a result of the union.[80] While £1,000 would be of "no consequence" to Trinidad, whose revenue was £500,000,

> to an impoverished place like Tobago – with its roads in places impassable; debts which under present circumstances it can never hope to pay; Grants in aid of Education reduced to already small dimensions; the allowance to the poor and aged slightly above starvation rations – this 1,000 pounds per annum would be equivalent to the saving loaf which prolongs the life of the perishing pauper.[81]

Low appealed to the governor to refund Tobago £4,926, the amount of alleged lost revenue for the first four years of union. Articulating we/they antipathies, he argued that Tobago's experience of loss of revenue since the union was an illustration that "the weaker vessel will suffer in a union with the larger and stronger".[82]

Collector of Customs John Fanning agreed that Tobago had lost revenue through goods escaping duty but disagreed with Low's rather high estimate.[83] Fanning proposed his own solution to the problem of lost customs revenue. He reasoned that Tobago should have its own customs and tariff system, as it had before union. On the other hand, Henry Fowler, the acting administrator of the colony, opined that the problem would be solved if both islands had "a common purse".[84] After reviewing the matter, the secretary of state ordered that the issue should be carried to the Legislative Council with a proposal of a yearly allowance from the Trinidad treasury to compensate Tobago, and that a select committee should decide the amount of compensation due.[85] He further ordered that the commissioner of Tobago should be present when the matter was discussed. This motion passed by the Council on 4 December 1893.[86] The select committee comprised the acting auditor-general as the chairman, the solicitor-general, the acting receiver-general and three unofficials: Mr Leotoud, Mr Cipriani and Mr Gordon. The committee's report had serious implications for the future political status of Tobago, but before the report was ready a call was made for total incorporation of Tobago into the administration of Trinidad.

At the end of 1893 a petition was prepared in Tobago recommending the island's incorporation as a ward of Trinidad. This was a joint effort of 1,016 individuals from the black labouring and middle classes, including labourers, artisans, teachers, two planters (from Trinidad) and one engineer.[87] The petition, spearheaded by C. L. Plagemann, "was decisive in shaping the views of the British officials on the future of Tobago".[88] Low described Plagemann as a "farrier, marshal's bailiff, amateur local radical and generally unsuccessful attempter of many things".[89]

Plagemann argued that Tobago was in a "deplorably low state" and that the situation could be easily remedied with the assistance of the secretary of state.[90] He contended that, so far, the union had proved "detrimental" to Tobago. Thus the island should be "incorporated more closely with Trinidad" by making it a ward in the colony.[91] He further requested establishment of a steamer service that would make stops at bays around the island. The revenue derived from the higher land tax that would result from Tobago's becoming a ward would provide an additional £2,000 per annum, which would pay for the service. Implementing this shipping proposal would facilitate regular transhipment of produce from Tobago to the Trinidad market and beyond. An itinerary appended to the petition showed that the steamer would call at Scarborough and sixteen bays around Tobago and then go to Barbados to connect with the Royal Mail steamers, finally moving on to Trinidad. "In other words, the signatories saw the need to integrate Tobago's village producers with international traffic and with the major nearby markets."[92]

Neither the governor nor Commissioner Low supported the petition. While Low thought the steamer service would be a "boon" for Tobago, he added sarcastically:

> I have no doubt the authorities of Trinidad will rejoice to incorporate as a ward an island with a revenue of £8,000, with an immediate prospect of being forced to spend £20,000, not to say the difficulty of collecting a land tax of one shilling per acre, when it is now found almost impossible to get in five pence.[93]

One senior official at the Colonial Office disliked the tone of Low's letter.[94] Low insisted that the petition was supported by only a few "names of weight or importance", that it did not represent "public feeling" and that it was the work of "an interested few – principally school teachers".[95] However, this petition caused the London officials to significantly change their thinking on the matter of Tobago's status and identity.

Wingfield agreed with the petitioners that "complete union ... would benefit Tobago, though for a time it would probably impose a burden on Trinidad".[96] He was convinced that neither the Legislative Council of the colony nor the Tobago Financial Board would be in favour of Tobago's becoming a ward. In response, Lord Ripon stated that while he was inclined to agree with the Crown's 1886 view that Tobago should be a ward of Trinidad, he was not yet prepared "to advise Her Majesty to adopt that measure, unless it is acceptable to the Legislative Council of the colony and the Financial Board of Tobago", and given Low's letter that such was not the case, no action would be taken on the matter.[97] However, Ripon did agree that the matter of the steamer service was worth consideration by the colonial government.

Ripon changed his mind about the proposal for making Tobago a ward after reading the report of the select committee on the loss of customs revenue to Tobago. The report was a blow to Commissioner Low's contention and may well have opened the floodgates for official pronouncements calling for Tobago to be made a ward of the colony.[98]

The report was laid before the legislature on 5 February 1894. Evidence on the amount of revenue Tobago had lost because of the union and the "consequent diversion of direct trade from Tobago to Trinidad" was gathered by the collector of customs, who had inspected the luggage of passengers en route to Tobago between 15 December 1893 and 14 January 1894. During this inspection for goods liable to duty but not entered on manifests, it was found that the duty on such goods amounted to only £3 12s. 3d., or approximately £45 per annum. Only 123 passengers travelled to Tobago during that period, and there was "no reason to believe that the average monthly traffic would be larger at any other time of the year".[99] The committee also discovered that Trinidad had given Tobago a credit of £3,928 11s. 8½d. during the first four years of the union, an amount more than adequate to cover any loss of revenue that Tobago had suffered as a result of diversion of direct trade to Trinidad. The committee also contended that exports from Tobago had fallen "considerably" since 1889, and that accounted for the reduced purchasing power of Tobagonians. The fall in revenue from imports could also suggest "the unsuitability of the Trinidad Tariff to the circumstances of Tobago".[100]

The committee recommended termination of free trade between the two islands and that each should be allowed to fix their own customs tariff and collect their own duties. At the end of the report a postscript by William Gordon-Gordon stated: "if Tobago could be converted into a Ward of Trinidad and its affairs managed economically its position and prospects would be materially altered in a few years and it would become a valuable adjunct to Trinidad".[101] If implemented, Gordon's proposal would undermine the remainder of Tobago's separate political and administrative identity, as well as the last vestiges of its autonomy. The island's political elite resisted this passionately, rejecting the idea and insisting on a separate customs union.

Agreeing with the majority report, the Tobago political elite called for separation. The Tobago Financial Board also sent a unanimous petition to the secretary of state requesting that "Tobago should have the right to manage her own Fiscal Affairs, and so make laws for the regulation of the Customs, Excise, and other duties which are at present imposed under the Laws of Trinidad".[102] Governor Broome doubted whether severing the customs union would be a good remedy to the problem; however, he had no objection to the proposal of the Financial Board.[103]

The London officials were not supportive of this idea. S. Oliver of the Colonial Office considered the Board's proposal to be "ill considered and retrograde".[104] Other officials, including Wingfield, concurred: "it should be plainly intimated that the Order in Council will not be amended in the sense proposed".[105] Wingfield argued that since the report of the select committee "exploded" the contentions of Commissioner Low, the loss to Tobago's revenue must be attributable to other causes, namely "the interruption of industrial progress caused by the mad proceedings of Sir John Gorrie[,] the effects of which are happily passing away".[106] He requested the opinion of Sir R. Meade, another official, on the matter. Meade suggested a "close[r] amalgamation" of Tobago with Trinidad[107] and advocated further consideration of Mr Gordon's proposal that Tobago should be made a ward of the colony. The secretary of state agreed with Meade.

Secretary of State Lord Ripon responded to the matter by first outlining his views on the causes of declining revenue in Tobago.[108] These included the abolition of import duties between the two islands; the fact that the Trinidad tariff imposed after the union was less burdensome than the previous one – an advantage to taxpayers but not to the Tobago treasury; recent trade arrangements with the United States of America – the 1892 McKinley tariff agreement – that further lowered duties on US commodities; and reduced consumption because of the adoption of higher Trinidad duties on spirits and tobacco. "[B]ut the most important cause of the failure of revenue has doubtless been . . . the collapse of sugar estate cultivation and the subsequent dislocation of trade and industry in the island in connection with the disputes between land-owners and metayers, resulting in the falling off in production and consequently in purchasing power."[109]

Tobagonian sociologist Susan Craig-James's elaboration is useful here. She argues that, since 1880, the four major sources of Tobago's revenue – import and other customs duties, excise duties, land and

Identity and Secession in the Caribbean

house taxes, and licences – had been falling steadily.

> Firstly, imports and exports had been considerably reduced because of the low prices for sugar, the low profits of most estates, the metayer disputes and the severe lack of specie. In addition, some of the dues on shipping had been reduced in 1882. Secondly, all but three of the thirty-two distilleries had already been closed by 1889, so reducing the excise duty collected. Thirdly, the crisis left many of the larger landowners unable to pay their taxes, and there was considerable forfeiture of land to the Crown in default. Finally, there was a marked export of animals by the middle strata and the labouring class after 1885, so reducing the license fees collected.[110]

Given all those factors, Lord Ripon contended, amending the Order in Council to once again give Tobago customs autonomy was not wise. "Rather than revert to the old system I . . . favour the policy advocated by Mr Gordon . . . namely to complete the union between the two islands by converting Tobago into a Ward of the Colony of Trinidad."[111]

At a public meeting held in Scarborough, neither the Financial Board of Tobago nor other members of the dominant class agreed with the secretary of state's suggestion that Tobago should be made a ward.[112] Given the sentiment of Tobago's upper class, Broome was convinced that the Legislative Council would not support such a move. Further, he argued, if Tobago was made a ward a considerable amount of Trinidad "public money" would be diverted to Tobago. The prospect of this financial burden was more significant to the governor than any sentiment in Tobago. Broome was continually concerned about how Tobago was going to "pay its way" in a virtually bankrupt state. He pointed out that on 30 June 1894 the island owed the Crown agents £1,622 and Trinidad another £5,000. He also explained that "the government of Tobago has lately again been driven to employ the proceeds of Post Office money orders, and Savings Bank fund, to pay salaries and current expenses".[113] Broome favoured Low's solution of reducing the salaries of government employees and amalgamating and abolishing certain positions in the civil establishment. Low had also suggested a loan of £10,000. Broome's remedy was an imperially guaranteed loan of £20,000 for road construction, for providing small, secured loans to "bona fide and specially selected cultivators" and for paying off debts owed to the Crown agents and to Trinidad. Broome ended his letter with this rhetorical question: "Tobago is an imperial possession, and, if it is worth keeping, is it not worth helping?"[114] Clearly Broome believed that the Crown had a moral obligation to assist Tobago.

The responses of Colonial Office officials and the secretary of state are similarly insightful. Wingfield declared that an imperial guarantee of a loan was "out of the question" and that the Trinidad government would not provide one.[115] However, Tobago could be given part of a loan made to Trinidad. Lord Ripon contended that while Tobago was in debt to the tune of £6,500, its revenue of 1893 exceeded its expenditure by £673. The prospect for a surplus in the current year was also good.[116] He did accede to a few of Low's recommendations for the abolition of offices. He did not approve the £20,000 loan, because it would have put an additional burden of £700 to £800 on the revenue and would most likely lead to increased taxation. Ripon also did not approve borrowing money to pay off the loan to Trinidad or to lend to small cultivators. However, he believed that a "moderate" loan of £4,000 to £5,000 could be raised locally, without an imperial guarantee, for road improvement and to pay off the Crown agents.

The negative financial situation of the Tobago government undeniably added to the problems of adjustment to the union. While local officials made attempts to resolve these problems, the situation did not improve. For its part the Colonial Office did not accept the view that Tobago needed a financial bailout by means of a huge loan. The London officials realized that the island had serious structural problems, given the sugar depression and the inability of its residents to pay taxes. While they wanted to honour the wishes of the leading classes in both islands to maintain, as far as possible, separate political and administrative systems, the Plagemann petition provided a fillip in the opposite direction. Thus, in the minds of the British, making Tobago a ward in the colony became the only rational solution, although it was seen as a measure of last resort.

If implemented, the solution proposed by the Colonial Office and the secretary of state would deal the final blow in eliminating Tobago's political and administrative autonomy and identity. Its prospects were viewed with serious foreboding by the planter/merchant class in the island. In a last ditch effort to dissuade the London officials and prevent the island from being completely subsumed by the Trinidad colossus, the dominant class, which stood to lose the most from total incorporation, invoked the issue of identity. Citing we/they antipathies, they insinuated that Tobago was a more purely British territory than Trinidad, whose "sentiment", religion and nationality were "alien" to the smaller island.

The Impact of Union on the Articulation of Tobagonian Identity

Everything seemed to be working at cross-purposes for the dominant class. Many of them had suffered personal misfortune in the bankruptcy of their sugar estates. They had played right into the hands of the Colonial Office, exchanging the old representative system of government for Crown Colony status without reaping the expected reward of an infusion of British capital. Having lost most of their political status and prestige with the union (Port of Spain had taken over as the locus of government administration), they could not accept the loss of the only semi-autonomous remnant of authority in the island, the Financial Board, for that would be an inevitable consequence of wardship. Their arguments that the union had contributed significantly to the continual decline in government revenue had been blown to bits by the report of the select committee that examined the impact of the union on the government's revenue.

The social prestige of the dominant class was gradually fading as more black and coloured Tobagonians moved up the economic ladder as shopkeepers, smallholders and planters themselves. Furthermore, in the Plagemann petition this upwardly mobile group had challenged the wisdom of the dominant class's solution to the Tobago problem. If Tobago became a ward of the colony, the latter knew that whatever vestige of political power and status they had left would disappear because Tobago would have only satellite status in the colony. The island's insolvency and their own straitened circumstances – many could not even pay property and land taxes – meant that they would not be socially equal to their more prosperous counterparts in Trinidad. Thus, preserving Tobago's separate identity and autonomy was worth the struggle.

Apparently nothing could cauterize the economic haemorrhage in Tobago. The continuing depressed economic state of the island led the planter/merchant class to support a petition calling for full separation from Trinidad and reunion with the Windward Islands federation. The developing autonomy movement in Tobago was being injected with new blood. The members of the dominant class can be described as the first secessionists, but their motivations for autonomy, outlined above, were self-serving. They cannot be placed on the far left of the autonomy continuum but rather several notches to the right of that position. They simply wanted to change partners, from Trinidad to the loose Windward Islands federation, in which they felt their political and commercial status would be preserved. Self-centred or not, they fought vigorously to achieve their goal.

On 10 December 1894 the elected members of the Financial Board wrote a letter to Commissioner Low complaining of "the intolerable nature of the present position of Tobago in relation to Trinidad, with regard to financial matters".[117] The unofficials referred again to the loss of revenue supposedly brought about by customs union with Trinidad. A petition to Queen Victoria accompanied their letter. It stated that the union had proved disastrous to Tobago and consequently invoked the resolution of 19 January 1887, which requested reversion to self-governing status.[118]

The petitioners made several charges concerning the negative effects of the union, in language that emphasized we/they antipathies and that also underscored grievances.[119] They effectively used issues of identity to make their claims. Besides the contention about loss of revenue, they charged "indifference on the part of Trinidad to any matter connected with the welfare of Tobago"; that the majority of the Legislative Council were unwilling to help Tobago out of its plight; and that the union had led to the introduction of "class prejudice" because of the

Identity and Secession in the Caribbean

actions of Trinidad judges [Gorrie in particular] and by the "general and admitted" lack of "sympathy" between the people of both islands, who were different in "religion and practically in nationality".[120] The memorialists also contended that the governor did not visit Tobago and that the Trinidad press wrote "disparagingly of Tobago" and disapproved of the union. Further, Trinidad's "elaborate and cumbrous" laws were unsuited to Tobago, especially those relating to customs, excise, prisons, education, Crown lands, vital statistics, registration of deeds and wills, and quarantine requirements.

Moreover, the petitioners thought it regrettable that the secretary of state refused to grant Tobago customs autonomy but instead advocated conversion of the island into a ward of Trinidad. They argued that if such a union occurred it would be "detrimental to the interests" of Tobago because (1) land taxes would immediately increase; (2) many Trinidad laws "unsuited to the requirements of a small community like Tobago" would come into operation; (3) expenditure on official salaries would increase; (4) diversion of the profits of trade from Tobago to Trinidad "would be ruinously increased"; (5) freedom of trade between the two islands did not benefit taxpayers in general but only a small body of "traffickers" who "speculate[d]" between the islands; (6) the development of Tobago's Crown lands would be checked; (7) corrupt practices in the Trinidad civil service would spread to Tobago, which was "dissimilar in sentiment, religion and race", and "finally, . . . Tobago refused to lose its identity and prestige by absolute incorporation with an Island alien in religion and practically in nationality".[121] Thus it had taken only four years of union for crystallization of Tobagonian identity in contradistinction to that of Trinidad and Trinidadians. In the years to come the identity issue would become even more politically charged.

Grievances, the secondary element in identity construction, were also highlighted. The petitioners cited the failed expectations of the union. Improved communication with Europe and America had not occurred. In fact, by the time of the petition the steamers of Scrutton's Direct Line from London had ceased calling at Tobago, and there was no direct communication with the United States. The petitioners lamented that all goods imported from America initially had to come through

Trinidad, resulting in "serious delay and much additional expense"[122] (autonomists of the 1970s continued to make this claim concerning goods imported from abroad). The expected influx of capital from Trinidad for development in Tobago had not materialized. The secessionists argued that because Trinidad had extensive and only partially developed tracts of Crown lands, she had neither the "capital, labour, nor willingness to assist in the development of Tobago".[123] Similar expressions of failed expectations would continue to dominate the complaints of Tobago's political leaders well into the next century.

Commissioner Low neither supported nor rejected the petition, which, he stated, was signed by two hundred persons who represented "the property and intelligence of the community".[124] However, he pointed out that while Trinidad was closer to Tobago than Grenada and the chief towns of those islands were "nearly equidistant from Scarborough", it was easier to get to Grenada by boat than to Port of Spain. He acknowledged that Tobago could not expect people of means from Trinidad to invest in Tobago; high rates of interest could be obtained on investments in Trinidad, where 700,000 acres of Crown land were available for sale. His own experience assured him that Tobago was not "regarded with favourable eyes". He agreed with the petitioners that only "traffickers" — the lower-class traders — benefited from trade between the islands. However, he argued that it was not difficult for them to lose in this trade, since they had to pay freight charges, steamer fare and their own upkeep for as many as eight days in Trinidad. This disparaging attitude towards the labouring class was characteristic of the political elite. Essentially Low was saying that blacks did not have the managerial savvy to determine whether they were making profits or not. Finally, he pointed out that Grenada, which controlled its own customs, also carried on a brisk trade with Trinidad, and thus provided competition for the Tobago traffickers.

While the Colonial Office did not accede to the petitioners' wishes, the responses of its officials provide useful insight into the relationship between the two islands.[125] S. Oliver did not think that reuniting Tobago with the Windward Islands government was a good idea, since granting

Identity and Secession in the Caribbean

Tobago customs autonomy would not satisfy their complaints.

Edward Wingfield argued that the Queen did not have the power to rescind the Order in Council because it was made under an act of Parliament; only additional parliamentary legislation could dissolve the union. He also pointed out that the petitioners had not provided any new evidence concerning the loss of customs revenue to Tobago. As to the allegations that Trinidad's laws were not suited to Tobago, Wingfield contended that the Legislative Council had the authority to pass special legislation for Tobago, and that it was the duty of the commissioner and the unofficial representative of Tobago on the Council to "represent the necessity for such legislation on any particular subject".[126] Even the quarantine laws about which the memorialists complained could be handled this way. Wingfield also argued that the fact that capitalists were not purchasing land in Tobago was no reason to dissolve the union. His strongest recommendation was that the governor should visit Tobago from time to time to "let the people see that he takes a personal interest in their welfare and remove the impression which evidently prevails that Tobago is neglected by the Colonial Government".[127] It is difficult to tell whether this was a genuine administrative gesture or a suggestion for window-dressing only. Notwithstanding, the acknowledgement of neglect – a major plank in the separatists' platform from the time of union until 1980 – was significant.

Another Colonial Office official even suggested that a commission of enquiry be formed to look into the matter of the union. That course of action was deemed unwise since it was felt that such a commission would not reveal more than was already known, and also because of the cost factor. Wingfield characterized such action as premature and blamed former commissioner Hay, who "took to drinking", for allowing "the whole administration to go to pieces".[128] Wingfield also blamed Sir John Gorrie, whose "zeal for the negro did scant justice to the planters and not only set the planters and metayers to quarrel but prejudiced in the eyes of the planters the connexion with Trinidad because he was a judge of that Island".[129] Wingfield was afraid that an inquiry would "revive the quarrels and racial antagonism" on the island.

Lord Ripon denied the petitioners' request to dissolve the union. He instructed Governor Broome to explain to them that their petition was "based in part on a misconception of facts", namely the issue of the loss of customs revenue.[130] While he admitted that Tobago's experience in its "administrative connexion" with Trinidad had so far not been fortunate, he urged the petitioners to understand that the causes of the problem were "exceptional" and would not be remedied by simply dissolving the union. "The real causes of stagnation [were] to be found in [the] depression of trade and agriculture which is not peculiar to Tobago, though it may be felt there at present with particular acuteness."[131]

The secretary of state also upbraided Governor Broome for not paying sufficient attention to Tobago. "I cannot resist the conclusion", he declared, "that, so far as administration can help the prosperity of a country, Tobago is suffering somewhat from the neglect and apparent indifference of the Executive Government".[132] (Ripon's assessment would echo down the corridors of time even several decades later.) He instructed the governor to visit Tobago as soon as possible and "investigate on the spot" the factors that led to the petitioners' complaints. He further insisted on lending to Tobago an official from the Botanic Gardens who was knowledgeable in growing and curing cocoa, to instruct local growers there as they had requested. Following Wingfield's lead, Ripon contended that special laws could be made for Tobago and that the representative from Tobago on the Legislative Council should take care of that obligation. For example, a law could be passed authorizing quarantine officials in either island to declare the other island or parts thereof infected.

Following Ripon's instructions, Governor Broome visited Tobago in early May 1895 and made a positive report on the state of the island's affairs, although he simply may have been trying to appease Ripon. Broome had not visited Tobago for two years. During his visit he commended the commissioner for good administration because the £2,000 debt owed to the Crown agents had been repaid, the island's revenue had covered its expenditure and a revenue surplus was expected at the end of 1895. Even the people seemed to be in better spirits and were better clad than when Broome had last seen them. They "looked well fed and prosperous".[133] Broome also observed more activity in housing construction and repair as well as in cultivation. Exports of animals to Trinidad during 1894 were valued at almost £18,000. Broome was happy to report that while the island had not made great strides, it was "distinctly emerging from its former hopeless condition".[134] From Commissioner Low he learned that purchase of Crown lands under the Crown Lands Regulation was satisfactory, and that Barbados was considering settling emigrants in Tobago.

Finally, to resolve the "burning question" of the alleged loss of customs duties, Broome authorized a search of passengers' luggage for one year from the beginning of June 1895 to determine conclusively the revenue loss to Tobago. Low felt that once that was settled there would be no reluctance in maintaining the union.[135] The abolition of certain offices, approved by the secretary of state, had been carried out, and a few investors had settled in Tobago. While Broome did not sanction Low's proposal that £5,000 should be loaned to owners of large sugar and cocoa estates, he did endorse a loan of £10,000 to improve the island's infrastructure. The secretary of state approved the loan for road construction and agreed with the governor that it was ill-advised to lend money to estate owners.[136]

In August 1895 the acting administrator of Trinidad and Tobago gave his unsolicited views on the situation in Tobago as depicted in the petition. C. C. Knollys lamented that "every possible difficulty caused by the union" had been "seized upon" by the petitioners. However, he opined,

> I consider the Union of the two Islands to be too close, or not close enough. The very best thing that could happen for Tobago would be [for it] to be made a ward of Trinidad, and I believe that opinion is shared by most if not all, disinterested persons who are acquainted with the circumstances of the two islands.[137]

His alternative solution was "to assimilate" the constitution of Tobago into that of St Lucia or St Vincent. In spite of these ideas, Knollys perceived that dissatisfaction with the union was "mostly caused by agitators working for their own ends".[138] He insisted that the union "ha[d] never really been given a fair chance".[139]

Two months later, in October 1895, Knollys visited Tobago for one week, apparently for the first time. He reported to the secretary of state that all the books were in good order and that many of the roads were better than could be expected, given the paltry amount that had been spent on them in recent times. He also reported, "I could not help being struck with the *insignificance and unimportance* of Tobago. It is not of more importance than one of the lesser wards in Trinidad."[140] For many years this image of Tobago in the minds of Trinidad government officials left a legacy of disparaging lack of interest in the island's affairs. Knollys had begun a trend of thinking that characterized the integrationists, viewing Tobago as one of the rural districts of Trinidad. Further, his visits to Tobago were based merely on the imperial obligations of his job, not made out of concern for Tobago's welfare.

Governor Broome also visited Tobago again between 26 March and 15 April 1896, probably the longest visit a governor had paid to Tobago in many years.[141] Broome reported, "I found the Dependency forgeing [sic] ahead, though slowly."[142] He commended the administration of Commissioner Low, who was "out early and late, and attends well to everything", including expenditure of the £4,000 first instalment of the loan for road construction.

Despite this report, the end of Broome's term in office set the stage for action on making Tobago a ward of the colony. The constant sentiment in that direction by British officials, the governor and the acting administrator; petitions deliberately seeking such a course or inadvertently supporting it; and, even more so, the depressed state of the island's economy all colluded to make the island seem more trouble than it was worth. So far the union had not resulted in much improvement to Tobago's fiscal affairs. In the words of Administrator Knollys, Tobago had become insignificant and unimportant. When Governor Hubert Jerningham took office in 1897, he was ready to make Tobago a "district or wardenship of Trinidad".

Identity and Secession in the Caribbean

Chapter 5

Making Tobago a Ward, 1897–1924

The period from 1897 through the first quarter of the twentieth century was one in which Tobago lost its semi-autonomous political and administrative status and identity. In 1899 Tobago became a ward, a mere administrative district, in the colony of Trinidad and Tobago. The period was also one of adjustment to the reality that Port of Spain was the seat of government and the administrative centre of the colony. The challenges of overcoming the physical and psychological distance between Tobagonians and the central government led to calls for Tobago to be given special consideration and concessions. The issue of representation on policy-making committees and in the institutions of legislative power became a major source of contention and ill will. During the first quarter of the twentieth century, letters and petitions listing various grievances and demanding greater devolution of power indicated a significant increase in the construction of Tobagonian identity in contradistinction to Trinidadians. At this juncture in the union the autonomists occupied positions just left of centre of the autonomy continuum. Their calls for separation were generally threats to effect more equitable treatment of the minor partner in the union.

Wardship: The Process

In 1897 Sir Hubert E. H. Jerningham became governor of Trinidad and Tobago, and soon he contemplated making Tobago a ward. In mid-August he visited Tobago for a week and reported to Secretary of State Joseph Chamberlain that he feared it would not be easy to alleviate the economic "difficulties under which this dependency is labouring".[1] After his very first visit to the island Jerningham thought it desirable to make Tobago a "district or wardenship of Trinidad". He reported on the poverty of the island, its poorly maintained roads and the need for capital and labour. He also stated that the people were "too lazy" to become farmers, a conclusion that could not be further from the truth.[2] Jerningham also expressed the view that unless Tobago became a "district" of Trinidad there was little hope for prosperity on the island. To him Tobago was truly a "dependency", and Trinidad was its saviour.

By January 1898 Jerningham had considered the report of the 1897 West Indian Royal Commission and became confident that his initial solution for Tobago's economic and administrative problems was sound. The commissioners did not mince words in their report, which not only gave their solution to Tobago's problems but also examined the fears of Tobagonians about their future prospects. They "recommend[ed] the complete amalgamation of Tobago and Trinidad, and the abolition of the separate account of revenue and expenditure. Tobago would then become a ward, or district, of Trinidad, and the two islands would have a common exchequer."[3] The commissioners, who believed that most Tobagonians were in favour of complete union, nonetheless pointed out that everyone did not share that view. Landowners and traders exhibited fears that the union would be established at their expense. Large landowners feared that complete union would lead to an increase in land taxes to the level prevailing in Trinidad. The commissioners explained that such an eventuality was not predetermined, since "Tobago in its present condition, has a good claim for a separate treatment in this matter".[4] Traders feared that union would reduce their business in imports and possibly exports. The commissioners conceded that that possibility was strong but did not think it was a significant enough argument against making Tobago a ward of the united colony.

To Jerningham the complete union of Tobago and Trinidad was absolutely necessary. He tried to convince Chamberlain that "in amalgamation lies salvation for Tobago".[5] He reported that Tobago's commissioner, William Low, concurred with this view. Since the majority of Tobagonians conducted trade with Trinidad, that was a "powerful reason" for believing they would favour a closer union with Trinidad. Jerningham ended his letter with the promise that if Chamberlain agreed with the amalgamation proposal, he would recommend that a delegation from both islands meet to discuss "the best means of treating Tobago with that equity and fairness which Mr Low claimed as a sine-qua non of the amalgamation".[6]

Commissioner Low was originally not in favour of Tobago's becoming a ward of Trinidad. His antagonism to wardship revolved around aspects of identity construction, especially we/they antipathies and historical memory:

> I must candidly confess that for the first 2 or 3 years of my residence here I was not an advocate for closer union with Trinidad: and even now the fact that an essentially English island, with such a brilliant page of history, will merge its identity on being amalgamated with an island largely permeated with Franco-Spanish ideas, although a mere matter of sentiment, causes a certain amount of regret.[7]

However, he could not dispute the view of the Royal Commissioners that Tobago's union with Trinidad in 1889 had not improved the island's financial and administrative position. Notwithstanding, he still argued that Tobago's financial and administrative condition was partly due to the fact that given

> [the] unsatisfactory nature of the present conditions of the union Tobago is in some respects considered and treated as a separate Government yet, financially, she is hampered by the Customs and Excise Laws and Regulation of Trinidad, and administratively her requirements are dealt with on the advice of officials resident in Trinidad and necessarily unacquainted with her local needs.[8]

The charge that Trinidad officials created ill-advised policies for Tobago because they were not resident on the island and, therefore, not acquainted with its circumstances continued to dominate the contentious relations between the islands for decades. Low had also formed such an attachment to the once prosperous little island that, while he felt compelled to recant his opposition to wardship, he insisted that Tobago should be annexed to either Barbados or the Windward Islands government if she would receive "anything less than equal, or, for the present, even generous treatment" in the union with Trinidad.[9] Low's suspicion that Trinidad would not regard Tobago with solicitous interest is significant. His long association with the island and conviction that Tobago was of purer British vintage than Trinidad gave him a strong sense of Tobagonian identity, at least in an official capacity, and in that regard he had separatist leanings. As a colonial administrator he probably had a very good idea of where Tobago stood in the pecking order of British West Indian colonies. Thus he tried to safeguard the island from the worst of the ignominious treatment that he was certain would be its lot.

Low's views on wardship for Tobago involved a moral obligation on the part of the larger, more prosperous island: "Trinidad [was] to be [held] responsible for the future upkeep of Tobago."[10] He cautioned that when Tobago became a ward, its depressed economy should "justify the exceptional treatment" in the matter of land tax, and warned that if the land tax was suddenly increased it would result in the remainder of the estates falling into the hands of the state by escheat. The situation was even more serious because "however impecunious the larger landowners are they form an important buffer between the Government and the peasant in a serious transitory state of things".[11] Low was of the same ilk as his superiors in the Colonial Office, whose racist views dictated that the political, economic and social development of black Tobagonians, and all West Indians, should be stymied as long as possible. Thus, despite his concern for the welfare of the island, Low supported the elite above the ordinary Tobagonian. His desire to protect, at any cost, the position of the planter and merchant classes places him among that group of London officials whose racial prejudice had clearly been manifested.

Low wished for some positive benefits for Tobago from the closer union of the two islands. These included improvement and extension of educational facilities and an increase in teachers' wages. He advised that the Trinidad officials who would be responsible for Tobago's affairs become well acquainted with the island and ensure "effective administrative supervision . . . over their subordinates stationed in a separate island".[12] The governor's administration of the island would become easier if telegraphic communication and a biweekly steamer service between the two islands were established. In Low's view, those two "necessaries" were of the greatest importance.

Next in the order of priority for Low was the extension of peasant proprietorship and setting up a botanic station as recommended by the Royal Commissioners. Low suggested making it possible for junior officials to be transferred to Tobago with proportionately lower salaries, because the cost of living in Tobago was less than in Trinidad. An increase in the police force and establishment of a volunteer militia corps were also recommended. Additionally, a warden whose duties would include that of sub-treasurer was proposed. Other suggestions included abolition of the separate account of revenue and expenditure, keeping Savings Bank funds separate from general revenue, paying the Tobago debt with a grant from the imperial treasury, and cancelling Trinidad's £5,000 loan to Tobago, since Trinidad would have benefited from the latter's customs revenue. Low's comments demonstrate his genuine interest in the welfare of Tobago. However, other ideas ran counter to his.

There was a lot at stake in wardship for Tobago, including its presence in the official name of the united colony. In July 1898 Acting Governor Sir C. C. Knollys expressed his integrationist philosophy in a letter to Chamberlain: "I suppose the name of the Colony will be 'Trinidad', Tobago being a district only."[13] It is not surprising that Knollys took this position. It was he who was the least impressed with Tobago, viewing it as insignificant and unimportant. Further, he embodied the official Trinidadian perception of the island that continued to vex Tobagonians for decades. Knollys's suggestion was rejected and the united colony was called Trinidad and Tobago. A magistrate-warden would become the chief administrator in Tobago. His salary was set at £500 per annum (later increased to £600), with provision of a horse and a travelling allowance of £35 per annum.[14]

From the beginning Tobago was considered a financial burden to Trinidad. In an 11 August 1898 letter to Chamberlain, Knollys pointed out that while Tobago would become a district of a prosperous colony and would share in its advantages and hopefully become prosperous itself, "at first it cannot but be an expense to Trinidad".[15] One of the expenses would be the cost of establishing a telegraph link with Tobago. For the West India and Panama Telegraph Company Limited to lay the cable would cost £7,820, which was too expensive for the Trinidad government to undertake at that time. The contention that Tobago was a financial burden to Trinidad would plague the relationship between the two islands throughout the twentieth century.

The British government took action on the recommendations of the 1897 Royal Commission. On 20 October 1898 an Order in Council revoked the 17 November 1888 Order by which Tobago was initially united with Trinidad.[16] The 1898 order made Tobago a ward of the colony of Trinidad and Tobago; the revenue, expenditure and debt of Tobago were merged with those of the united colony and Tobago's debt to Trinidad was cancelled. Ironically, Tobago had become partially a ward of itself. In reality, however, it became a satellite of Trinidad.

All laws in force in Trinidad took effect in Tobago, and all future laws of the colony applied to Tobago. However, the legislature had power to enact special and local ordinances – called regulations – applicable only to Tobago. The 1898 Order in Council also provided that the governor could levy a separate land tax in Tobago that would be lower than that in Trinidad. In addition, licence fees authorized by the Licence Regulation (1893) were to continue in force in Tobago, notwithstanding those in the rest of the colony. However, no licence fees could be charged for horses (stallions), geldings, mules, mares and asses, a concession that was much appreciated by the people.[17] The Tobago licence fees for spirits would continue in force, notwithstanding Trinidad ordinances to the contrary. The 1898 order also prohibited taxes, rates or charges in Tobago from being used to raise funds for East Indian immigration, which applied only to Trinidad.

With reference to the composition of the legislature, additional instructions were made to the effect that unofficial members would no longer be chosen as representatives of any particular district of the colony.[18] However, a special exception was made: one unofficial member would be chosen from the residents of Tobago to promote the interests of the smaller island. This type of consideration was needed, and was demanded by later autonomists, to give Tobagonians the sense that they had a stake in the colony. On 8 December 1898 Governor Jerningham proclaimed that the 1898 Order in Council would take effect on 1 January 1899, thus making Tobago a ward of the colony from that date.[19] On 24 October 1898 he recommended James T. Rousseau, chief clerk and assistant to the sub-intendant of Crown lands, to be the warden-magistrate of Tobago.[20] On 30 November 1898 Chamberlain approved Rousseau's appointment.[21]

Wardship: Problems and Possibilities

The reorganization of the civil establishment in Tobago was the first order of business after the island was converted into a ward. After the first three months of operation it was clear that staff arrangements had to be made. The warden, whose duties "necessitated his frequent absence from office", requested a clerk who had knowledge of the procedures of a magistrate's court.[22] The work of the sub-treasury, which included the post office and customs and other duties, was also deemed too heavy for its staff; thus an assistant harbour-master was appointed.

Other problems cropped up after Tobago became a district in the colony. A petition from some residents of Tobago concerning various needs of the island was sent to the secretary of state during the first half of 1899.[23] Two points of contention were the administration of justice and the investigation of land deeds. While Acting Attorney-General Vincent Brown and Attorney-General N. Nathan wished to transfer all trials of the Supreme Court from Tobago to Port of Spain, the Executive Council advised that the Tobago assizes should continue in operation.

The petitioners complained that the Tobago rules of court stated that initiation and trial of any action in the ordinary jurisdiction of the Supreme Court was forbidden. They argued that this procedure would "so enormously increase the cost of litigation . . . as to amount to an entire denial of justice".[24] Brown indicated that the petitioners misunderstood the law, since "ordinary jurisdiction" meant actions that exceeded £200 in value. He claimed that in Tobago only a limited number of such cases occurred. Thus the abolition of the Tobago assizes would affect only very few Tobagonians. Even so, abolition of the Tobago assizes would make it inconvenient for Tobagonians to access the services provided by government. Trinidad officials did not usually sympathize with the difficulty Tobagonians faced in having to travel to Trinidad to access government services. Hence autonomists in the twentieth century continued to emphasize Tobago's special circumstances, especially its isolation from the centre of government, when justifying their claims for decentralization and even secession.

The petitioners also complained about the transfer to Trinidad of the register of deeds, wills and other related documents. Brown, an ardent integrationist, was convinced that operation of the Trinidad system of registration "absolutely" necessitated "that there should be but one Register where all indexes are kept, judgments recorded and *lis pendens* filed".[25] He could not envisage working the system with two registers. The use of one register located in Trinidad became a bone of contention from 1899 onwards. The fact that Tobagonians had to go to Trinidad to register deeds and wills reveals the government's insensitivity towards meeting their needs and giving due consideration to their peculiar circumstances as an island separated by water, with very unreliable sea communications. This matter was taken up by the elected representatives of Tobago from 1925 onwards, and was used as a rallying point to galvanize support for the autonomy movement in the 1970s. Brown suggested that the union could be successful only if "frequent direct communication existed". Since that was not then a reality, he should have found some other way to deal with the registration of deeds and wills in

Identity and Secession in the Caribbean

Tobago. Brown's emphasis on frequent communication demonstrates that he did not envisage Tobago's becoming an important administrative centre in the colony. In his mind the Trinidad government should not be required to make allowances to suit the Tobago situation, and Tobagonians should go to Trinidad if they wanted access to the full range of government services.

Despite Brown's position on the matter, a solution was found. In March 1900 the legislature passed an ordinance entitled *An Ordinance to provide for the receipt in Tobago and transmission to Port-of-Spain of deeds and assurances executed in Tobago and required to be registered in the office of the Registrar General.*[26] The Executive Council had taken its first step in considering the special circumstances of Tobago. Had the government continued down that path, it is likely that demands for secession would have been delayed.

In August 1899 C. C. Knollys, serving again as acting governor, visited Tobago and gave a glowing report of "marked signs of improvement" compared to his visit three years earlier. He wrote, "[T]here is now more trade and more life; many of the old houses are being repaired and painted, and several new ones are being built."[27] Most of the abandoned estates in the Windward district had been purchased and planted in cocoa and rubber. Warden Rousseau was commended for his work on the island. In a letter to Chamberlain, Knollys insisted that everyone was satisfied with Tobago's status as a ward, except the island's nominated representative in the Legislative Council, George. H. McEachrane. No detail was given of McEachrane's grievances. However, Warden Rousseau observed that there was room for improvement in the administrative structure of the island.

Not long after Tobago was constituted a ward, Rousseau advocated for "greater powers than the Warden of any other ward" in the colony.[28] This situation developed when the governor's office returned Rousseau's supplementary warden's report for January to March 1901. The colonial secretary stated that Rousseau's inclusion of information concerning departments not under his purview constituted unacceptable procedure: "The Governor [C. A. Maloney] wishes you to send in your *departmental* report, which should be confined entirely to the matters connected with the departments under your charge."[29] Rousseau's response was that as warden of Tobago he was the representative of the sub-intendant, ex-officio supervisor of excise, superintendent registrar, ex-officio sanitary inspector, inspector of schools for Tobago, stipendiary magistrate and representative of the director of public works. All these responsibilities, as well as other factors, led him to conclude that the chief officer in Tobago should have more powers than wardens in Trinidad. Rousseau pointed out that wardens in Trinidad styled their reports "administration" reports. Thereby, he implied, he was the head of administration in Tobago as much as they were in their wards; as such, he included items in his report that the wardens in Trinidad included in theirs.

Rousseau further contended that Tobago "should not be treated in the same manner as any other ward".[30] He referenced the 1884 Royal Commission report, which stated that the warden should be regarded as the "representative of the governor", with the authority of interference in departmental matters only in cases of "extreme emergency". He also argued that Governor Jerningham had held this view and had communicated the same to him in instructions and later in private letters.[31] Given Jerningham's instructions shortly after taking office, Rousseau began submitting reports "embracing the whole administration of the Island"; thus he continued the practice during Governor Maloney's administration.

Rousseau further defended his action in terms of the distinct identity of the island and with regard to its isolation from the centre of government:

> Tobago can never be the same as any other ward of Trinidad – it is divided from that Island by twenty miles of ocean – it has a different people and a history of its own – it is recognized as different in the commercial world by being included in the routes of the different steamship companies, and its growing importance under altered circumstances will increase the difference every year.[32]

He insisted that "from a purely administrative point of view there ought to be a head to the Service in Tobago, that is to say an officer to whom in an emergency any matter might be referred, and whose decision would be final pending a reference to Trinidad.[33] He further explained that referring matters to the receiver-general, collector of customs or postmaster-general meant "a delay of at least a week, and in the meantime the public may be put to serious inconvenience".[34] Rousseau certainly had his finger on the pulse of the negative administrative impact of the union on Tobagonians. What is significant about his comments is that they remained germane for decades afterwards, and were still on the laundry list of grievances of the separatists in the 1970s.

Taken at face value, Rousseau's comments may lead one to conclude that he should be placed on the left of the autonomy continuum. He was in fact a centrist. As a senior government officer he was interested only in effective and efficient administration. Like Commissioner Low before him, Rousseau was basically interested in governance. Low had recommended that Tobago be reunited with the Windward Islands government rather than suffer marginalization and neglect from Trinidad. Rousseau pointed out that the difference between working as an administrative subordinate in Tobago and as one of equal rank in Trinidad meant that the former was working at a disadvantage. Subordinate officers in Trinidad, despite their distance from the centre of administration, could quickly confer with their supervisors by telephone or telegraph. Thus Rousseau recommended that, at least "until telegraphic communication is established, the officer occupying the post of Warden and Magistrate [in Tobago] should be entrusted with fuller powers".[35]

Rousseau's proposal led to official consultation on the matter. The governor solicited comments from key officials in Trinidad. Director of Public Works Walsh Wrightson contended that Rousseau wanted increased supervisory authority. He had "strong objections to a Warden assuming charge of the work of this Department, in which much technical knowledge is requisite, and of giving orders to the District or other officers".[36] However, he welcomed the "assistance" of the warden, and in the case of an emergency expected him to give instructions of a non-technical nature. Wrightson demonstrated his integrationist philosophy in other remarks on the matter. He contended that Rousseau's claim that Tobago's special circumstances made it different from other wards was "without any solid basis". He did not understand why government officers in Tobago should be treated differently from those in Trinidad. Furthermore, he thought "the proper policy to pursue is to eliminate points of difference, to promote the solidarity of the Colony and not to accentuate differences between the two Islands forming it".[37] Wrightson was a classic integrationist Trinidadian official who saw Tobago as just another rural district of Trinidad.

Receiver-General S. W. Knaggs was equally stuck in the integration-ist mould. He declared that Rousseau's proposal was "detrimental to the public service".[38] Similarly situated to the right of centre on the autonomy continuum was Collector of Customs R. H. McCarthy. He was convinced that "no benefit" would come from adopting Rousseau's suggestion. McCarthy believed that Rousseau's proposal would under-mine the union of the two islands: "The powers sought by Mr Rousseau for the Warden are quite inconsistent with the ideas which underlay the annexation of Tobago; they would logically bring about the loosening of the union between the two Islands."[39] He further argued that Tobago was less isolated than Mayaro or Toco (two rural villages) in Trinidad, and that the pending steamer service and telegraphic communication on the island would soon end its isolation. Finally, McCarthy posited that Rousseau's suggestion might stem from jealousy, because the "very conscientious" sub-collector of Tobago had brought the work of the receiver-general's department in Tobago from "chaos into an admirable condition. In doing so he had necessarily aroused some resentment".[40] McCarthy minimized Rousseau's concerns as personal peeves. Similar charges would be laid at the feet of separatists during the mid-twentieth century.

Deputy Inspector-General of Police A. Douglass Owen did not take kindly to Rousseau's recommendation. First, he declared that the police in Trinidad were not under wardens or stipendiary mag-istrates. Second, he contended that putting a civilian warden "over the Sub Inspector" would be "detrimental to discipline".[41] Reiter-ating McCarthy's point, Owen argued that Tobago was no more inaccessible than other rural districts of Trinidad such as Toco,

Mayaro and Erin, and that it would soon benefit from a biweekly steamer service.

The comments from all these officers made Rousseau's recommendation seem trivial and petty. It was obvious that the Trinidad officials did not understand or appreciate the special circumstances with which Tobagonians and government officials working in Tobago had to contend as a result of the island's physical separation from the seat of government. These officials were on the far right of the autonomy continuum and thus were not sensitive to some of the negative effects of the union on Tobago. For example, the argument that Tobago was no more isolated than certain rural districts in Trinidad was used continually to counter the claims of the autonomists.

Secretary of State Chamberlain simply rubber-stamped the ideas of the colonial officials in Trinidad. He asked Governor Maloney to inform Rousseau that "the Warden of Tobago should be in the same position as any other Warden in the Colony".[42] He also agreed with Maloney that Rousseau should be moved from Government House and provided with other, adequate accommodations or a housing allowance. On his next visit to the island, in November 1902, Acting Governor C. C. Knollys reported that Rousseau had vacated Government House and was "provided with a very good house at the Fort".[43] From the perspective of the integrationists, occupying the chief residence had given the senior official in Tobago an unrealistic desire to be governor of the island. Interestingly, about fifty years later the same would be said of the separatist elected representative of Tobago, A. P. T. James – although he never lived at Government House!

Knollys's two-week visit to Tobago from 12 November 1902 allowed him to observe firsthand developments and problems in Tobago. His report to Chamberlain, for the most part, was glowing:

I found a very marked improvement in the general condition of the Island. Everyone is now satisfied that the close union with Trinidad has resulted in great advantage to Tobago. Work is more abundant, wages higher, and visible signs of improvement appear in the better state of repair of both houses and cottages and the extended cultivation of the land.[44]

That few residents asked to see him compared with his last visit, when he was "besieged by applicants", was to him proof of his conclusions. He boasted that the coasting steamer was a great success that opened up the island and encouraged small cultivators. The ships made trips around the island and docked at various bays, making it easy for farmers to sell their produce and livestock. The system also had the advantage of a produce agent on board the ships, which guaranteed that middlemen did not defraud the farmers.[45]

Notwithstanding the good news, Knollys was forced to admit that Tobago was isolated from the centre of government and trade in the colony. During his visit one of the steamers was dry-docked, and as a result, he lamented, "The isolation is complete and is much felt by those engaged in trade and agriculture. This isolation makes it difficult for the Governor to pay more than a flying visit to Tobago. I cannot too strongly urge that the project of wireless telegraphy should be pushed on."[46] Knollys had to learn the hard way about the realities of life in the island-ward after the union. During his two-week visit he received news from Trinidad on only one occasion. It was this experience – of walking in the shoes of Tobagonians – that Trinidadian officials, and Trinidadians in general, lacked. They were hardly ever on the spot, and most never visited Tobago, which explains their integrationist philosophy.

Besides experience, a certain calibre of leadership was required of the official who was directly in charge of the isolated ward of Tobago. In December 1903 the satisfactory administration of Tobago became an issue. In a confidential letter to Alfred Lyttelton of the Colonial Office, Governor Maloney reported that he was "far from satisfied" with the work of the acting warden of Tobago, W. C. Nock, whose substantive position was warden of the Montserrat district in Trinidad: "Mr Nock, I regret to say, appears to me to be lacking in the energy, appreciation of the responsibilities of his post, and in some of the qualifications necessary to the satisfactory performance of his duties."[47] In 1903 the duties and qualifications for the office of "Warden and Supervisor, Sub-Registrar and Stipendiary Magistrate of Tobago" were:

Duties: As Warden – General supervision and advancement of his Ward Union. The collection of Ward and other Rates and Taxes. As Magistrate – The ordinary duties of a Stipendiary Justice of the Peace, and such other duties as the Governor may from time to time direct. *Qualifications*: As Warden – Energy, tact and a keen appreciation of the responsibilities of the post. As Magistrate – Knowledge of law and practice in Summary Jurisdiction.[48]

Obviously Nock did not carry out these duties very well. As a result, Maloney recommended R. S. Rowbottom, clerk of the peace of San Fernando, at the time acting stipendiary magistrate of Couva, for the job. Mr Bourne, a senior official at the Colonial Office, noted that he was not surprised that Nock was "not a complete success". He also did not think that Rowbottom was the right person for the job, but recommended his provisional appointment until he proved his capability.[49]

In March 1904 Governor Maloney withdrew his recommendation of Rowbottom and surprisingly recommended James T. Rousseau, the former warden of Tobago, who was at the time sub-intendant of the Department of Crown Lands. Even more surprisingly, he also recommended that Rousseau be allowed to occupy Government House when the governor was not on the island. Given his previous position on the matter, Maloney's rationale was almost shocking:

> My reasons for making these recommendations are twofold. I consider that, owing to its comparatively isolated position, the Ward of Tobago occupies a status different to that of any other Ward of the Colony, and that experience has shown that it is necessary for the Warden to be an officer of considerable standing and experience, capable, should the necessity arise, of affording advice and assistance to the other Government officers, not directly under his control, who are stationed in the Island.[50]

Maloney's views echoed Rousseau's earlier position that the warden in Tobago should have more authority than those in Trinidad. Over the years the governor may have come to acknowledge the problems inherent in the union, problems from which Tobago suffered acutely.

Maloney's second reason for his proposals was that Rousseau had successfully completed the work for which he had been transferred to the Crown Lands Department; the department was now considered overstaffed. In addition, Rousseau was the best man for the wardenship of Tobago, "in spite of his ambition to be regarded as Governor of that island".[51] Maloney most likely recognized that the Tobago case needed a capable officer who was sympathetic to the needs and circumstances of the island. In fact, Tobago needed its own administration. As a proven efficient centrist administrator, Rousseau was the best officer the government had in the local colonial service. The numerous retrenchments and amalgamations of positions in the Tobago civil establishment prior to union and during its first ten years may have prevented Tobago residents from achieving the seniority needed for the position of warden. In addition, many of the senior officials in the colonies had been recruited from Britain. Chamberlain agreed to Rousseau's reappointment but denied the request that he should reside at Government House,[52] and by April 1904 a warden's quarters had been constructed on the island. His lobbying efforts for greater authority as warden of Tobago finally vindicated, Rousseau died on 28 October 1910.[53] While his efforts to give the senior government official in Tobago greater powers remained unfulfilled, he left a significant legacy of advocacy for that position.

In September 1912 Governor Sir George R. Le Hunte recommended that the title of warden of Tobago be changed to "commissioner". In writing to Undersecretary of State Harcourt, Le Hunte argued, "Tobago is . . . the most isolated Ward in the Colony and the position of the Warden is one of greater responsibility than the others."[54] However, Le Hunte did not intend "to alter the Executive or judicial status of the Office except as far as I may find it expedient to give more freedom in matters of minor executive detail".[55] The officials at the Colonial Office were somewhat leery about Le Hunte's proposal, but one stated that if the governor wanted the change he would not object. Another official was more apprehensive, pointing out that

> [t]he present warden is liable to transfer to a Trinidad ward. Tobago is only a ward or parish of Trinidad, & we do not want to encourage any centrifugal tendencies. "Commissioner" usually implied leadership of a separate, though subordinate, political entity . . . e.g. the commissioners of . . . Montserrat & the

Virgin Islands, & the Commissioner of Turks & the Caymans. On the other hand, the magistrate of Carriacou is called "commissioner of the Carriacou District" of Grenada, & the officers in charge of the Bahamas Out-Islands are called "commissioner".[56]

Henry Lambert, who approved Le Hunte's proposal on behalf of the undersecretary of state, made it abundantly clear that the new title would be "purely honorary" and that the Colonial Office would regard the senior government official in Tobago in the same way as it did the commissioner of the Carriacou district of Grenada or of the Bahamas Out Islands. In addition, the Tobago official was to be called "commissioner and warden" so as to avoid any perception that the status of the officer had changed. The new title became effective from 1913 and remained so until 1918, when it was discontinued; in that year the magistrate and warden was provided with an assistant warden.[57] These demands for special concessions underlined the fact that the central government should have treated Tobago as a special case, and Le Hunte recognized this need more than the other governors.

The Tobago Planters Association and the Problems of Wardship

Other needs arose as the decades of wardship wore on. Tobago residents, especially those of the middle and upper classes, made requests of the central government to improve the social, economic and political status of the island. The Tobago Planters Association (TPA) was at the forefront of demanding certain improvements from the government in Port of Spain. An outbreak of dysentery in 1912 prompted a call by Tobagonians for improved medical services. These included the provision of an additional medical officer, the appointment of a qualified sanitary inspector, the establishment of dispensaries at Moriah and Sandy Point, the reduction of fees charged by medical officers, compulsory notification of residents in cases of dysentery, immediate attention to the well-water supply of the island, and installation of a public latrine in Scarborough. Letters demanding these improvements were sent to the government by three individuals: the secretary of the TPA, on 17 September 1912; Reverend H. R. Davies, who also forwarded a resolution passed at a public meeting held on 18 September 1912; and the Honourable H. L. Thornton, a resident proprietor in Tobago and the appointed representative for Tobago on the Legislative Council.[58]

The Executive Council did not respond favourably to most of the TPA's recommendations. The Council indicated that the financial position of the colony made the appointment of a fourth medical officer impossible. It pointed out that Tobago was better served by medical officers than Trinidad; the former had one such officer for every 6,916 residents while the latter had one for every 9,775 inhabitants.[59] (There were only thirty-five medical officers in the entire colony.) Provision for the appointment of a sanitary inspector was tabled for the next year's budget. The government did not view the building of a dispensary at Moriah as a necessity because there was a dispensary at Concordia, which was two and a half miles (four kilometres) from Moriah. However, the Council accepted the need for a dispensary in the Sandy Point district but indicated that such a project would be considered when the financial condition of the colony improved. The fees charged by medical officers were reportedly under examination. The surgeon-general intimated that compulsory notification in cases of dysentery would not result in any advantage to the population. However, the well-water supply was receiving the attention of the government. Providing a public latrine in Scarborough was scheduled for consideration in the 1913–14 budget. Despite the small gains from these demands, Tobagonians continued to voice their concerns and did not stifle their grievances for long.

The reduction of the civil establishment on the island was another issue against which they protested. The abolition of the office of clerk of the peace by Governor John Robert Chancellor in 1919 led forty-seven inhabitants, including the black druggist James A. A. Biggart (later the first elected representative of the island on the Legislative Council) to petition Secretary of State Viscount Milner to re-establish the position. Biggart and the other "taxpayers" argued that the action taken by the governor resulted in there being only one magistrate on the island "to receive complaints, advise on the charge to be laid, and then adjudicate on the same".[60] Obviously this matter involved a conflict of interests. The petitioners demanded that the duties of the clerk of the peace "should not be vested in the Magistrate" but should be performed instead by another official.

The petitioners outlined several problems with the new arrangement.[61] First, it led to inconvenience, because the magistrate (who was also the warden) and his clerical assistant could not attend to the public on court days because they were involved in court proceedings. Second, the petitioners did not take kindly to the fact that they would have to give partial evidence to the magistrate, who would be the one adjudicating the case, before a summons could be issued. Since the magistrate had to travel to Roxborough (seventeen miles [twenty-seven kilometres] from Scarborough) to carry out some of his duties, at those times it would be impossible to get him to issue summonses and warrants. Lord Milner did not accede to the prayers of the petitioners, but asked the governor to inform them that he would wait on reports of how the new arrangements worked before he dealt with any specific complaint.[62]

Provision of adequate sea communications and local representation on the Legislative Council of the colony were other matters taken up by the TPA. On 3 March 1919 the secretary of the TPA, Edward B. Smith, wrote to the Development Committee of the colony concerning steamer communication between the islands. The committee, chaired by the governor, recommended development projects for the colony. Smith's letter advised that the committee was "under a certain disadvantage in considering matters connected with Tobago, owing to the fact that there is not upon it any member who is a resident in Tobago, and acquainted with the local condition and needs".[63] (The lack of Tobagonian representation on policy-making committees remained a sore point in the Tobago/Trinidad saga for decades.) The TPA made several recommendations. It requested resumption of the pre-war inter-island service of two ships and improvement of facilities for handling cargo at Scarborough, Roxborough and Milford. The TPA also made suggestions concerning public health matters. These included construction of a district hospital at Roxborough, and government control and inspection of the conditions under which meat was sold in Scarborough and the outlying districts of Tobago. In addition the planters requested provision of a supply of ice for Tobago and a water supply for Scarborough. Not satisfied with the response from the colonial government, the TPA then petitioned Lord Milner, their primary concern being sea communications.

The TPA claimed to represent the "entire planting interest" in Tobago; it also took credit for bringing at least £200,000 into the island since 1900. The association contended that because Tobago had no representative on the Legislative Council it was "very difficult for the Island to bring its needs and views to the notice of the Government". Furthermore, no Tobago resident had been invited to sit on the Development Committee.[64] The TPA charged that with the exception of the governor and the director of public works, no other member of the committee had "any knowledge of the island or of its local conditions and characteristics, its coast, ports or special requirements".[65] The other members had either never visited the island or did so only occasionally, on trips to Scarborough, but knew nothing more of the island. Given this contention, the TPA was outraged that the committee did not heed the "expert" maritime suggestions of Captain Dadd of RMS *Belize,* the coastal steamer; Captain Dewar, superintendent of the London and Glasgow Direct Line of steamers; and Sir Norman Lamont, all of whom were acquainted with the needs of the island and whose ideas were allegedly the same as the views of the TPA. The planters recommended that a ship of at least one thousand tons was needed to satisfy the coasting trade, because the *Belize* would soon prove too small unless she made weekly instead of fortnightly trips.

Mayo Short, chairperson of the TPA, and the secretary, Edward Smith, also took the opportunity to bring to the attention of the secretary of state several other items relevant to Tobago's development. They advocated for a main road from Speyside via Charlotteville and the Northside district to Scarborough; a main road from Roxborough to Parlatuvier; bridges over the Mount Irvine and Parlatuvier rivers; extension of telephone service to the Leeward district and Parlatuvier; and alignment of medical districts so as to make them smaller, along with all the other requests made by the secretary in the March 1919 letter to the Development Committee. Lack of representation was a major grievance. While the TPA conceded that two Tobago planters had presented testimony before the Development Committee and the views of the association were known to it, Short and Smith lamented that the "inhabitants feel that they have been completely left out of account and wish to assert their *right* to representation on the Development Committee".[66]

Acting Governor W. M. Gordon sent the association's petition, as well as his comments thereon, to Lord Milner. Gordon contended that the current steamer service, using one ship, was more than adequate, since its full cargo capacity had never been achieved. Thus the Development Committee reasoned that the government's best course of action would be the establishment of its own coastal steamer service after the contract with the Royal Mail Steam Packet Company ended in 1923. To accomplish this proposal, the government would initially procure a vessel of 500 to 600 tons, and then a second vessel if the traffic warranted it.[67] Gordon was "unable to say" why no representative of Tobago had been appointed to the Development Committee. However, he opined that because meetings were held frequently it would have been inconvenient and impossible for a Tobago resident to attend them (at that time the coastal steamer made only fortnightly trips to Tobago).

Gordon had a definite reason for there being no resident Tobagonian on the Legislative Council. Since the death of the H. L. Thornton some years earlier, it had been

> found impossible to obtain the services of a suitable resident willing to devote his time to legislative duties and . . . it has been arranged that the interests of Tobago should be represented on the unofficial side of the Council by the Honorable Adam Smith, C.M.G. The attendance of an unofficial member necessitates frequent absences from home and as the Council usually sits once a fortnight and occasionally more often, a member for Tobago, if he did not reside in Trinidad, would find such constant absences from his ordinary duties almost intolerable.[68]

The lack of representation by Tobagonians on committees and boards and in political institutions such as the legislature and (later, during the independence period) in the Senate continued to be a major grievance. Tobagonians also perceived it as an abrogation of their rights.

The TPA's concerns about representation on the Legislative Council received significant attention from the colonial government and the Colonial Office in 1920. As the year began, Governor Chancellor, in a confidential letter to Milner, stated that he agreed with the TPA that a Tobago resident should be an unofficial member of the Legislative Council. Chancellor concurred with Gordon that finding a suitable representative in Tobago was difficult because "acceptance of a seat on the Council involves a considerable sacrifice of . . . time to the service of the public".[69] Notwithstanding, in his attempt to redress the wrong, Chancellor took advantage of the absence of a Council member, who was away on six months' leave, to invite T. L. M. Orde, manager of the Louis d'Or Estate in Tobago, to act as a provisional member of the Council. In his communication with Orde he extended to him an offer to serve a further five-year term when a vacancy arose.

In their minutes to Chancellor's letter the officials at the Colonial Office agreed to wait on Orde's response before addressing the TPA's petition. One official made an interesting additional comment about his rationale for waiting: "[T]here is a question pending as to negro representation on the Council. Till it is settled, prospective vacancies should not be mortgaged."[70] Clearly racial discrimination was a factor that limited the choice of "suitable" Tobago residents as representatives on the Legislative Council.

Milner had also requested Chancellor's comments on the TPA's petition. Chancellor declared that the charge that the Development Committee had ignored the interests of Tobago was "unfounded". He presided over all the meetings and "took pains by hearing numerous witnesses to obtain the best available information on the subject that came under discussion".[71] He further argued that since the issues affecting Tobago would have been discussed at only two or three meetings of the committee, he did not "consider it necessary to ask a resident of Tobago to make the considerable sacrifice of his time that membership of the Committee would involve".[72] He intimated that the decision about the steamship service had been

made after consideration of the testimony of a number of knowledgeable people. The committee's members, declared Chancellor,
were "impressed by the statement of the Agent of the Royal Mail
Steam Packet Company that the present service was carried on at
a loss in spite of the substantial subsidy received from the Colonial
Government".[73]

With regard to the other recommendations made by the TPA,
Chancellor pointed out that the committee viewed most of them
favourably,[74] including the recommendations for construction
of two main roads, the bridge at Louis d'Or and extension of the
telephone service. Provision for the bridge at Mount Irvine was
scheduled for the future. Some matters, such as the "Allotment of
Medical Districts" and provision for a hospital at Roxborough, were
not within the terms of reference of the Development Committee.
The members of the committee also found the improvement of
harbour facilities "highly desirable" but required financial estimates
before they could advise on the practicability of those projects. The
ice supply was a matter for private enterprise to handle. A scheme
for the supply of water to Scarborough and the Leeward district had
already been estimated to cost £40,000, and was to be undertaken
when the financial situation of the colony allowed. The matter of
the sale of meat was referred to the central board of health. Chancellor opted to deal with the question of representation of Tobago
on the Legislative Council in a separate despatch.

On 12 February 1920 Chancellor wrote to Milner informing him
that Orde had declined the position on the Legislative Council. The
frequent visits to Trinidad, which would last four to six days each,
were more than he could spare.[75] Chancellor instead offered the
position to A. H. Cipriani, a merchant residing in Port of Spain who
owned large coconut estates in Tobago. Cipriani consented to serve
in the temporary vacancy and to regard himself as the "representative of Tobago". From then until 1925, when elected representatives
began serving on the Council, Trinidad residents oversaw Tobago's
interests in the corridors of power. Tobagonians were available for
tenure in the legislature, but the elitist and discriminatory policies

that characterized the political system in the colonial period prevented people of African descent from serving.

The TPA can be placed just left of centre on the autonomy continuum – they were not radicals by any means. They insisted that the views of Tobagonians should be taken into account in policy decisions; that Tobago should have representation on the Legislative Council; that special consideration should be given to Tobago because of its isolation from the centre of administration, since sea communications were so infrequent between the centre and periphery of government. As the planting elite they were absorbed in their own commercial interests. However, although they did not represent the black masses, the elite's advocacy for amenities in Tobago would have redounded to the benefit of the labouring class.

The TPA remained an influential organization for quite some time, even beyond World War I and the constitutional changes that came in its wake. After the war, political pressure from citizens of all races in the British West Indian colonies led to constitutional change, making it possible for elected representatives to sit in the legislature. The constitutional changes in Trinidad and Tobago opened the door for elected representatives from Tobago to influence significantly the relationship between the two islands in the union, so much so that the aspirations and needs of its inhabitants were no longer taken for granted. The last year in which nominated officials represented the interests of Tobagonians in the legislature was 1924. Elections to the Legislative Council in 1925 launched a new era in political relations between Tobago and Trinidad. It was an era in which elected representatives with a strong sense of Tobagonian identity – such as James A. A. Biggart – were able to serve their native island and people.

Chapter 6

James A. A. Biggart's Crusade for the Development of Tobago, 1925–1932

By the beginning of the second quarter of the twentieth century the people of Tobago had more than two decades of experience of being governed from Trinidad. The disadvantages of being isolated from the seat of government were clear. As a satellite ward, Tobago needed strong advocacy in the legislature if it were to achieve any significant development. Constitutional changes in the colony that allowed some members of the legislature to be elected provided an opportunity for Tobagonians to play an advocacy role, thereby keeping the special circumstances and needs of the island before the government.

This chapter and those that follow examine the role of the various Tobagonian representatives as advocates of the interests of the island's inhabitants. They also show that these legislators articulated a number of grievances – the secondary sources of identity construction – to justify their demand for self-government. Some of these legislators were not passionate advocates of Tobago's cause but others identified very closely with their fellow islanders and displayed a strong sense of Tobagonian identity. Coincidentally, the white legislators were integrationists while most of the black legislators were separatists. The latter were vigilant in demanding that the government make concessions to Tobago because of its peculiar circumstances. The separatists also insisted that the government make development in Tobago a priority. James A. A. Biggart, a black Tobago legislator from 1925 to 1932, laid the groundwork on which other autonomists later built. He addressed a number of issues in the legislature that persisted as grievances in Tobago for many years after his tenure in office.

Biggart: Biography and Philosophy

The end of World War I brought a demand for constitutional change in Trinidad and Tobago. To a great extent this demand was initiated by men such as Captain Arthur Andrew Cipriani, an officer in the British West Indian Regiment who returned from the war with reformist ideas. Cipriani revived the Trinidad Workingmen's Association, which had been inactive during the war, and entered colonial politics by forming the Trinidad Labour Party, which had strong ties to the British Labour Party.[1] The movement for constitutional reform led the British government to send out the parliamentary undersecretary of state for the colonies, the Honourable E. F. L. Wood, to investigate the demand for changes in the colonial governments. Wood opposed responsible government (a fully elected Legislative Council) in Trinidad and Tobago but recommended limited elected representation on the Council, with an increase in its membership. As a result the unofficial side of the Council was increased from eleven to thirteen legislators, with seven elected members and six nominated. The official members were increased from ten to twelve, and the governor retained his original and casting votes to ensure an official majority.[2] Thus, for the first time since 1877, when Tobago was reduced to Crown Colony government, Tobagonians had the right to elect a representative to the legislature.

The local franchise commission worked out the details of the franchise and established the boundaries of the constituencies. It set the qualifications for candidates and voters at a level that severely limited participation in the political process.[3] Candidates were required to own real estate that was worth a minimum of $12,000 (British West Indian dollars) or from which they derived an annual income of $960, or they were to have an income of more than $1,920 per annum. They were to have been resident in their constituency for one year or own real property there worth $24,000 or from which they derived a yearly income of $1,920. Only literate men aged twenty-one and over were eligible for election. Thus only those who possessed considerable property or had a fairly high income could be candidates, and the vast majority of the black population was effectively disfranchised. Council members were not remunerated (until 1939), although a subsistence allowance of $5 was granted to the member for Tobago "when attending meetings".[4]

The franchise was also very limited by high property and income qualifications. The requirements for a voter were

> Occupation as owner for one year of property of $60 rateable value in a borough or $48 elsewhere; occupation as tenant paying $50 per month rent in a borough or $48 elsewhere; or payment as a lodger for one year of $60 rent or $300 rent and board combined; or occupation as owner or tenant under agreement of property paying at least $2.40 per annum land tax; or annual salary of $300.00.[5]

Clearly the working class and even the lower middle class remained disfranchised. The minimum voting age was twenty-one and voters were required to understand spoken English. Anyone who had received poor relief six months prior to the date of registration as a voter was disqualified.

The first election was held on 7 February 1925. The electorate comprised only 5.9 per cent of the population of the entire colony.[6] In Tobago, of 1,800 registered voters, only 547 went to the polls.[7] James Alpheus Alexander Biggart (1878–1932), a black druggist, won the Tobago seat. Governor Sir Horace A. Byatt reported to Secretary of State Lieutenant Colonel L. S. Amery that no Europeans contested the elections in Tobago.[8] Given the qualifications for candidacy, Biggart must have been one of Tobago's well-to-do, politically astute, educated black professionals.

Biggart began his pharmacy career in 1892 as an assistant druggist apprenticed to or supervised by various private doctors and government medical officers, who wrote letters certifying his education and experience in the field of pharmacology. Walter H. Ince, the acting government analyst and a professor of chemistry, certified that Biggart had taken a course in practical and theoretical chemistry and passed the examination. Another medical professional, E. Gerald Blanc, certified that Biggart had taken courses from him in Latin and dispensing. Under his tutorship Blanc found Biggart to be a "painstaking, apt, and very intelligent pupil who made considerable progress in a short time".[9] Biggart owned the only pharmacy in the Windward district several years before wardship in 1899.[10] He was the only dispenser in Tobago who had completed a systematic course of practical and theoretical chemistry at the government laboratory in Trinidad, under Professor Ince.

In the Colonial Office records, James Biggart is introduced by a 1903 petition to the secretary of state requesting permission to take a licensing examination for druggists in Tobago. He filed the petition because the extension of Trinidad's laws to Tobago as a result of wardship obligated him to travel to Trinidad to do the exam. He believed that was unfair to him.[11] Before that time druggists did not have to be licensed to practise on the island. However, with wardship, medical professionals in Tobago were subject to the regulations of the Medical Board of Trinidad, including being required to pass examinations to be licensed. Biggart argued that Governor Hubert Jerningham, under whose administration the island became a ward, promised "the inhabitants including Professionals who were in the field prior to the annexation every reasonable consideration".[12] In September 1900 Biggart had applied to take the licensing examination for assistant druggists, scheduled for the following month in Scarborough. Apparently the medical board cancelled the examination. Biggart petitioned both the board and the governor, without success, to have the exam held in Tobago. The justification for his petition was twofold. First, he had applied to do the examination when it was being offered in Tobago. Second, he could not bear the expense of travelling to Trinidad. These grounds justified either an exemption or another chance to take the examination in Tobago.

Based on Biggart's petition, the medical board agreed to send the theoretical part of the examination to Tobago and to have him tested orally in practical pharmacy by Dr. Blanc.[13] The board made it clear that the exception made for Biggart was not intended to establish a precedent. The entire experience reveals the impact of the union on the lives of Tobagonians. It shows the Herculean efforts they made to adjust to the new realities of being isolated from the centre of administration. It demonstrates the insensitivity of the colonial government to the disadvantageous circumstances in which the union had placed many Tobagonians. The fact that simple solutions could be found to deal with some of the problems arising from the union indicated that officials in Trinidad were not willing to make concessions to Tobagonians, and probably saw doing so as burdensome. This experience may have made Biggart particularly sensitive to the plight of his fellow islanders. In addition, it may have made him willing to participate in politics as an advocate of their interests.

Biggart's advocacy of the interests of Tobagonians began in 1919 over the abolition of the office of the clerk of the peace (see chapter 5).[14] His respectability and undoubtedly his popularity, as one of the few medical professionals on the island, along with his involvement with proprietors and merchants in the 1919 clerk of the peace case, may have earned him the backing of the enfranchised upper-middle and upper classes in Tobago. His re-election for a second term in 1927 testifies to that fact. The *Minutes of the Proceedings of the Legislative Council* of Trinidad and Tobago for 1925 to 1932 reveal that he was an untiring advocate for Tobagonians and for the development of Tobago.

James Biggart constantly campaigned for development of the island's infrastructure; improvement of sea communications and education; establishment and improvement of markets, post offices and wireless and telephone services; and provision of government services in Tobago that would have made it unnecessary for Tobagonians to go to Trinidad to access those services. Indeed, Biggart began a tradition of strong advocacy on behalf of Tobagonians and the development of their island that was carried on by autonomists such as A. P. T. James and A. N. R.

Robinson in the latter part of the twentieth century. The issues Biggart raised in the legislature continued to be addressed by other Tobagonian representatives until 1980, when the island received internal self-government status within the Republic of Trinidad and Tobago. Many of the grievances highlighted by the spokesmen of the autonomy movement in Tobago in the 1970s were long-standing ones that were never satisfactorily addressed by the central government. Thus, in time, Tobago's elected representatives felt a need to wrest control of the destiny of their island and of their fellow inhabitants from the central government in order to establish policies that would reflect their priorities for development and to establish easily accessible administrative services. Biggart can be viewed as the one who laid the foundation on which the 1970s autonomy movement was built.

As noted earlier, the elected officials of Tobago can be placed along a continuum from integrationists to separatists. Separatists such as Biggart were not necessarily secessionists who wished to undermine the union. They saw Tobago and its inhabitants as possessing a distinctive identity and culture. The separatists argued that the union placed Tobagonians in disadvantageous circumstances because of Tobago's isolation from the centre of government, politics and the economy in Port of Spain. This isolation created a need for the government to treat Tobago as a special case with respect to development and the provision of government services on the island. Separatists believed that the government should respond with understanding and sensitivity to those circumstances and needs by making concessions and by not ignoring economic and social development of the island. They contended that officials in Trinidad did not have firsthand knowledge of the problems and conditions in the smaller island and as such could not make informed decisions on matters that affected the island. They insisted that Tobagonians should be represented on policy-making committees and boards and in institutions such as the Executive Council, the Senate and the Cabinet. James Biggart can be placed just left of the mid-point of the autonomy continuum.

Biggart and Education

Little has been written on this early-twentieth-century advocate of Tobago's cause. However, Professor Carl Campbell has written about Biggart's role in seeking development of education for Tobago within the wider context of development in education in the colony in the aftermath of the union.[15] Campbell presents Biggart as a separatist who challenged the integrationist approach to education. The education authorities in Trinidad were integrationists. Campbell argues that they tended to see few problems in the educational system in Tobago and appraised Tobago's schools as just as good or bad as schools in rural Trinidad. The separatist viewpoint, which Campbell asserts was held exclusively by Tobagonians, presented the school systems of the two islands as not meshing together easily. At the time of union Tobago had only denominational primary schools, while Trinidad had both primary and secondary schools along with a teacher-training institution; some of these schools were owned and operated by the government.

As a separatist, Biggart requested special consideration for education in Tobago, including increased funding, college exhibition (government scholarships to secondary schools) set aside for Tobago students, special representation on the board of education for Tobagonians, and a resident inspector of schools for the island. He challenged the notions held by Trinidadian officials that the government was wasting money on education in Tobago and that Tobagonian children were not intelligent. He was at the forefront of efforts to establish secondary education in Tobago.

James Biggart made provision of affordable secondary education in Tobago a major plank of his election campaign. His manifesto stated:

> ... as matters stand educationally only the rich and well-to-do people of Tobago are able to give their children a good education. This is so because the centre of education is so far removed from us, to say nothing of the cost by virtue of the situation. My aim is to bring to the notice of the Government the necessity of a school of Higher Education where the boys and girls of our Island will receive a good foundation, which is so necessary to meet the requirements of

modern civilization. My object is to request that such a school be placed within the reach of the poor man's pocket, and bring to his door educational benefits, which are now only open to those who are able to send their children to Port of Spain and other centres.[16]

Biggart's crusade to improve education on his native island began two months after he was sworn in as a member of the Legislative Council. On 17 April 1925 he called on the government to promise that it would either establish or subsidize a secondary school in Tobago in order that Tobago's youngsters could have access to secondary education without having to travel to Trinidad.[17] While Tobagonians were able to pay school fees, they were unable to pay the cost of board and lodging in Trinidad. The government doubted that a "secondary school at which fees are paid would receive sufficient support in Tobago to justify its establishment, since the number likely to take advantage of it would probably be small".[18] The government's response demonstrates how Trinidadian officials perceived Tobagonians. Clearly the government did not think that Tobagonians had the financial resources to pay secondary school tuition. Second, and probably more important, the government saw Tobagonians as lacking the ambition to improve their children's lives and future prospects through education.

In spite of these negative perceptions, the government pledged that when funds were available it would support any private secondary school established in Tobago. The caveat was that the government had to be satisfied first that the school was necessary and had achieved a certain standard. The scepticism about whether there would be sufficient interest in secondary education was ludicrous. The warden's report for 1924 showed that there were thirty-six government-assisted primary schools on the island, with a total enrolment of 5,716 students.[19] Bishop's High School was established in Tobago in 1925 by the Anglican Church and received a government grant.[20] In 1927 the school had an enrolment of forty-nine pupils and, along with five other schools, was affiliated with Queen's Royal College in Trinidad.[21] In 1930 Biggart's advocacy for education in Tobago led him to request two annual government scholarships tenable at Bishop's High, just as there were for Queen's Royal College.[22] The board of education advised against it.[23] Biggart wanted to secure educational opportunities for Tobagonians similar, if not equal, to those the government provided for Trinidadians.

Assuring quality elementary education in Tobago was also important to Biggart, and in 1926 he requested reappointment of a resident inspector of schools[24] – the office of the Tobago inspector of schools had been abolished at union. In 1928 Biggart again pleaded with the government for a resident assistant inspector of schools, because he did not believe that Tobago schools were receiving the same kind of supervision as schools in Trinidad.[25] The government admitted that Tobago schools had not been as well supervised as those in Trinidad since the resident inspector was withdrawn. In May 1928 the government informed Biggart that "arrangements have been made for the schools in Tobago to be more frequently visited in the future, which will give them the same supervision as schools similarly situated in Trinidad".[26] The government's response proves that, with regard to the supervision of schools, Tobago was treated as a far-flung rural district of Trinidad, not easily accessible to inspectors. Fortunately a resident inspector was reappointed in 1930.[27] Inspector E. B. Grovesnor not only inspected Tobago's schools but conducted in-service courses for teachers as well.

Not satisfied with just a resident inspector, Biggart lobbied for appointment of a representative of Tobago on the board of education, "one who knows the educational needs and aspirations of the people of the Island-Ward".[28] Tobago had had its own board of education up to the time it became a ward. This request by a separatist for Tobagonian representation implied that Tobago's interests could be served best only when Tobagonians were in a position to influence policies that would affect the island and its inhabitants. Further, it suggested that officials in Trinidad did not see Tobago as a significant part of the colony, and thus had to be reminded constantly that its inhabitants deserved equal treatment. Despite Biggart's untiring efforts on behalf of Tobagonians, however, the planters were not pleased that he was their representative in the colony.

The TPA's Attempt to Undermine Biggart's Status

Biggart had served about four months in office when in July 1925 the TPA made similar claims for Tobagonian representation on the Executive Council. The TPA was also interested in increasing the powers of the warden of Tobago. The association wrote to Governor Horace Byatt requesting appointment of a commissioner-warden, with membership on the Executive Council, after the incumbent retired.[29] Since Byatt did not agree with its proposals, the TPA passed a resolution that was sent to the secretary of state for the colonies. In the resolution Chairman Mayo Short laid out the TPA's case:

> The members of the Association feel strongly that Tobago, from its past history, and comparatively isolated position, should not be on quite the same footings as the other wards of the Colony, but that it should have an Official of rather a higher standing than an ordinary Warden, who has no authority over Officials of other Departments in the island.[30]

This was the same claim James Rousseau had made more than a decade earlier. The TPA also recommended that the commissioner-warden should not be a local man, but preferably an officer from England, or at least another colony, "who would have no outside interests". Its members wanted a person with no allegiance to pressure groups in the colony. The new officer would be not only the official head of the administration but also the "social head" of the island. The members of the TPA foresaw that such a person with representation on the Executive Council "would be of the greatest use in furthering the island's interests".[31]

The TPA pitched its request in terms of identity. The planters noted the tensions in the relationship between Tobago and Trinidad that had existed since the time of union. They pointed out that Trinidadians had "strong feeling[s]" against Tobago being made a ward and argued that in the past some of the unofficial members of the Legislative Council had "looked upon matters connected with Tobago as a nuisance".[32] They felt that it was unfair that

> [w]hile Tobago is not given credit by the general Public in Trinidad for the amount of revenue she contributes to the Colony's Treasury in the shape of import Duty on all household supplies, clothing, estate stores etc. which have

Identity and Secession in the Caribbean

to come into the island from and through Trinidad, she usually gets the credit for all the expenditure connected with the running of the local steamers, although as a matter of fact, the steamer occupies more time in visiting the various ports in Trinidad than it does in Tobago.[33]

A. P. T. James made the same claim around the middle of the twentieth century.

It was necessary to address these complaints to the secretary of state because it seemed that no one was interested in presenting them to the "Trinidad authorities", a problem that would be resolved if a commissioner-warden were appointed. That officer would have an intimate relationship with the Tobago community and the government. His authority would enable him to "settle urgent matters without delay".[34] One of the major problems of union was the delay in taking action on matters connected with Tobago. Therefore, at this early stage of union, Tobago's planter class believed that the solution was to have a representative in the highest policy-making body in the colony, and thus one possessed of significant government authority and influence.

Governor Byatt rightly believed that the TPA's concerns stemmed from its members' conviction that "Trinidad is very much occupied with its own affairs and that the interests of Tobago consequently drift into a position of secondary importance".[35] Tobago had indeed become marginalized in the union, although the governor disputed that fact and insisted, "Tobago in the past has received special and detailed attention." However, he acknowledged that because of "financial reasons" the government found it impossible to satisfy all the "demands for improvements" on the island. He justified his position by listing the capital projects that had received attention since the union. These included a weekly steamer service, operated at a "heavy loss"; a telephone service; wireless telegraph installation; "an excellent system of roads"; improvement and expansion of the hospital; and an almost completed "extensive" water supply to the southern half of the island, which was estimated to cost £74,000.[36]

With regard to the appointment of a commissioner-warden, Byatt argued that if such an officer were to attend meetings of the Executive Council he would have to be absent from Tobago each week from Thursday to Tuesday. That would result in his being unable to perform his "ordinary duties" and would lead to the appointment of someone else to function in Tobago while he attended the meetings.[37] This argument did not take into consideration other options, because the Tobago representative did not have to attend every meeting; he could attend selected ones at which he would advocate for the welfare of the island.[38]

Byatt argued that it had been difficult to find Tobagonians who were willing to serve as nominated members of the Legislative Council, and thus a Trinidadian had to be selected as a substitute. When Byatt thought of suitable Tobagonians, he restricted his choices to Europeans. He pointed out that in the "recent [February 1925] election no European came forward as a candidate for Tobago, and the planters have themselves very largely to blame, both now and formerly, if they are not satisfied with their representation".[39] Racial discrimination was a factor in the selection of representatives to the legislature. The planter elite's request for a commissioner-warden recruited in England to be the administrative *and social* head of Tobago also demonstrates the racial prejudice of this group, which explains their dissatisfaction with Biggart's representation and their desire to undermine his status on the island.

As the Tobago member of the Legislative Council, Biggart, a black man, officially represented the planters as the official political and social head of the island. Being represented in the corridors of political power by someone of African descent negatively affected the planters' social standing in the colony, at least in the eyes of their peers in Trinidad. Their wish to have someone qualified to sit on the Executive Council (as opposed to Biggart's position on the Legislative Council) had more to do with their racial preference than anything else. As the planter/merchant class they really wanted someone with whom they could form an intimate relationship. Thus their desire for a European commissioner-warden was aimed primarily at overshadowing Biggart's social status in order for them to retain pride of place in the social and political order of the colony. The members of the TPA, therefore, were not separatists who had Tobago's interest at heart; their motivations were self-serving.

The secretary of state denied their request. If the planter elite were dissatisfied with James Biggart's representation after only three months, the masses were very pleased, because their interests were being served.

Biggart's Advocacy for Infrastructure Development

Biggart's advocacy for the improvement of the infrastructure on the island testifies to his passion for the development of Tobago. Even before the union, Tobago's roads and bridges were poorly maintained and its social infrastructure needed improvement. The annual reports of the director of public works for 1924 to 1928 show that the mileage of roads maintained in Tobago remained the same throughout the period – 135.56 miles (217 kilometres) of main roads and 8.94 miles (143 kilometres) of local roads.[40] Throughout his tenure in the legislature Biggart called on the government to improve and increase the roads and bridges in Tobago.

In 1925 he called attention to the "deplorable condition of the Northside main road, from Mount Dillon to Bloody Bay" and pushed for conversion of the Charlotteville-Speyside main road into a motor road.[41] These roads were located in Tobago's rural corridor, in the Windward district, Charlotteville being the farthest village from Scarborough. The Windward Main Road, subject to landslides and thus narrowing from time to time, also concerned Biggart. One part of the road was only eight feet wide, and he blamed its narrowness for a major accident between a car and a lorry that sent the car hurtling sixty feet (18 metres) down an embankment.[42] In response to all these problems the government cited the heavy expenditure needed to redress them as justification for not being able to attend to the roads immediately. However, the government indicated that it was contemplating converting the Charlotteville-Speyside road into a cart road and probably diverting or building a retaining wall along the most dangerous section of the Windward main road. On 16 October 1925 the legislature approved £1,070 to build two retaining walls on the Windward main road.[43] Biggart's crusade for improvement of infrastructure in Tobago had won its first victory.

Biggart also devoted his attention to bridge construction and repair. In 1922 the government had allocated some money for construction of a bridge over the Louis d'Or River on the Windward main road. Apparently the work had been started some years before Biggart took office, but it had been abandoned. In May 1925 he began lobbying to get the work resumed.[44] His efforts on this project continued throughout 1927, but to no avail. The government cited "many urgent claims in other districts" that made it impossible to resume construction on the bridge even in 1928.[45] Biggart continued to lobby the government throughout his tenure in the legislature for the maintenance and extension of main and local roads and bridges. He also sought the upgrading of roads to make them suitable for wheeled traffic[46] and for repair and extension of local roads such as those in the villages of Moriah and Mount St George, in the Windward district, and Bon Accord, Canaan and Plymouth, in the Leeward district.[47]

For the most part the government indicated that the colony could not bear the expenditure for the repair, upgrading and construction projects that Biggart brought before the legislature. However, there were some positive results. The warden's report for 1928 stated that some improvements had been made to the Windward main road – "several dangerous corners were removed and the culverts widened".[48] Biggart's advocacy on behalf of the development of infrastructure showed that the needs of Tobago had to be constantly kept before the government. This applied to sea communications as well.

The provision of adequate sea communications between Tobago and Trinidad remained a major bone of contention. Tobagonians needed not only passenger transportation but also cargo space for their agricultural crops and livestock produced by the planters and peasants. Since the union, Port of Spain had become the largest market and the only transhipment point to markets beyond the colony. The government's coastal steamers were the main form of transportation by sea. Thus, keeping that service operational and adequate was crucial to Tobagonians' livelihood and to their access to government and other services in Trinidad. In addition, mail came to the island via the government steamers. Therefore, because sea transportation was vital to

Identity and Secession in the Caribbean

all Tobagonians and because he had to use the service himself to get to Legislative Council meetings, James Biggart kept the issue of sea communication constantly before the government during his tenure in office.

The disruption of steamer service in November 1924 led to great inconvenience and hardship for the residents of Tobago[49] when the *Belize,* the only government steamer serving the inter-island route, ran aground off Toco, on Trinidad's northern coast. In March 1925 Biggart called on the government to appoint a committee to examine the issue of external communication with Tobago, with a view to avoiding future inconvenience.[50] Disruption of service occurred periodically because of accidents, routine maintenance and other factors; it affected the peasants the most, because they could not get their goods to market. The effect on the planter class was not as severe; they preferred to hire sloops to take their staples, such as copra, to Trinidad, because the sorting of the *Belize*'s cargo at the Port of Spain jetty made their goods vulnerable to the elements and, therefore, spoilage.[51] The government did not agree that appointing a committee would serve a useful purpose, because the solution was to charter or purchase another steamer.[52] Further sea communication fiascos continued to demonstrate the tenuous nature of the situation. Mail delivery was seriously hampered by the unexpected withdrawal of the *Belize,* apparently for repairs, during the middle of February 1927.[53] This made Biggart even more determined in his efforts.

In April 1927 he made an attempt to provide Tobago's planters and peasants with access to worldwide markets by asking the government to take steps to have the Canadian Merchant Marine Temporary Service steamers call at Tobago. A 1925 agreement with Canada did not allow for such calls, which Biggart considered "vital to the future progress" of the island.[54] The Canadian ships subsequently called at Tobago's ports from 1929, but not for very long.[55]

Biggart's persistence led the government to appoint a committee on 15 May 1928 to look into the problems of sea communication between the islands. After the withdrawal of the *Belize* from service for seven weeks in 1929 – notwithstanding substitution of the Canadian cargo steamers

– Biggart again demanded that the government set definite policies to prevent recurrence of "such a regrettable state of affairs".[56] In November 1929 the government reported that plans were being made to procure two steamers for the inter-island service, as recommended by the Tobago Sea Communications Committee. Biggart's advocacy for improved sea communications also included provision of a jetty at Roxborough and extension of the one at Scarborough. The government rejected his 1931 request for these facilities on the grounds that passenger traffic and general cargo had not increased, although livestock traffic had grown. The cost of those projects was estimated at £20,000, which the government held that it could not afford at that time or "for sometime to come".[57] Towards the end of his tenure in office, Biggart requested a reduction in passenger rates on the coastal steamers. The government rejected that recommendation because the steamer service was operating at a loss.[58]

Besides education, infrastructure and sea communication, James Biggart was also concerned about the disparity in wages paid to government workers in the two islands, the reduction of unemployment in Tobago and the establishment of industries on the island. One of the first issues he drew to the government's attention when he took office in February 1925 was the disparity in wages between the labourers employed by the public works department in Trinidad and those in Tobago.[59] The department utilized the cantonnier system: a cantonnier was a labourer in charge of maintaining a specific portion of road approximately four miles (6.4 kilometres) long. The government provided him with tools and he worked alone. Labourers on the public roads in Trinidad received between forty and sixty cents per day, while Tobago workers were given forty to fifty cents remuneration for a day's work. Trinidadian cantonniers received sixty cents per day, while those in Tobago received fifty cents; female labourers on the former island were paid twenty to thirty-five cents per day, while those on the latter earned twenty-four to twenty-eight cents per day.[60] No explanation of this disparity was offered. In March 1925 Biggart moved a motion calling on the government to appoint a commission of enquiry to look into the matter of wages paid to Tobago labourers in the public works department, the government farm and the botanic gardens, with a view to determining whether similar government workers on both islands should be paid the same wages.[61]

Biggart also tried to alleviate the unemployment situation in Tobago. In March 1928 he requested replacement of the cantonnier system with the older custom of employing from time to time as many labourers as required.[62] The government did not see the wisdom of this recommendation, since in its view the system was working satisfactorily on both islands. In 1929 Biggart also pressured the government to fulfil its promise to establish a lime-juice factory in Tobago.[63] At that time the director of the department of agriculture was developing plans for the factory and the agricultural adviser for Tobago had already been given "a general outline of the proposal to discuss informally with those concerned".[64] The factory was later established and the first meeting of the Tobago Lime Growers Association was held in 1930.[65]

Biggart also attempted to get a market built at Roxborough, a police station at Moriah, in the Northside district, and a fire station with modern fire-fighting equipment at Scarborough.[66] In addition he sought to make government services more convenient for the rural population. In October 1926 he requested that the government make provision at Roxborough for stamping of scales and weights of retail shops and of licensed cocoa dealers from the Windward district. This would make it unnecessary for them to travel the long distance to Scarborough to get their scales and weights stamped. The proposal was accepted.[67]

As a health professional himself, James Biggart had a vested interest in increasing the number of medical personnel and improving medical facilities in Tobago. In 1928 he lobbied for a resident dentist.[68] The government was not able to provide one, and stated that its previous attempts at arranging periodic visits by dentists from Trinidad had failed because experienced practitioners were "unwilling to interrupt their private practice by frequent absences".[69] In October 1926 Biggart requested a motor ambulance service for Tobago, which was especially needed by people in the Windward and Northside districts, who found it difficult to take their sick to the Scarborough Colonial Hospital.[70] He also requested establishment of a health office at Delaford village for people in the Windward district, who had to travel long distances to

Roxborough for medical attention and vaccination of their infants. The government could not make provision for the ambulance in the 1927 budget but indicated that steps were being taken to establish a health office at Delaford.[71]

Geriatric care was also a concern of James Biggart. In 1926 he brought to the attention of the government the condition of the Scarborough Poor House, whose residents could be seen begging daily on the streets of the town. Biggart requested that the government "take full control of this institution, and thereby cause the aged inmates to be taken care of and treated in a similar manner to those in Poor Houses here [in Trinidad]".[72] The government responded positively to this request – the warden's reports for 1926 reveal that the poor house was remodelled, repaired and painted and the floor was finished with crude oil. In addition, a qualified nurse and matron were appointed, and residents could not leave the institution without permission, resulting in a considerable reduction of mendicancy.[73] The Scarborough commercial class of merchants and shopkeepers also assisted by contributing weekly to a fund in support of the institution.

The extension of telephone and wireless services in Tobago received Biggart's attention as well. In 1927 he requested extension of telephone services to Bethel and Les Coteaux, and in 1929 he recommended replacement of the bamboo poles used to support telephone lines between Moriah and Parlatuvier with more durable poles, since destruction of the bamboo poles resulted in disruption of service.[74] The government could not justify expenditure on those projects because the Tobago telephone system was operating at a loss of £550 per annum.[75] In addition, Biggart recommended appointment of a second wireless operator to the Scarborough wireless station. If the sole operator fell ill, service had to be discontinued until a substitute arrived from Trinidad, which could take days, given the uncertain nature of sea communications at that time.[76] He also suggested extension of the station's hours of service to make things easier for the public. The government did not accept any of these recommendations because, as in the case of the telephone service, the wireless system was being operated at a loss.[77]

Identity and Secession in the Caribbean

Biggart proposed the extension of other government services in Tobago. In 1928 he requested establishment of a post office/money order office/savings bank at Moriah to provide easy access to the services of such an institution for the people in the Northside district.[78] His request was partially satisfied; the government indicated that the limited use of postal services by the residents of Moriah and its environs would merit providing a service that initially, from April 1929, would allow them only to purchase inland and imperial postal orders. Apparently the demand grew and, in response to other pleas from Biggart, the government decided to include provision for a sub–post office at Moriah in the 1931 budget. It further promised to convert the institution into a money order office with full postal facilities if the demand warranted it.[79] For the capital of the island, Biggart recommended construction of a postal pillar-box at a central location and a letter-box by the Customs House for the convenience of the people of Scarborough.[80] The post-master-general was given permission to arrange for the erection of the postbox.

Decentralization of government services was very important to Biggart in order to prevent Tobagonians from having to travel to Port of Spain to procure documents and services. Having to attend meetings of the legislature in Trinidad every two weeks and his own experience in 1903 with the druggist's licensing examination must have made him very sensitive to the problems of Tobago's isolation from the centre of the government. In 1928 he made efforts to get the government to enable the procedure of legitimating children born out of wedlock to take place in Tobago.[81] The Legitimacy Ordinance conferred on the person "legitimated" and his family the right to inheritance and the full status of a child born in wedlock. The government insisted that something so important should be done only at the registrar-general's office in Port of Spain, because that official had custody of the registers of births and marriages for the entire colony.

The government was insensitive to the hardship and expense for travel, food and lodging that Tobagonians had to endure when travelling to Trinidad to procure government services. It insisted that, since

> the act of legitimation is one which can be performed but once in a life-time and the fees charged are negligible ... no undue hardship is entailed by insisting that the person seeking to be legitimated and his parents or surviving parent, as the case may be, should attend at the office of the Registrar-General in Port-of-Spain and sign the entry of the necessary particulars of re-registration.[82]

This problem of over-centralization continued to be a thorn in the flesh of Tobagonians up to the 1970s; even then they had to travel to Trinidad to procure official documents such as birth certificates and to get land deeds embossed. Travelling to Trinidad involved expenditure of money, sacrifice of time (usually more than one day) and the frustrations of coping with the bureaucracy in Port of Spain. The persistence of grievances such as these encouraged the burgeoning development of a sense of identity among Tobagonians, as one people enduring the same woes in their dealings with the central government.

James Biggart's strong Tobagonian identity and pride are seen in his insistence on preservation of Tobago's history. On 15 February 1929 he requested that the government "collect the necessary information regarding things of historical interest in Tobago, including the literature of the Island-Ward, with a view to preserving them for future reference".[83] His concern for preservation of Tobago's historical records undoubtedly reveals his sense of pride in his native island and the importance he attached to passing on the legacy to future generations. Biggart believed that history was a very important vehicle of Tobagonian identity.

Biggart's response to the Tobago school crisis of 1930 sheds light on his convictions. The affair stemmed from a visit to Tobago by Governor Sir Claude Hollis and Director of Education James Marriot in July 1930. Their comments about education in Tobago and about Tobagonians were not complimentary. Hollis "told Tobagonians that their school buildings were sub-standard, their teachers were poorly qualified, and that there were too many small schools wasting government money [while Marriott] said or implied that Tobagonians lacked 'brains'. . . ".[84] Biggart, who attended the function at which the remarks were made, was much offended, and retorted,

If a history of Tobago were written all these things would be made clear to people, and they would be able to realise that we Tobagonians are not the non-entity as some people imagine, and that the children have brains. We have been tutored in representative institutions: we had what Trinidad did not have.[85]

That comment provides insight into the essence of Biggart's legislative tenure and that of later separatists such as A. P. T. James. The separatists were on a crusade for recognition of Tobago and Tobagonians as a legitimate part and partners of the united colony. They were on a mission to prove that despite the island's economic misfortunes, Tobagonians still retained their pride and their humanity. Thus their history was important, and they had a legitimate stake in the colony and should not be treated as second-class citizens. Furthermore, by referring to Tobago's legislature of the past, Biggart in effect retold the story of Tobago's proud history, thereby invoking strong sentiments of identity. His retelling of the stories of past greatness was coupled with we/they antipathies – Tobago had had a representative government while Trinidad did not. Biggart's contribution to the construction of identity in that manner, along with his oft-repeated litany of grievances, showed that he invoked Tobagonian identity as a strategy in his struggle to wrest more equitable treatment for Tobago from the central government. In this respect he laid a solid groundwork for the separatists who would follow him.

Biggart must have been pleased, yet concerned, with the government's proposal in March 1929 that called for examination of the records in Tobago "with the object of destroying those of no value and putting the others into order and cataloguing them".[86] The government decided to put a vote for that purpose before the Finance Committee. The warden's report for 1929 stated that the "[o]ld Records of Tobago were collected, sorted and indexed by L. P. Guppy who was appointed for this purpose".[87]

James Biggart served his constituents well. When he had been only six months in office, Governor Byatt described him as "specially active in bringing the interests of the Island before the Legislature".[88] His persistent advocacy for the interests of Tobagonians and for development of the island, along with his vehement defence of Tobagonian children (thus, all

Tobagonians), reveals that he shared in the plight and perceptions of his people and his native island. His experience shows that Tobagonian pride and sense of community were strong at the time of union. His attempts to redress the disadvantages faced by Tobagonians ironically prove that the union played a major role in enhancing Tobagonian identity. Trinidad and Trinidadian officials became the other, the entity that did not understand and was insensitive to their woes. To make matters worse, Trinidadian officials so looked down on Tobagonians that they were brazen enough to come to Tobago and speak disparagingly of its institutions and people. By the time Biggart died in 1932 it must have been clear to the majority of Tobagonians that they were not seen as equals and as deserving of attention from the central government and, thus, from Trinidadians. On the contrary, they were regarded as rural, backward fiscal parasites and administrative burdens. This negative perception by Trinidadians served only to bind Tobagonians more closely together and to enhance their identity.

The Biggart era was followed by an interregnum of two white integrationist legislators. The first, Isaac A. Hope, was a right-leaning centrist planter, while the second, George de Nobriga, was a wealthy, established upper-class manager and planter in the colony.

Chapter 7

The Integrationists' Interregnum
Isaac A. Hope and George de Nobriga, 1932–1945

The passion that James Biggart brought to the Legislative Council on behalf of Tobagonians diminished after his death in 1932. Two white integrationists, Isaac A. Hope and George de Nobriga, succeeded him in office. Unlike the separatists, the integrationists viewed Tobago as a ward of Trinidad and not an equal partner in the union. To them Tobago was simply another rural administrative district of Trinidad, just like Toco or Erin, and thus not entitled to any special concessions from the central government. The integrationists believed that Tobago's isolation from the centre of government was no more of a challenge than that of the rural districts in Trinidad. Tobago was also perceived as a ward in the sense of its dependence on Trinidad for economic survival and sustenance. As far as some integrationists were concerned, Tobago's depressed local economy made it – from the very outset of union – a fiscal parasite, using resources that should have been allocated for development in Trinidad. Furthermore, it was considered an administrative burden to most of the Trinidadian legislators and administrators.

Integrationists fit a certain profile. In the Tobago case they were either government officials, Europeans, individuals allied with the planter/merchant elite or members of the ruling political party. Their advocacy for Tobago's interests was not as passionate as that of the separatists. They also believed that the development of Tobago would naturally and automatically take place, in conjunction with that of Trinidad. They trusted the central government to seek Tobago's welfare without much prodding or protestation.

The Tenure of Isaac A. Hope

Isaac Arbuthnot Hope was born around 1865.[1] After Biggart's death he ran unopposed in the 1932 by-election. He was a planter and business-man with a general store in Scarborough who had started his career as a merchant clerk. He also owned considerable property in Roxborough. An adult when the colony was united, Hope knew well the difficulties Tobagonians faced: "I lived all my time in Tobago and I know the inconvenience we suffer."[2] He remembered when the services of the *Belize* had been withdrawn for three months and the residents of Tobago "had to depend upon a passing boat from Demerara once a month to establish communication with Trinidad. For three months we were there hanging out like pelicans in the wilderness."[3] He also claimed to have helped pack the first ten bags of cocoa produced on the island.

I. A. Hope was right of centre on the autonomy continuum. While he knew the disadvantages Tobagonians experienced because of the island's isolation, his advocacy on their behalf reveals that he expected the government to advance Tobago's welfare without much prodding. Hope was sworn into office on 21 October 1932 and represented Tobagonians until 1938.

Hope's first request was for unemployment relief, by encouraging the government to engage in capital projects in Tobago. He advocated dredging work at the mouth of the Steel River, in the vicinity of Lambeau village, on the island's southwest side.[4] He also called for extension of the water service to Patience Hill and for measures to arrest erosion in the Charlotteville Bay Road area that threatened houses there. The government declared that neither the street nor the houses were in immediate danger, but the situation would be monitored with a view to undertaking protective works.[5] Concerning the extension of water service to Patience Hill, the government argued that the estimated cost of £4,500 was too heavy for the colony to bear.[6] In February 1937, five years later, the government moved to approve various district water schemes, which included extension of the Scarborough project to Patience Hill at a cost of $4,800.[7] A 1937 outbreak of typhoid in Roxborough led the government to approve a pipe-borne water supply project for the town at an estimated cost of $7,500.[8] Hope expressed joy and gratitude that the government had made prompt provision for the emergency at Roxborough. To avoid further outbreaks of typhoid he recommended extension of the service for another three miles, to the village of Belle Garden. An established cocoa farmer, in August 1932 Hope supported a recommendation from the Finance Committee that funds from the colony's surplus be set aside to assist peasant proprietors to establish cocoa fermentaries.[9] Cocoa had emerged as a significant cash crop, and the various districts needed fermentaries; even the large fermentary in Roxborough required expansion and equipment. Hope also supported the imposition of additional duties on certain imports to protect industries in the colony and reduce unemployment.[10]

Isaac Hope emerged as an advocate of affordable health care for children. In the debates on the colony's 1933 budget he opposed a recommendation for imposition of a two-shilling fee on parents who took their children for medical attention at government medical facilities. Previously medical attention and medicines had been free to the children, and Hope was concerned that imposition of the new fee would adversely affect children, mostly those of poor parents.[11] In February 1933 he moved for the reduction or elimination of fees charged to children under employment age of agricultural and other labourers who were in "straightened [sic] circumstances". This became a major plank in his 1933 election campaign platform, since it was a "burning question which affect[ed] directly or indirectly nearly every household".[12] Using statistics for the prices of major export crops between 1921 and 1931 (listed in Table 2), Hope showed that

TABLE 2
PRICES OF AGRICULTURAL COMMODITIES, 1921–31

Commodity	Price in 1921	Price in 1931
Sugar	33–36 shillings	13–9 shillings
Cocoa	35 shillings	29 shillings
Coconut	94 shillings for selects	63 shillings
Coconut	54 shillings for culls	44 shillings for culls
Copra	19 shillings	10 shillings
Coffee	20 cents	9 cents

Source: Debates, 10 March 1933, 53.

a significant reduction over the ten-year period had affected the wages of workers throughout the colony; and consequently parents' ability to pay for medical attention.[13]

In his arguments for the reduction or elimination of medical fees, Hope's declaration that Tobago was just like the other agricultural districts in Trinidad, and thus needed no special concessions, revealed his integrationist philosophy:

> My district is a purely agricultural one, and in that respect it is not unlike nearly every district in Trinidad. When agriculture is depressed it also depresses every other industry of the community. . . . I am not asking for any special treatment for the Island of Tobago, because our circumstances are very much the same as those of the districts of Trinidad. Being purely agricultural our wants are very much the same as those here, and I do not wish that Tobago should be regarded as any water-tight compartment of this colony or should receive any special treatment in that respect. I believe that it is the most important duty of every member of this Council to assist Your Excellency in solving the problems with which this colony is beset, and I can think of no problem that is more serious at the present time than that of alleviating the lot of the labouring men and women and their children.[14]

As an integrationist, Hope believed that what benefited Trinidad would automatically benefit Tobago, and thus the ward was not to be viewed as a "water-tight compartment" of the colony, with a need for special treatment.

Based on the response of the surgeon-general, Hope realized that there were ordinances in place that allowed children younger than eight years old to receive free medical attention by obtaining pauper's certificates. Although he suggested this, he was aware of its dehumanizing effect. The surgeon-general opposed free medical care because he contended that the infant mortality rate in Tobago had been, for many years, much lower than that of Trinidad, even close to that of England and Wales.[15] Given those realities, Hope withdrew his motion.

Providing water for Tobagonians was another of Isaac Hope's concerns. In February 1933 he asked the government to consider controlling the Des Vignes Road spring in order to assist with the water supply to the village of Moriah, especially in the dry season.[16] The government explained that an agreement was being worked out with the owners of the land on which the spring was located.[17] However, two years later Hope revisited the matter – the government had not resolved it.[18] Hope believed that Tobagonian representation on the Central Water Board would result in greater attention to matters relating to water services on the island. In 1936 he asked, "Will the Government consider the advisability of appointing a ratepayer of Tobago upon the Central Water Board so as to give the taxpayers of that section of the Water Area some measure of representation in the deliberations of that body?"[19] Apparently no action was taken on this suggestion. However, the request for Tobagonian representation on the board as a strategy to secure better services on the island reflected the extent to which Tobagonians felt that their priorities were not those of officials in Trinidad.

The development of Tobago's roads was another issue that Hope championed. In February 1933 he requested work on a portion of the Culloden Road near the village of Les Coteaux to allow for wheeled traffic "and so relieve the hardships of many house-holders in that vicinity".[20] The government replied that the road was open to wheeled traffic but not to motor traffic, because of its sharp curves and narrow width. In addition it stated that the expenditure of £2,600 could not be justified because the Arnos Vale Road was an alternative route. Hope also expressed concern that nothing was being done about the Crown traces, or paths, on the island that were falling into disrepair; large sums of money had been expended on their construction.[21] In his last year as Tobago's representative on the Council, Hope requested reopening of the road from Parlatuvier to Charlotteville in order to give access to labour and capital for the fertile cocoa lands in the district.[22] The government insisted that the road was open, but the need for improving it would be investigated.[23]

The Great Depression had a significant effect on the economy of the Caribbean region. Declining prices for the major exports gave rise to increased unemployment, mainly because of lack of money to pay workers. Hope urged the government to create employment through capital expenditure on various projects such as dredging the mouths of tidal rivers. He related harrowing stories in which lack of employment had left many Tobagonians without money to pay their rates and taxes and government officials had confiscated their personal belongings. In Hope's view the situation in Tobago was "reaching a serious crisis".[24]

Hope also tried to reduce the tax burden on the poorer classes. In May 1933 he called on government to consider reducing taxes on agricultural land from £1 to 9d. an acre, as well as reduction of produce licences from £5 to £2 10s.[25] The government did not consider that course of action advisable. In 1937 Hope supported repeal of the Trade Licensing Ordinance (No. 37 of 1935), which allowed for a special tax for relief of the cocoa industry.[26] The tax was burdensome to the poorest class in society, and many people had to obtain extensions in order to pay it. However, the Finance Committee recommended that a loan of £250 be made to both the Roxborough and the Pembroke cooperative cocoa fermentaries. Captain Arthur Cipriani, the member for Port of Spain, thought that putting money into cocoa and coconut in Tobago was the same as throwing money "into the sea" because of the marked decline in prices for those products. He believed that the better course of action would be to expend one million dollars on establishing a livestock industry in Tobago to supply the Trinidad market with beef and pork.[27] Hope disagreed with Cipriani. He pointed out that he had been present at the inception of the cocoa industry, that he had seen it grow and flourish and that it had resulted in appreciation of land values on the island; he still believed that production of cocoa in Tobago was viable. As a cocoa farmer, Hope was defending his livelihood.

During his tenure on the Legislative Council Hope tried to secure as much relief for his constituents as possible. He addressed the disparity in funds allocated for poor relief in the colony as a major issue, especially since he was a member of the Poor Relief Board. In 1934 the sum of £14,000 was voted for poor relief in the colony. Of that sum only £300 was allocated to Tobago, an amount that could "hardly" be described as "fair and reasonable".[28]

The growth of business ventures in Tobago also received Hope's backing. He supported the Finance Committee's recommendation of a loan to the Tobago Producers Co-operative Association to build an ice plant and cold storage facility costing approximately £2,650, and a warehouse at Scarborough for £1,280.[29] He believed the ice plant would help the fishing industry's need for storage and would relieve the situation in which there was no ice in Tobago from Thursday to Tuesday because the coastal steamers did not sail on those days.

The improvement of sea communications and wharf facilities in Tobago was another matter that received Hope's attention. In March 1934 he called for extension of the Scarborough jetty. While the government acknowledged the "considerable increase since 1929 of the amount of cargo handled at Scarborough", it pointed out that extending the jetty would necessitate building an expensive breakwater to protect the ships queued at the jetty from damage due to the drift and strength of the swells in that area. The government recognized the need, but the total cost of the project, which exceeded £15,000, was more than the government could afford.[30]

During discussions of the colony's budgetary estimates, Hope often took advantage of the opportunity to bring the medical needs of Tobagonians to the attention of the government. At the discussion of the 1935 budget in November 1934, Hope lamented that no budgetary allocations had been made for an X-ray machine at the Scarborough District Hospital. There was no allocation for the appointment of an assistant medical officer at the hospital, or for subsidized dispensaries in rural areas such as Charlotteville and

Castara. In the discussion of the 1936 budget a year later, Hope again made a plea for a fourth medical officer for the Colonial Hospital (previously the District Hospital).[31] He also contended that the job of resident surgeon should be a full-time position.

However, Hope complimented the government on the hospital's progress. Its status had been promoted to that of colonial hospital. It possessed some of the best equipment and it had a fine staff of nurses and a fully qualified matron. Nevertheless, the need for more medical staff was not met. One year later, when discussing the 1937 budget, Hope again raised the matter of an additional medical officer for Tobago. He lamented the fact that for four years he had been making the same recommendation without success. He pointed to the "enormous expansion of the [budget] vote [for health] in Trinidad" while provision was not being made for additional officers in Tobago.[32] Hope even argued that the failure to provide more medical officers for Tobago was discriminatory and contrary to the Order in Council of 1898 that made Tobago a ward of the united colony. He clearly felt that the central government had an obligation to provide basic services as a matter of course. Thus, after four years of trying, he was "very sore" that he had not received any "consideration" in the matter. Hope should have realized that development in Trinidad did not automatically trickle down to Tobago.

Other matters affecting Tobagonians were brought to the government's attention. During the budget discussion on 9 November 1934, Hope advocated reducing passage rates on the steamers by 20 per cent. The governor, in his address to the Council on 15 February 1935, attributed the reduction in revenues of the coastal steamers partly to a reduction in deck fares and freight rates on certain articles and the decline in the number of deck passengers;[33] this suggests that the rates had been reduced. Hope also focused attention on the deteriorating condition of the roads on the island: "The road service has got so bad in Tobago that previously I could drive twenty miles without feeling it, but now I can do only six."[34] In addition, he reminded the government of the lack of fire-fighting equipment on the island.[35]

Identity and Secession in the Caribbean

As a farmer, I. A. Hope was very much interested in agriculture and animal husbandry. He recommended extension of the local stud farm to the government property at Mount St George or other areas, for the convenience of stock-raisers in the Windward district. Government officials stated that they would examine the matter when a veterinary officer was stationed on the island.[36] The Supplementary Estimate for 1936 showed that a full-time veterinary surgeon and a manager had been appointed for the Tobago Government Farm. However, it also showed a great disparity in expenditure on Tobago's farm compared to those in Trinidad. Of the $120,000 allocated to farms in the budget, Hope noted that only $820 was earmarked for Tobago.[37]

In 1936 Hope lamented that the wireless services of the colony would be sold to the Cable and Wireless Limited Company on the pretext that service would be improved, even though no extension of the hours of operation of the Tobago station would result. The wireless station in Tobago operated for only six hours per day, from eight to eleven o'clock in the morning and then from two to five o'clock in the afternoon.[38] One year later Hope revisited the matter in the legislature. On that occasion he requested arrangements with the wireless station in Tobago so that emergency calls could be made outside the limited six-hour period at higher rates.[39] The government agreed to allow emergency calls at twice the normal rate.[40] These were the kinds of services that made the cost of living in Tobago higher than in Trinidad – Tobagonians had to pay extra because of their isolation.

Sea communication between Tobago and Trinidad was a critical issue all of the time. In February 1937 Hope stressed the inconvenience caused by withdrawal of the steamer *Tobago* from its regular duties, and called for early resumption of its usual itinerary.[41] The ship had been withdrawn to serve as a tender for passenger steamers in the Port of Spain harbour. In March Hope called for resumption of the steamer's regular itinerary. He pointed out the inconvenience of not having a second ship on the Trinidad–Tobago route, a situation that amounted to "putting back the hands of the clock".[42] Tobagonians had lobbied hard and long to get a two-ship steamer service, but the expansion project at the Port of Spain harbour was preventing ships from berthing. As a result, tourists and other passengers needed a smaller ship to take them to shore, and to serve this purpose *Tobago* was occasionally withdrawn from its customary itinerary.

The scant courtesy shown to Tobagonians in this matter angered Hope:

> I know there is a section of the public who looks upon the Island-ward as some forlorn child of an unlawful union to be treated to the crumbs – but I submit, Sir, that the union is perfectly lawful and was made by letters patent, signed by that greatest of Empire builders "Victoria the Good" of blessed memory. And this Government should regard it as a duty to implement her acts, instead of putting stumbling blocks in the way.[43]

He implied that the government should see Tobago as an integral part of the colony and therefore should not treat it as though it had second-class status but rather should necessarily seek its best interests. The integrationists failed to acknowledge the folly of this line of argument. Tobago's priorities were not the same as those of the government in Trinidad.

Hope blamed the government for marketing Trinidad to tourists without making sufficient preparation for the burgeoning tourist trade and the ocean liners that brought them to the shores of the colony: "I submit, Sir, that we have been like the foolish virgins who awaited the bridegroom without oil in their lamps, and now, behold he cometh, we are found without oil in our lamps and, like bullies, we would pounce down and seize what is not ours."[44] Despite his integrationist philosophy, Hope was not afraid to deride the government for treating Tobago as an orphan.

Governor Murchison Fletcher sympathized with Hope's concerns. He noted that a little more money was being made by using the *Tobago* as a tender, but declared that money was not as important to him as "the desirability of getting this regular service which the people could rely upon year in, year out".[45] He wished that the steamers would run on their usual itinerary but pointed out that the extra money to get a ship to serve as a tender was too much for the colony to bear; however, if the members of the legislature thought differently they were free to vote their conscience on the issue. The governor then made a significant point. He hoped that the director of the Department of Works and Transportation would "not be too much impressed with the necessity for making this service pay for itself. There is no more reason why a ferry service of this nature should be self-supporting than a road should be self-supporting."[46] Unfortunately, the motion lost, eight to thirteen. In November 1937 Hope insisted that the time had come for the government to look into the expanded trade between the islands and make proper accommodation for it.[47] Sea communication continued to be a sore point in relations between Tobago and Trinidad even into the late twentieth century.

During his tenure on the Legislative Council, while Isaac A. Hope addressed many issues that concerned Tobagonians, he still saw the government as the saviour of Tobago and believed that it should be trusted to look after the welfare of the smaller island. While some of his comments in the legislature may be interpreted as more centrist than integrationist, the overall impression one gets is that he was right of centre and thus an integrationist. He did not have the same sense of identification with the average Tobagonian that James Biggart displayed. The fact that he had lived on the island all his life and was affected by all the inconveniences of its isolation from the centre of government was not enough to make him see Tobago as an entity separate from the rest of the colony. In his view, Trinidad should make adequate provision for Tobago because it was its "duty" to implement the acts of the imperial government. Hope may have felt that the many years of union should have, as a matter of course, made the merger of the islands organic. However, that was not the reality. Unlike Hope, separatists tended to see Tobago as a "water-tight compartment" in the colony, different from Trinidad and thus deserving of special treatment. Despite his integrationist philosophy, Hope represented Tobagonians well in the Legislative Council, and another integrationist succeeded him.

The Tenure of George de Nobriga

In 1938 George de Nobriga (1886–1972) became the elected representative for Tobago. He was a powerful landowner, a racehorse owner and a businessman. The *Tobagonian,* a monthly magazine featuring articles about Tobagonians and the development of the island, provided a bio-graphical sketch of the newly elected representative.[48] De Nobriga was born in Port of Spain on 23 July 1886. He was educated at Queen's Royal College, where in 1902 he passed the senior Oxford and Cambridge examinations. In 1903, at the age of seventeen, he became overseer of the Aranguez sugar estate in San Juan, Trinidad, which was owned by John Alfred Rapsey, chairman of the Commercial Telephone Company. Rapsy soon offered de Nobriga a job at his company; there he moved up through the ranks and became general manager, serving for more than fifty years. He was at the helm of the telephone company when it was taken over by the government in November 1960.

George de Nobriga also became general manager of the electric company in 1928. When that company was taken over by the government in 1937 and the Trinidad Electricity Board was formed, he remained its chairman. He retained that position when the board gave way to the Trinidad and Tobago Electricity Commission in 1946, and served until 1962. De Nobriga was also a leading manager of many other business concerns. In 1938 he was managing director of Trinidad Consolidated Telephones Limited, the Electric Ice Company Limited and Tobago Plantations Limited. He was a director of the Trinidad Jewellery and Loan Company Limited, Charles McEnearney and Company Limited, Zenith Oil Fields Limited and the British Colonial Film Exchange Limited. He was also vice-president of the Coconut Grower's Association Limited. In summary, George de Nobriga was an extremely wealthy and influential member of the commercial sector of the colony.

He was also a sports enthusiast. De Nobriga was a "crack tennis player between the years 1915 and 1927, when he had the honour of representing the Colony".[49] He was interested in golf, and was responsible for purchasing the Maraval Golf Course and for the design and construction of its first nine holes. He loved the "sport of kings" – horse-racing – and was a member of the Race Clubs of Trinidad and Tobago. His horses participated "at every race meeting"; he bred horses and owned an "excellent stud". He even imported Restigouche, supposedly one of the best stallions ever brought to the colony. In 1941 he was elected president of the Tobago Race Club and vice-president of the Trinidad Turf Club.[50]

George de Nobriga was tall, good-looking and approachable. He possessed the ability to win people's respect and affection, but he was also made of "stern stuff and just the person to get what he wants done."[51] He was compared to a military commander – "a man born to lead men". The editor of the *Tobagonian* believed "that under his leadership Tobago will make up and give a good account of herself in the near future".[52] Tobagonians hoped that de Nobriga would bring his influence and managerial skills to bear on the government as he advocated for the needs of the island.

The Sea Communications Committee Report

The first major issue that de Nobriga addressed was sea communications between Tobago and Trinidad. In March 1938 he recommended the appointment of a committee to inquire into the "satisfactory and adequate accommodation to meet the present and growing requirements of the [steamer] service".[53] On 1 April 1933 the government announced that a six-man committee headed by J. F. Nicoll, the acting colonial secretary, and including de Nobriga, had been established for the purpose. De Nobriga deserves great credit for initiating the formation of this committee and for the excellent assessment of the economic needs of Tobago that the committee's June 1933 report highlighted.[54]

The committee's members interpreted its terms of reference widely to include recommendations for accelerating economic development in Tobago, because, as they pointed out, "[t]ransport is essentially ancillary to the economic life of the area it serves and a substantial expenditure on transport facilities for Tobago can only be justified if a vigorous policy of economic development is pursued both by the government and the people of Tobago".[55] The steamship service between the islands was operated by the 605-ton *Trinidad* and the 537-ton *Tobago*. These ships had replaced the 1,498-ton *Belize* in 1931. They operated on alternate nights, ferrying both passengers and cargo. In addition there was a weekly service to Roxborough and a fortnightly service around Tobago. The committee contended that "the service constitutes the only link, apart from a few sloops, which Tobago has with the outside world. It must therefore be regarded as a public utility service and we are satisfied that it is now so regarded by the Government."[56] The ships were occasionally diverted from service to serve as tenders for tourist ships in Trinidad, which led to several complaints. However, the committee pointed out that if the tourist trade was not fostered in Port of Spain, Tobago would suffer "immediate loss" because she benefited from the trade herself. Tourism had long been accepted as a major potential industry in the island. The committee reported that, since 70 per cent of Tobago's shipping was done through the port of Scarborough, the "round the island" service needed investigation.

The committee's report, known as the Nicoll Report, also pointed out that accommodation for the third-class or deck passengers – mostly peasant proprietors – who made up the bulk of the travellers, was very unsatisfactory.[57] The ships usually carried more than their capacity of deck passengers and there were no seating accommodations, so most of the passengers had to sit or lie on the deck. In addition to the overcrowding, conditions for passengers worsened during rough weather, which resulted in seasickness. Embarking and disembarking of passengers at Scarborough and the other Tobago ports were treacherous because the ships could not come alongside the jetty at Scarborough, and the other ports did not have jetties. Privately owned boats thus engaged in a highly competitive ship-to-shore service. Cargo handling was also poor, resulting in delays in clearing goods on both islands. The Port of Spain jetty lacked space, and at Scarborough there was inadequate lighterage service and wharf accommodation. The other beach landings in Tobago were described as "primitive".[58]

The report then focused on the relationship between transportation in Tobago and economic development of the agriculture and tourism industries. During the five years before the report and as a result of the Great Depression, the volume of exports from the island had stagnated. There was a worldwide slump in the cocoa and coconut industries. The committee recommended diversification in foodstuffs production to include onions, small and large livestock, poultry and eggs, and the appointment of at least one other agricultural officer to advise, to supervise and develop agriculture on the island and to assist in cooperative marketing. The committee also suggested establishment of an auction market at Port of Spain for livestock, and that the practice of shipping livestock only once a week from Tobago should be abandoned for more frequent trips. Further, it suggested improvement in the handling of livestock.

The Nicoll Report also examined the road transport system, which was another major obstacle to development in Tobago. The roads, developed from bridle paths, were not suitable for motor traffic. The report advocated a "comprehensive programme for the survey, re-alignment and metalling of the existing system".[59] In addition, the committee recommended construction of a road between Charlotteville and Castara to close the gap in the island's road system, to open up rich agricultural lands and to facilitate the tourist trade in that beautiful section of the island. The Tobago legislators who served prior to de Nobriga had made this recommendation as well. Since the hilly terrain of the area made road construction very expensive, the report suggested that landowners should donate to the government the land used to build the roads. The committee also suggested the establishment and operation of a "Motor Transport Service" for passengers and goods, by the government or by a concessionaire in conjunction with the Coastal Steamer Service. After establishment of the proposed road system, Nicoll and his team recommended disbanding the "round the island" steamer service. However, Scarborough and King's Bay were to remain ports of call and were to be properly equipped for handling passengers and cargo.[60]

Given the high cost of establishing a jetty at Scarborough capable of berthing the steamers, the committee called for improvement of the lighterage wharf, extension of storage on the wharf and the purchase of at least one new lighter. The erection of a jetty capable of berthing the steamers, as well as the construction of storage sheds, was recommended for King's Bay. The *Trinidad* would be used as the main cargo ship, with alterations to improve accommodation for livestock.

The purchase of a new ship, to be used primarily for carrying passengers, especially tourists, was also recommended.[61] The proposed ship had to be capable of providing a fast daylight service of five hours between the islands, with accommodations for 80 first-class, 120 second-class and 200 third-class passengers. In addition, the vessel should provide cargo space for five motorcars and valuable livestock such as horses. The committee recommended equipping the ship with cold storage for perishable freight, as well as wireless communication for emergencies. If all the recommendations were put in place, the committee suggested that the *Tobago* should be taken out of regular service and used as a reserve ship to ensure regularity of the entire sea communications service.[62] It also proposed immediate construction of a boat landing, sheltered by a breakwater, at Scarborough, along with a government-maintained ship-to-shore service.

Toby McIntosh, the editor of the *Tobagonian,* was quite pleased with the "progressive and far-reaching" recommendations of the Sea Communications Committee Report. He pointed out that while "many persons . . . regarded the Island more in the nature of a liability than an asset to the sister Isle [Trinidad]", he was grateful that the committee was not of that opinion.[63] Two years later, in May 1940, de Nobriga made a tour of Tobago to visit his constituents. "The inadequate and irregular steamship communication" was the gravest complaint brought to his attention.[64] Nothing had been done to implement the recommendations of the Nicoll Report, which was shelved during World War II.

Infrastructure and Social Service Concerns

Besides sea communications, de Nobriga attended to other issues that affected Tobagonians. In March 1938 he requested that the government provide suitable accommodation for teachers in some villages of Tobago where it was difficult to find places to rent. Transportation to these villages was poor and sometimes non-existent. He pointed out that some teachers were forced to use the schools as living quarters.[65] The government's response on 1 April indicated that, of the thirty-three primary schools in Tobago (all were denominational and assisted by the government), seven principal's quarters were supplied by the denominational board and the teachers themselves owned

Identity and Secession in the Caribbean

fourteen. Of the remaining twelve quarters, which were rented, only three were more than one mile (1.6 kilometres) away from the school (Patience Hill Roman Catholic, Delaford R. C. and Franklyn Methodist), whereas the school principals lived between three and five miles (five to eight kilometres) from their school.[66] The government did not consider those distances far enough away to warrant teachers sleeping in school buildings. It further pointed out that quarters were being provided for the head and assistant teachers at the new Mason Hall government school that was being opened that day.

Other matters also received a listening ear. On 29 November 1940 de Nobriga presented a petition to the government from the residents of the northern districts of Tobago. The residents cited the need for better roads and medical facilities in their area. Another petition from the Bethel section of the Tobago Peasant Proprietors Association sought help to secure the ownership of certain lands.[67] On 16 May 1941 de Nobriga presented yet another petition, from residents of Roxborough, regarding acquisition of lands for building purposes, provision of free milk and medical attention for schoolchildren, improvements to roads and so on.[68] These concerns may not have been attended to because of the reduced expenditure occasioned by World War II.

During the war years George de Nobriga was quiescent in the Legislative Council. An examination of the *Minutes of the Legislative Council* for those years might lead one to think that he had abdicated his role as the representative of Tobago and, indeed, as a Council member. Apparently he sensed the futility of requesting financing for projects when Trinidad and Tobago, and all the colonies in the British Empire, had drastically reduced expenditure to financially support Britain and her allies in the war effort. Nevertheless, the *Tobagonian* portrays de Nobriga as politically active during the war, especially in terms of keeping in touch with his constituents. The March 1939 issue indicated that he was interested in getting to know the needs of his constituents by making a weekend tour of the Windward district and holding meetings with villagers. First he met with the people of Charlotteville at a meeting chaired by Captain C. A. Turpin, a "wealthy landed proprietor".[69] The inhabitants of

Charlotteville inquired about the cocoa subsidy and complained about the telephone service.

Similar issues concerned the villagers at Speyside. They were "loud in their denunciation of the hardships they suffer[ed] in the matter of securing medical aid".[70] They also pointed out that while they could make phone calls to Scarborough, the reverse was not possible. De Nobriga also met with the people of Roxborough, who shared the view that if the previous elected Tobago representatives had been able to travel as easily as did de Nobriga, "Tobago would have been very much better off at the present time".[71] The grievances raised by Tobagonians during de Nobriga's tenure echoed those made in the years before, and they continued to persist in the decades after. These grievances, the secondary elements in identity construction, festered in the consciousness of Tobagonians. It made them see the government seated in Trinidad as not particularly concerned about their plight.

De Nobriga proposed ways to deal with the challenges caused by the war. He encouraged the rearing of goats because of the difficulty of getting shipments of condensed milk to the colony, and he offered a prize for a milking competition on the island.[72] He also promoted a "Win the War" drive in August 1940. De Nobriga represented the interests of Tobago's cocoa growers when he was appointed to the Cocoa Subsidy Board in 1940 – the first time that Tobago had a representative on that board.[73]

In early 1943 de Nobriga visited Tobago again and met with his advisory committee to discuss various matters affecting the island. He assured the members that the Tobago telephone service, which the government had recently acquired from the Tobago Development Company, would be improved by having more than one line serving the Windward district.[74] Various other matters were discussed at the meeting, including procuring a weighing scale for the purchase of animals by the government, the shipping of livestock, food storage and preservation, the milk supply, the coastal steamers, acquisition of land for the peasantry in Charlotteville, health and sanitation, education, nurses for the hospital, and matters pertaining to the Tobago Government Farm. The members asked de Nobriga to bring those issues before the legislature.

In March 1944 he again visited Tobago and travelled all over the island holding meetings. In May 1944 de Nobriga was nominated to a seat on the Executive Council, a position of tremendous political influence.

In that year a bus service was started in Tobago – a project that de Nobriga had urged. Unfortunately the bus fares were high; de Nobriga explained that the condition under which he was able to secure the bus service was that it be financially self-supporting.[75] Speaking at a joint meeting of the Tobago District Agricultural Society and the Tobago Chamber of Commerce held at the Court House in November 1944, de Nobriga gave an account of his stewardship from March 1944 as representative for Tobago. He had supported the proposed harbour scheme for Scarborough; construction at Port of Spain of a quay and warehouses for handling cargo from Tobago, to avoid congestion; construction of a medical centre for Scarborough; and a survey of Charlotteville by the Planning and Housing Commission. He informed the attendees that a jitney for transporting patients from the Windward district to the hospital would soon arrive on the island. In addition he promised that in the near future Tobago would have wireless telephone communication with Trinidad.

Probably because George de Nobriga was a businessman, he treated his job as the island's representative much like that of the manager of a firm rather than as a man of the people. He made official visits to his constituents, consulted with Tobagonian advisers and made attempts to address their concerns in the Legislative Council. Given the great interest his visits generated, and the fact that he managed so many business concerns in Trinidad, de Nobriga obviously did not spend much time in Tobago. It is unlikely that he was very close to his constituents or identified with them, since he was not a native son. He also did not speak much in the Council, so it is difficult to get a full picture of his advocacy for Tobagonians.

In all fairness, it should be noted that his tenure on the Council coincided with World War II, a time when the colony reduced its expenditure in order to support Britain's war effort. Thus George de Nobriga may have found it incongruous to demand costly development projects for Tobago. However, it is also arguable that even with very urgent matters, such as those considered by the Sea Communications Committee, de Nobriga (and the other committee members) dealt with Tobago primarily as a business opportunity needing judicious investment. It is fair to assume that, for the most part, de Nobriga viewed Tobago as another of his business concerns requiring good management, with the government as the chief steward.

None of de Nobriga's comments indicate that he felt a close affinity to Tobagonians. He was a white Trinidadian representing Tobagonians. He did not exude a Tobagonian identity. He simply owned Tobago Plantations Limited (known locally as Lowlands Estate) on the island. Taking everything into consideration, George de Nobriga was an integrationist. Tobagonians did not support him at the polls in 1946, probably because they had expected so much from him that he did not deliver. In many respects A. P. T. James, his successor – a political newcomer but a "son of the soil" – was his antithesis.

Chapter 8

A. P. T. James and the Union, 1946–1961

In 1946 universal adult suffrage was granted to Trinidad and Tobago and elections were held.[1] Prior to that the franchise was extremely limited: only the upper-middle and the upper classes could vote and serve on the Legislative Council. The election seems to have generated great interest – approximately 73 per cent of the 11,509 electors turned out to vote.[2] Before the polls opened on 1 July, the *Tobagonian* reminded its readers of Tobago's distinctiveness and needs:

> Tobago's problems are different from those of any other Colony. We are an island compact in ourselves. In many respects we are a[n] entity. More than any other part of the colony we need a Representative who will not only know and understand our needs, but who will press for them in and out of season, for unless our problems are kept continually before the minds of the powers that be we will inevitably become more . . . backward than we already are.[3]

Toby McIntosh, the editor, had taken a decidedly separatist position that invoked the issue of identity. He realized that Tobago would not get fair and equitable treatment from the central government if it was not constantly pressured to do so. Six candidates contested the single

Tobago seat. Alphonso Philbert Theophilus James (1901–62), a labour contractor, won 50.9 per cent of the votes while his nearest rival received only 19.7 per cent; only 7.2 per cent of the voters supported George de Nobriga.[4] James, a spirited, passionate representative of Tobagonians in the Council, rose to meet the *Tobagonian*'s high expectations.

This chapter examines A. P .T. James's advocacy for the interests of Tobago and Tobagonians and his views on the relationship between Tobago and Trinidad. It also assesses his role as a legislator. His career as the elected representative of Tobago spanned an unbroken fifteen-year period from 1946 to 1961, which coincided with the last years of his life.

James was born in Patience Hill, Tobago. He served a short stint as a pupil teacher[5] and then migrated to Trinidad, where he worked as a labourer at the La Brea pitch lake. He rose through the ranks to foreman with the Brighton Company and later became an independent contractor who "employed hundreds of workers and from all records he paid his workers handsomely".[6] James was a member of the Trinidad Labour Party. He was also involved with the Uriah Butler labour movement in the 1930s and was an advocate for labour issues. He can be considered Tobago's most ardent advocate for political, social and economic development.

James believed strongly that Tobago, though disadvantaged by years of neglect by the British government and the central government in Trinidad, was an equal partner in the union and not a subordinate, dependent adjunct. He contended that Tobago should have separate representation and a separate voice on all issues and in all forums, even in the Parliament of the British West Indies Federation. He expressed the view that if Tobago's infrastructure, sea communication and social services were improved and its agricultural, fishing and tourism resources developed, the island could once again achieve economic viability and thus free itself from dependence on the Trinidad treasury.[7] Probably the most significant of James's convictions was that Tobago should once again be granted administrative autonomy and that the island should become a separate political unit independent of Trinidad. James was a separatist *par excellence*. Until the end of his career and life he maintained the view that Tobago should secede from Trinidad. Thus he can be placed on the far left of the autonomy continuum, although initially he began just left of centre.

A. P. T. James and the Colonial Government

Two of the first issues that A. P. T. James addressed in the Trinidad and Tobago Legislative Council were Tobago's sea and land communications. The steamship service between the islands was a constant bone of contention. The two steamers operating in 1946 were old, slow and unreliable. James constantly called upon the government to purchase new ships to service the inter-island route. The steamer service was crucial to the commercial viability of the island, as well as for transporting Tobagonians who needed to access government services in Port of Spain. The poor state of the island's roads made the steamer service even more important.

During his tenure on the Council, James argued that Tobago was an integral part of the colony and that the government was responsible for maintaining the island's sea link with Trinidad, just as it was duty bound to maintain road communications with any and all of the other areas of Trinidad.[8] In this regard he echoed the earlier sentiments of Governor Sir Murchison Fletcher and the Nicoll Report. He objected strenuously to the view that by subsidizing the coastal steamer service the government was only being charitable to Tobagonians.[9]

By January 1950 James was calling on the government to replace the coastal steamer *Tobago,* which was in a state of disrepair.[10] In his 1953 contribution to the colony's budget debate, he demanded replacement of one or both of the ships that operated between the islands.[11] In May 1955 he moved a motion calling on the government to consider replacing both of the coastal steamers, the *Tobago* and the *Trinidad,* with modern ones. He reminded the government that the steamers served not only Tobagonians but the entire colony. They were used to transport produce from Tobago for consumption in Trinidad and for transhipment overseas, they served as the "highway which link[ed] the Island-Ward with its bigger sister, Trinidad" and they supported the tourist trade.[12] In February 1957 the government withdrew the steamers from service and sold them.[13] Three years later James's advocacy for two new ships bore fruit.[14] The new steamers were called the *Scarlet Ibis* and the *Bird of Paradise*.

In his attempts to get roads in Tobago constructed and improved, James applied as much political pressure on the government as he used to procure the new steamers. He constantly asked the government to declare how much of the colony's budget was allocated to road development in Tobago, which roads were under construction, and the nature of road improvement work on the island. Construction of the North Coast Road was a matter that he kept before the legislature. That road linked the rural areas, where much of the agricultural produce was grown, to Scarborough, the main town and port. The North Coast Road was the key to stimulating agricultural development on the island, since it allowed planters and peasants direct ground access to the capital for shipping their produce.[15]

James was also concerned about the disproportionate amount of money being spent on maintaining roads in Trinidad as compared to similar expenditure in Tobago. He asked the government to increase its 1949 budget allocation for roads in Tobago in order to put it on par (proportionally) with expenditure on roads in Trinidad. The government insisted that the high volume of traffic in Trinidad's urban and industrial areas necessitated expenditure "far in excess of the cost in a rural district like Tobago".[16] This official view of Tobago as a rural backwater, not worthy of much attention, was a legacy from the time of union. That attitude incensed Tobagonians and led them to view the central government and Trinidadians as the insensitive other.

Another factor that made the need for roads in the rural areas of Tobago urgent was the inability of the coastal steamers to dock at some ports during bad weather.[17] For example, between 27 December 1949 and 12 February 1950 the steamers were unable to dock at Bloody Bay and Parlatuvier. Food supplies were affected and the government had to use Jeeps and trucks to deliver supplies to those areas. The condition of the roads did not help, and James appealed to the government to improve the roads between either Castara and Parlatuvier or Roxborough and Parlatuvier.[18] In the debate on the 1951 budget, James again urged the government to construct the North Coast Road. He argued that the road would reduce the cost of operating the coastal steamers, since they would only have to operate between Port of Spain and Scarborough, not around the island as well. The Nicoll Report had also recommended this strategy. To James's proposal that the road would cost $400,000, one Council member retorted, "But Tobago is not worth that."[19] In the eyes of the Trinidadian legislators, Tobago was at the bottom of the infrastructure totem pole, undeserving of significant capital development.

In 1952 James continued urging the government to construct the North Coast Road, which by then was estimated to cost $500,000.[20] In 1956 the PNM government, led by Dr Eric Williams, came to power. During its first term of administration a special development programme was devised for Tobago that included construction of the North Coast Road.[21] Tobago was given special consideration by the new government and its expenditure was separated from that of Trinidad. A Ministry for Tobago Affairs, with a permanent secretary, was proposed.[22] James welcomed these plans for Tobago and urged their immediate implementation.[23]

A. P. T. James desperately wished to change the image of Tobago as the "forgotten child" and the "Cinderella" of Trinidad and the Caribbean. His charges of neglect served to strengthen we/they antipathies between the people of the two islands and cemented Tobagonian identity: "Tobago is no longer prepared to sit and merely take the crumbs that fall from Trinidad's table."[24] Further, the government's neglect of social services in Tobago led James to exclaim, "[T]he position is such that I am tempted to ask whether Tobago is the backyard of Trinidad."[25]

Attempting to improve Tobago's image, in 1946 he urged the government to implement the recommendations of the 1944 report on the medical and health policy of the colony, which called for additional medical staff for Tobago as well as the erection of health centres and extension of ambulance services on the island.[26] In a speech in the Council in January 1949, James highlighted a litany of woes concerning conditions at the Tobago Colonial Hospital. He contended that the officer in charge of the hospital did not have an office; there were only six beds for females in the general hospital; there was no X-ray machine (I. A. Hope also advocated for X-ray equipment); boilers for sterilization, which had been promised seven years earlier, had not yet been delivered; the thirty-one-year-old Norwegian stove used for that purpose had failed periodically; the operating theatre was not separated from the ward, so patients could observe doctors performing surgical procedures; and sanitary conditions were not satisfactory, especially with regard to waste disposal. Above all, there were no separate wards for patients with infectious diseases.[27] In 1951 the government provided $3 million for improvements to various health facilities in the colony, including the Tobago hospital.[28]

As a former pupil teacher, A. P. T. James was also very much concerned about education in Tobago.[29] During his fifteen years in the legislature he demanded that the government build and maintain schools in Tobago, as many of the existing ones were very dilapidated. In 1947 he requested that a "proper school" be built in Roxborough, the island's second town, to replace the "two old shacks" there.[30] In 1950 James urged the government to construct at least one other secondary school in Tobago. He also kept before the legislature the need for repairs to the elementary schools.[31] At that time Tobago had only one secondary school – Bishop's High School in Scarborough, which was an Anglican school.

James's philosophy of education promoted the study of agriculture, which he believed was Tobago's greatest asset. He advocated the establishment of a farm school in Tobago. The government expressed interest in such a school, but again cited cost as the mitigating factor in undertaking the venture.[32] In the December 1951 budget debate James urged the government to give more scholarships for the study of agriculture, even up to 50 per cent of the total scholarships awarded.[33] He deplored the emphasis that was placed on the professions at the expense of agricultural work. He asked the government to "consider adopting measures whereby children could be taught at school not to consider their schoolmates socially inferior or to be lacking in character if they happen to take up agriculture for a livelihood".[34] This was a serious matter to James and to all Tobagonians because of the almost purely agrarian nature of Tobago's society. To suggest that people who did agricultural work were socially inferior to those who were in the professions was equivalent to adding to the stigma of Tobagonian inferiority.

In 1952 James recommended establishment of a trade school in Tobago and a secondary school in the Windward district.[35] So frustrated was he with the government's lethargy in establishing a secondary school in the rural section of Tobago that he set up his own school in Roxborough – James' Foundation Secondary School – "and devoted a class exclusively to the subject of agriculture".[36] He was happy to hear that the government had made provision in the 1957 Tobago Development Programme for a school at Roxborough.[37] During James's tenure in office the government built at least two elementary schools, one at Bon Accord and the other at Montgomery, to replace some of the nine dilapidated schools acquired from the Moravian board.[38]

The conviction that Tobago could regain economic viability, mainly through the development of its agricultural and fishing industries and also by encouraging tourism, fuelled James's passion. He believed that Tobagonians would be willing to make sacrifices in order to foster such development. Thus, in January 1947 – without success – he suggested that the government "consider the feasibility of levying a cess on exports from Tobago with a view to raising funds to finance various improvement schemes which are vital and necessary to the well-being of the Island's inhabitants and which Government might not be able to allocate money for in the near future".[39] As a self-made man he felt that Tobagonians could pull themselves up by their own bootstraps and by dint of sacrifice. His ultimate goal was to rid Tobago of economic dependence on Trinidad. The stigma of Tobagonian inferiority was tied to the fact that the island came into the union in a dependent economic condition. James probably felt that this negative association jeopardized Tobagonians' pride, or at least made Trinidadians view them as inferior. James was fiercely protective of the image of Tobago and its people, and as such of their identity.

His continued emphasis on the development of industries in Tobago was partly aimed at stemming the constant migration of young Tobagonians from the island in search of employment in Trinidad. In early

1947 he suggested that if the government gave Tobagonians opportunities to develop the economic potential of their island, the entire colony
would benefit. Tobagonians would then be able to establish a cement
factory, develop a flourishing trade in tobacco, operate a cooking oil
factory, produce sugar commercially and raise enough cattle to "supply
Trinidad with most of the meat she need[ed]".[40] In January 1948 James
requested government consideration for "resuscitating the sugar industry in Tobago, so that unemployment in the Island-Ward may be eased,
and revenue added to the funds of the Colony".[41] He saw Tobagonians as
a self-reliant people who could achieve industrial development if provided with the appropriate support.

Not confident that the government would support economic development in Tobago, James sought help overseas. In 1948 he paid his
own fare to London to take his constituents' grievances to Secretary
of State for the Colonies Sir Arthur Creech Jones. This act was also
symbolic of James's lack of trust that the Trinidad government would
promote the island's welfare. Thus he sought an authority higher than
the colonial government because the latter was unsympathetic to the
cries for development in Tobago. In that regard he acted as a separatist. In a memorandum to the secretary of state written by James
and Louis A. Peters (both prominent members of the Tobago Citizens
Political and Economic Party, discussed below), James outlined the
needs and potential of Tobago in the areas of animal husbandry, production of dairy products and cocoa, secondary processing industries,
telephone service, electrification, health personnel and services, education, road development and other areas.[42] He also raised the issue
of Tobagonians having greater authority in determining policies that
directly affected them.[43]

In London James recommended that the Colonial Development
Corporation provide $15 million for the island's development. He
urged the corporation to conduct a survey aimed at increasing local
food production and formulating a long-range plan for establishing
light industries and training skilled workers.[44] His distrust of the government's intentions to develop Tobago is evident in the memorandum
submitted to Jones:

> While it is true that the present administration has already set up a standing economic committee to advise it on industrial and agricultural expansion, no faith can be placed in any policy it might formulate. The government's past indifference to recommendations for improvement is well known and its failures too conspicuous.[45]

James had all but given up hope that any remedy for Tobago's problems would come from the colonial government.

In 1949 he prodded the government on the issue of developing the fishing industry of Tobago and of the colony in general. The government's response was that no planning could be done until experts carried out surveys to indicate the area's potential for fishing.[46] Similarly, in 1950 he called on the government to "set up a committee . . . to enquire into the possibilities of re-establishing in Tobago either one or all of the following industries: sugar, tobacco, cotton".[47] He contended that if Tobago's economy were given a chance to become viable, the view held by some legislators – that Tobago was "only suited for the export of goats" and that it was a liability to Trinidad – would change.[48]

The electrification of Tobago was always a cause for concern. A. P. T. James lobbied hard for providing Scarborough with electricity. He was incensed that no provision was made for electrification of the island when the government embarked on a $6 million island-wide electricity scheme for Trinidad in 1949.[49] Scarborough finally received electricity in 1952.[50] Such examples of uneven development eventually led the autonomists of the 1970s to demand internal self-government for Tobago so that Tobagonians could set their own development priorities. Indeed, this was the thrust of James's advocacy throughout his tenure in the legislature. He also demanded a better water supply for Tobago. While the Hillsborough dam was completed in 1952, he continued to press for extension of water distribution in Tobago,[51] urging the government to provide the pipelines needed for that service.[52]

The development of tourism in Tobago was another rallying point for James. In 1947 he chided the government for setting aside $80,000 for tourism, from which he alleged that Tobago had not benefited. Because of the government's lack of action on the issue of tourism development in Tobago, James threatened separation from Trinidad:

> Tobago is prepared to remain with Trinidad as long as Trinidad is prepared to
> have us as equal partners, but we are not prepared to continue at the present
> rate at which we are going and we shall use every constitutional means to see
> to it that we are not going to be the slave of Trinidad.[53]

James insisted that "since Tobago forms part and parcel of the Colony, we cannot consider it progressive unless we make the people of Tobago as progressive as those in Trinidad".[54]

As the years passed, James grew increasingly frustrated with the snail's pace at which the government attended to development in Tobago. In 1951 he requested a progress report on the 1947 infrastructure projects for Tobago; six major projects had been scheduled for completion in 1947.[55] One was the development of Lower Scarborough. This project had been reallocated to the 1951–56 five-year development plan and accorded a low priority. Second, "preliminary works" were undertaken on the development of Charlotteville but no funds had been provided for further development. Work was in progress on the drainage of swamps at Bon Accord, Golden Grove, Friendship and Louis d'Or. The construction of the Hillsborough dam was also underway; it was completed in 1952 at the cost of $1.7 million. The fifth project involved improvements to the Tobago harbour; this was postponed until the latter part of 1951. Finally, construction of an "all-weather" road from Moriah to Charlotteville was abandoned because the ratio of the cost to the population that would be served was considered too high.[56] These kinds of delays and disappointments supported James's contention that the government did not have Tobago's interest at heart.

In that 1947 speech James raised other issues as well. He called on the government to alleviate the high cost of living in Tobago and provide a good water treatment plant, housing and medical facilities, as well as electricity.[57] In 1948 he continued to lobby the government to develop tourism. He moved to make lands in the Crown Point–Storebay area in south-western Tobago available to individuals who were interested in building hotels and developing the tourist trade.[58]

James must have been convinced that he would get his constituents' support if he called for separation. At least he knew that they shared his

Identity and Secession in the Caribbean

frustrations and wanted to see some positive action taken to improve economic opportunities on the island. The 1947 threat of secession was not his last. His plan to use constitutional measures to effect separation from Trinidad indicates that James was not a radical secessionist. His visit to the Colonial Office, the locus of imperial power, shows that he believed that the British government, with its sovereignty over the colonies, could be persuaded to dissolve the union between Tobago and Trinidad. His 1948 memorandum linked development of Tobago, which he was confident would result after separation, with the benefits of ensuring essential material and foodstuff for Britain.[59] James was willing to do anything that would redound to the benefit of his native island. He continued to seek a better deal for Tobago by attempting to garner greater representation on the Legislative Council for Tobagonians.

Constitutional development in Trinidad and Tobago was one of James's major concerns. Before 1925 all the members of the legislature were nominated. After 1925 seven members were elected, with only 6 per cent of the population of the colony being qualified to vote,[60] and Tobago was given one seat on the Legislative Council. In 1941 the number of elected representatives was increased to nine, with Tobago retaining a single seat.[61] Constant calls were made for full representative government, that is, for all the members of the Council to be elected. James was a champion of this cause, and he supported the 1948 Constitutional Reform Committee's minority report written by Dr Patrick Solomon. Solomon and James both insisted that the Council should be fully elected.[62]

James submitted his own minority report, dated 14 November 1949. In it he objected to the fact that "population was the sole consideration" for deciding how many seats Tobago should have in the legislature:

> I have all along maintained, especially in the Legislature and in my representations to the Secretary of State for the Colonies, that Tobago, which at one time had its own government, should have at least two seats in the new Legislature under the new constitution. In my opinion, any attempt to condemn Tobago to one seat in the new Legislature can only mean that she has not benefited politically from the new constitution granted the Colony.[63]

Representative Roy A. Joseph, Member for the borough of San Fernando, supported James's advocacy for increasing Tobago's representation in the legislature to two members, and he requested the same for his constituency.[64]

In 1950 James similarly deplored the fact that the new constitution, which increased the number of elected representatives on the Legislative Council to eighteen, did not grant Tobago two seats. Convinced that Tobago was not being treated fairly, James referred to the resolution passed by the Tobago House of Assembly in 1887, which stated that if the union did not benefit the island, two-thirds of the residents could petition the secretary of state to have the union dissolved. While he declared, "I am not advocating such a procedure at this moment", he went on to "warn the government that unless Tobago receives fair and just treatment – better treatment than is meted out to the Island Ward today – perhaps she might be forced to take the best course which she believes will bring untold benefits to her sons and daughters".[65] This was his second threat of secession, a threat made to effect better treatment for Tobago as well as to garner a greater share of the economic pie from the central government. The Tobago County Council, of which James was the chairman, also protested against the failure to grant Tobago two seats in the legislature. The councillors argued that

> . . . as a detached county in the colony [Tobago] claims the right to a better representation in the Colony's Political affairs due to her geographical position and lack of proper inter-Island Communication which renders it humanly impossible for any one single representative to address himself satisfactorily to the various and varied problems peculiar to the Island.[66]

Governor Hubert Rance disagreed with the councillors' contention that communication between the islands was poor and thus a "serious disability" to the Tobago representative. The two coastal steamers, "which made several trips every week, and . . . a daily aeroplane service, provided [sufficient] inter-island transportation".[67] In addition, he argued, the government's wireless and "radio telephonic" communication systems were available in Tobago. However, Rance noted that choosing a nominated member from Tobago, which was

suggested by the Tobago Citizens Political and Economic Party, constituted a "convenient solution", but the competition for representation
in the legislature did not make that a viable option. Despite the protests
from James, Joseph and the Tobago County Council, Parliamentary
Undersecretary of State James Griffiths let stand the Electoral Districts
Delimitation Committee Report. The majority report was submitted
to the governor on 4 November 1949 and was accepted by the Executive
Council on 21 January 1950. Thus Tobago retained only one seat in the
legislature.

The demands for increased Tobagonian representation envisioned
not only more seats on the Legislative Council but involvement in
the Executive Council and other committees as well. James tried to
impress upon the government that, because Tobago was separated
from Trinidad by sea, no one on the larger island was "conversant
with the condition" or "competent to state what actually happens in
Tobago" except resident Tobagonians.[68] As early as 1947 he contended,
"I consider it very much a necessity that Tobago should be perma-
nently represented on bodies such as the Estimates Committee [which
made the colony's annual budget], and peradventure, the Executive
Council."[69] Throughout his political career James continued to press
for Tobagonian representation in the government. He believed that
only "persons who [were] actually on the spot" could provide the government with the information "to arrive at a decision as to the real
needs of Tobago" and to ensure that "the rights of Tobago[nians were]
well preserved".[70] James wanted Tobagonians to have sole authority to
determine the policies that affected their island and their destiny.

The Tobago Citizens Political and Economic Party, of which James was
a member, also took up the matter of increased Tobagonian representation. This self-proclaimed "organ and mouthpiece of the majority of
the population" protested the "discrimination" against Tobago regarding increased representation in the corridors of power.[71] Its members
passed a resolution to that effect on 29 October 1950 and sent it to the
secretary of state, the governor, the speaker of the Legislative Council
and senior members of all the legislatures in the British West Indies,
including Alexander Bustamante, leader of the Jamaica Labour Party;

Michael Manley, leader of the Jamaican opposition party; Grantley Adams, leader of the Barbados Labour Party; and W. Crawford, leader of the Barbados opposition party.[72] Signed by S. E. Roberts, the chairman, and Louis Peters, the secretary, the resolution was also sent to the chairmen and members of the Tobago County Council, the Tobago Chamber of Commerce and the Tobago District Agricultural Society.

The resolution began by invoking Tobago's identity. It referred to Tobago's glorious past when the island was "independent . . . with its own Administration".[73] The Tobago Citizens Political and Economic Party revisited the disallowed 1887 pledge aimed at returning Tobago to independent Crown Colony status if its relationship with Trinidad proved disadvantageous after the union (even the autonomists of the 1970s invoked this pledge). The members of the Tobago Citizens Political and Economic Party lamented that Tobago's status in the union had not improved despite many constitutional reforms that had consistently increased the number of representatives in the legislature. Not only was Tobago denied an increase in elected representation, the island was not granted any nominated representatives. More important, Tobago was also denied representation on the Executive Council, "the chief instrument of Government Policy". The Tobago Citizens Political and Economic Party declared that as a result of these deficiencies in the 1950 constitution, Tobago had suffered a "demotion" in status within the colony.

The signatories of the resolution also argued that Tobagonians should be seen as a "Minority Group"; in all democratic countries such groups were accorded "privileged" representation. They deplored the fact that, even with representative government, Tobagonians were not included in the administration of their own island unless their representative chose to align himself with the ruling Trinidadian party that controlled the government; the autonomists of the 1970s made this claim as well. The members of the Tobago Citizens Political and Economic Party authorized the Tobago member of the Legislative Council to take "every constitutional means at his disposal (even to the extent of leading a delegation of the Party to Downing Street [the Colonial Office])" to press for an amendment to the 1950 constitution. This amendment would include provision for Tobagonians to have a permanent representative on the Executive Council. In addition, the party demanded creation of a special ministry to handle Tobago's affairs. Finally, the amendment would provide representation for Tobago, separately from Trinidad, in the proposed West Indies Federation. The purpose of this was "to enable Tobago to express its views as the other small Islands of the Caribbean".[74] James gazed at the forthcoming federation with eyes yearning for autonomy. He realized that even if Tobago gained significant representation in the Legislative Council, its representatives would still be outnumbered. Procuring a guaranteed autonomous voice in the federation would be the crucial step in releasing Tobago from the stranglehold of the Trinidad government in which he had no faith.

Governor Rance objected to every claim made in the Tobago Citizens Political and Economic Party's resolution and advised Griffiths to deny its requests.[75] However, he sympathized with the Tobago Citizens Political and Economic Party's wish for greater representation for Tobago at all levels of the government:

> I would have liked if possible to meet their desires. . . . Tobago had a chance of having its representative being appointed to the Executive Council but the Legislative Council voted otherwise. I would have liked to have nominated a person from Tobago to the Legislative Council but in making this decision I could not allow sentiment to play a part in a matter of such importance, and there was no resident of Tobago whom I considered suitable.[76]

Rance's last statement harkens back to similar remarks by previous governors who contended that no "suitable" — meaning white — Tobagonians could be found to serve as nominated members of the Council. Tobago's majority black population always posed an impediment in the implementation of such racist policies.

Rance pointed to resistance from the Legislative Council in his attempts to secure greater Tobago representation. He was also convinced that the resolution was "inspired" by James: if James had been appointed to the Executive Council the resolution would not have been produced. Rance dismissed the claim of minority status with a classic integrationist argument: "I do not consider [that] . . . the people of

Tobago constitute a group which can be separated, whether on political, ethnical or religious ground, from the rest of the Colony."[77] On the issue of neglected infrastructure development, he believed that Tobago received "its fair share" of capital expenditure. He cited the Hillsborough waterworks then under construction, estimated to cost more than $2 million, as well as five projects in the 1950–55 five-year economic programme. These included improvements to the Tobago Colonial Hospital to the tune of $300,000; construction of additional health centres, a central administration building and quarters for public officers; completion of the Tobago deep-water harbour; and "re-planning the town of Scarborough at a cost of $750,000".[78]

In addition, Rance contended that Tobagonians' "main complaint" of neglect in capital expenditure had developed in them an "ultra-sensitivity which can best be described as a neglection complex".[79] This, he declared, was not justified, because Tobago was not being

> milked financially by Trinidad, but the reverse is the case and Tobago benefits more than she actually would if she had to depend on her resources alone. Tobago, standing alone, would undoubtedly be an impoverished colony. United to Trinidad, she benefits from the relatively greater economic strength of the latter.[80]

Like other integrationists, Rance believed that Tobagonians should simply be grateful for the few capital development projects undertaken on the island since the union – and be quiet.

Governor Rance provided approximate revenue and expenditure figures for 1947 and 1948 to bolster his contentions. In 1947 Tobago's revenue was $216,000 while its expenditure amounted to $926,000, leaving a deficit of $710,000; the 1948 revenue was $200,000 and the expenditure stood at $1.127 million, leaving a deficit of $927,000.[81] However, it is important to note that after Tobago became a ward, accurately disaggregating the island's revenue and expenditure from those of the larger colony was extremely difficult. Tobagonian separatists always argued that the government was not revealing the true amount of revenue generated on the island, while at the same time emphasizing its expenditure. Tobagonians, who never trusted the government, always saw something sinister in this aspect of its reporting. The government had allocated the cost of purchasing and operating the costal steamers solely to Tobago's expenditure – another sore point in inter-island accounting. Rance, unlike his predecessor Governor Murchison Fletcher, argued that the ships were operated "for the benefit of Tobago" and, further, this was done at a "loss of approximately $245,000 in 1949 and $325,000 in 1950".[82] Fletcher and others saw the maintenance of inter-island sea communication as a service that the government was duty bound to carry out, in the same way that it was obligated to maintain the roads in the colony. Thus the issue of what figures were entered into Tobago's revenue and expenditure equation was debatable.

On the matter of the Tobago representative's having to ally himself with a Trinidad party to gain access to executive power in the administration, Rance argued that Tobago was "no worse off than several of the other constituencies".[83] This patent failure of Trinidadian officials to understand the negative effects of separation by water on a "detached county" bred an insensitivity that was particularly evident in Rance's "neglection complex" argument. Trinidadians never really understood what it was like to be marginalized far from the centre of government activity. In the years ahead, especially during the struggle for internal self-government in the 1970s, Trinidadians would continue to be oblivious to the disadvantages Tobagonians suffered from being separated by the ocean.

Governor Rance did not accede to the idea that Tobago should be given a minister – a very predictable response from an integrationist. Citing Scotland, for which a secretary of state had been appointed, Rance argued that Tobago could not be compared with it in terms of "population, economic or financial strength, or inaccessibility".[84] Tobago's supposed economic weakness was always used to justify the extent to which the island should not be given special consideration. James understood this rationale. Thus he always pushed for economic development so that Tobago could gain political leverage in the colony.

Concerning constitutional arrangements in the proposed West Indies Federation, Rance argued that the colony could decide to give Tobago one of the nine seats that would be allocated to Trinidad in the Federal Parliament. However, realizing that the Tobago Citizens Political and Economic Party wanted more than mere equitable representation and that its goal included separation from Trinidad, Rance countered, "If the petitioners mean that the representation of Tobago should be entirely separate from that of Trinidad then I would suggest that this is impossible under the existing constitution."[85] The Tobago Citizens Political and Economic Party had authorized James, in his capacity as the Tobago member of the Legislative Council, to use any constitutional means at his disposal to effect Tobago's independent representation at the highest level. Becoming a federal unit was his strategy for accomplishing this goal.

As early as 1948 James had articulated his view of Tobago's place in the federation: "I believe in a federation in which every individual unit will be able to express its views as a true voice of the people."[86] Some of James's colleagues in the legislature interpreted his strong advocacy for matters concerning Tobago as an attitude tending towards secession. In January 1948 he brought this matter to the attention of the governor: "Your Excellency, whenever I attempt to speak in the Council, there is a tendency among certain members to interpret me as wanting either to separate Tobago and Trinidad or[,] as one member puts it[,] I am trying to become Governor of Tobago."[87] Clearly James was not a radical secessionist.

Notwithstanding, he took issue with the resolutions of the Conference on the Closer Association of the British West Indian Colonies held in Montego Bay, Jamaica, in September 1947. As the government attempted to get those resolutions passed in the legislature in 1948, James pointed out that Tobago was not mentioned in them. He noted that all the other smaller islands were included and he reminded the members of the Legislative Council of Tobago's glorious past, a period when the island "boasted of a constitution far greater than anything Trinidad has ever seen".[88] He insisted that Tobago was entitled to the same degree of representation as the other islands. He further suggested an amendment to the motion, calling for the Council to accept the conference resolutions on the condition that wherever the word "Trinidad" appeared in them it should read "Trinidad and Tobago".[89] James refused to allow Tobago's identity to be swallowed up in the generic designation "Trinidad". As his successor A. N. R. Robinson would later argue, such societal biases tended to creep into official circles and documents. James's reiteration of Tobago's glorious past during the dispensation of the old representative system was a strategy of invoking Tobagonian identity and including we/they antipathies in the discussion of autonomous representation for Tobago at the federal level.

As the years went on, A. P. T. James's advocacy for the needs of Tobago was accompanied by ambivalence about Tobago's place in the union. His frustration with the government's lacklustre attempts to develop Tobago, and his wounded pride over the view that the island was considered a financial burden to Trinidad, led him to hint at the possibility of separation. In January 1949 James declared,

> Tobago should not be considered a drag on Trinidad. . . . I am satisfied beyond the shadow of a doubt – and I am not speaking in a tone of Tobago being placed by itself or I should not advocate such a move at this moment, but when every individual is considering federation and when we believe that the only hope of assisting us to make ourselves a people is by unity – in this strain I cite this only to convince members of this Council who believe that we will always be a drag – that Tobago may well support itself and even become of assistance to the Colony.[90]

James was clearly concerned about Tobagonian identity when he mentioned the "hope of . . . mak[ing] ourselves a people". He implied that the corporate Tobagonian self could not reclaim its adulthood (lost at the time of union) until the island achieved economic independence. The thought that Tobago was "considered a drag on Trinidad" was unacceptable to him. He preferred separation for Tobago rather than having the island treated as a dependent minor. Thus James proposed that a $10 million grant from the imperial government for development of Tobago's agricultural resources would make the island economically viable in ten years.

In 1951 James and the Tobago Citizens Political and Economic Party wrote a memorandum addressed to the secretary of state for the colonies "Setting out the Grievances, Disabilities and Complaints of the Inhabitants of Tobago".[91] He delivered the document to the governor to be forwarded to London. He also made a second visit to London that year and presented the demands outlined in the memorandum to the officials at the Colonial Office.

The signatories of the memorandum proclaimed that they were not seeking secession, because they considered themselves "ardent believers in the Policy and Principles of Federation".[92] They contended that Tobago had not benefited politically or economically from the union with Trinidad and that it should have more than one seat on the Legislative Council and a representative on the Executive Council. The signatories advised that a "Grant-in-Aid, coupled with better communication and Free Trade with the outside world, would not only increase the island's population, but would produce a wealthy and prosperous Tobago".[93] It recommended establishment on the island of cotton, tobacco and sugar-cane cultivation by the peasants and development of the fishing industry. The potential for development of citrus and banana production was also highlighted, as was establishment of a tourist industry. Furthermore, the signatories complained about the lack of electricity and cold storage facilities on the island. They declared that the absence of those services retarded the establishment of some of the industries they wished to see develop on the island.

The memorandum of the Tobago Citizens Political and Economic Party also cited the lack of proper roads and the non-existence of communication with the outside world, leading to transhipment of perishable items from Trinidad. While the signatories graciously noted the efforts of the central government in dealing with Tobago's problems, they argued that "the results of these efforts are almost imperceptible and cannot effectively combat the evils occasioned by past neglect".[94] The memorandum requested (1) amendment of the constitution to provide Tobagonians the fullest representation possible in the union; (2) authorization for Tobago to enter the federation not as a ward but as a "recognized Unit of the combined Colony of

Trinidad and Tobago with similar status" as that of the other units of the Windward and Leeward islands; and (3) allocation of £1.5 million from the imperial government as a grant-in-aid for the development of Tobago. On 1 August 1951 James met with the parliamentary under-secretary of state and reiterated the claims and requests made in the memorandum.[95] From the resolution and the memorandum of the Tobago Citizens Political and Economic Party, it is obvious that James and his supporters had a vision of an administratively autonomous and economically vibrant Tobago.

With every change of government, A. P. T. James continued his advocacy for the development of Tobago. By 1956 the colony of Trinidad and Tobago had achieved internal self-government within the British Empire. The legislature was fully elected and accounta-ble to the people. The colony was still under the ultimate leadership of a British-appointed governor, but a chief minister from the party that won the general elections was chosen to lead government busi-ness. Trinidad and Tobago was moving from a purely colonial state towards independent nationhood. By 1958 the colony had joined the British West Indies Federation as one of its principal partners; the capital of the federation was established in Trinidad. Tobago was not accorded separate status in the federation, but received one par-liamentary seat. In the five years after 1956 James battled with the ruling PNM government for the development of Tobago, as ardently as he had done in the previous decade.

A. P. T. James and the PNM Government

In 1956 the advent on the political scene of the PNM, led by Dr Eric E. Williams, gave James hope that development in Tobago would be has-tened. However, Williams and the PNM government posed a threat to James's political hold on Tobago, and this seems to have radicalized his views on the place of Tobago in the union.[96] The prospect that the British West Indies Federation would soon be established gave James additional leverage to wrest from the government better treat-ment and even administrative autonomy for Tobago. Constant taunts from members of the government and its supporters, who castigated him as an overambitious and physically unattractive political relic, may have pushed him over the political edge. Hence, by the end of his political career James had become a strong advocate for secession from Trinidad.

Initially James favoured the government's plans for Tobago. The PNM won the 1956 general elections and by mid-1957 Eric Williams had announced the Tobago Development Programme. For Williams, Tobago was a test case of Trinidad's ability to be the leader in the federation, which was finally constituted in 1958 (but dissolved in 1962). "If Trinidad cannot develop Tobago, then Trinidad's claim to be the principal partner in the Federation, Trinidad's claim to accept the responsibility of the smaller islands (formerly entrusted to the United Kingdom), falls to the ground," Williams proclaimed.[97]

Like James, Williams believed that over the years the Trinidad government had neglected Tobago. During his explanation in the legislature of the Tobago Development Programme, Chief Minister Williams declared that Trinidad had a "moral obligation" to Tobago, given the many years of neglect the smaller island had experienced. He promised to grant Tobago administrative autonomy as a "self-contained unit, independent insofar as day-to-day administration is concerned, independent of Trinidad, independent of the present . . . restriction requiring the simplest matters of office routine to be referred by a junior officer in Tobago to a senior officer in Trinidad".[98] He further proposed to establish a separate Ministry for Tobago Affairs with a minister who would be a member of the Executive Council. The chief minister promised $9.2 million for economic development of the island over a five-year period. The programme envisioned the development of agricultural industries, cottage industries and tourism, catering especially to Trinidadians. One significant aspect of the development plan was that Tobagonians were to be consulted on implementation of the programme.[99]

These pronouncements must have been music to James's ears, for he had lobbied hard for similar policies over the years. Even the separate administration for Tobago had been his idea; as shown above, it

Identity and Secession in the Caribbean

had already been set out in the 1950 resolution of the Tobago Citizens Economic and Political Party:

> The principle of having a Permanent Secretary in Tobago to deal with administrative matters was advocated by me years ago. Indeed and in fact when the Commission [was] set up by this Government to investigate the administrative arrangements in Tobago, I recommended that there should be somebody like a Commissioner responsible for all the different Departments; because there were times when one found himself in Tobago on official business but there seemed to be no one responsible.[100]

After two years of PNM rule, James seems to have become impatient with the government and suspicious of its plans for Tobago. In December 1958, during the debate on the 1959 budget, he lambasted the government's development programme as one "based primarily on vote-catching".[101] He urged the minister of agriculture and lands to reveal his plans for the development of agriculture in Tobago with respect to coconuts, cocoa, coffee, cattle rearing, poultry and fishing. He was fearful that the government's proposals for Tobago would not be implemented.

By 1959 relations between James and the government had become strained. Members of the Legislative Council teased him about self-rule for Tobago; even his fellow parliamentarian and friend Uriah Butler remarked on 7 June 1957 that he would support such a move for Tobago. On 1 May 1959, while Williams was explaining the government's proposal entitled *Reorganisation of the Public Service,* James interrupted him on four occasions regarding points of dispute, as well as for clarification. On the fourth occasion when James rose to speak, Williams refused to give way, stating, "If you want me to discuss Tobago affairs and give you some idea of the pattern that should be developed when you secede from Trinidad, I am ready to deal with that."[102] Williams was obviously aware that some Tobagonians were considering secession.

In July 1959, in his response to the Throne Speech, James expressed dissatisfaction over the governor's compliment to the government on its progress in developing Tobago. He argued that construction on the North Coast Road (begun in 1957) had caused unnecessary inconvenience to Tobagonians because the advice of paid technicians was not heeded. This resulted in destruction of private food gardens and in unnecessary acquisition of private property by the government, and agricultural access roads were not being constructed along with the main road. Moreover, the PNM's policy of denigrating agricultural work and promoting the professions above agriculture was ruining the island.[103] James said that he no longer considered Tobago "part and parcel" of Trinidad but rather a "partner". Thus he repudiated the status of ward, viewing Tobago as on equal footing with Trinidad in the union.

The government's practice of debiting the entire cost of the new steamers *Scarlet Ibis* and *Bird of Paradise* (delivered in 1960) from the Tobago development account also incensed James. The ships served both islands; their cost should have been divided equally between their accounts.[104] James's dissatisfaction over that and other issues led him, at the end of his 12 April 1960 speech on the budget, to hint at the possibility of secession: "Sir, we the people of Tobago do not believe in charity. We are conscientious and we accept the principle of self-sufficiency. We believe that if we are marching along to Independence, whether separately as an entity of the Territory of Trinidad and Tobago, or not, we want to contribute."[105] The next day, as the budget debate continued, he called on the government to provide land for the peasants so that local food production could increase, and he urged an increase of agricultural staff in Tobago to provide them with advice. In addition he pressed for development of the Scarborough harbour to allow for direct communication with the outside world and, finally, he requested that the government negotiate with the federal government for ships in federal service to call at Tobago.[106] Facilities for communication with the outside world had been important to Tobagonians since the time of union. They lamented the fact that Port of Spain served as the entrepot of the entire colony, effectively cutting off direct links between Tobago and the wider world. If secession were to be meaningful, the island would have to establish its own links with the international trading community.

By 1960, two years after the federation had been established, James was convinced that Tobago needed to separate from Trinidad if the island's economic potential were to be exploited profitably. He believed that the Trinidad government was blocking economic development on the island. He strenuously objected to the government's treating Tobago as an "orphan" and minor subordinate dependant. James wanted independence for Tobago but he realized that the island had to take an intermediate first step; the federation provided an opportunity for Tobagonians to break away from Trinidad's control. By 1960 James had allied himself with a group called the Tobago Independence Movement (TIM). The TIM considered itself a "prominent group" of Tobagonians and others residing on the island who were investigating the possibility of Tobago's attaining internal self-government status, which the colony as a whole had obtained only four years earlier. Commander Horace Whittaker, president of the Tobago Chamber of Commerce, chaired the committee studying internal self-government possibilities.[107] In a July 1960 interview with the *Trinidad Guardian* newspaper, James came out strongly in favour of internal self-government for Tobago, despite his detractors' view that Tobago could not support itself economically.[108] He contended that the TIM was forced to consider this option because of the "Trinidad Government's obvious intention to conceal the amount of revenue collected in Tobago from all sources, while feeding their party machine with propaganda that they are spending so much money in Tobago".[109]

In addition, James argued that it was retrograde to continue living on "charity while other West Indian people are striving to become self-supporting and self-sufficient".[110] Furthermore, Trinidad was denying Tobagonians the "right and privilege" to have control over their internal affairs while the current trend among West Indians was to move towards "nationhood". The TIM sought to "unite all Tobagonians in their struggle for a direct voice in their own affairs".[111] If this effort succeeded, Tobago would become a federal unit independent of Trinidad or a federal district directly under control of the federal government. In spite of these goals, James still insisted that the prevailing view, which held that the TIM adopted a "separatist attitude", was "absolutely unfounded".[112] This ambivalence may have been because the TIM was still assessing strategies that would allow Tobago to gain independent representation in the federal Parliament, with or without separation from Trinidad.

After the summer of 1960 the issue of independence for Tobago was hotly debated in the press. In October one Tobagonian, writing in the *Trinidad Guardian* under the pseudonym "Disenchanted", took umbrage at Premier Eric Williams's suggestion at a press conference that "people should never go back to the land".[113] Disenchanted argued that the premier's tone indicated that agricultural workers were not well educated and that they were "degraded form[s] of life". The writer saw few alternatives for economic independence if agriculture were to be abandoned in Tobago: "We sometimes wonder whether it is not the intention of Government to make Tobago so completely dependent upon Trinidad as to make any form of independence, not merely political, completely out of the question." He or she railed at the government's arrogance in making decisions concerning Tobago without consulting Tobagonians: "We do not appreciate Government's high handed attitude towards Tobago affairs. This bland assumption that Government can assess Tobago's needs more accurately than Tobagonians themselves does not please."[114] These grievances continued to be articulated for the next twenty years, until Tobago was granted internal self-government. The need for consultation with locals and the desire for economic independence were both contentious issues for Tobagonians.

While Tobagonians clamoured for independence, former government officials such as Trinidadian Albert Gomes thought the idea ludicrous. Commenting on the TIM's proposal for economic development of Tobago through political independence, Gomes argued, "They are definitely wrong in their assumption that independence would enhance Tobago's chances of securing a better future for Tobagonians."[115] In classic integrationist fashion he insisted that the best way for Tobago to secure a better future for her citizens was in "becoming, both politically and economically, an important adjunct of the larger sister island".[116] Gomes, like most Trinidadian government officials, saw Tobago as only an appendage drawing sustenance from Trinidad. This view infuriated James.

In his rebuttal article James countered: "it was this same attitude of Mr. Gomes and his government that prevented the development of Tobago before".[117] He claimed that when he went to England in 1948,

Brigadier Mount, comptroller of the Colonial Development Corporation, had agreed that Tobago could get a special development grant if the Trinidad government supported the idea. The government, of which Gomes was a part, did not support James's "claim for special consideration for Tobago".[118] Thus, to prevent recurrence of a situation in which the government's actions signalled that it did not care about Tobago, James contended that he and his colleagues were seeking self-government.[119]

The PNM certainly did not support Tobagonians' quest for self-government. The party's weekly newspaper, the *Nation*, declared that in advocating secession James was "selling their [Tobagonians'] birthright for a mess of pottage".[120] The correspondent argued that secession would result in "economic slavery" because it would once again place the population at the "mercies of the plantation owners", who had a reputation for paying low wages. These estate owners were selling their beach-front properties at extravagant prices to hoteliers and wealthy aliens. The paper also warned that, with the peasants also selling land and "grasping at big money", Tobagonians would soon become landless. Having lost their land, they would have to work for the new estates – the "hotels and wealthy private people". The upshot would be that the "independent Tobago peasant of today will become the poor hired man and domestic servant of tomorrow, begging for whatever wages he can get".[121] In a rebuttal piece another columnist argued that secession was a "string of pearls", contending that "[t]he middle man of Trinidad is today your foreign investor who is reaping the benefit of Tobago's labour".[122] (Tobagonians considered Trinidad businessmen rapacious and not to be trusted.)

By 1 November 1960 the TIM had produced a document that the press considered a "manifesto" that proposed Tobago's separation from Trinidad. The document recommended holding a referendum on the issue of separation. A two-thirds majority vote in favour of the measure would justify a demand for constitutional separation from Trinidad.[123] If there was a majority vote in favour of secession, the TIM proposed three options: (1) Tobago could become a federal unit without "individual financial responsibility"; (2) Tobago could become independent and remain within the federation like the other smaller islands; or (3) like British Guiana, Tobago could become independent but not a member of the federation.[124] The document cited four benefits of independence: (1) reduction in the cost of living by importing directly from other countries, thus bypassing Trinidad; (2) freedom to attract small industries and thus improve the island's economy; (3) freedom to determine agricultural policy; and (4) freedom to control development of the tourist industry. The document argued that Tobago's development was being stymied by the inability of foreign investors to secure permits to invest in the island, by the Tourist Board's lack of initiative in attracting tourists, and by "non-existent sea transport, due to local firms not being sufficiently organized to arrange mutual benefit buying from abroad".[125] Clearly the goal of this "civic movement" was to effect the economic development of Tobago, which its members believed would not happen if the island remained under control of the Trinidad government.

James argued that the Trinidad government was not solicitous of Tobago's interests. Tobago was treated more like an "orphan" than a sister island. Furthermore, Tobagonians were no longer satisfied with "crumbs from Trinidad's table"; "by handling their own affairs [they would] be able to achieve the political and economic independence they desire[d]".[126] Tobagonians also believed they had nothing to lose if they separated from Trinidad: "Tobagonians feel . . . that they will be much better off without being tied in any way to Trinidad", for "Tobago is confident that, as a unit of the Federation, she will be no worse off than St Lucia, St Vincent, Antigua or St Kitts"[127] — islands similar in size to Tobago.

On 4 November 1960 James raised the issue of secession in the legislature:

> While I am on this phase, let me tell the Minister, I came here today not to talk about any separationist move. The people of Tobago are quite competent to speak when the time comes, and they will speak. You better believe that they will speak at the proper time and place, so if I happen not to say anything about any separationist move today, do not believe that I do not accept your challenge. I accept your challenge but postpone the day of the fight.[128]

These words were prophetic. Later in his speech, which was apparently directed at Williams, James stated that, during the days of the colonial government, whenever "I raised the question of independence for Tobago I got very little support and I had to give it up". But, he went on, it was the "dissatisfied and disgruntled people in Tobago" who were calling for independence.[129] James declared further that it was a "memorandum to the Secretary of State for the Colonies which was published in your paper, *The Nation* . . . which spurred on the people to set up a committee to enquire into the possibility [of independence for Tobago]. So do not blame James."[130]

It was on 20 May 1960 that the *Nation* had published the memorandum (dated 3 May 1960) to which James referred. It was captioned "We Want More Representation in the Federal Legislature". In that memorandum the arguments James used to demand two seats in the Trinidad and Tobago legislature were used to demand more seats for Tobago in the federal legislature. Among the signatories to the memorandum was A. N. R. Robinson,[131] a founding member of the PNM and James's political rival. (Later in his career Robinson led the autonomist movement of the 1970s after he broke with the PNM.) James insisted that the memorandum was the result of a PNM address delivered in Scarborough on May Day, 1960. Given that information, and the fact that Premier Eric Williams proclaimed that "every people should have the right to decide for themselves", James wondered why the ministers of government and "even the Premier" were "so intrigued and getting so groggy about internal self-government for Tobago".[132]

In James's view, the PNM government possessed a colonial mentality. He insisted that colonialism, whether from the United Kingdom or Trinidad, should be opposed. He further contended that while Tobagonians were grateful for the benefits they gained in association with Trinidad, they should be given a chance to decide for separation. He insisted that his stance was not a political position: "When the time comes for me to take or play my part in the fight I will resign the Party to which I belong and fight Tobago's issue."[133] He again declared that Trinidad should know that "[W]e are not satisfied to continue to take the crumbs falling from their table. We are able to go out and pull our weight . . . ."[134] James softened his rhetoric soon after by asking (probably in response to an interjection), "What are you talking about 'separatists'? Who told you we are separating? We are saying that we want to have a direct say. We are saying that we would not like to see, if Trinidad say they are pulling out of the Federation we would automatically have to pull out; or if Trinidad say, they are remaining in the Federation we would have to remain also. We want a direct voice . . . ."[135] Sometimes it seemed that James preferred administrative autonomy – a significant devolution of government power in Tobago. However, secession was always a solid option for him. His ambivalence reflects the fact that he was not a radical secessionist and that from time to time he would move back and forth along the left side of the autonomy continuum.

Horace Whittaker, a self-proclaimed PNM supporter, president of the Tobago Chamber of Commerce and a member of the TIM, supported James. In November 1960 he complained that "practically nothing has been implemented [in Tobago] since 1956".[136] He referred to the PNM's election promises and its five-year development plan. The only exception he noted was the North Coast Road, which was "badly planned" because it did not open access to agricultural lands, since the first phase of the road passed through the protected rainforest region into Bloody Bay. Whittaker also contended that, because the government did not develop agricultural and tourism policies for Tobago, the island had become the "laughing stock of the Federation". These grievances and disappointments over unkept promises from the government tended to push the separatists farther and farther along the left side of the autonomy continuum.

However, not all Tobagonians favoured separation. A. Moore, a Tobagonian living in Maracas, Trinidad, did not support the TIM; he seemed to be an ardent federalist. He described the TIM as a "provocative Movement for the separation of Tobago from its sister, Trinidad".[137] Moore questioned whether the average Tobagonian supported secession. He admitted that "more often than not" Tobago had been relegated to the role of "Cinderella". With the advent of the federation, he was convinced that "brighter days" had come for Tobago. In addition, Moore believed that after sixty years the people of both islands had come to accept each other: "Today, in all parts of Trinidad, the Tobagonian is welcomed and is admired for his ambitious approach to life. The same can also be said of the Tobagonian attitude towards Trinidadians who take up residence in Tobago."[138] Moore questioned the motives of the TIM leaders. He wondered whether they were truly federalists or just "using the federation conveniently, to meet their own ambitious ends".

Indeed, James was using the federation, not out of self-interest, but in order to get Tobago out from under the economic and political control of Trinidad. His advocacy from 1946 testifies to this. The leaders of all the territories in the federation saw the institution as a first step in gaining independence from Britain, especially the leaders of the larger territories such as Trinidad and Jamaica. Therefore it is not surprising that James would share that vision for Tobago. Moore held a centrist position but, despite his misgivings about the TIM, supported James's referendum recommendation because he believed that Tobagonians should "decide their own destiny".

The TIM was also opposed by Lionel Mitchell, a Trinidadian educator who lived most of his adult life in Tobago. A staunch supporter of the PNM, Mitchell wrote articles in the *Nation*. His solution to the Tobago dilemma was that a ministry of Tobago affairs should be established, with a minister who had representation in the Cabinet (the successor of the Executive Council). Like the magisterial reformers during the Protestant Reformation, Mitchell believed that the system could be reformed from within. Like the other members of the PNM, he was an integrationist. He argued that if his policy of "ministerial independence" were implemented, "no sensible Tobagonians would breathe the words secession or independence".[139] The developments of the 1970s would prove him wrong.

During his last year on the Legislative Council, A. P. T. James kept alive the issue of self-government for Tobago. In a discussion on the draft order of the Boundaries Commission in March 1961, he argued that the PNM government had finally voted in favour of Tobago's having two seats in the legislature not because its members believed Tobago would be better represented, but because the PNM had gained much support in Tobago and felt confident that it could win the two seats in the 1961 elections. James also alleged that the PNM was feeling somewhat insecure in Trinidad in the upcoming elections, thus the need to have the two Tobago seats to offset possible losses in Trinidad.[140] He warned the PNM government, "Let me make it perfectly clear that two seats for Tobago is not going to fool Tobago into discarding their intention of having their own legislature and taking their rightful place among the units of the West Indies."[141] He was aware that the PNM could use its support for increasing Tobago's representation in the legislature to assuage the passion of the separatists or to swing the middle-grounders back to the right.

In 1961 Williams described the TIM as a "reactionary group" opposed to the PNM government's policy for Tobago.[142] By that time the TIM was dying a slow death. A mammoth meeting planned for Scarborough to explain the ideas of the movement "flopped", as did its handbill campaign.[143] Even an essay competition organized by the group worked against it: "The winning essay contained a fairly scathing attack on Tobago Independence."[144] The organization declined because of a number of factors: "The frequent visits of various Ministers of government, along with Tobago's share in the current Five Year Development Programme of Trinidad and Tobago and such public relations gestures as the Leased Bases talks here [in Tobago] in November–December of the last year are all quietly working against it."[145] In addition, infrastructure development projects, such as roads and schools and the improvement of beach facilities for fishermen, all tended to leave the impression that the government was paying attention to development in Tobago. Thus the PNM implied that independence was not absolutely necessary for development of the island.

In a Legislative Council speech in April 1961 James was the last person to mention the TIM, defending the group from Williams's vicious characterization of its members as "reactionaries" (Williams had also called it the "Tobago Idiotic Movement"). James explained that the TIM's twenty-one-page "questionnaire" (which the press called a manifesto), titled "Calling All Tobagonians", examined the possibility of Tobago's gaining independence within or outside the federation.[146] However, both the federation and James were passing from the scene of action, and along with them went the TIM.

James lost the 1961 general elections to A. N. R. Robinson, the brilliant young lawyer whom he had beaten in the 1956 election for the Tobago seat. James died of a cerebral haemorrhage on 5 January 1962, one month after he lost the election.[147] The federation was dissolved in 1962 and Trinidad and Tobago became an independent nation that same year. While his vision for Tobago did not materialize, to James's credit it can be said, without equivocation, that Tobago was a better place because of his unrelenting advocacy for the interests of its inhabitants in the Trinidad and Tobago Legislative Council. The political pressure he put on the central government forced Trinidadian officials to abandon the view that Tobago should be considered only a rural backwater, not worthy of much administrative attention, devoid of political consciousness and having little economic potential. A. P. T. James changed the political status quo of the relationship between the two islands. One of the best tributes paid to him was by his friend Uriah Butler, a trade union leader and fellow legislator. In 1957, during the debate in the legislature on the PNM-sponsored Tobago Development Programme, Butler stated, "Since his advent here I am certain that I speak the truth when I say that Tobago has never had in this hon. Chamber a greater champion of its cause."[148]

James Biggart prepared the soil and A. P. T. James planted and watered the seeds of the autonomy movement that grew in the 1970s. However, the decade after his death was characterized by peaceful coexistence between Tobagonians and the central government. There are a number of reasons for this. First, as a result of James's political pressure, the PNM took a special interest in Tobago that resulted in provision of electricity, extension of pipe-borne water services, construction of schools and health centres, and similar development projects. Tobagonians felt that the government was finally paying them some attention. Second, since Robinson was a member of the Cabinet, Tobagonians felt assured that he would protect the welfare of the island. Third, with the establishment of the Ministry of Tobago Affairs in 1964, there was a feeling that the island and its people had regained a limited measure of control over their internal affairs. Finally, there was no one personality championing self-government who commanded the respect and loyalty of the majority of Tobagonians during the 1960s, which were the honeymoon years of the PNM regime in Tobago. In fact, the period from 1956 to 1976 constituted an era in which the PNM's agenda held sway in the country. However, the 1960s proved to be the calm before the storm – the autonomy movement was dormant but not dead. By the end of the decade Dr Rhodil Norton had begun the clarion call for secession. In 1970 Robinson, the former deputy leader of the PNM, broke with the party and thereby freed himself to champion the movement for internal self-government for Tobago.

Chapter 9

The PNM and Development in Tobago, 1956–1976
Hope and Disappointment

The death of A. P. T. James in January 1962 silenced for a while Tobago's radical voice in the Legislative Council. With the nationalist PNM candidates as Tobagonians' representatives in the legislature, the ruling PNM government was left to determine Tobago's destiny unopposed. The government gave special consideration to administrative, infrastructure and economic development of the island between 1956, when the party won the national elections, and 1976, when the Ministry for Tobago Affairs was hastily dismantled after the PNM lost the two Tobago constituencies in that year's election.

Some development programmes characterized the first two decades of PNM rule. Tobago was marked for special consideration because Eric Williams acknowledged that the island had been neglected in the past and that it was isolated from the centre of government.[1] In addition, within the context of the ill-fated West Indies Federation, Tobago was to be a model, a showpiece of how development in the smaller territories would take place under the leadership of Williams and the government in Trinidad.

Those were the honeymoon years – years of great expectation. Signs of progress were manifested in capital development projects and administrative upgrades. The PNM government displayed a concern for Tobago that the island had not experienced since the union. Experts conducted studies in connection with the proposed development of the island, and some of their recommendations were implemented. The North Coast Road was constructed, electrification of the island was carried out, schools were built, pipe-borne water distribution increased and the administrative arrangements were enhanced. While Tobagonians appreciated all the positive developments that blossomed during the golden era of the PNM's dominance, they continued to harbour a number of real grievances and were still feeling a psychological distance between themselves and the central government seated in Trinidad – and, by extension, Trinidadians, as discussed in chapters 10 and 11.

The focus of this chapter is the administrative and economic developments in Tobago associated with the PNM honeymoon period. This was also the era when Tobago-born A. N. R. Robinson held many Cabinet positions, including that of minister of finance. Robinson appeared satisfied with the PNM's agenda for Tobago, and it is fair to assume that he believed development in Tobago would go hand in hand with national development. In that regard he can be considered an integrationist during this period, identifying with government policies up until 1970, when he broke with the PNM. When that party came to power it promised to give priority to the needs of Tobagonians. However, after twenty years of its administration, Tobagonians were not satisfied.

Administrative Arrangements for Tobago

The seeds of nation-building in the colony of Trinidad and Tobago were sown with the advent of Eric Williams and the PNM in 1956. In that year the colony was granted limited internal self-government within the British Empire. Crown Colony government was coming to an end and party politics was being introduced. The PNM won thirteen of twenty-four seats in the 1956 general elections and formed the first party government in the colony, with Eric Williams as the chief minister.[2] The governor, who represented the Crown, remained head of the Executive Council. The PNM was in control of the legislature, and it fostered a nationalist agenda. Up to 1959 the ruling party had to work within the context of a government that was still under the watchful eye of the Crown, through the Executive Council. However, with the advent of the West Indies Federation in 1958 and ministerial government in 1959, the PNM party became fully responsible for setting the agenda of the two islands.

For the first ten years after union, the administrative arrangements for Tobago involved a Financial Board, which was presided over by a commissioner. As discussed in previous chapters, the Financial Board was responsible for collection and expenditure of local revenue and made policy decisions concerning the projects on which that revenue was spent. By virtue of office, the commissioner was an official member of the Legislative Council. The Board had authority to enact local regulations, but these had to be approved by the legislature in Trinidad. Along with the nominated member from Tobago, the commissioner represented the interests of Tobagonians in the corridors of power.

After 1899 Tobago was administered as a ward under a senior government official called the warden. "Wardens were virtual governors in their districts. There was no significant reduction in their powers until March 1946 when a system of county councils was introduced."[3] The county councils of the united colony were locally elected bodies with jurisdiction over the counties previously supervised by the wardens. They were responsible for constructing, maintaining, repairing and lighting roads and bridges, except for main roads; maintaining burial grounds; providing, maintaining, managing and controlling markets, public pastures and recreation grounds; providing financial and other assistance towards maintenance of community, district and village halls; distributing truck-borne water; providing, maintaining and controlling local government buildings and homes for the aged; and constructing and maintaining all drains and watercourses except main watercourses, as well as other duties assigned by the head of state.[4] The county councils therefore simply carried out prescribed duties with funds provided by the central government; they had no policy-making power. That was reserved for the central government, whose control of their finances severely circumscribed the "volume and nature of the tasks that the Councils were able to initiate".[5]

Despite the inception of county councils, the wardens remained the highest-ranking government officials in their jurisdictions. In the 1950s they became the chief executive officers of the county councils, responsible for "efficient administration of County Council functions pertaining to the County".[6] After 1960 this role was taken over by a full-time officer paid by the central government.[7] The wardens remained responsible for collection of taxes and gave annual reports covering revenue and expenditure, population statistics, maintenance of roads and the other matters outlined above in the list of duties of county councils. They also reported on general development in their counties. Thus, when the PNM gained control of the government in 1956, the warden of Tobago was still the chief government administrator on the island. He had no executive power and had to refer matters to officials in Trinidad for decisions before anything outside the scope of his or the county council's ordinary duties could be implemented.

One aspect of the PNM government's agenda was to enhance the administrative arrangements for Tobago. In 1957 two reports, both concerned in whole or in part with improving the administration of Tobago, were requested by and presented to the government. The first resulted from a directive of the Executive Council. The *Report of Committee for the Re-organization of the Administrative Arrangements of Tobago* was submitted in March. Led by Organization and Methods Officer D. J. A. Briggs, the four-man committee first outlined the long-standing and often-repeated weakness of Tobago's administration:

> At present, Tobago is administered as a Ward of Trinidad. There is no co-ordinating authority for all the various activities of government in Tobago. The Warden of Tobago has officially no greater powers than a Warden in any County of Trinidad, although in practice he is looked on by many of the public as the head of the administration of Government resident in Tobago. As a general rule, there is little or no devolution of authority to the departments in Tobago,

Identity and Secession in the Caribbean

and most matters requiring a decision, even in some cases on the most petty question, are referred to Trinidad.[8]

The report recommended the "maximum amount of devolution to the Government officials in Tobago" and consequently "minimum reference of matters of detail back to Trinidad".[9] With this in mind the committee proposed the appointment of a commissioner for Tobago at a salary equal to that of a permanent secretary. The permanent secretaries were second in command of government ministries and the ministers above them had seats in the Cabinet. The commissioner, as head of the administration in Tobago, would represent the governor, the chief minister, the colonial secretary, other ministers and the financial secretary. It would be his duty to coordinate all government activities and ensure that government policies were carried out and the public was given efficient service. In addition he would have to keep the heads of government departments informed on actions he took, and they in turn were to correspond with him on various matters so that he would be "kept completely in the picture".[10]

Under these proposed arrangements the heads of departments in Trinidad were to continue to be responsible for the "functional direction" of the work of their staff in Tobago. All policy matters were still to be determined in Trinidad. Within the scope of those policies and "finances made available", the commissioner and the officers in charge of the departments in Tobago were to make the decisions for administration of government on the island. At the time of the report the committee had not worked out the division of authority between the commissioner and the heads of departments. However, they believed that "with working experience it should be easy to determine the allocation of responsibilities between them".[11] The committee recommended preparation of separate budgetary estimates for Tobago and establishment of a branch of the accountant-general's department on the island. This branch would be responsible for the "receipt of revenue, detailed vote control, authorization of payments and accounting without prior reference to Trinidad".[12] The establishment of Tobago branches of the audit and inland revenue departments was also suggested. Despite the new position of commissioner, the committee recommended retention of the position of warden and chief executive officer for district administration and local government work.

Not long after the committee on reorganizing Tobago's administration submitted its report, a team of experts that visited Tobago in March and April 1957 submitted its report on development proposals to Chief Minister Williams. As it was led by A. deK. Frampton, agricultural adviser to the comptroller, the team's report is commonly called the Frampton Report.[13] The team's goal was to suggest plans for development of the island. Some of their recommendations pertained to the need for administrative changes in Tobago, within the context of proposals for a comprehensive economic development plan that Williams later labelled the Tobago Development Programme. This programme was presented to the legislature in June 1957.

Citing the Frampton Report in his comments on the Tobago Development Programme, Williams pointed out that Frampton and his team had consulted with the Tobago County Council and the Tobago Advisory Board. Echoing the sentiments of James Rousseau years before, he indicated that such consultation was necessary because "Tobago, as an island detached from Trinidad, cannot simply be put on the same footing as the County Council of Caroni, or of Victoria, or of some other part or district in Trinidad".[14] Furthermore, "[n]othing would be gained by imposing on Tobago today the views of a government, however benevolent".[15] Williams's ideas were very enlightened; he seemed to understand something of the negative impact of centralization on the island and its people.

Published in August 1957, the Frampton Report recommended significant administrative changes for Tobago. First, the team gave credit to the job done by the island's small staff, who worked with little or no technical supervision and advice from Trinidad and who laboured "under a natural dislike of isolation in a backward territory".[16] However, Frampton and his colleagues noted that government services on the island were inadequate for "any real progress". They pointed out that the claim that conditions in Tobago were no worse than those in the rural areas of Trinidad was "an unsatisfactory criterion to apply, considering the size of Tobago and its potentialities in agriculture and fisheries, and in the tourist industry".[17]

The team also noted that the recommendations of the Committee for the Re-organization of the Administrative Arrangements of Tobago did not take into account "development which might take place outside the ordinary run of government activities".[18] The administration of the island under a warden whose "effective responsibility [was] really confined to matters of what might be described as Local Government functions" was inadequate for supervision of a development programme. The administration, in which each ministry and department of the government had separate branches in Tobago, with the officers of those branches directly responsible to their supervisors in Trinidad, was insufficient. Given Tobago's isolation within such an administrative structure, it was impossible to exercise effective supervision of government works, especially since senior personnel had visited Tobago only sporadically. Thus, among other things, the development programme required "a considerable devolution of power to some person on the spot".[19]

Frampton and his associates also recommended various high-level staff appointments for Tobago:

> We consider that Tobago needs, and that the possibilities of development justify, the appointment of a top-class administrator of the rank of the Administrator of one of the Leeward or Windward Islands. Indeed, since those territories, not even excluding Dominica, have suffered less from neglect and inadequate administration during the last 50 years than has Tobago, the rehabilitation and development of the island will, we think, call for someone of an even higher standing.[20]

The team had put its finger on the pulse of the problem, and the report reflected the stance of those on the left of the autonomy continuum.

The suggestion of "top-class administrator[s]" included appointment of two administrative officers, one of higher rank than the commissioner recommended by the committee for reorganization of Tobago's administration, and the second of the rank of senior assistant secretary. The report also proposed the appointment of a development commissioner for agriculture, fisheries and forestry and a senior engineer to direct the road programme, as well as other officers. Finally, in terms that highlighted Tobago's distinct identity, the report stated that Tobago was "sufficiently a separate entity" to justify direct dealing at the ministerial level between the administrator and the government in Trinidad:

> We therefore suggest that there should be one Minister with an appropriate title responsible solely for Tobago affairs to whom the Administrator of Tobago should have direct access. The Minister would be responsible to the Central Government for initiating action on Tobago matters; he should, if possible, be a member of the Executive Council. This would be similar to the arrangement in the United Kingdom, where there is a Secretary of State for Scotland, with a seat in the Cabinet, who is responsible for bringing matters of interest to Scotland to the attention of his colleagues; even though constitutionally Scotland and England are one.[21]

A. P. T. James and the Tobago Citizens Economic and Political Party had been making this suggestion since 1950. The team further suggested that if the present constitution did not allow for a separate minister of Tobago affairs, another minister could be assigned the role. His parliamentary secretary would do the daily job of coordination while the minister handled Tobago matters on the Executive Council.

The appointment of a central advisory development board or council for Tobago was also proposed. This body would allow representatives from a wide cross-section of the island to share their views on development. The team agreed with the committee for reorganization of Tobago's administration that separate budget estimates should be prepared for Tobago and that the administrator should be the controlling officer for expenditure of money on the island.[22] The report cautioned that providing separate revenue estimates would be valuable only for statistical purposes, although it would be interesting to see the relationship between Tobago's revenue and expenditure. Echoing James's sentiments, the report cautioned that "the ascertaining of revenue attributable to Tobago may not be as straightforward as it seems, because income earned in Tobago can go to the Trinidad head offices of companies operating there; or to individuals living in Trinidad, who make no

Identity and Secession in the Caribbean

declaration of income tax as Tobago residents".[23] The report also called for establishment of a Tobago development fund into which all development and welfare grants and loans raised for the Tobago programme, as well as contributions from the Trinidad government, would flow.[24] The funds so provided would not lapse from year to year, and once allocations were agreed upon, the administrator would be responsible for authorizing disbursements from the fund.

Given the proposals from the Committee for the Re-organization of the Administrative Arrangements of Tobago and the Frampton Report, the PNM government made various administrative changes in Tobago between 1956 and 1976. First, the Department of Tobago Affairs, headed by a permanent secretary for Tobago affairs, was created, effective from 1 January 1958. G. W. Gordon, the director of surveys and sub-intendant of Crown lands, was appointed permanent secretary for Tobago affairs as of 10 March 1958.[25]

The duties of the permanent secretary for Tobago affairs were laid out in detail in Secretariat Circular No. 4 (Staff) of 1957, and issued to the heads of all government departments.[26] The permanent secretary was the head of administration for the government on the island. He represented the minister responsible for Tobago affairs and was responsible for administering and coordinating the government's activities to ensure that its policy was carried out effectively and that an efficient public service was maintained. While copies of minutes of the Executive Council pertaining to Tobago were to be sent to the permanent secretary, the actual implementation of those policy decisions continued to reside in the various ministries headquartered in Trinidad. Only decisions from the chief minister's office were exempt from that proviso. The permanent secretaries in Trinidad were to advise the permanent secretary for Tobago affairs of decisions that would affect the branches of their department in Tobago. The permanent secretary for Tobago affairs could, however, communicate directly with other permanent secretaries about the execution of decisions that would have an impact on Tobago. He was also responsible for keeping the respective permanent secretaries and their various ministries informed about actions he planned to take. Those officials in turn were to keep the permanent secretary for Tobago affairs informed about their activities that would affect Tobago. It is clear that too many decisions still had to be made or approved in Trinidad. The effort to coordinate all government activities on the island would still lead to a cumbersome machinery requiring either consulting with or informing several departments and ministries in Trinidad.

In addition, all policy matters were still determined in Trinidad. However, the permanent secretary for Tobago affairs did have the authority to make "all day-to-day decisions" necessary for efficient administration of government in Tobago. Those decisions were to be in keeping with general lines of policy, within the scope of available funds and, where necessary, after consultation with the officers in charge of government departments in Tobago. The permanent secretary also had the authority to issue requisitions to authorize expenditure for Tobago. Consequently, internal departmental releases of funds by the Works and Hydraulics Department were under his jurisdiction. All personnel and disciplinary matters affecting officers in Tobago were subject to consultation with the permanent secretary for Tobago affairs, who communicated with the colonial secretary on those matters. Only issues relating to police officers could, when unavoidable, escape this proviso.

Various personnel functions also formed part of the responsibilities of the permanent secretary for Tobago affairs. Leave relief from duty had to be approved by him, and officers in charge of departments in Tobago could not visit Trinidad without his approval. All other officers had to obtain permission to leave Tobago from the officers in charge of their departments. Further, requests from officers working in Tobago to leave the colony were to be forwarded through the permanent secretary for Tobago affairs. He also had authority to make temporary appointments of persons who were not working in the civil service to non-establishment positions in Tobago. Similarly, when candidates could not be found in Tobago to fill temporary junior positions in the civil service, the officers in charge of departments in Tobago had to obtain the permanent secretary's consent before making a recommendation to the head of department in Trinidad.

The permanent secretary for Tobago affairs certainly had more executive powers than the warden of Tobago. Establishing a separate department concerned primarily with the issues and realities facing Tobago and Tobagonians was a step in the right direction. However, it seemed that the central government was giving authority with one hand but taking it back with the other. In addition, restricting determination of both policy and government budgetary allocations to officials in Trinidad meant that Tobago's destiny continued to be directed by persons and forces outside the island. And the decisions made by officials in Trinidad were not necessarily in the best interest of Tobago and its people.

Other administrative arrangements for Tobago were considered in the late 1950s. In November 1957, Premier Eric Williams requested Parliamentary Secretary the Honourable Ulric Lee to make recommendations for reorganization of the public service.[27] Lee submitted his report on 24 June 1958. It came at a time when the colony was on the verge of gaining full internal self-government, with its focus being on achieving independence within the West Indies Federation. Thus Lee's administrative proposals were made in the specific context of potential constitutional changes.[28]

One chapter of the Lee Report dealt specifically with "Tobago Affairs". Lee recommended making Tobago affairs a division in a ministry "responsible for the administrative control of all departments in Tobago".[29] He suggested that the premier be responsible for Tobago affairs, assisted by a permanent secretary. Lee proposed that the permanent secretary be responsible for the Division of Tobago Affairs and to the Public Accounts Committee for all financial matters in Tobago. Given the small size of the staff units in Tobago and for the purpose of economy, Lee suggested that the departments in Tobago should be "adequately assisted by their counterparts in Trinidad". A similar rationale led him to restrict decision-making on "policy matters affecting Tobago" to officials in Trinidad, with consultation of the premier. Further, "in this context the Ministries and Departments in Trinidad ought readily to appreciate the peculiar position of the Division of Tobago Affairs and to co-operate fully with it even though inevitably it will demand many things and appear to give nothing in return".[30] Lee was not prepared to provide the level of devolution of power sought by James in the 1950s. No specific provision was allowed for involvement of Tobagonians in the administration of their island.

Based on Lee's proposals, the staff for the units of finance, the establishment and personnel, as well as the works unit, came under the general administration section. The finance unit was responsible for financial control of the whole island, including "self-accounting", or internal auditing. In addition, assignment of a separate finance staff to the works unit was proposed because of the volume of work involved in its operation. Similarly, the inland revenue unit, which dealt with income tax assessment, was assigned a separate staff because of the confidential nature of its work. Lee also suggested disbandment of the district administration (the warden's office) and distribution of its work and staff between the county council and the inland revenue unit. No provision was made for the police, fire services, audit and judiciary departments.

Lee's report was submitted when various political developments were taking place in the colony. In 1959 the cabinet system was introduced in Trinidad and Tobago. Under this system the premier (formerly the chief minister) presided over the Cabinet (formerly the Executive Council), "the Governor ceased to be a member of the Cabinet, and the ex-officio members, retained for the sake of continuity and on the basis of their experience, were not allowed the right to vote".[31] The introduction of the cabinet system paved the way for Tobago to gain direct representation in the highest policy-making body of the colony, through the minister responsible for Tobago affairs.

Some of the proposals of the Lee Report were not easy to implement. The establishment of certain branches of government departments proved difficult in Tobago. A branch of the Inland Revenue Department did not begin operation as scheduled, resulting in inconvenience to Tobagonians who wished to procure clearance certificates needed to travel overseas. This also affected the provision of other services that only the Inland Revenue Department could supply. Obviously, without a branch of the department on the island, Tobagonians would have to travel to Trinidad to procure those services. The acting accountant in the Ministry of Tobago Affairs complained to the permanent secretary that officers who had been appointed to positions in the newly established, but as yet unopened, Tobago branch of the Inland Revenue Department had not yet gone to Tobago because they were "apparently awaiting more favourable circumstances", even though office accommodation and quarters were ready on the island.[32] Trinidadian officers saw appointments to positions in Tobago as banishment.[33] Permanent Secretary for Tobago Affairs G. W. Gordon endorsed the accountant's view and forwarded his memorandum to the permanent secretary in the Office of the Premier. Gordon also wrote to the permanent secretary to the Ministry of Finance, Planning and Development, soliciting his help "to bring about the speedy establishment of this department before the year ends".[34]

Reorganization of the public service in Tobago continued throughout the 1950s and 1960s. In accordance with the recommendations of the Lee Report, a move was made to integrate the inland revenue branch in Tobago with the warden's office[35] as of 2 August 1960. By 1961, as a result of the administrative changes in Tobago, the civil establishment on the island had increased from 360 employees in 1958 to 442.[36]

In 1962 Trinidad and Tobago became an independent nation, but this did not affect the administrative arrangements for Tobago. However, it soon became evident that the Department of Tobago Affairs could not satisfy the need for efficient administration on the island. The combined administration of Tobago by the Department of Tobago Affairs and the various branches of ministries located in Trinidad proved cumbersome. Thus, in 1964, the Ministry for Tobago Affairs was established. Prime Minister's Office Circular No. 1 of 1964 outlined the new administrative arrangements and powers.[37] It granted executive functions in Tobago to a senior civil servant who had full control of and responsibility for not only the duties of the permanent secretary of Tobago affairs – matters formerly dealt with jointly by the Department of Tobago Affairs and the other ministries – but also execution of the rehabilitation programme (to repair damage caused by 1963's Hurricane Flora, especially to housing and agriculture) and all aspects of the development programme. The Ministry of Tobago Affairs was "responsible for its own problems and . . . [had no] need for exporting such problems to other ministries".[38] Because the functions of the Ministry for Tobago Affairs encompassed the activities of all the other ministries, the Cabinet appointed Prime Minister Williams as the minister for Tobago affairs. Director of Personnel Administration Victor E. Bruce, who had served as the permanent secretary for Tobago affairs, was appointed the commissioner for Tobago affairs.[39]

As the new head of administration, the commissioner for Tobago affairs was directly responsible to the minister of Tobago affairs, and for the execution of all matters under the minister's portfolio. All permanent secretaries and other technical officers in other ministries were to communicate directly with the commissioner. They could not issue instructions to or through any junior officer in the Ministry of Tobago Affairs.

Given the small size of the administration in Tobago, the Ministry of Tobago Affairs was not expected to be self-sufficient. Thus the ministry still depended on other ministries for staff, substantive appointments, transfers, replacements and advice on technical and other matters. The commissioner and the permanent secretaries of the various ministries were therefore to have cordial relations and to hold consultations from time to time. They were to coordinate activities through the Committee of Permanent Secretaries, on which the commissioner sat on equal terms with the other members. The staff, plant and equipment of the various ministries were to be at the disposal of the Ministry of Tobago Affairs, for consultation, among other matters, on transfer, on loan and on hire. The commissioner was designated a "Corporation Sole" for the purpose, *inter alia,* "of making loans on mortgage where necessary in connection with the rehabilitation and development plans".[40]

Two years after the Ministry of Tobago Affairs was established there was official complaint that Tobago was not being served well by the permanent secretaries of the other ministries. The permanent secretary in the Ministry of Tobago Affairs, H. Leacock, complained that the other permanent secretaries in Trinidad did not visit the divisions

Identity and Secession in the Caribbean

of the Ministry of Tobago Affairs that formed part of their ministries. He reminded them that the "proper administration of the Ministry of Tobago Affairs depend[ed] to a large extent on the technical advice received from and occasional discussions with Officers of other Ministries in addition to the ever present desire to establish a feeling of comradeship with other Permanent Secretaries".[41] Leacock suggested that his peers pay quarterly visits to the divisions of the Ministry of Tobago Affairs that related to their respective ministries. Integration of the ministry into the national administrative structure suffered from the problem of isolation about which Tobagonians had complained for a long time. This difficulty also indicated the limitations of the administrative arrangements for Tobago up to that time. It is not surprising that this system was eventually replaced.

The need for the various government ministries in Trinidad to work closely with the Ministry of Tobago Affairs was reiterated in a 1971 memorandum to all permanent secretaries and heads of departments from Dodridge Alleyne, the permanent secretary to the prime minister and head of the civil service. He outlined the responsibilities and authority vested in the permanent secretary for Tobago affairs, and in his ministry, by the Cabinet. He also reminded the various officials that they were to "ensure that the Ministry for Tobago Affairs [was] provided with all the facilities necessary for the effective performance of its duties".[42] Alleyne urged closer and more effective relations between the ministries in Trinidad and the Ministry for Tobago Affairs. The Committee of Permanent Secretaries was directed to assist in achieving these objectives. Despite the elevation of the Department of Tobago Affairs to ministry status, Trinidadian officials still treated the island as not worthy of their time and efforts. In official thinking, Tobago remained a mere appendage of Trinidad even in the 1970s.

The establishment of the Ministry of Tobago Affairs certainly did not solve the problems of administration in Tobago. Having to coordinate matters with ministries and departments in Trinidad proved difficult. A significant part of the ministry's problem was that, while it had to coordinate the functions of other ministries in Tobago, "in many instances, the Prime Minister's Office, line ministries and the treasury retained more or less direct control over government and administration in Tobago".[43] The ultimate weakness of the ministry – its Achilles heel – was its lack of permanence. Like all the other ministries, the Ministry of Tobago Affairs existed at the pleasure of the prime minister.

In the 1976 general elections the ruling PNM party lost the two Tobago seats to the DAC, headed by A. N. R. Robinson, who had resigned from the PNM five years earlier. The loss of these seats led Eric Williams, in an apparent act of political reprisal against Tobagonians, to dismantle the Ministry of Tobago Affairs. All government departments in Tobago reverted to the control of their respective ministries in Trinidad. This retrograde step led to great administrative chaos and inconvenience to Tobagonians. Many government workers did not get paid for several weeks. A number of temporary workers were laid off. Some families with two or more members working in the Ministry of Tobago Affairs were separated when one member was reassigned to a department in Trinidad.[44] General confusion reigned in the administrative services on the island. The incident showed Tobagonians that they were not considered important in the eyes of the ruling party – except when their political loyalty was guaranteed. More significantly, it revealed that the administrative arrangements for Tobago were inadequate and subject to capricious leaders in the central government. This incident demonstrated Tobago's need for a permanent administrative institution possessing executive powers and political clout. With the Ministry of Tobago Affairs disbanded, other arrangements had to be made for administration on the island.

On 23 December 1976 the acting administrative officer V in the Ministry for Tobago Affairs – the most senior official under the permanent secretary – Alfred Geyette, made recommendations to the permanent secretary in the Ministry of Local Government, Joseph H. Herrera, concerning new administrative machinery for Tobago that would take effect on 21 January 1977. Herrera had requested the suggestions after he visited Tobago on 16 December 1976. As a prelude to his proposals, Geyette noted that no financial provisions had been made for the Ministry of Tobago Affairs in the draft budgetary estimates of expenditure for 1977. Further, he pointed out that the ministry itself had to be "divided, with the parent Ministries based in Trinidad being responsible for the operation of the relevant Divisions formerly under the Permanent Secretary for Tobago Affairs with effect from 21st January, 1977".[45] The administrative staff and sections of the ministry were reallocated as follows: the personnel section was placed under the Ministry of Local Government, other service sections were amalgamated with the general administration unit of the Ministry of Local Government, and the development, printing and binding (including office machines) sections, as well as the finance sections, were placed under the umbrella of the Ministry of Finance (Planning and Development).

The recommendations basically called for the general administration unit of the Ministry of Local Government in Tobago to continue functioning, in order to ease the transition problems that would result from dismantling the Ministry of Tobago Affairs. Geyette suggested that the general administration unit should continue handling duties pertaining to the Public Service Commission regarding the submission of staff reports to various ministries and supervision of officers' personnel records. In addition, he proposed that the unit should be given the authority to deal with leave, discipline and other functions of the director of personnel administration on behalf of all ministries with sections in Tobago. The general administration unit was also to be given responsibility for processing retirement benefits for monthly and daily paid staff. The functions of the chief personnel officer regarding various allowances, government quarters, scheduling of positions and settlement of disputes arising from representations by trade unions were recommended to be retained by the unit, as was the classification of positions. Retention of the old procedure of settlement of disputes with workers and their union representatives was recommended to facilitate one-day sessions at monthly meetings in Tobago instead of having workers attend such meetings at the headquarters of their respective ministries in Trinidad.

Geyete proposed that authority for government quarters, rest houses and government buildings should also be given to the general administration unit. Responsibility for dealing with visits from local and foreign officials to and from Tobago was to be placed with that unit as well. The authority to award contracts under $2,000 and to purchase items costing up to $1,000 could either be performed by the ministries or delegated to the senior officer (administrative officer V) in the general administration unit. Geyette also suggested that the administrative officer V have the authority to perform other functions previously carried out by the permanent secretary, namely arrangements for various functions such as Independence Day parades and Remembrance Day celebrations, and the coordinating functions of the National Emergency Relief Organization. He proposed establishment of a new section in the administration unit to deal with duties previously performed by the finance branch of the defunct ministry, even though those duties now fell under the Ministry of Finance.

Prophetically, Geyette envisioned some problems regarding payment of workers in Tobago if their pay sheets were to be submitted to the various ministries in Trinidad for processing. He pointed out that, under the current system, pay sheets were often submitted later than the scheduled dates for processing, and sometimes on the very dates on which they were due for payment. This affected daily paid workers more than other civil servants. He suggested serious consideration of this matter when the new administrative arrangements were being finalized. Herrera forwarded Geyette's recommendations to all the permanent secretaries, the chief personnel officer and the director of personnel administration for their comments.[46]

The permanent secretary in the Ministry of Finance, Frank Barsotti, also wrote to all the permanent secretaries and heads of departments, warning them of potential trouble. He reminded them that, from 1977, a centralized unit for the execution of accounting services in Tobago on behalf of the various ministries and departments would no longer exist. He further instructed the accounting officers to

> take the necessary steps to ensure that personnel at all levels are informed of their duties and responsibilities to ensure the prompt and speedy processing of vouchers, pay sheets and similar matters, and also to make appropriate arrangements for the safe custody of financial and accounting records between divisions in Tobago and their respective head offices in Trinidad.[47]

Identity and Secession in the Caribbean

Barsotti's instruction did not make the transition any easier. Despite all these warnings, administrative chaos reigned in Tobago for weeks during the transition.

Given the above, it is clear that during the first two decades of PNM rule in Trinidad and Tobago a systematic effort was made to upgrade the administrative arrangements for Tobago. Based on the Report of the Committee for the Re-organization of the Administrative Arrangements for Tobago, the Frampton Report and the Lee Report, it was well-known that the island needed a senior government officer with executive powers and direct representation in the Cabinet. Attempts at achieving this went through various stages. First, in 1957 Tobago affairs became part of the portfolio of the premier. By 1959 a Department of Tobago Affairs had been created, headed by a permanent secretary. Both of these developments were integrationist in nature. Finally, in 1964 the Ministry of Tobago Affairs was established, with direct Cabinet representation. While this measure was left-leaning in intent, in that it reflected the goals of separatists such as James, the fact that the ministry was under the control of a Trinidadian minister (and the head of state) places it on the integrationist side of the autonomy continuum. In addition, it was subject to the whims of the prime minister, and was disbanded after Tobagonians decided that the government in power was not acting in their best interest.

Central Administrative Services Tobago replaced the Ministry of Tobago Affairs. This unit, presided over by a permanent secretary, was similar to the previous Department of Tobago Affairs. The permanent secretary has no executive power and the unit had no direct representation in the Cabinet. Therefore, Central Administrative Services Tobago sat firmly in the integrationist camp and was fraught with the same problems as the departments established before the Ministry of Tobago Affairs came into existence. Central Administrative Services Tobago represented a backward step in administrative status for Tobago, imposed by an uncaring and vindictive government in Trinidad. In terms of the administration of Tobago, its separation from Trinidad was not only physical but also ideological.

The struggle for a permanent administrative and political institution that would be responsive and sympathetic to the needs and aspirations of Tobagonians is the focus of chapter 11. However, the PNM's record on economic development in Tobago during its first two decades of political control must first be assessed.

Economic Development in Tobago

Proposals for the economic development of Tobago were made just before the PNM came to power. The catalyst for these plans was A. P. T. James's consistent advocacy for development of the island. As early as October 1955 Governor E. Beetham sent a telegram to the secretary of state for the colonies stating, "I have in mind initiation of a comprehensive planned drive for development of the economic potentialities of Tobago."[48] The telegram pointed out the necessity of conducting aerial, soil and socio-economic surveys of the island. It also proposed to seek technical assistance from outside the colony. Agricultural development was seen as a matter of "some urgency". The governor also provided several statistics for the secretary of state's consideration. In 1954 Tobago exported to Trinidad 73 short tons of bananas, 12 short tons of plantains, 396 short tons of ground provisions, 107 short tons of corn and 16 short tons of peas.[49] The island's population in 1953 stood at 33,000. Of its 74,392 acres, 42,000 were under cultivation of cocoa, coconuts, sugar and limes; the Hillsborough dam and the Scarborough wharf had been completed in 1952 and 1953 respectively. Two land settlement schemes, a forty-holdings (or divisions, comprising 275 acres) project and a twenty-holdings project (150 acres), were completed in early 1955 at Louis d'Or and Mount St George respectively. The settlers were to grow coconuts, cocoa and vegetables as well as to raise livestock.

The proposed development of Tobago was discussed at a meeting held in the Colonial Office on 27 October 1955. A number of Colonial Office and Trinidad government officials were in attendance. They included Victor Bryan, minister of agriculture in Trinidad; L. N. Blanche-Fraser, financial secretary of Trinidad; the director of colonial surveys, Brigadier Hotine; assistant agricultural adviser L. Lord; P. Rogers of the Colonial Office; and other British officials including W. I. J. Wallace, J. W. Vernon, W. G. Wilson, P. J. Kitcatt and W. W. Wallace. Victor Bryan opened the discussion by sharing the governor's view that Tobago could be greatly developed agriculturally and that certain surveys were needed as a prerequisite. Bryan explained that "Tobago has not been entirely neglected in the past, but money had been spent on unrelated requirements due to the absence of any co-ordinated plan".[50] That was the government's official position. Tobagonians obviously thought otherwise.

Rogers pointed out that, while the financial and other difficulties could probably be overcome, "it was most important not to overlook the human aspects of the problem and the need to enlist the co-operation of the people of Tobago in any development schemes that might be put in hand".[51] Bryan replied that he and the governor had considered the matter and thought to place an executive officer, similar to a development commissioner, in Tobago to take charge of the plan. The proposals for economic development of Tobago received the blessing of the Colonial Office and the plan was initiated by completion of an aerial survey in early 1956.

The PNM's advent on the national scene in 1956 further raised Tobagonians' hopes for economic development. The 1956 political manifesto of the PNM guaranteed special consideration for Tobago. Section IV of the manifesto, "PNM's Programme for Tobago", recognized the island's "special needs, problems and potential" and promised

> an efficient steamer service between Trinidad and Tobago; around the island road transport; an expanded water distribution system; greater publicity for the recreational amenities and natural beauty of the island; direct communication between Tobago and the outside world by West Indian and international steamship lines; increased facilities for secondary education; marketing facilities for peasant farmers and fishing operatives; minor industries based upon agricultural products; provision for the ordinary amenities of civilization in rural districts, such as postal services, district nurses, telephone communication and library services.[52]

The PNM seemed genuinely interested in placing Tobago on a firm economic footing, as well as in providing basic social services.

The PNM's candidate in Tobago in the 1956 general elections, A. N. R Robinson, must have had some input into this section of the manifesto. Based on the document alone, Tobagonian voters had plenty of reasons to support the PNM and its candidate. However, they decided to stick with the tried and true, and thus voted to re-elect A. P. T. James to the Legislative Council for his third consecutive term. This was a blow to the PNM and to both Eric Williams and Robinson. Williams was very upset over the PNM's loss:

> I wanted that seat badly. . . . My first reaction to the loss was to hell with Tobago, but Mr Robinson insisted that Tobago had a special say in the manifesto and hence the setting up of a Tobago Affairs Department which was incorporated in my portfolio as Minister of Tobago Affairs.[53]

Williams's attitude towards rejection by the Tobagonians was insensitive, and foreshadowed his future contempt when his party lost the Tobago constituencies again in 1976.

Despite its loss of the Tobago seat, the PNM attempted to be true to its election promises. On 7 June 1957 Williams sponsored the Tobago Development Programme in the Legislative Council. In soliciting support for his proposal, he cited "the many years of neglect and betrayal" of Tobago by the government during the colonial period. In a very persuasive speech he underscored the need to "correct the past and set Tobago on a new course".[54] Developing Tobago's economic potential would also help to stem the tide of migration from Tobago to Trinidad, which had resulted in over four thousand persons leaving the island between 1952 and 1955.[55] Williams reasoned that reducing migration from Tobago would help ease the pressure on jobs, social amenities and health services in Trinidad.[56]

Another goal motivated Williams to promote the economic development of Tobago. He wanted Trinidad to be the "principal partner" in the soon-to-be-established West Indies Federation. He believed that promoting development in Tobago would prove him worthy to be leader of the federation, since he could show that his program for development in Tobago would also be effective in other underdeveloped territories:

> Tobago is a test case. If Trinidad cannot deal with Tobago, if Trinidad cannot develop Tobago, then Trinidad's claim to be the principal partner in the Federation, Trinidad's claim to accept the responsibility of the smaller islands falls to the ground. Tobago is being watched as an indication. The test of sincerity of the Trinidad Government's pronouncement with respect to the development

of the smaller islands has been the most important question that we face as far as Federation is concerned.[57]

While it cannot be said that the PNM government totally neglected Tobago, capital expenditure on the island testifies to uneven development when it is compared to Trinidad. The government consistently funded development projects on the island, but the statistics reveal that, on average, only 7 per cent of its capital expenditure budget was allocated to Tobago between 1956 and 1980.[58] The economic plan for the first term of the PNM's rule testifies to this imbalance.

The PNM's *Five-Year Economic Programme 1956–1960* provided for development projects in the colony; it was approved by the Legislative Council on 21 December 1956. The document detailed proposed expenditures for 1957. The government estimated that expenditure on that year's development projects would be $24,830,521. Of that sum, the planned expenditure on Tobago was only $672,594 (see Table 3).[59] Thus, less than 3 per cent of the funds earmarked for development in the colony in 1957 were allocated to Tobago. However, it should be pointed out that an additional $50,000 was estimated for improvement of fishing beaches throughout the colony, and a small portion of that would have been allocated to Tobago.

Notwithstanding, the plans in the PNM's Tobago Development Programme were aimed at surpassing the former government's five-year economic programme (1950–55). Williams stated that the programme was important "first and foremost as the fulfilment of a moral obligation on the part of the people of Trinidad to the people of Tobago".[60] The development of Tobago, Williams claimed, was a "matter of highest priority" to the government. The programme for Tobago was based on the recommendations of the 1957 Frampton Report. Its proposed cost was $9.2 million over five years. In response to Williams's sponsorship of the Tobago Development Programme, A. P. T. James contended that the former had based much of his development plan on the memorandum that he had taken to the Colonial Office in April 1948,[61] when James had asked the Crown for a grant of $10 million for development in Tobago.

TABLE 3

PROPOSED EXPENDITURE ON DEVELOPMENT PROJECTS IN TOBAGO, 1957

Project	Cost ($)
Water	
Island-wide water scheme	400,000
Agriculture	
Roads and bridges, Louis d'Or	994
Water supply, Mount St George	5,400
Roads and bridges, Mount St George	5,000
Roads and Bridges	
North Coast Road	50,000
Public buildings	
Fire and ambulance station, Scarborough	26,000
Completion of central administration building, Scarborough	40,000
Housing	
Quarters for warden	31,000
Quarters for senior assistant librarian	17,600
Quarters for technical officer, works department	17,600
Health	
Completion of renovation, remodelling and extension of hospital	75,000
Payment of outstanding accounts for Roxborough Health Centre	4,000
Total	**$672,594**

Source: Trinidad and Tobago, *Five-Year Economic Programme 1956–1960: Memorandum for 1957.*

In 1957 the team led by Frampton contended that the focus of development in Tobago should be agriculture, with fisheries and forestry playing an important but minor role. Tourism also had "considerable possibilities for development". However, all development in Tobago depended upon provision of adequate communications, particularly roads.[62] A cheap ferry service between the two islands to cater to Trinidadians wishing to visit Tobago was also suggested. Minor improvements were to be made to the airfield at Crown Point but a permanent runway was not deemed necessary at that time. The agricultural thrust envisioned cultivation of major crops such as cocoa, bananas and coconuts, with coffee, mixed orchard crops and food crops of all kinds for consumption within the colony. Land settlement schemes were proposed to boost the cultivation of cocoa. Further, provision of agricultural credit to small and medium farmers was recommended. Development of the livestock industry was also a possibility. With expansion of the road programme, a small timber and furniture-making industry could be established by means of controlled exploitation of the forest reserve. There was also a need for development of administrative structures for improved marketing, such as a marketing board for the island.

Frampton's road improvement proposals included, first, extension of the main road from Roxborough to Parlatuvier, a distance of 11 miles (17.6 kilometres). The second priority was construction of the North Coast Road, in two sections: first, from Parlatuvier to Moriah (12 miles, or 19 kilometres); second, from Parlatuvier to Charlotteville, a distance of 14 miles (22.4 kilometres). Other miscellaneous road extension projects covering 30 miles (48 kilometres) were also envisaged. Maintenance of roads and bridges and construction of wooden jetties at the Parlatuvier and Speyside bays were also suggested.[63] Expenditure on road maintenance in Tobago would increase from $160,000 to $247,000 a year.[64] A second dam was considered a necessity in the near future and the electricity commission was encouraged to establish a secondary generating plant at Roxborough, with the view of extending the electricity supply to the north coast areas.

In the field of education, the Frampton Report recommended construction of five new schools to provide accommodations for five hundred additional students. A primary school was to be constructed at Mason Hall and senior schools were proposed for Roxborough, Scarborough, Plymouth and Mason Hall. Existing schools were to be partitioned to allow for teaching in separate classes, and Bishop's High School was to be expanded to cater for a "technical stream" of thirty pupils.

The estimated cost of Frampton's development programme for Tobago was $11 million over a five-year period. This included $1.16 million for employing staff connected specifically with the development plan.[65] Funding for the development programme would be achieved in the following way: 16 per cent from colonial development and welfare grants, 50 per cent from loan funds and 34 per cent from the colony's budget or surplus balances, and a development fund was to be established for financing the programme. The proposals in the Frampton Report laid the foundation for future development plans.

In 1958 the government established a new five-year development programme for 1958 to 1962. The colony's total expenditure on development in 1958 amounted to $28,445,343.[66] In 1958, for the first time, Tobago's budgetary estimates and expenditures were separated from those of Trinidad,[67] providing specific figures on expenditure in Tobago.[68] Only $1,488,807 was spent on development projects in Tobago that year (see Table 4). As in 1957, only about 3.3 percent of the expenditure on development for 1958 was allocated to Tobago. The projects that received the greatest financial outlay were the North Coast Road and expansion of electricity service. Miscellaneous improvements to other roads and bridges received significant funding, as did expansion of water distribution and construction of primary schools.

In 1959, the second year of the development programme under the PNM, $38 million was spent on development projects in the colony.

TABLE 4
CAPITAL EXPENDITURE ON TOBAGO, 1958

Project	Cost ($)
North Coast Road	794,987
Miscellaneous improvement to roads and bridges	195,715
Electricity supply	296,995
Fire and ambulance station, Scarborough	2,306
Primary schools	84,364
Alterations to Tobago Hospital	17,217
Water	152,000
Self-help housing	15,241
Local government (local and orphan roads, recreation grounds)	81,982
Total	$1,488,807

Source: Five-Year Development Programme 1958–1962: 1958 Report, Part II.

Identity and Secession in the Caribbean

Of that amount, only $1,681,018 was spent on capital projects in Tobago (see Table 5).[69] The amount expended on Tobago represented only 4.4 per cent of development expenditure in the country in 1959. The major projects were further construction on the North Coast Road and extension of electricity and water services. Various minor roads were also maintained. Only $84,000 was spent on primary schools, and a fire and ambulance station was constructed in Scarborough.

TABLE 5
CAPITAL EXPENDITURE ON TOBAGO, 1959

Project	Cost ($)
Agriculture (coffee establishment, planting subsidies, pedigree livestock, artificial insemination, hillside conservation, aid to farmers)	17,269
Aviation (night lighting, runway improvement)	70,858
Electricity	187,190
Public buildings and amenities (fire and ambulance station, quarters)	74,127
Education (primary schools)	97,309
Health (Tobago Hospital)	4,573
Water supply	231,270
Local government (minor roads, recreation grounds, public conveniences)	94,922
Labour and social services (playground development and equipment)	3,500
North Coast Road	900,000
Total	**$1,681,018**

Sources: Five-Year Development Programme 1958–1962: Report of the Premier on Development Projects for the Year 1959; Five-Year Development Programme 1958–1962: Projects for 1960.

Development projects in 1960 cost $38.6 million.[70] Of that amount only $2,513,652 was spent on Tobago (see Table 6).[71] One of the major accomplishments of 1960 was the completion and delivery of two coastal steamers, Scarlet Ibis and Bird of Paradise. These ships cost $3.6 million, and their entire expenditure was debited from the Tobago account.[72] This was unfair to Tobago, since the inter-island ferry service was a necessary government obligation. Furthermore, the ships served the entire colony, not Tobago alone. Also in 1960, the northern village of Mason Hall received pipe-borne water for the first time. That year only 6.5 per cent of government development funds was spent on projects in Tobago. This inconsequential sum led to criticisms of the PNM government.

A. P. T. James, for example, chided the government for complaining that the pre-1956 government had earmarked only $4.5 million for Tobago out of a total proposed expenditure of $57 million, while the PNM government spent $6.5 million of its $191-million budget on Tobago.[73] In other words, PNM spending amounted to 4.1 per cent less than the colonial government had allocated for development projects in Tobago. This led to further questioning of the government's commitment to development in Tobago. James accused the government of wasting resources and failing to keep its promises to Tobagonians.[74] In part the emergence of secessionist feelings in Tobago was due to Tobagonians' frustrations over these unfulfilled promises. They were no longer satisfied with "the crumbs falling from [Trinidad's] table".[75] Now they were prepared to threaten the unity of the state.

TABLE 6
CAPITAL EXPENDITURE ON TOBAGO, 1960

Project	Cost ($)
Agriculture (coffee establishment, forage grass propagation, planting subsidies, hillside conservation, markets, etc.)	15,173
Forests (construction of forest quarters)	341
Fisheries (landing facilities, minor improvement to beaches)	5,258
Roads and bridges (North Coast Road, miscellaneous improvements)	1,241,517
Aviation (night lighting, runway improvements)	294,926
Electricity supply	334,279
Public buildings and amenities	99,992
Education (primary schools)	187,531
Health (Tobago Hospital)	26,122
Water supply	147,067
Housing (self-help housing, acquisition and development of sites, slum clearance)	64,801
Local government (minor roads, recreation grounds)	94,490
Labour and social services (playground development and equipment)	2,155
Total	$2,513,652

Source: Five-Year Development Programme 1958–1962: Report of the Premier on Development Projects for the Year 1960. [Trinidad]: Office of the Premier, 1962.

Tobago's portion of the government's capital budgetary allocation between 1958 and 1962 was similarly small (see Table 7).[76] The statistics do not show actual expenditure, which was usually less than the amount budgeted. It is clear that, before 1963, government capital budgetary allocations for Tobago never reached 7 per cent, even though development in Tobago was supposedly accorded high priority after 1956.

TABLE 7
PROJECTED CAPITAL EXPENDITURE IN TRINIDAD AND TOBAGO, 1958–62

Year	Total ($million)	Tobago's Share ($million)	Tobago's Share (%)
1958	28.4	1.8	6.33
1959	38.2	1.8	4.70
1960	38.6	2.5	6.47
1961	52.6	3.1	5.90
1962	60.7	3.5	5.76

Source: Ragoonath, Development in Tobago: Twentieth Century Challenges.

On 30 September 1963 Hurricane Flora devastated Tobago. Thirty people died and agriculture, forestry and fisheries were severely affected.[77] The major export crops of coconut, cocoa and bananas suffered severely – five thousand of seven thousand acres of these trees were decimated.[78] Except for livestock, agricultural development was arrested. A substantial portion of the fishing fleet of the villages was also either damaged or destroyed.[79] Approximately 2,750 of the 7,500 houses on the island were ruined, and another thousand were severely damaged; thus about 50 per cent of the housing was no longer suitable or safe for habitation.[80] Public buildings, schools and water and electricity supplies were also severely affected. In early October the government appointed a team to formulate a long-term rehabilitation program for Tobago. The Report of the Tobago Planning Team (1963) recommended $43,375,300 for the rehabilitation project over a five-year period.[81]

Based on that report, the government modified its Draft Second Five-Year Plan 1964–1968, which had been published just two months before the hurricane. The Second Five-Year Plan 1964–1968: Modifications to Draft Plan proposed capital expenditure on Tobago to the tune of $38,068,900, or

12 per cent of the total capital expenditure for the country.[82] In the five years before Hurricane Flora, Tobago had been allocated an average of 6 per cent of the capital expenditure in the unitary state. The increase to 12 per cent was because of the hurricane and did not affect the proposed capital outlay for Trinidad.[83] In fact, by the end of the period only $23 million had been used on projects in Tobago: $7.4 million in 1964, $6 million in 1965 and $10 million between 1966 and 1968 was spent on development projects in the island; thus Tobago's share of the capital expenditure fell to under 5 per cent.[84] "Moreover, such a position was retained during the entire decade of the 1970s and even until the 1980s. Put differently, Tobago's share of developmental expenditure hovered between 5% and 6%."[85] The government tried to resuscitate the Tobago economy with this minuscule expenditure, but without success.

In the five years after Hurricane Flora, government expenditure in Tobago resulted in some improvement of and additions to the development projects.[86] In an attempt to resuscitate agriculture, $7 million was spent, mostly on cocoa, coconut, bananas, food crops and vegetable production. Despite government provision of capital through loans, grants, subsidies, plants, seedlings, fertilizers and herbicides, the acreage in production of all these commodities had fallen drastically by 1982, signifying a marked departure from agriculture in the post-Flora era.[87] The condition of roads in Tobago left a lot to be desired, especially secondary and agricultural access roads, which were in a general state of ill repair, if existing at all. The government spent $6.4 million on roads on the island in the five years after the hurricane – an attempt to improve the road network – but it remained in an unsatisfactory condition through the 1970s. With regard to fishing, the government financed seventy-nine new boats and twenty-five new outboard engines in the immediate post-Flora era, thereby replacing and extending the Tobago fishing fleet. In addition it supported expansion of the tourism sector via provisions for resuscitating agriculture, fisheries and the road system, and also by granting loans to boat owners and operators in the tourist industry. Thirty-two Tobagonians completed a course for hotel workers between 1964 and 1968. However, it was direct private-sector investment that led to an increase in hotel and guest-house rooms from 185 in 1960 to 448 in 1972 and an additional 200 by 1982, giving a total of 651.[88]

In spite of the government's efforts in the economic sphere, unemployment and poverty in Tobago were still above the national levels in 1981. Thus, compared to Trinidad, Tobago faired worse. In the country as a whole, unemployment and poverty rates for 1981 were 10.4 per cent and 3.5 per cent respectively; in Tobago they were 15.5 per cent and 6 per cent.[89]

The Tobago Planning Team stated in its report that the health-care system in Tobago was inadequate. It recommended improvements and extension of the Scarborough hospital and the provision of four mobile health units and two ambulances, because there were not enough health centres. Despite these proposals, only improvements to the hospital were provided for in the modified five-year plan;[90] a revision of the plan provided funds for rebuilding one health centre. After 1968 other health centres were rebuilt and a maternity delivery centre was completed and opened at Roxborough in 1977. By 1980 Tobago had a ninety-six-bed hospital, fifteen health centres and the maternity delivery centre.[91]

Other developments in social services occurred after the hurricane, but not all met the needs of the island's populace. By 1968 two steel water reservoirs with a capacity of 333,000 gallons (1.3 million litres) had been built[92] and the pipe-borne water supply had also been extended. After 1968 the Courland, Richmond and Highland waterworks and treatment plants were established and upgraded, and sewers for Scarborough were laid in the late 1970s. In the field of education, the government rebuilt the two schools destroyed by the hurricane and repaired others. More places were created for secondary school pupils by extending the Scarborough Secondary School and constructing a similar school at Roxborough, increasing secondary school enrolment significantly. In 1963 only 765 students were enrolled in government-owned and government-assisted secondary schools in Tobago. By 1969, however, 1,434 students were registered at these schools.[93] Private secondary schools also increased their enrolment from 651 to a thousand in the years from 1964 to 1968.[94] There was, however, still a deficiency, and the government built Signal Hill Secondary School in 1978, by which date government-owned and government-assisted secondary schools in Tobago were able to accommodate 2,400 students.[95] Despite these developments, "in 1980 more than 1,000 students sought entry into secondary schools; less than 40% were actually placed, due primarily to the lack of an adequate number of secondary school places".[96]

The government also assisted with housing after Hurricane Flora. The modified draft five-year plan allocated $11 million for housing, of which 80 per cent was to be made available through loans; 1,008 persons accessed these loans.[97] Another three thousand people constructed houses in Tobago from 1964 to 1969; by 1970 there were over eight thousand houses in Tobago. In addition, under various housing schemes the government built more than two hundred houses in Tobago in the 1970s, with an overall count of 1,356 new houses built in that period by government and private citizens.[98]

Economic development in Tobago during the first two decades of PNM control proceeded gradually. The level of government commitment to such development, as indicated by capital expenditure on the island, suggests that while Tobago was not left out of national development, it cannot be argued that the island was granted its promised priority. The "moral obligation" to Tobago expressed by Williams in 1957 was never fulfilled, even after Trinidad was made the capital of the West Indies Federation in 1958. Tobagonians constantly complained about the government's broken promises, and these complaints fuelled their identity construction and desire to control their own affairs. The central government did not provide the infrastructure and resources necessary for economic growth in Tobago. Meanwhile, the petroleum, petrochemical, steel and various lighter industries were doing extremely well in Trinidad and were being nurtured with government support. On the other hand, until 1980 Trinidadians still considered Tobago as a rural, if not backward, island.

Tobagonians continued to harbour many grievances against the central government, all of which were tinder to the fire lit by the autonomists. Prominent Tobagonians were convinced that the government could not be trusted to develop Tobago. For example, James's sentiments, expressed in the memorandum to the secretary of state in 1948, were equally true in 1976: "no faith can be placed in any policy it [the government] might formulate".[99]

The voices of the autonomists were not completely silenced after James's death. Individuals such as Rhodil Norton and A. N. R. Robinson insisted that Tobago was not receiving its fair share of the economic pie, and therefore should secure significant devolution of government power – or secede.

Chapter 10

"The Question Now Is: To Secede or Not to Secede"

During the 1960s and 1970s various prominent individuals, singly or as groups, championed the cause of greater autonomy for Tobago. A few called for outright secession from Trinidad. Continuing on the path paved by A. P. T. James in the 1940s and 1950s, these autonomists argued that Tobagonians were treated as second-class citizens, that the island had not been given its fair share of the national economic pie, that the government had not fostered economic development on the island and that government services were not easily accessible to Tobagonians. Many autonomists rehearsed a litany of grievances that heightened Tobagonian identity and galvanized support for their stance. They demanded that the government deal with Tobagonians as equals or face an assault on the union.

Rhodil Norton and the Call for Secession

The first of the autonomists to gain recognition in the 1970s was Rhodil Norton, a medical doctor. Norton began his advocacy for secession in

1969. At the time he was president of the Buccoo Reef Association, a group of tour guides engaged in shuttling visitors to and from the famous reef in glass-bottomed boats. Norton was also a long-standing member of the Tobago Chamber of Commerce who had been expelled the month before he made his May 1969 call for secession.[1] He was expelled because of his refusal to apologize for his "disorderly behaviour" at an annual general meeting of the chamber held the previous March.[2] Norton also aspired to political office. He had contested the 1966 general election on the Democratic Labour Party ticket but had lost to the PNM candidate, Benjamin L. Basil Pitt (known locally simply as Basil Pitt) in the Tobago West constituency.[3] (Pitt later became the minister of state responsible for Tobago affairs in the Office of the Prime Minister.)

Norton's demand for secession involved complaints by the residents of Buccoo over what they called a "great injustice" with respect to their livelihood as operators of shuttle boats to and from the Buccoo Reef. The government appointed a committee to investigate the matter. However, "not . . . even one representative of the boatmen [was included] on the committee. This was one of the reasons advanced by Dr Norton as to why Tobago should secede".[4] Lack of consultation of Tobagonians on matters directly affecting their lives was a long-standing complaint that reflected the government's arrogance. Norton expressed his conviction that "the only way to eradicate it [the injustice] was to go it alone".[5] Norton was on the far left of the autonomy continuum. His call for secession seemed spontaneous and he lacked a broad-based following.

Trinidadians opposed Norton's views, expressing a decidedly integrationist philosophy. One individual, in an article in the "What We Think" section of the daily *Evening News,* reminded Norton that "except for the narrow division by water, Tobago is just another part of the State as any other ward. And to suggest that Tobago should consider leaving the State, would be comparable to asking any other Ward in Trinidad to do the same".[6] Whenever the issue of self-government was discussed, Trinidadians often came to this illogical conclusion. Tobago's natural ocean boundaries made severing its ties from Trinidad a viable option; no other district in Trinidad could make such a claim. That argument represented Trinidadians' lack of knowledge of Tobago's history in the union, as well as their failure to understand Tobagonian identity. It also reflected their disregard of the problems Tobagonians faced as a result of the island's isolation from the centre of government and power. Further, Tobagonians' lack of control over their own destiny and their powerlessness to determine development priorities for the island were the basis of many disputes. These factors seriously affected Trinidadians' assessment of the Tobago situation.

Many, like the newspaper columnist, had accepted the ruling PNM's propaganda that the government had been spending an enormous amount of money on capital development projects in Tobago. They even characterized the government's attention to and expenditure on Tobago after Hurricane Flora as beyond the call of duty: "Within the last 10 years or so, Tobago has had more attention paid to her than she ever had in previous history. . . . As a matter of fact, so much emphasis has been placed on Tobago in all-round development that she has become the envy of some Wards in Trinidad."[7] Such statements reveal that most people were unaware of the minuscule amount of capital expenditure that the government provided for Tobago. Thus secession was not the allegedly ludicrous idea; instead, it was the view that Tobagonians should not seek separation that was an "absurd proposition".

Tobagonians who opposed secession were principally members of the ruling PNM government. In June 1969 Basil Pitt criticized the advocates of secession at the inaugural meeting of the Tobago Jaycees, a cultural club. Pitt and other government officials were integrationists. They viewed the island as an "integral region of the nation".[8] Supporting Pitt's view, the president of the club contended that there was no need to secede because "the island was making great strides in development and had become famous for its Buccoo Reef and Calypso Rose".[9]

Other Tobagonians expressed their views on the issue of secession. Cyril Garcia, a Scarborough merchant, although he condemned secession, argued that a claim that top government officials were promoting secession was just a smokescreen to hide the fact that "it was the poor people, the youths and the oppressed who are calling for secession".[10] Tobagonians were no longer following the "elite

Identity and Secession in the Caribbean

conmen" (upper- and middle-class leaders) who spoke in integrationist terms to satisfy the PNM politicians. Garcia insisted that the majority did "their own thinking . . . and they know when they are being neglected and treated as Second class citizens".[11] While Garcia opposed secession, he listed a number of grievances, including (1) the Ministry of Tobago Affairs was ineffective and a rubber stamp of the central government; (2) its officials were "afraid to make decisions" or made bad ones when they did, and (3) the government had failed to keep its promises to develop Scarborough and construct a new airport runway. He also feared that another generation or more would pass before those projects would be completed.

More critical charges emerged from the debate on secession. Garcia declared that Trinidadian government officials in Tobago were corrupt and practised nepotism and other irregularities.[12] No one took action against these officials. Further, Trinidadians were appointed to vacant positions on the island instead of Tobagonians, reducing opportunities for Tobagonians to be promoted in the civil service. Adding fuel to the flames was a high rate of unemployment among youth, who had to compete with retired personnel who were being re-employed as daily paid workers with high salaries. This frustration over unemployment contributed to flirtation with drugs, especially marijuana use, a practice unknown before 1969.[13] In addition, the government was doing nothing to curb the increasing cost of living, especially the prices of food and clothing. University scholarships were not set aside for Tobagonians, and they were not selected for national sports teams. The frustrations endemic in Tobago's society led Tobagonians to become hostile to Trinidadians, who were being heckled and even assaulted on the island.[14]

Norton's demands and the many grievances in Tobago (secondary sources of identity construction and catalysts for secessionist claims) forced the PNM to court the favour of Tobagonians in 1969, when it held its annual convention on the island. In addition, Tobagonians were well represented in the government, even in the Cabinet. Basil Pitt was minister of state with responsibility for Tobago affairs, and A. N. R. Robinson, member of Parliament for Tobago East, was the minister of external affairs. Furthermore, the Tobago County Council was "dominated by the elected representatives of the ruling party".[15] Prime Minister Williams took a personal interest in Tobago and appointed himself minister for Tobago affairs. Along with Pitt and Robinson, as well as eight others, including two permanent secretaries, Williams established a special Tobago Affairs Committee on 3 October 1969 to examine the problems on the island. Trinidadians criticized Williams's decision. Many agreed that Tobago was "a special case" but they reverted to the argument – one that would be replayed over time – that certain areas of Trinidad, such as Laventille, could not secede "or even threaten to secede".[16] However, they noted that if Tobago switched political loyalties and "rallied round the banner of some vocal secessionist, she could conceivably do . . . serious damage to the prestige and position of Trinidad in the West Indian community".[17] Thus the potential for wounded pride made the PNM government pay attention to the problems of Tobagonians.[18]

On 10 October 1969 the Tobago Affairs Committee made decisions aimed at accelerating development on the island.[19] It approved construction of thirteen agricultural access roads, provision of public access roads to three beaches – Pigeon Point, Arnos Vale and Little Bacolet Bay – and establishment of a pest control unit to assist farmers. Under the jurisdiction of the forestry division, the unit comprised six temporary game wardens and one temporary motor vehicle operator. The Ministry of Agriculture was also directed to make a special study of the cocrico, one of the two national birds, which had become a major pest, damaging the crops of Tobagonian farmers. The Ministry of Public Utilities was requested to undertake an immediate study and report within the month on providing a special cargo ship to operate between Trinidad and Tobago. The attorney-general was mandated to prepare legislation no later than 30 November to protect the reefs at Buccoo and Speyside. The committee also agreed to approach Parliament with a request for $500,000 to facilitate acquisition of Tobago real estate, significant portions of which were still in the hands of absentee landlords.

Those stopgap measures did not stifle the demands for secession. In the same month that the Committee was formed, J. Bayliss Frederick, a prominent Tobagonian lawyer, declared that the time had "come for geography and politics to go hand in hand".[20] Frederick contended that "foreigners [were] bleeding Tobago dry". To him the foreigners were "Trinidadians – businessmen in particular"; his contention was based on the fact that 90 per cent of all the money spent on clothing, building materials and foodstuff in Tobago went into the pockets of Trinidadian businessmen. Decrying Tobago's dependent status in the unitary state, Frederick wrote, "The most embarrassing thing for anyone to do is accept something he has not earned, and this is what Trinidad is doing to Tobago. We are being humiliated instead of being developed."[21] Frederick complained that no encouragement was given to Tobagonians to form cooperatives that could compete with foreign-owned businesses. He bemoaned the loss of agriculture's "tremendous" potential and the failure of industrial growth independent of Trinidad. Promoting the latter would retain profits, provide capital for investment in businesses operating on the island and foster economic development.

The tourist industry provided a good example for the critics. It failed to provide living wages or reduce unemployment. Tobagonians were not educated for managerial positions since there was no training school on the island, as in Trinidad. Local employees in the hotel industry were chambermaids and waiters and the more prestigious and better-paying jobs went to Trinidadians, although a few light-skinned Tobagonians were included.[22] Even taxi drivers were not gaining maximum benefit from the booming tourist industry, because foreign-owned car rental companies were monopolizing the tourist transportation business. Where local taxis were used, the fares were strictly regulated. In addition, boat owners plying their trade to and from the Buccoo Reef were being paid "starvation wages". Frederick returned to the call for locally owned, small cottage-type hotels as one solution to the problem, as these smaller guesthouses would allow Tobagonians to benefit from the tourist industry. In the 1970s these and other issues led Tobagonians to organize around the demand for secession.

The Tobago Emancipation Action Committee, chaired by Rhodil Norton and derisively described as a "mysterious band of 'doctors, councilors, union executives, teachers, and local businessmen'", called for secession in 1970.[23] Labelling Norton the "Apostle of Secession", the *Express* newspaper dismissed "all this secession talk [as] fiddlesticks".[24] However, Eric Williams and his Cabinet were not so casual about secession in Tobago. The government sought funding from the Inter-American Development Bank to finance infrastructure for the tourist industry, including an international airport, access roads to a proposed new airport, and sewerage facilities for the existing Crown Point airport and the surrounding south-western area of Tobago.[25] At the time a joint mission of the Inter-American Development Bank and the Food and Agriculture Organization was advising the government on preservation of the Buccoo Reef and development of land adjacent to it. To assuage the calls for secession, the government allocated funds in its 1970 budget for construction of agricultural access roads; acquisition of estates for agricultural purposes; land distribution for livestock, dairy and food crop production; harbour development; construction of a spur road to Parlatuvier; and redevelopment of lower Scarborough.[26] Once more the integrationist PNM government was responding to the grievances of Tobagonians as though the island were in a crisis situation, as in the case of Hurricane Flora. In spite of the government's record of failing to keep most of its promises, the *Express* considered it "folly" that Norton and his followers would be "driven by sheer frustration into a spurious plan for secession".[27]

The police began surveillance of the activities of the Tobago Emancipation Action Committee. At its meeting in Delaford on 4 January 1970 to inform the public about its demands for independence, Norton told the large crowd that if Tobago seceded it would be able to sustain itself economically with annual revenue from four sources: a casino, which could earn approximately $225 million; the hotel industry, which could earn $3.7 million; and tourism and agriculture, which would generate revenue in an independent Tobago.[28] Norton also charged the government with providing easy loans to "expatriates in Trinidad while refusing financial assistance to Tobagonians" for investment in Tobago.

Adopting James's earlier contention, the new group of secessionists believed that Tobago would be no worse off if it were separated from

Trinidad. "Orlando" wrote in the *Express* in 1970, "The history of Tobago separated from Trinidad can never be as horrible as its history in association with Trinidad."[29] Orlando based his support for secession on the uneven development in Tobago: "While Trinidadians continue to enjoy the benefits of oil, asphalt, tourism and hundreds of factories, Tobago continues to be without one single factory. And while Trinidad is receiving meaningful economic development plus first class facilities for sport and recreation, Tobago continues to be hoodwinked with talk of 'unspoilt charm.'"[30] He pointed to unfulfilled government promises and the failure of tourist revenue to benefit Tobagonians: "Tobago is waking up to the realization that since no body cares about her, she must care for herself. Beautiful beaches cannot fill empty stomachs. We cannot wear 'rustic charm' on our back; we cannot find happiness in empty promises which are even emptier by their repetition and frequency."[31] He lamented that the Tobago-born representatives in Parliament – Basil Pitt; Lionel M. Robinson, minister of agriculture, lands and fisheries; and A. N. R. Robinson, the former minister of finance – were more loyal to their political party, the PNM, than to their island. Walling E. B. Lewis, a contributor to the *Trinidad Guardian*, also blamed Tobagonians in top government positions for the lack of development on the island.[32]

Not all Tobagonians supported Norton's call for secession. One *Express* columnist described him as a "Joker in the Pack" because he suggested a casino as a revenue-earner for Tobago.[33] While some Tobagonians did not support secession, they took umbrage at the article's description of Norton's followers as "crazy" and "gullible". One person, writing under the pseudonym "Crusoe", contended that even those Tobagonians who did not support secession at that time felt that, if the island continued to be neglected by the central government, "someday one of our many brilliant sons would avail himself to lead us to true independence".[34] This response foreshadowed things to come. Robinson, the former PNM senior government official and deputy political leader, broke with the ruling party in 1970, freeing him to champion the Tobagonian cause.

In 1973 a government constitution commission, headed by the notable jurist Sir Hugh O. B. Wooding, investigated Rhodil Norton's demand for secession. The commission reviewed the claim that Tobago was like any other rural area in the country. It ruled that while Tobago was closer to Port of Spain than Moruga and other areas in Trinidad, it was a "sea-girt island, distinct and apart from Trinidad, with its own territorial waters and dependent in its association with anywhere outside Tobago upon sea and air communications".[35] Citing Tobago's distinct identity, the commission also recognized that after union and "until the advent of County Councils, Tobago had no representative organ to express the hopes and aspirations, the fears and apprehensions, or even the day-to-day actualities of its people", especially since the people, culture and customs of the two islands were so different.[36]

At hearings in Scarborough on 10 and 11 March 1973, Tobagonians presented their views to the commission. They contended that other West Indian islands of similar size were independent; yet Tobago did not even have a "Deeds Registry or a Record Office where certificates of births, marriages and deaths [could] be obtained".[37] They also argued that much of the government's development expenditure in Tobago was on tourist promotion projects, that the vessels of the West Indian Shipping Service did not call at Scarborough and that the higher cost of living in Tobago was due to the Trinidad government's indifference to Tobagonians' welfare and prosperity.

The commission noted that the "relatively small group of Tobagonians" who advocated secession from Trinidad had modified their demands. The autonomists at the hearing requested a constitutional provision that would permit secession, contingent on a majority vote in a referendum. However, the commissioners unequivocally took an integrationist stance in their final recommendation: "[W]e do not and cannot recommend the inclusion in the Constitution of any provision pointing towards secession. Rather, our recommendations are and must be aimed at strengthening the natural unity of Trinidad and Tobago."[38] Tobagonians rejected this integrationist position, and a couple of years later one of its "brilliant sons" demanded internal self-government for Tobago.

Identity and Secession in the Caribbean

The Quest for Internal Self-Government: The Trigger Factor

The 1970s were eventful years – the Black Power movement had taken hold in the country and there were calls for constitutional reform. The tensions between Tobago and Trinidad increased and came to a head as a result of the 1976 general elections. The PNM lost the two Tobago seats to the DAC, which increasingly became identified as a Tobagonian political party. The central government responded by disbanding the Ministry of Tobago Affairs, triggering a renewed demand for self-government. Tobagonians now perceived the DAC members of Parliament, Robinson and Dr Winston Murray, as representing solely their interests. Once more their elected representatives passionately articulated Tobagonians' grievances and the plight of the island. This focus on grievances enhanced Tobagonians' sense of community and solidarity because they all shared the same woes and had a common enemy. Thus Tobagonian identity became the driving force behind the autonomy movement.

Dismantling the Ministry for Tobago Affairs constituted and has remained the major crossroads in the relationship between Tobago and Trinidad since the union. This apparent act of political reprisal by the ruling PNM government against Tobagonians, for not supporting the PNM at the polls in 1976, demonstrated unequivocally that the central government was insensitive to the circumstances and concerns of Tobagonians. The administrative chaos and inconvenience caused by disbanding the ministry was unjustified, and Tobagonians experienced much anguish. Consequently they resented the PNM and its leader, Eric Williams.

Williams's attitude hardened towards Tobagonians for supporting the party of his rival, Robinson, who was once his right-hand man and deputy political leader of the PNM. Robinson was also a co-founder of the PNM and had held numerous top Cabinet positions in the government. He had become increasingly disenchanted over various improprieties among government officials, whom he charged with corruption, exemplifying what Eric Roach referred to when he wrote that Tobagonians took the "island's strong peasant conscience and integrity into the Trinidad administration".[39] Robinson now empathized with the nation's masses, who were increasingly discontent with social and economic conditions in the country. This discontent came to a head in the so-called Black Power Revolution of 1970. On 13 April 1970 Robinson, who was minister of external affairs at the time, resigned as a member of Cabinet because he disagreed with Williams's handling of this social disturbance, which constituted a public expression of no confidence in the government. He believed that "sufficiently serious attempts [had not been] made by the government to remove the underlying causes of the present situation in the country".[40]

The civil unrest in Trinidad began on 26 February and lasted until 21 April 1970. Geddes Granger, a spokesman for the National Joint Action Committee, a radical ideological group that eventually became a political party, led the civil disturbance. During the unrest, antigovernment protests and politically motivated violence were directed against both the foreign and local elites.[41] Radical intellectuals, university students and the urban dispossessed highlighted various grievances, including the racist policies of the commercial elite. They claimed that the PNM government had failed to transform society and improve living standards. The disturbances subsided after the threat of a general strike, scheduled for 21–22 April. The government declared a state of emergency on 21 April and imposed a dawn-to-dusk curfew. The military supported the government, and during the curfew fifteen Black Power leaders were arrested, which brought an end to the disturbances.

The government remained intact but Robinson resigned from the PNM party on 20 September 1970. He cited as his reasons abuse of power by the political leader, Eric Williams, the party's failure to submit to disciplinary procedures, scandalous improprieties of government ministers close to the prime minister, and corruption and vilification of party members (such as Robinson himself) who had tried to expose and remedy the abuses.[42] Robinson was the first high-ranking government official to take a public stand against Williams. His continuous public denunciations of Williams and the government led to an enduring enmity between the two men.

Severing ties with the PNM allowed Robinson to identify more closely with the issues that for so long had confronted Tobagonians.[43] He immediately created a political base of supporters called the Action Committee of Dedicated Citizens. On 15 October 1970 this group published *The Road to Freedom,* which reflected Robinson's interest in launching a strong opposition to the PNM, declaring that the government needed transformation. On 24 December 1970, the Action Committee of Dedicated Citizens (ACDC) and the Democratic Labour Party (DLP) combined efforts to "work towards the emergence of a new organization that would reflect the basic desire of Trinidad and Tobago and the Caribbean for meaningful change".[44] The merger was called the ACDC/DLP. On 3 April 1971 the first national congress of that group renamed itself, forming a political party called the Democratic Action Congress (DAC),[45] with Robinson as its leader. In its first publication, *Guide to Change for Trinidad and Tobago* (April 1971), the DAC drew attention to the need for economic development and greater autonomy in Tobago.

In the section of *Guide to Change* titled "New Direction for Tobago", the DAC discussed issues affecting the island. The document focused on agriculture, tourism and the commercial potential of the island. It called for a "serious attempt" by the government to develop Tobago's "human and material resources", and to end Tobago's isolation from the outside world by providing a "harbour capable of accommodating ocean-going liners" and by improving airport facilities to meet "international standards".[46] The document favoured protection of Tobago's beaches and marine life from pollution by the mining activities of petroleum companies operating in the waters around the island. Also emphasized were the development of tourism, expansion of cooperatives and resolution of the long-standing problem of disputed land titles.

Guide to Change highlighted various grievances and stressed that Tobago was in a disadvantageous position in its relationship with Trinidad. One of the most significant statements in the document invoked Tobagonian identity and pointed to the need for Tobagonians to be in charge of the destiny of their island:

> Above all there is urgent need for the people of Tobago to be more involved in decisions affecting their livelihood and future prospects. This means that as far

as practicable, decisions regarding Tobago's future must be taken in Tobago. The island is a district community with a life of its own. It must not be regarded as a mere adjunct or appendage of Trinidad.[47]

Self-government for Tobago was on the DAC's agenda from the inception of the party. Contrary to what some have argued, Robinson's interest in Tobago did not emerge suddenly after the 1976 dissolution of the Ministry of Tobago Affairs.[48]

The DAC placed great emphasis on the principle of self-determination. A newspaper article that discussed the 1973 DAC National Congress, held at Queen's Hall in Port of Spain, stated:

> A Recognition of the right of Self-determination for Tobago is incorporated in a wide-ranging Democratic Action Congress (DAC) manifesto. The programme for the sister island by the DAC, led by Tobago-born Mr. A. N. R. Robinson will be designed to achieve the following: Rapid improvement of the Tobago economy; and Involvement of residents in the planning of their future.[49]

This continuous interest in the development and better administration of Tobago persisted until 1977, when Robinson presented a motion in Parliament calling for internal self-government for Tobago. However, it was the dissolution of the Ministry of Tobago Affairs that triggered the parliamentary struggle to grant Tobago self-government.[50]

Between 1970 and 1976, opposition to the PNM government grew steadily. The other political parties wanted to break the PNM's domination of the national political arena. As it related to Tobago's position in the union, 1976 proved to be a critical juncture in the political history of the country.[51] First, the election manifestos of three political parties – the DAC, the Tapia House Movement and the United Labour Front – advocated greater autonomy for Tobago. Second, the disbanding of the Ministry of Tobago Affairs resulted in untold inconvenience and administrative disruption in the island. Third, another post-election fallout was Williams's implication that Tobagonians' rejection of the PNM at the polls was tantamount to support for secession. This was also the year when initial steps were taken by the Regional Action Committee of the DAC, the

Tobago arm of the party, to lobby Parliament for self-government for Tobago.

The political parties allied with the DAC were vocal in their support of self-government for Tobago. The Tapia House Movement's political leaflets advocated "Home Rule" for Tobago. Statements in the United Labour Front's documents were also highly charged: given the "super-exploitation which Tobago has had to endure, complete internal autonomy concerning Tobago affairs" and "the fullest democratic participation on the part of the masses of the people in the political administration of the island" were necessary to get Tobago out of the "mess" into which the "puppet PNM regime" had put it.[52] In reality the PNM had inherited the "mess" from the colonial administration, but had done little to improve the island's development.

The DAC's programme for Tobago recommended "rapid development and diversification of the Tobago economy . . . ; involvement of residents in the planning of their own future; promotion of self-help and self-reliance . . . ; and devolution of executive authority and of administrative responsibility to broaden the area of local decision making".[53] The right to self-determination was trumpeted also in the DAC's 1976 political manifesto. Tobago's special circumstances, its problems, its potential, the grievances of its residents and, even more so, willingness to remedy those issues were included in the major parties' plans for better government as they contested the elections of 25 September 1976.[54]

The results of the elections probably stunned both the DAC and the PNM. The DAC did not win any of the thirty-four constituencies in Trinidad; however, it carried the two Tobago seats. Robinson was the successful candidate for the constituency of Tobago East and Winston Murray won Tobago West. The election results clearly indicated Tobagonians' support for greater autonomy and development of their island – and could have been taken as a bad omen, considering the PNM's political stranglehold on the country.

The PNM's leader did not take the loss well. Williams denied that he was angry with Tobagonians, but his rhetoric two days after the election results were published showed otherwise. In his post-election speech, Williams told Tobagonians:

> If you want to go, go. We are not holding you. I'm not going to send any Coast guard or ship or army to hold them back. What for? They want to go, go! Everybody understands today that whatever used to be said in the past, we don't live in any world of true eternal love. The greatest thing today is the divorce celebration. O.K. Let's have a divorce celebration! It is a financial matter; what terms do we agree on without bitterness, without any emotion? All they have to tell me is what it is they want and how to do it. I appoint somebody to do it. I have more important things to do. So whenever they are ready, my friends, and they have voted one way, O. K., I for one wasn't too bothered about this. I always suspected that within the ranks of the PNM so-called there has been a solid section surreptitiously supporting the secession. It is not a crime. There are places that are there already. Others will come. I will be particularly careful not to do anything in my position as the Prime Minister of the country to keep Tobago by force. I am against it and I would advise the population not to do that. I told Tobago long time ago when this thing came up: "You all talk about Tobago seceding from Trinidad; no big thing. The thing that you have to worry about is when the movement starts for Trinidad to secede from Tobago . . . that would be serious." I am for neither.[55]

Williams was concerned about his political image and the effect the Tobago election results might have on electoral districts in Trinidad in future elections. His hard-line stance against Tobagonians may have been the politically astute thing to do in an obviously embarrassing situation.

The PNM's response to Tobago's rebuff at the polls was swift and severe: the government dismantled the Ministry of Tobago Affairs. This only "helped to fan the fires of anger and pride in Tobago".[56] Tobagonians, who were incensed over such an insensitive move, viewed the government's hasty action as an act of political reprisal, and it became the trigger factor in the movement for internal self-government. On 26 November, two months after the election, a regional congress of the DAC, held at the Caribana Club House in Scarborough, authorized the Tobago representatives "to introduce a motion in Parliament at the earliest opportunity, and to take all other proper and necessary steps to achieve internal self-government for Tobago in 1977".[57] Robinson's motion was placed on the parliamentary order paper for introduction on 10 December 1976. Coincidentally, that day was also being observed as Human Rights Day. But Tobagonians' efforts to exercise their right to self-determination were thwarted by the government for three long years.

Chapter 11

Tobago's Struggle for Internal Self-Government, 1977–1980

Tobagonians exercised their right to self-determination not by radical secession, but by using constitutionally available options through the parliamentary process. Their goal was passage and implementation of a motion for internal self-government. This led to a protracted struggle in Parliament as the PNM government engaged in a great deal of filibustering. The DAC and its supporters pressed on and even tried to bring regional pressure to bear on the government. Their efforts paid off in 1980, when the Tobago House of Assembly was re-established.

The Motion for Internal Self-Government

The parliamentary struggle for self-government in Tobago did not begin without a hitch, and its entire three-year duration was fraught with challenges. Though initially carded to be placed on the order paper for introduction on 10 December 1976, A. N. R. Robinson's motion was mysteriously omitted. Robinson was informed beforehand that discussion of the national budget was scheduled for that day as well and was accorded priority as government business, but he was also told that the matter would remain on the order paper in case there was a chance it could be introduced. It seems that the PNM government had participated in the "illegal" removal of the motion from the order paper,[1] and no explanation was given for this action. It is clear that the government was attempting to railroad the campaign for internal self-government from its inception. Between 10 December 1976 and the next sitting of Parliament on 14 January 1977, PNM supporters circulated a petition against self-government in Tobago. More than four thousand signatures were obtained, but many were deemed bogus.[2]

Undaunted by attempts to sabotage his motion, Robinson presented it in Parliament on 14 January 1977: "Be it Resolved: That this honourable House is of the opinion that all proper and necessary steps should be taken to accord the people of Tobago internal self-government in 1977."[3] Fellow DAC parliamentarian Winston Murray seconded the motion. During a ninety-minute speech, Robinson reiterated the tale of woes that Tobagonians had experienced under the colonial and post-colonial governments, both of which had failed Tobago. Robinson focused on the Ministry of Tobago Affairs, pointing out that it had no executive power and thus was an administrative failure. In addition to the potential for a viable tourist industry, Robinson raised the issue of the presence of commercial quantities of petroleum deposits in the seabed offshore of Tobago. He contended that Tobagonians should govern themselves and secure the economic development of their own island.

Further, the motion advocated a permanent administrative structure for the island that would include an elected body responsible to the people of Tobago. The system demanded was not status-oriented but rather functional in nature. By demanding internal self-government, Tobagonians were exercising their right to self-determination under international law. The PNM parliamentarians, in classic integrationist mode, denounced the motion. On 21 January 1977 Attorney-General Selwyn Richardson claimed that Robinson and Murray were really interested in self-aggrandizement and secession.

However, opposition parliamentarians supported the motion. In an attempt to unseat the PNM, the political parties of the Opposition saw the Tobago issue as one that could weaken the ruling government's power base. Hence their remarks were generally supportive of greater autonomy for Tobago. At the end of the day's sitting, the leader of the opposition United Labour Front and member for Siparia, Raffique Shah, moved an amendment to the motion: "That this Honourable House is of the opinion that all proper and necessary steps should be taken to hold a referendum to ascertain the views of the people of Tobago on internal self-government in 1977."[4] Shah continued his remarks on 28 January, the third day of the debate, and charged that the motion was not being treated seriously.[5] Since the PNM government's "stewardship" of Tobago had not resulted in "any meaningful economic benefit to the people of Tobago", he affirmed their right to self-determination.[6] Shah also castigated the government's laissez-faire attitude towards Tobago, which, he charged, had resulted in the island's being treated as a vacation resort by most Trinidadians, who went there for sea bathing. They purchased nothing, carrying over to the island all they needed. The United Labour Front supported decentralization on the grounds that Tobago was a "special case".[7] Shah's call for a referendum was aimed at convincing the people of Trinidad that Tobagonians really wanted self-government, but Trinidadians were sceptical because of the petition against self-government with four thousand signatures.

The third day's debate continued with an attack on Robinson by the minister of works, transport and communication, Hector McClean. He accused Robinson of seeking power and secession under the guise of internal self-government, since he had never raised the issue while a ranking minister of the government.[8] Robinson would later argue that when he was with the PNM he did indicate that action should be taken to give greater autonomy to smaller dependent islands of the West Indies that were parts of confederated states.[9] Towards the end of his contributions, McClean accused Robinson of suffering from "political tabanca [lovesickness]", because he was attacking the PNM government from whose good graces he had fallen. [10]

The next speaker, Winston Murray, rose, "happy" to make his contribution that would "mark the departure from the simple and specious sophistry that we have been having here during the entire debate".[11] He argued that the government was allowing Tobagonians to be dispossessed from their land gradually by outsiders from Trinidad, including East Indian businessmen. Murray called for the preservation of Tobagonian culture, especially such values as collectivism. Minister of Finance Overand Padmore responded to Murray on the fourth and final day of the initial parliamentary discussions of the motion for self-government.

Padmore insisted that Murray's comments smacked of secessionist sentiment.[12] He also tried to disprove allegations of the PNM's neglect and underdevelopment by citing expenditure statistics on contemporary government projects in Tobago. Padmore also moved an amendment to the motion that led to its final version as voted on by Parliament. The government would agree to the motion for internal self-government if it were amended so that the measure would not contradict the unitary statehood of Trinidad and Tobago and the views of the majority of Tobagonians, and if it took into consideration the financial and economic realities of both islands and the impact on other parts of the country.[13] Padmore promised that if the amendment were accepted, the government would introduce a motion to refer the matter to a joint select committee of Parliament already established to consider another matter. It is clear that, from the outset, the PNM government had a scheme for dealing with the DAC's bid for increased autonomy for Tobago.[14]

Lionel Robinson, A. N. R. Robinson's brother and representative for Toco/Manzanilla, made his comments after Padmore. He agreed that the government should be blamed for not providing Tobago with an international airport and similar infrastructure, but he argued that the charge of neglect was unfair: the government had provided, among other things, electricity to the island.[15] Lionel conceded that the government's "attempts to restructure the administration [of Tobago] had not been very successful".[16] However, he defended the hasty dissolution of the Ministry of Tobago Affairs on the grounds that it would have been "morally objectionable" to leave a PNM minister in Tobago after the party had lost the elections there, and also because an opposition member could not have been placed in that position, since by virtue of office he would become a member of the Cabinet.[17] Lionel Robinson failed to realize that it was also morally objectionable to allow Tobagonians to suffer the inconveniences brought about by dismantling of the Ministry of Tobago Affairs. Some other, reasonable solution should have been found. In the final analysis, the purpose of his remarks was to persuade the House of Representatives to accept the amendment proposed by the government.

By the end of the debate Shah had withdrawn his amendment for a referendum and other, slight changes had been made to the government's version. The version of the motion unanimously accepted by the House read:

> Resolved: That this honourable House is of the opinion that all proper and necessary steps should be taken to accord to the people of Tobago internal self-government in 1977, in such measure as will not be contradictory to the constitutional reality of the independent unitary state of Trinidad and Tobago, such proper and necessary steps to take into account:
> (a) The views of the majority of the people of Tobago;
> (b) The cultural, financial and economic realities and potential of Trinidad and Tobago;
> (c) The impact of any such change on other parts of Trinidad and Tobago.

The motion was severely restrictive, but it was the best that the Tobago representatives could procure from their integrationist colleagues, who had the majority of votes in the Parliament.

A. N. R. Robinson continued to vilify the government for disbanding the Ministry of Tobago Affairs and for having no Tobago representatives in the Senate or in the Cabinet. He maintained that "Tobago will be satisfied with nothing less than legal and constitutional guarantees [because] Tobago's experience has shown that nothing less than a permanent structure of government will do".[18] In addition, he described the government's policies towards Tobago as "bankrupt".

At the end of four days of debate the first phase of the parliamentary struggle for internal self-government for Tobago was over. The road ahead was long and filled with hurdles. Victory would demand

Identity and Secession in the Caribbean

patience and determination to cope with three more years of delays, filibustering and deliberate attempts by the government to derail legislation intended to give Tobago an autonomous institution with significant executive power to enable it to determine policy. Obviously the government (reluctantly) voted for internal self-government because "it would have been politically embarrassing for Dr Williams and the PNM to vote unequivocally against the [original] motion".[19]

The government's amendment centred around two issues: first, its thinking that the DAC's real motive was secession, and second, Williams's view that Robinson was the enemy. Williams was haunted by his perception of a secessionist element in Tobago society. He was correct, but secessionists made up only a small fraction of the population. Whether small or significant, this group posed a threat to his political superstructure. While the PNM won the majority of seats in the 1976 general election, the votes indicated that other political parties were undermining its dominance in the country.[20]

Initially Tobago was, and continued to be, a thorn in the flesh of the PNM. In that party's first foray into the political arena, in the 1956 election, Tobagonians shocked the PNM when James defeated Robinson at the polls. Twenty years later they again embarrassed the PNM by rejecting the party at the polls. While Williams conceded that he would eventually lose the war for internal self-government, he was intent on winning many of the ensuing battles. Since the PNM government was being forced to act as midwife in the rebirth of a politically and administratively autonomous Tobago, it made sure that the delivery would not be without complications.[21]

The Meaning of Internal Self-Government

The debate on internal self-government for Tobago tended to be confusing because the two principals in the debate, the PNM and the DAC, interpreted the term differently. From the inception Robinson argued that secession was not part of his agenda. In his opening remarks in the House on 14 January 1977 he explained:

> The purpose of this motion is to place a substantial part of the responsibility
> for the conduct of Tobago's affairs fairly and squarely where that responsibil-
> ity belongs; that is to say, in the hands of residents of Tobago themselves.
> This is not secession, sedition or separation; it is rather a matter of historical
> justice. It is consistent with contemporary notions of human rights and it
> accords with realism.[22]

Robinson's definition of internal self-government included significant devolution of government power to Tobagonians so that they could determine the destiny of their island and select priorities for development. Officially the disintegration of the unitary state of the Republic of Trinidad and Tobago was not part of his thinking, even though some of his supporters may have thought privately that secession was a viable option.[23] From his former integrationist stance while part of the PNM government, Robinson had now moved to mid-left of centre on the autonomy continuum.

Various DAC leaflets, distributed to educate Tobagonians on the issue of internal self-government, clarified Robinson's ideology. These leaflets were didactic in tone and replete with definitions. One, titled "What Is Internal Self Government & Examples", explained:

> Internal Self Government is the devolution of Central, National or Federal
> Power. Internal Self-Government is understood to mean, an island, country,
> ward, region, area, commune, province, municipality, land, or State within
> a dominion, Kingdom or Confederation which is given the opportunity to
> control its domestic internal affairs. It is autonomous and enjoys self-adminis-
> tration. This is not separation or independence. Other names for Internal Self-
> Government: Self Administration, Home Rule, Self-Determination, Greater
> Autonomy, Devolution of Executive Authority and Decentralization.[24]

The fifty states of the United States of America and the twenty-five cantons and half-cantons in Switzerland, as well as the ten provinces of Canada, were cited as specific examples.

Everette E. John, secretary-treasurer of the Regional Action Committee of the DAC, defined internal self-government the same way in a 4 May 1979 letter to the committee's members. The letter detailed areas that would remain under sole purview of the central government if internal self-government were granted to Tobago. Listed were "defense, foreign policy, coinage, posts, granting of citizenship, internal security and the higher levels of justice".[25]

Vesta John, Everette's wife and also a member of the DAC, echoed the DAC's definition in a letter to the editor of the *Express*. Taking issue with Mervyn Stewart's article titled "Selfish", which appeared in the paper on 19 September 1979, she thought it "necessary to clear up the ignorance and misconception" that internal self-government meant secession.[26] Such a misconception may have been perpetrated by the PNM's implication, both in and outside of Parliament, that Robinson and his followers were really interested in secession. Selwyn Richardson's comment in the House of Representatives during the initial debate on the issue demonstrates this quite well. He stated that Robinson was "asking this honourable House to preside over the liquidation, or rather the fragmentation and disintegration of the Republic of Trinidad and Tobago".[27] Richardson argued that to grant Tobago internal self-government would necessitate amending the constitution of the republic, which would result in "legalized secession". He insisted that such a measure would require Tobago to have its own senate, governor or president and also the authority to pass its own laws, excluding those relating to foreign affairs and defence. Further, he insisted, Tobago would have to establish its own public service and judiciary.[28]

During the parliamentary debate on 14 February 1977, Overand Padmore's view was similarly tunnel-visioned and integrationist. As far as he was concerned, Robinson and Murray were part of the "secession–self-government crowd" and were "putting the people of Tobago at risk [of losing funding from the central government] to satisfy . . . personal aggrandizement", aspiring to be "kings, princess, dukes and lords in this tiny island".[29] This charge is reminiscent of that levelled at A. P .T. James almost twenty years earlier.

The PNM's official definition of internal self-government is found in its 1977 publication *Data Relating to the Question of Internal Self-Government for Tobago*. The opening pages of the book contain two memoranda from Williams, dated 13 May and 15 June 1977. The appearance of the memos and the fact that Williams was the leader of the PNM indicate his sanction of the views of the book. The publication provided the following explanation:

> The term Internal Self-Government when employed without any restriction may be defined as a form of government possessed by a political unit in which that unit more or less controls its own domestic affairs. Its defense and foreign affairs are usually handled by a state from which it would normally have obtained that status by legislation. Internal self-government would in the ordinary course entail that the self-governing territory would have:
>
> (1) A Head of State
> (2) An Executive
> (3) A Parliament
> (4) A Judiciary
> (5) A Civil Service
> (6) Police Force
>
> Possibly its own citizenship, and almost all the institutions associated with an independent state.[30]

It was this definition, "employed without any restriction", that the PNM held and that it presented to the nation. "In view of Williams' opposition to Robinson, the adoption of such a strict definition can be seen", as one DAC leaflet stated, as a "deliberate attempt by others to misinform and scare the masses".[31] Clearly Williams intended to present the definition that came closest to independent statehood in order to convince the citizenry that Robinson's true goal was secession. Notwithstanding, Robinson and the DAC had solid reasons for their position.

The DAC's Case for Internal Self-Government

The DAC's position on internal self-government included political and economic considerations as well as various grievances. It argued that the colonial solution — making Tobago a ward — was a failure. So too were Trinidad's administrative measures vis-à-vis the Department of Tobago Affairs and the Ministry of Tobago Affairs, because these arrangements lacked executive power. The head of the Tobago administration still had to refer matters to Trinidad for approval. The party insisted that Tobago needed a representative, democratic and permanent governing body, independent of the vagaries of party politics. The DAC's spokespersons also expressed gross dissatisfaction that there was no Tobagonian representative in the thirty-one-member Senate. Further, they objected to the fact that representation at the executive level of government depended on voting "in accordance with the majority of the Trinidad electorate . . . [and] the whim of the Prime Minister in forming his Cabinet".[32] Since self-determination was a basic human right guaranteed by the United Nations charter, Tobagonians could not be denied this right.

Movements for greater autonomy in other parts of the world in 1977 informed the DAC's demand for internal self-government, and the party's leaflets cited various examples of the devolution of power. On 26 March 1977 the Republic of the Philippines granted autonomy to a "large area covering the island of Palawan, the Sulu archipelago and roughly half of Mindanao (one of the largest of the Philippine islands)".[33] On 23 March the island of Aruba in the Caribbean decided not to become part of the proposed Independent Netherlands Antilles Federation. Furthermore, by the Barbuda Local Government Act of 1977, Antigua granted Barbuda, a West Indian island much smaller than Tobago, greater autonomy.[34] Thus the DAC showed that granting internal self-government was a legitimate contemporary practice, even among Caribbean states.

The political arguments alone were sufficient justification for internal self-government. However, the DAC's arsenal contained another salvo: its economic rationale (the economic arguments regarding neglect and uneven development have been fully explored earlier). Very little infrastructure for economic development had been put in place in Tobago since its union with Trinidad. The DAC's economic arguments also revolved around the island's identity. One of the party's documents contended, "[T]he economic case for internal self-government for Tobago starts from the indisputable and immutable fact that the island is a geographical and economic entity."[35] Thus economic development in Trinidad "does not and cannot automatically benefit Tobago since important economic resources are not freely transferable between the two islands . . ."[36] Petroleum exploitation in Trinidad, for example, did not create employment opportunities in Tobago. Claims abounded that oil companies in Trinidad had exploited petroleum resources in Tobago's waters without giving the island credit as the source. Tobagonians had to migrate to Trinidad to take advantage of jobs in the country's petroleum sector. By the same token, DAC supporters claimed that the "expansion of industry in Trinidad does not spawn service industries in Tobago – no workers' housing, no plant mainte-nance and repair, no haulage and transport services will develop in the smaller island as a result of industrial expansion in the larger".[37] Only through official policy, such as transfer of revenue via the gov-ernment budget, could Tobago procure any meaningful share of the fruits of national economic development.[38]

However, transfer of national revenue to Tobago via the annual budget had proved problematic. Those funds had strings attached, as they were tied to policies established by the central government. Tobagonians needed an administration with the authority to decide development policy on its own and to allocate funds accordingly. Without that kind of control, the DAC feared that the central government would continue its policies of developing Tobago's economy to complement that of Trinidad. The DAC objected to this policy of dependence[39], a relationship that the government in Trini-dad had fostered with respect to Tobago[40] throughout the history of the union. This policy was manifested in its failure to construct an international airport and a deep-water harbour of international standard that could give Tobagonians independent access to the international commercial community. Providing "direct communi-cations between Tobago and the outside world" was a hallmark of the PNM's 1956 election manifesto.[41] However, the promised deep-water harbour and international airport were conspicuously absent in its 1961 manifesto. Instead there was an emphasis on peasant farming, cottage industries and domestic tourism – "vacationers from Trinidad".[42] Large-scale economic activities in Tobago were not part of the PNM's vision, and Eric Williams considered international tourism anathema to national development.[43]

DAC documents underscored the government's lack of interest in Tobago's economy and its failure to encourage the development of industries on the island. In 1976, out of the 649 firms that received government concessions, only four were in Tobago.[44] These were the Tobago Garment Factory, the Tobago Metal Fabricating Company Limited, Betterbloc Limited and Tobago Banking Services Limited. The issue seemed even more alarming when statistics on government-assisted companies were examined:

(a) Of 36 Assisted Enterprises starting production during 1976 NONE was located in Tobago.

(b) Of 17 Assisted Enterprises in the construction stage during 1976, NONE was in Tobago.

(c) Of 59 Assisted Enterprises in various stages of planning in Trinidad and Tobago in 1976, only two (2) were in Tobago.

(d) NONE of the major new industries projected in the petro-chemical and energy fields involving billions of dollars of new investments will be located in Tobago.[45]

In 1977 Robinson contended that the government was concealing the fact that there were commercial oil deposits in Tobago's waters.[46] His claims proved true. The Deminex-Agip group, a consortium of seven West German companies formed in 1969, acquired a licence in June 1970 to explore for hydrocarbons in the waters off Tobago. In 1975, with the assistance of Tenneco, a US company, Deminex drilled well LL9-1 eight and a half miles (13.6 kilometres) off Tobago's north-west coast; it tested positive for natural gas.[47] A second well, KK6-1, located five miles (eight kilometres) south-west of the first one, also tested positive for gas. The fact that Tobago possessed gas reserves was a powerful argument that Tobago's economic potential could provide adequate financial support for its people.

Apart from the political and economic arguments in favour of internal self-government, the DAC articulated a host of grievances. As stated in chapter 2, grievances are the secondary basis of identity construction. They promote we/they antipathies and demonize the other. By articulating various grievances, Tobagonians strengthened their common bonds and heightened their distrust of and antagonism towards the Trinidadian government.

DAC supporters reiterated the often-made complaints that the island was not receiving its fair share of economic and social services, including education, provision for convenient inter-island communication, water supply, road development and maintenance, internal transport services and jobs.[48] In 1977 Robinson also pointed out that there was no resident judge on the island. He noted that a broken bridge over a river in Parlatuvier had gone unrepaired for many years. That bridge, inherited from the colonial government, was the same one that Williams had used as an example of that government's neglect in his 1956 speech in the legislature. After twenty years in office, his government had done nothing to fix it.[49]

In addition, Tobagonians were annoyed that the government's five- and ten-day temporary jobs under the special works projects were given only to PNM supporters. "The Special Works Programmes must be seen, not only as an important form of patronage to party supporters and clients of the local 'Barons' but also as a medium of control over dissidents."[50] These jobs included cleaning the beaches and other minor projects, which provided ready cash for the lower classes; many in Tobago argued that the day jobs lured the young away from agriculture. "The Special Works projects were infamous for providing a whole day's wage while the labourer worked only for a couple hours each day."[51] The movement away from agriculture made Tobago a net importer of food after the 1950s; prior to that it had been a net exporter and was considered the breadbasket of Trinidad.[52]

Other grievances included the high cost of living in Tobago. In 1979 the cost of living was almost 29 per cent higher than in Trinidad.[53] This was caused in part by the extra cost for freight and handling of goods transhipped from Trinidad, which was caused in turn by the long-standing problem of absence of an international airport or deep-water harbour in Tobago to facilitate direct deliveries from overseas.[54] Shortages of certain food items, especially price-controlled goods with low profit margins, sugar, rice, cheese and butter, were prevalent in Tobago.[55] The lack of adequate storage facilities in Tobago also contributed to this problem.

Tobagonians were also disturbed by the influx of Trinidadian businessmen, especially those of East Indian descent, into Tobago.[56] These businessmen bought land on the island, which Tobagonians found particularly irksome since they considered land as part of their cultural heritage. The purchase of land by these entrepreneurs also drove up property values to a level that Tobagonians could not afford.[57] Tobagonians were incensed when the East Indian firm of Kirpalani's was given permission to build a large department store in the centre of downtown Scarborough, while the town and country planning division had denied Tobagonian businessmen permission to build or even to improve their existing structures.[58] Tobagonians were prevented from building in Scarborough ostensibly because the Scarborough Development Plan, aimed at improving downtown Scarborough, had not been finalized. The development plan did not get off the ground until the 1980s.

The most frequent and nagging grievance continued to be the inconvenience Tobagonians faced in accessing basic government services. They were forced to travel to Trinidad to procure birth, marriage, death and tax clearance certificates, as well as title deeds for real estate. They also went to Trinidad to be interviewed for government jobs, even those located in Tobago.[59] Travelling to Trinidad cost money and time and resulted in lost wages. On many occasions Tobagonians could not get confirmed return reservations on the limited and unreliable air-bridge service; many were forced to stay overnight at the airport in Trinidad.[60] This resulted in a great deal of inconvenience and frustration, especially after a long day spent battling the red tape of government bureaucracy in Port of Spain. Tobagonians were sometimes forced to pay bribes in order to get certain documents from government officials in Trinidad.[61] The need to go to Trinidad for almost everything of importance was a continual thorn in the sides of Tobagonians. The "excessive centralization of the bureaucratic system" was one of the key factors responsible for the problem.[62] The DAC argued that devolution of government power to an elected assembly would alleviate the problems Tobagonians faced.

Other issues plagued Tobagonians. As late as June 1979, a six-member ministerial committee reported on problems dealing with eight key issues on the island. These included shipping cargo from Trinidad to Tobago, inadequate health and sanitation facilities, problems of administration, difficulties in the Tobago County Council, concerns in the Tobago special works division, the condition of the roads, and water and electricity supplies.[63] These grievances, along with social and economic underdevelopment of the island and the disbanding of the Ministry of Tobago Affairs, led Robinson to present his motion in Parliament demanding internal self-government for Tobago. However, the government was slow in implementing the provisions of the internal self-government motion.

The Parliamentary Process: Central Government Filibustering

Approval of the motion for internal self-government was the first phase in the struggle to secure self-government for Tobago. The second phase was tedious and exacting; it involved deliberations of a joint select committee of the government to examine the motion and make recommendations for implementing the measure. This phase also included drafting legislation to give effect to the motion. During this period the DAC became very impatient with the filibustering tactics of the government. The party held rallies to protest the inordinate delay and also tried to put pressure on the government to hasten the process by taking its concerns to the regional community of the Caribbean.

The House of Representatives, at its sitting on 25 February 1977, and the Senate, in session on 1 March, agreed to appoint a joint select committee to make recommendations for effecting the 4 February 1977 parliamentary resolution for granting internal self-government to Tobago.[64] The committee comprised twelve members, six from each house of Parliament.

The meetings of the Joint Select Committee were all held in the Parliament's Chamber of the Red House in Port of Spain. No special arrangements were made to hold even one of the eight meetings in Tobago, and thus Tobagonians wishing to testify before the committee had to travel to Trinidad. DAC supporters were outraged.[65] The first meeting was held on Monday, 9 May 1977. With a 30 September

1977 deadline, the public was given two and a half months to submit comments in writing. Most of the twenty-eight memoranda received before the deadline arrived close to the end of September. Eighteen memoranda came from individuals, three were from political parties (the DAC, the PNM and the Tapia House Movement) and seven were from organizations, including the Trinidad and Tobago Association of Village Councils and the Trinidad and Tobago Chamber of Industry and Commerce.

The committee submitted its report to the House of Representatives on 21 July 1978 – one year and five months after Parliament had agreed to grant Tobago internal self-government. The report noted that, to satisfy the need for the "greatest possible measure of participation" by Tobagonians in the policy-making and implementation stages of matters affecting them, a great degree of devolution of government functions and powers was necessary in the system of internal self-government.[66] Tobago's geographical and other circumstances warranted special consideration. The need for an organization in Tobago to coordinate government functions and services was also emphasized. The committee confirmed that the former arrangements had "resulted in uncertainty, misunderstanding and delay". It acknowledged the need for a government structure with "appropriate constitutional and/or legislative safeguards to ensure permanence".[67]

The committee recommended the appointment of a senior public officer as head of the administration. This person would "supervise the operation of all departments of the Central government located in Tobago and make on-the-spot decisions to ensure that government services [would be] executed with the same efficiency and dispatch as elsewhere in the Unitary State".[68] It was also suggested that, among other things, the administrative structure should provide for issuing of birth, death and marriage certificates in Tobago and registration of title deeds, as well as a facility for initial processing of passports and citizenship documents.

Legislation to provide for the establishment of an elected body called the Tobago Island Council was deemed necessary; that institution would replace the Tobago County Council. The Island Council would have jurisdiction over finance (except foreign borrowing); economic development in the areas of agriculture, industry and tourism; the environment; infrastructure relating to internal communications, water and electricity; physical planning; community services such as education, health, sports, culture and the arts; and "such other subjects as may be needed".[69] The Joint Select Committee also suggested that no committees be specified by the legislation, but that such matters be left to the discretion of the Island Council.[70]

The committee operated from an integrationist standpoint. Thus the recommendations did not really cater to significant devolution of central government power.

> The proposals were almost identical to those which had been advanced four years earlier by the Constitution Commission and fell far short of what the DAC had been asking for. Curiously enough, although the Committee recommended that the function exercisable by the Council would encompass finance and economic development, it was silent on the question as to the taxing power of the Council, and what power the legislature and executive would have to veto or vary decisions of the Island Council, whether such decisions were of a financial, administrative or legislative nature.[71]

Undoubtedly the influence of the PNM on the committee was strong. The DAC did not protest, and accepted the report.

The third major phase of the struggle for internal self-government involved drafting legislation. This phase spanned the period between the submission of the report of the Joint Select Committee and the date that legislation was passed to grant Tobago internal self-government. On 8 September 1978 Lionel Seemungal, senior counsel, was employed to draft the legislation.[72] Seemungal submitted the draft on 20 November 1979, just over one year later. In the interim, Robinson and the DAC supporters became very impatient. Therefore Robinson, also a barrister-at-law, prepared draft proposals for internal self-government for Tobago. The DAC also organized a huge rally at James Park in Scarborough, protesting the delay in implementing the 4 February 1977 resolution of Parliament.[73] At the rally, held on 1 May 1979, Robinson presented his proposals, which he claimed were "unanimously approved by accla-mation . . . of several thousand residents of Tobago".[74] The following day he personally delivered two copies of his proposals to the attor-ney-general, Selwyn Richardson.

In protest of the delay in granting Tobago internal self-government, Robinson moved another motion in Parliament on 22 June 1979: "Be it Resolved: that this House expresses its displeasure at the continu-ing failure of the Government to honour its major obligations to the people of Tobago, and in particular, its commitment to a system of internal self-government on the island."[75] Once again Robinson rehashed the inconveniences that Tobagonians were experiencing, such as paying airfare to Trinidad to obtain birth certificates and other official documents. Robinson emphasized that such realities reflected the government's "deliberate design to reduce Tobago to a state of dependence".[76]

During his speech Robinson charged Seemungal with procras-tination. He also pointed out that the government had not given Seemungal a deadline to complete his work, and that lackadaisical attitude was typical of the government's lack of interest in Tobago.[77] Richardson countered that illness and the sheer immensity of the task was accounting for Seemungal's slow progress. In a letter to Richardson on 26 April 1979, Seemungal had indeed declared that he had been "confined to bed for the past few weeks with a painful and crippling slipped spinal disc" and, further, that as one not specialized "in the severally involved fields of Constitutional Law, Local Government, Legal Drafting and Tobago Affairs", he needed to become familiar with them. Thus he was taking a "thorough, comprehensive and studied approach, rather than a rushed one", which could lead to legislation with serious litigious consequences.[78] By submitting his own draft bill, Robinson highlighted Seemungal's inexperience and put pressure on him and the government to produce the draft legislation.

Winston Murray continued the debate on Robinson's "motion of dis-pleasure". He had been suspended from the DAC during the latter part of 1977 for making public his convictions that Tobago should secede.[79]

Murray had subsequently formed a small political party called the Fargo House Movement, named in honour of A. P. T. "Fargo" James. By founding his own political party, Murray repudiated both Robinson and the PNM government.[80] He rejected the report of the Joint Select Committee and shared his conviction that the government was intent on giving Tobago a "modified form of County Council" instead of internal self-government.[81] He also rejected Robinson's proposed draft bill.

Robinson's motion received support from opposition parliamentarians such as Basdeo Panday, the representative for Couva North and a United Labour Front member. He castigated the government for treating Parliament with "contempt" by not apologizing or showing any contrition over its failure to grant Tobago internal self-government. Two years had passed since Parliament had agreed that Tobago should be granted internal self-government. Despite support from opposition parliamentarians, the motion of displeasure was denied because of insufficient support – eight members voted in favour and sixteen opposed it.[82] Undaunted by that outcome, the DAC continued its protest outside the parliamentary arena.

In October 1979 a three-member delegation from the Tobago Committee for the Defence of Human Rights embarked on what they styled a "Caribbean Mission" to garner regional support for internal self-government for Tobago. The purpose of the mission was to "create a Caribbean awareness of the plight of Tobago in relation to the inordinate delay by government to implement parliamentary approval for internal self-government for the island".[83] The team also planned to disseminate information about human rights violations in Tobago. They visited Grenada, Barbados, St Vincent and St Lucia between 19 and 29 October 1979. Neville S. Gibbes, past president of the Tobago Chamber of Commerce and a practising barrister-at-law; Agatha Keens-Dumas, secretary of the Tobago Christian Council of Churches, president of the Tobago Women's League and secretary of the Tobago branch of the Red Cross Society; and County Councillor Hochoy Charles, also past president of the Tobago Youth Council, comprised the team. The mission, funded by the Caribbean Conference of Churches, met with several government officials and the officers of various organizations.[84] It placed added pressure on Williams and the PNM government to speed up the process of granting greater autonomy to Tobago.[85]

In November 1979, not long after the delegation from the Tobago Committee for the Defence of Human Rights returned home, Seemungal submitted his draft legislation. However, there was still another hurdle to jump. The government rejected the Seemungal draft bill, "An Act to make provision for, and in connection with the Internal Self-Government of Tobago, and all matters incidental thereto", because it gave Tobago too much autonomy. In March 1980 the government publicly presented its objections to the draft bill. Certain portions were deemed contrary to the constitutional reality of the unitary state of Trinidad and Tobago, even though "these very provisions were intended to satisfy some of the recommendations of the Joint Select Committee".[86] As a result, on Friday, 29 February 1980, the Cabinet appointed a committee to consider the Seemungal proposals, along with the attorney-general's comments thereon and their relation to the report of the Joint Select Committee. The committee held five meetings between 25 and 28 February 1980. Based on its findings, the Cabinet and the attorney-general, Selwyn Richardson, rejected major provisions of the Seemungal draft bill.

Their objections were numerous,[87] and a few are highlighted here. Clause 7(c) of the draft bill gave the Tobago representative in Parliament membership on the Island Council. The government thought that this clause would open the way for a Cabinet minister to be subordinate to the chairman of the Island Council and also to the chief secretary, who was given ministerial status. Clauses 49 to 52, which dealt with the responsibilities of the Council and its exercise of executive authority and remuneration, as well as the disqualification and removal of secretaries, were also problematic to the government. These secretaries were to have various portfolios such as health, tourism and sports. The government was concerned that those secretaries would form a "Tobago Cabinet", and asked for clarification on the relationship between the chairman of the Island Council and the chief secretary. The government also had difficulty accepting clauses 58 to 62, which gave the Island Council authority over remuneration and allowances for its employees. The government demanded information about the body to which the Council would be accountable in those matters (in Trinidad and Tobago such matters were routinely presided over by the Salaries Review Commission).

Clause 66 of the Seemungal draft bill also gave absolute privilege – with reference to the law of defamation – to the proceedings of the Island Council. The government stated that such privilege belonged only to Parliament. Clauses 68 and 69 were also objectionable since they empowered the Island Council to make by-laws called council laws. The government wanted Parliament to have a supervisory function over such matters, along with veto power. Clauses 78 to 80 gave the Council authority to appoint a chief clerk, a function already under the jurisdiction of the service commissions department of the government. The power to legislate and impose taxation was the subject of clauses 113 and 114, giving the Island Council unlimited power in that sphere.

The Council's right to borrow funds locally was also rejected by the government. The draft bill gave the Council authority to borrow up to one-third of its expenditure of the previous fiscal year. However, it allowed an increase of that amount if a majority vote of the Council supported it and if the secretary responsible for finance approved it. In the government's view, the Council's power to borrow locally was thus limitless. In addition, the draft bill did not take into account the question of guaranteeing loans. The government insisted that the minister of finance should give his consent before the Council was allowed to borrow money. Similarly, clause 117 allowed the Council to borrow money internationally, via the minister of finance and subject to government approval. The government declared that it was inappropriate for the Council to engage in international financial transactions. It also objected to clauses 153 and 154, which guaranteed that the act establishing the Island Council could not be amended or repealed except by a three-quarters majority of both houses of Parliament. The government contended that such a concession would make it virtually impossible to amend or repeal the act. These were some of the objections the government had to more than thirty clauses or subsections of clauses in the Seemungal draft bill. Given these objections, it rejected the bill in its entirety.

The government published a document containing the Semungal draft bill, its objections to the bill, comments from the attorney-general, the Cabinet's comments and the legislative action needed to give effect to the Cabinet's comments if they were approved. The public was given one month – March 1980 – to express it views on the document in writing. Almost two thousand individuals commented on the government's publication. The majority were residents of Tobago who signed a petition, the preamble of which quoted Article 1 of the International Covenant on Human Rights: "All peoples have the right to self-determination. By virtue of that right they freely determine their political status and freely pursue their economic, social and cultural development." The petitioners supported the Seemungal draft bill unequivocally and demanded its prompt implementation. The petition read, "We the people of Tobago state categorically that we accept the Seemungal Draft Bill as is and, therefore demand its IMMEDIATE IMPLEMENTATION. WE WANT INTERNAL SELF GOVERNMENT FOR TOBAGO, A PERMANENT ADMINISTRATION IN TOBAGO, NOT HERE TODAY AND GONE TOMORROW. WE THY SERVANTS HUMBLY PRAY . . . ."[88]

Letters of support for the draft bill were also sent to the secretary of Cabinet. Many respondents expressed the view that the bill faithfully followed the report of the Joint Select Committee. DAC stalwart Hochoy Charles contended that the government's failure to publish that report had led to confusion among the citizens.[89] Other Tobagonians such as Neville Gibbes of Scarborough, Caedmon Murray of Mesopotamia and Everette E. John, secretary-treasurer of the Tobago Regional Action Committee of the DAC, insisted that the government's rejection of the Seemungal draft bill had resulted in erosion of the authority of Parliament. The Regional Action Committee charged the PNM with pursuing a "rigid one-party line on the issue".[90]

The committee also accused the government of making an "unprecedented attempt . . . to intimidate, prejudice and mange public opinion by publishing its own adverse comments on the Draft Bill, while pretending to await the guidance of the very public opinion before formulating its own opinion".[91] Pamela Nicholson, a DAC member from Mount Pleasant, further castigated the government for including the attorney-general's comments with the Seemungal draft bill: "In my opinion, this method of approach smarts of perfidy and treachery and its main purpose can only be to undermine Tobago's cause, and confuse, bribe and shade the population's understanding of the Draft itself in the Government's quest to tilt opinion in its favor."[92]

Nicholson, Gibbes and Nathaniel Moore of Scarborough believed that the government intended to draft legislation that would institute only an upgraded county council in Tobago instead of a powerful island council with significant executive powers.[93] From that perspective Nicholson declared, "[I]t seems to me that the Government's aim is to maintain its vicious stranglehold and to leave the Island Council totally powerless, and at the same level of a glorified County Council."[94] Gibbes took the same stance: "The thinking seems to be merely concerned with replacing the Tobago County Council with similar limited authority."[95] Moore insisted that "there should be no whittling down of the power and scope of the proposed Island Council".[96] Tobagonians who commented on the government publication indicated that they did not trust the central government to draft legislation that would produce an island council with significant executive powers.

Despite the comments of the public, in July the government made motions in the House and in the Senate rejecting the Seemungal draft bill. Selwyn Richardson's motion in the Senate required the preparation of legislation to establish the Tobago Island Council.[97] As a result, the attorney-general's office prepared the Tobago House of Assembly bill: "to establish the Tobago House of Assembly for the purpose of making better provisions for the administration of the island of Tobago and for matters connected therewith" (hereafter called the THA bill). The THA bill was completed during the month of August and was read for the first time in the House on 5 September 1980. On 12 September the bill passed by a majority vote.

Robinson disapproved of the THA bill because it did not provide for certain measures. These included the resuscitation of agriculture, control and production of water by the people, generation of electricity, control of communications to the outside world, protection of Tobago's environment from pollution, emergency operations in case of natural disasters, moderation of the cost of living, job and career opportunities to stem the tide of migration to Trinidad, and representation in the Senate.[98]

Robinson also objected strenuously to section 21(1) of the bill, which dealt with the functions of the Assembly. This section stated:

> The Assembly shall formulate and implement policy on all matters referred to it by the Minister and the Minister of Finance shall consult the Assembly on matters of national importance such as the annual national budget, development projects and the operation and use of long-term funds as they relate to Tobago and subject to this Act, the Assembly shall be responsible for implementing in Tobago, Government policy relating [*inter alia*] to, (a) Finance, (b) Economic planning.[99]

That clause implied that the Assembly would have to implement the government's policy whether it served Tobago's interest or not, and it was also subject to interpretation. Section 21(1) became a bone of contention and a thorn in the flesh of the Assembly after it was established.

Section 4(c) was also odious to Robinson. It assigned a clerk to the Assembly with responsibility for efficient administration of all its functions.[100] Robinson argued that this clause resulted in overlapping functions and conflict of interest, since the clerk would be appointed by a government agency such as the service commissions department. That department was responsible for appointing all public officials, and under the constitution it was sworn to remain loyal to the government in power. Robinson objected to the Assembly being placed under the jurisdiction of a central government department – the government was giving with one hand and taking back with the other.

In addition, the financial provisions for the Assembly disturbed Robinson. Clause 47 stated:

> Upon the commencement of this Act there shall be appropriated and credited to the [Tobago House of Assembly] Fund, a sum of money which in the opinion of the Minister of Finance is reasonable to enable the Assembly to engage immediately upon the discharge of its functions under this Act.[101]

The bill left the central government with sole authority to determine how much funding the Assembly would receive from the national coffers. The Assembly was not even given a consultative role. The government wanted to retain as much control of the Assembly's operation as possible, and thereby limit its effectiveness.

According to Robinson, the "biggest joke of all" was clause 54, which dealt with allowances for certain officers of the Assembly. The clause stated:

> The President may make regulations prescribing – (a) the allowances to be paid to the Chairman, Deputy Chairman and other members of the Assembly for the purpose of defraying reasonable out-of-pocket expenses; (b) the allowances to be paid to the Chairman for the purpose of defraying the cost of entertainment and reasonable travelling expenses incidental to his office; (c) an honorarium to be paid to the Chairman.[102]

This clause indicated that the officers of the Assembly would not be salaried workers.

Clause 27 was equally unsavoury. It provided for regular monthly meetings of the Assembly and for special meetings convened by the chairman. It also authorized any three Assembly members – one of whom had to be a councillor – to call a meeting of the Assembly if the "Chairman neglects or refuses to call a meeting within seven days of receiving a written request thereof". This small quorum was inadequate to carry on the business of the Assembly.

Robinson's articulation of his objections to the THA bill had gone on for approximately fifty minutes when DAC supporters in the public gallery of the parliamentary chamber burst into applause in agreement. Speaker of the House C. Arnold Thomasos immediately ordered the police to clear the gallery. On that cue Robinson walked out of the meeting, in solidarity with his supporters.

Nonetheless, the debate continued. Winston Murray's criticisms were more biting. He suggested that secession would be the best solution for Tobago. Murray had moved to the very far left of the autonomy continuum. He stated that he and his supporters had raised "our flag" and had sung "our anthem" on 31 December 1977.[103] The flag-raising ceremony, conducted at Fort James in Plymouth, Tobago, not only protested the delay in granting Tobago internal self-government in 1977, it also signalled the Fargo House Movement's repudiation of Trinidadian sovereignty over the island.[104]

During the debate, Murray requested clarification on whether the clerk or the chairman would be the ultimate authority in the Assembly – an issue Robinson had already raised. Murray held that the members of the Assembly should be paid salaries, and he also moved an amendment to clause 20, to increase the term of office in the Assembly from three years, similar to the county councils, to four years.[105]

After other amendments were approved, the Tobago House of Assembly bill was read for the third time and passed by a parliamentary majority. On 23 September 1980, Ellis Clarke, president of the Republic of Trinidad and Tobago, assented to Act No. 37 of 1980, the Tobago House of Assembly Act: "An Act to establish the Tobago House of Assembly for the purpose of making better provision for the administration of the Island of Tobago and for matters connected therewith." Thus Tobago was granted internal self-government.

On 24 November 1980 the first Tobago House of Assembly election in modern times was held. Of an estimated 25,000 people eligible to vote, 15,893 Tobagonians (63.5 per cent of the electorate) showed up at the polls,[106] demonstrating that internal self-government was a significant issue to most Tobagonians. The DAC won eight of the twelve seats contested by capturing 53 per cent of the vote; the PNM garnered 44 per cent and the Fargo House Movement received a paltry 2 per cent of votes.[107] The DAC's success showed that most Tobagonians had separatist leanings and were willing to fully throw off the PNM's yoke. However, their lack of support for the Fargo House Movement indicated their rejection of secession. The PNM's performance was significant. It revealed that many Tobagonians were unsure of what the future would hold under the new system of administration, and perhaps insecure about how the central government would deal with them and their island from that point on. Despite these uncertainties, a new chapter in the history of Tobago had begun.

Presided over by President Clarke, the inaugural meeting of the Assembly took place on Thursday, 4 December 1980. Robinson was elected chairman of the Assembly and Hochoy Charles was appointed leader of Assembly business. Three councillors were also selected: Dr Jacob D. Elder, Everette E. John and James Ivan Ogieste.

The Assembly had many confrontations with the central government in the first few years of its operation. The issue of significant devolution of central government power and the allocation of financial resources bedevilled their relationship. The persistent tension between the islands also strengthened Tobagonian identity.

The tense relations between the Tobago House of Assembly and the central government during the past decades continue to lead some Tobagonians to think that secession – though rejected in 1980 – remains an option that Tobagonians will never give up. While the ghosts of James and Norton still haunt its historic forts and scenic waterfalls, many years after the granting of internal self-government the moderating sea breezes of politicians such as Robinson continue to have a calming effect on the populace. An assessment of the post-1980 era of Tobago's relationship with Trinidad will be critical for providing clues as to whether Tobagonians feel that they are partners in the union or that they are still ill-perceived by their countrymen because they continue to receive financial allocations from the central government. More important, Tobagonians will have had sufficient time to reflect on what self-rule has meant for them and how it has affected their identity and their future prospects.

Notes

Abbreviations

Admin.	Administration
CEO	Chief Executive Officer
Circ.	Circular
CO	Colonial Office (papers)
Confl	Confidential
CP	Council Paper
CSO	Central Statistical Office
DAC	Democratic Action Congress
Debates	Trinidad and Tobago Legislative Council Debates (1931–61)
Desp.	Despatch
EEJL	Personal library of Everette E. John
encl.	Enclosure
Hansard	*Parliamentary Debates* (from 1962 onward)
HCL	personal library of Hochoy Charles
HoR	House of Representatives
Memo	Memorandum
Mins Exec Co	*Minutes of the Executive Council*
Mins Leg Co	*Minutes of the Legislative Council*
PMO	Prime Minister's Office

PNM	People's National Movement
PRO	Public Record Office
Rpt(s)	Report(s)
Tdad	Trinidad
Tgo	Tobago
TPA	Tobago Planters Association

Chapter 1

1. *Microsoft Encarta Encyclopedia 2000*, "Trinidad and Tobago".

2. Ibid.

3. Thomas C. Holt, *The Problem of Freedom: Race, Labor, and Politics in Jamaica and Britain, 1832–1938* (Baltimore: Johns Hopkins University Press, 1992), 263–309.

4. Michael Anthony, *Historical Dictionary of Trinidad and Tobago* (Lanham, MD: Scarecrow Press, 1997), 600–601.

5. Ibid.; [Trinidad and Tobago], *Education 1800–1962: Trinidad and Tobago Independence Exhibition* (Port of Spain: Government Printing Office, 1962), 2, states that the Education Ordinance of 1870 recognized two types of schools: "the State or Government Schools supported wholly by public funds, and the Assisted Denominational Schools receiving financial aid from the Government".

6. Anthony, *Historical Dictionary*, 600–601.

7. Ibid.

8. Roger Scruton, *A Dictionary of Political Thought* (New York: Harper and Row, 1982), 213.

9. Anthony D. Smith, "Nationalism: A Trend Report and Bibliography", *Current Sociology* 21, no. 3 (1973): 8–52.

10. This study relies heavily on the typology of Caribbean identity advanced by Ralph R. Premdas, who was kind enough to share his ideas with me and also to provide copies of his work on the subject, besides pointing me to other useful material. I owe him a great debt of gratitude.

11. Ralph R. Premdas, "Ethnic Identity in the Caribbean: Decentering a Myth" (keynote address to Association for the Study of Ethnicity and Nationalism, London School of Economics and Political Science, 21 March 1995), 10.

12. Ibid., 11.

13. Ibid.

14. Ibid., 11, 48.

15. Ibid., 48.

16. A. N. R. Robinson, "Unity and Change in the Caribbean Region", in *Forging a New Democracy* (Freeport, Trinidad: HEM Printers, 1985), 44.

17. Ralph R. Premdas, "Public Policy and Ethnic Conflict", *Management of Social Transformations (MOST)*, Discussion paper series no. 12 (1997): 7.

18. Ibid., 7, 8.

19. Premdas, "Ethnic Identity", 22.

20. Ibid., 13, 14.

21. Ralph R. Premdas, "Identity and Secession in Nevis", in *Identity, Ethnicity and Culture in the Caribbean*, ed. Ralph R. Premdas (St Augustine: School of Continuing Studies, [1999]), 457.

22. Premdas, "Ethnic Identity", 23.

23. Ibid.

24. Ibid.

25. Ibid.

26. David L. Niddrie, *Tobago* (Middleton: Litho Press, 1980), 99.

27. Susan Craig-James, "The Evolution of Society in Tobago: 1838 to 1900" (PhD diss., London School of Economics and Political Science, 1995).

28. Ralph R. Premdas, "The Caribbean: Ethnic and Cultural Diversity and a Typology of Identities", in *Identity, Ethnicity and Culture in the Caribbean*, ed. Ralph R. Premdas (St Augustine: School of Continuing Studies, [1999]): 7.

29. Ibid., 7, 8.

30. Ibid., 8.

31. Carl Campbell, "Tobago and Trinidad: Problems of Alignment of Their Education Systems at Union: 1889–1931", *Antilia* 1, no. 3 (April 1987): 21–27.

32. Ibid., 22.

33. Ibid.

Chapter 2

1. Craig-James, "Evolution", 54.

2. Craig-James explains that up to 1897, Tobago, Fiji, British Honduras, St Helena, the Falklands, the Turks Islands, St Helena and Papua New Guinea were the only places in the British Empire without the telegraph: "The telegraph widened the gap between places with and without it." Ibid., 422. Tobago received the telegraph around 1906–7.

3. Reverend William Carrington (educator and Anglican clergyman), unrecorded interview by author, Scarborough, 23 January 1998.

4. Professor Edrick Gift, interview by author, tape recording, St Augustine, 26 February 1998.

5. Allan Richards (chief clerk, Tobago House of Assembly), interview by author, tape recording, Scarborough, 10 February 1998.

6. F. E. Nunes, "A Ministry and Its Community: Tobago – A Case Study in Participation", *Social and Economic Studies* 23, no. 2 (June 1974): 176.

7. Gift, interview. For examples of dialect phrases, proverbs and their meaning, see H. B. Meikle, "Tobago Villagers in the Mirror of Dialect", *Caribbean Quarterly* 4, no. 2 (December 1955): 154–60; and Verlene Bobb-Lewis, "Proverbs", and Winford James, "Tobagonian Dialectology: Form and Character", both in *Conference on Culture and the Cultural Heritage* (Scarborough, Tobago: n.p., 1984). See also Niddrie, *Tobago,* 106, 107.

8. Niddrie, *Tobago,* 105, erroneously contends that many of the lighter-skinned people in Tobago came from other islands, such as Grenada.

9. Carrington, interview, 23 January 1998; Robert P. Ingram, "Damsel in Distress", *Weekend Express,* 4 October 1969; "Tobago Sons Are Responsible", *Trinidad Guardian,* 10 January 1970.

10. Nunes, "Ministry", 177; Clarence Warner (justice of the peace), interview by author, tape recording, Government House Road, 27 January 1998.

11. Carrington, interview.

12. Roger D. Abrahams, "Public Drama and Common Values in Two Caribbean Islands", offprint no. 82, Institute of Latin American Studies, University of Texas at Austin, reprinted from *Trans-action* (July–August 1968): 62–71. Abrahams includes a significant discussion on the spirit of cooperation among Tobagonians, especially those in the town of Plymouth, where he did most of his investigation.

13. Gift, interview.

14. Ibid.

15. Doddridge Alleyne (retired permanent secretary, Office of the Prime Minister), interview by author, Petit Valley, 19 November 2000.

16. Joe Radcliffe, "In Crusoe's Isle I Found a Tropical Paradise", *Sunday Mirror,* 30 August 1964, 16.

17. Ibid.

18. Ibid.

19. Ibid.

20. Horace Leighton-Mills, "Tobago's Just One Big Happy Family", *Express,* 18 January 1976, 11.

21. Ibid.

22. Ibid.

23. Ibid.

24. Therese Mills, "Everybody Wants Tourism for Tobago", *Sunday Guardian,* 5 November 1972, 8.

25. Ibid.

26. Niddrie, *Tobago,* 102.

27. "The Question Now Is: To Secede or Not to Secede", *Express,* 28 October 1969, 5.

28. Selwyn Ryan, "Tobago's Quest for Autonomy: From Colony to Ward to . . .", *Caribbean Review* 14, no. 2 (1985): 7.

29. Ibid., 8. Ryan also provides some useful details on religious diversity in the country: "The 1980 census shows Roman Catholics in Trinidad and Tobago constitute 33.6 percent of the population, Hindus 25 percent, Anglicans 15 percent, Muslims 5.9 percent, Presbyterians 3.9 percent, Pentecostals 2.5 percent, Baptists 2.4 percent, Seventh Day Adventists, 1.5 percent, Methodists 1.4 percent, Jehovah's Witnesses, 0.8 percent and others 8 percent. In Tobago the distribution is radically different. Anglicans, the largest denominational group, make up a full 35 percent of the population, followed by the Seventh Day Adventists 10.6 percent, Methodists 10 percent, Roman Catholics 9.5 percent, Pentecostals 5.6 percent, Baptists 2.4 percent, Jehovah's Witnesses 0.73 percent, Hindus 0.45 percent and Muslims 0.26 percent."

30. Eric Roach, "Why Nearby Tobago Is So Different". This article was found in the newspaper clipping files on Tobago at the Heritage Library in Port of Spain, Trinidad. From the internal evidence the article appears to have been written before 1975 and most likely between 1972 and 1973, probably for the *Trinidad Guardian,* for which Roach wrote another article, titled "Tobago Dialect Is Not Pot Pourri", in the 13 April 1972 issue of the paper. In the latter article Roach was responding to Horace Leighton-Mills's article "Tobago Lingo: A Pot Pourri", *Trinidad Guardian,* 7 April 1972. Calls for secession from Dr Rhodil Norton and others triggered an ongoing debate on the culture of Tobagonians in 1972 and 1973.

31. Ibid.

32. Ibid.

33. Ibid.

34. Ibid.

35. Ibid.

36. "Disenchanted", "Tobagonians Resent Premier's Attitude", *Trinidad Guardian,* 3 October 1960.

37. Fitzroy Fraser, "Independence Movement in Tobago", *Gleaner,* 8 February 1961. *Picong* and *fatigue* refer to negative and derogatory statements apparently made in jest but most times based on reality or on the perceptions of others. They are meant to hurt and embarrass the people about whom the comments are made.

38. Roach, "Why Nearby Tobago".

39. Ibid.

40. Ibid.

41. Ibid.

42. Willis E. Lewis, "Tobago – Restrospect and Prospect", *Tobagonian,* June 1940, 15.

43. Premdas, "Identity and Secession", 451.

44. Ryan, "Tobago's Quest", 7. Ryan states that the 1980 census put Tobago's African-descent population at 93.5 per cent, as opposed to Trinidad's 40.8 per cent.

45. Premdas, "Identity and Secession", 452.

46. On various aspects of culture see other papers in *Conference on Culture and the Cultural Heritage* (Scarborough, Tobago: n.p., 1984) and various articles in the *Tobagonian,* a monthly magazine published between 1938 and 1948. One particularly useful article is Thomas A. Telemaque, "Customs in Crusoe's Isle", *Tobagonian,* June 1940, 9–13.

47. Ryan, "Tobago's Quest", 8.

48. Bakes are made of flour dough flattened into a circle and baked in an oven or iron pot over a wood fire. Chocolate tea is made from dried roasted cocoa beans that are pounded in a mortar until the mixture becomes warm and viscous; it is then rolled into a ball and left to solidify. The chocolate ball is grated and put to boil in water with bay leaves, other spices and milk, and sweetened with sugar. The "tea" has a very robust aroma.

49. C. R. Ottley, *Tobago Legends and West Indian Lore* (Georgetown: *Daily Chronicle,* 1950), 49. See also C. R. Blackette, "The Len Han: Tobago's Traditional Fold Co-operative", in *Conference on Culture and the Cultural Heritage* (Scarborough, Tobago: n.p., 1984); and Liley

Reid (close associate of A. P. T. James), interview by author, tape recording, Hyatts-ville, MD, 24 November 2000.

50. Ottley, *Tobago Legends,* 49. See also Abrahams, "Public Drama", for a discussion of Tobago's communal ways, especially in the town of Plymouth.

51. Ottley, *Tobago Legends,* 50.

52. Ibid., 51.

53. Ryan, "Tobago's Quest", 8.

54. Ibid., 8.

55. J. D. Elder, "Tobago's Peculiar Culture", in *Conference on Culture and the Cultural Heritage* (Scarborough, Tobago: n.p., 1984).

56. Elder, "Tobago's Peculiar Culture".

57. Ibid.

58. Ibid.

59. Ibid., 5.

60. Ibid.

61. Ibid., 11.

62. Ibid.

63. Ibid.

64. C. R. Ottley, "How They Dance the Reel in Tobago", *Tobagonian,* June 1941, 19–22; J. D. Elder, "The Tobago Reel Dance", in *Conference on Culture and the Cultural Heritage* (Scarborough, Tobago: n.p., 1984). Niddrie, in *Tobago,* 99–100, tells a story of a seventy-six-year-old man he met in the Scarborough market who related his grandparents' account of the arrival of indentured Africans. The old man stated that on their first free day, a Sunday, they "hollowed out the trunk of a silk cotton tree, stretched a hide over it, and proceeded to beat out a wild dance rhythm in front of the Methodist Church". Tobago continued to have direct infusions of liber-ated Africans into the 1860s.

65. Elder, "Tobago's Peculiar Culture", 12.

66. Ibid.

67. J. D. Elder, "Tobago Folk Songs", in *Conference on Culture and the Cultural Heritage* (Scarborough, Tobago: n.p., 1984).

68. Elder, "Tobago's Peculiar Culture", 12.

69. Elder, "Tobago Folk Songs".

70. Premdas, "Identity and Secession", 454.

71. Ibid.

72. Rita Pemberton, "The Emergence of a Peasantry in Tobago and Its Impact on the Colony of Trinidad and Tobago 1838–1950", *Antilia* 1, no. 3 (April 1987): 38–49.

73. C. E. R. Alford, "A Settler in Tobago", *Tobagonian,* September 1938, 19.

74. George S. C. M. Robley (former county councillor), interview by author, tape recording, Goodwood, 25 January 1998.

75. Craig-James, "Evolution", 119, 120. Craig-James further states: "Central to the transition from slavery was the provision ground/internal marketing complex, through which the enslaved asserted their humanity, enterprise, dignity and desire to

accumulate. In the attachment to the provision grounds and the markets, we discern the desire for a new order struggling to free itself from the integuments of the old" (p. 122).

76. Ibid., 124.

77. Ibid., 155–63.

78. Granville St John Orde Browne, *Labour Conditions in the West Indies* (London: Her Majesty's Stationery Office, 1939), 123–25.

79. Gift, interview.

80. *Debates,* 7 June 1957; PNM, "PNM 1956 Election Manifesto", in *Major Party Documents,* vol. 1 ([Port of Spain]: [1966]).

81. Craig-James, "Evolution", 356, shows that a pattern of migration to Trinidad developed soon after the union. In 1891 there were 3,307 Tobagonians in Trinidad and 16,942 in Tobago. In 1901 the comparable figures were 5,334 and 17,241 (p. 354). "Thus between 1891 and 1901 the Tobago-born living in Trinidad increased by 60 per cent, and the proportion of Tobagonians living in Trinidad increased from 16.3 per cent to 23.6 per cent. Expressed another way, the increase of Tobagonians in Trinidad between 1891–1901 was five times the increase of the Tobago population" (p. 398).

82. Before 1961 Tobago had one seat in the Legislative Council; after that date the island was divided into two electoral constituencies.

83. Quoted in Selwyn Ryan, *Revolution and Reaction: Parties and Politics in Trinidad and Tobago 1970–1981* (St Augustine, Trinidad: Institute of Social and Economic Research, University of the West Indies, 1989), 119.

84. Learie B. Luke, "Tobago's Struggle for Internal Self-Government 1970–1980" (MA thesis, Morgan State University, 1992), 100.

85. Premdas, "Identity and Secession", 467.

86. Ibid.

87. A. N. R. Robinson, *The Mechanics of Independence: Patterns of Political and Economic Transformation in Trinidad and Tobago* (Cambridge: MIT Press, 1971), 24.

88. Reid, interview.

89. Premdas, "Identity and Secession", 473.

90. *Debates,* 31 July 1959, 80–81.

91. Ryan, "Tobago's Quest", 7–9, 38–39.

92. *Debates,* 14 April 1950, 783.

93. Peoples' National Movement Special Convention, *Perspective for the New Society: Peoples' Charter 1956,* revised (n.p., 1970), iii.

94. "Tobago Welcomes You", *Tobagonian,* April 1947, 4.

95. A. N. R. Robinson became prime minister of the country in 1981; under his government a deep-water harbour and an international airport were built in Tobago.

96. Selwyn H. H. Carrington, "The Union of Tobago and Trinidad: The Emergence of Underdevelopment and Dependency", in *Forging a New Democracy,* ed. Ralph Sebastien (Freeport, Trinidad: HEM Printers, 1985), 55–66; see also J. D. Elder, "The Dependence Syndrome: Tobago as a Special Case with Reference to the Areas of Politics and Economics", in the same work, 67–71.

97. Luke, "Tobago's Struggle", 80.

98. The political system in Trinidad and Tobago operated in the following manner: Under Crown Colony government, a majority of members of the Legislative Council represented the government's interests. They were paid senior public servants and were called official members. These included the colonial secretary and the attorney-general. There were also nominated members chosen by the governor, as well as elected members. The nominated members were expected to serve the government's interests, but they represented the planter, merchant and industrial classes of society. The Legislative Council made laws for the colony. The Executive Council formulated government policy; it comprised senior government officials such as the colonial secretary, attorney-general, auditor-general, receiver-general, commandant of the local forces and others. In 1956 party politics was introduced to the colony, and the party that garnered the most votes in the general elections became the ruling party. It was allowed to chose the chief minister, who carried on government business, although the governor was still the head of state. In 1959 ministerial government was introduced and the chief minister became the premier. He chose his Cabinet, which replaced the Executive Council as the chief policy-making organ of government. In 1962 Trinidad and Tobago became an independent nation and the premier became the prime minister. The Legislative Council became Parliament, which had an elected lower chamber called the House of Representatives and a nominated upper house called the Senate. In 1976 Trinidad and Tobago became a republic with a president as head of state. However, because the country follows the Westminster style of government, the prime minister is the one who has control over the government. Cabinet remains the highest locus of executive power.

99. *Hansard* (House of Representatives), 28 January 1977, 1361.

100. Luke, "Tobago's Struggle", 103.

101. Ibid., 83.

102. *Hansard* (HoR), 4 February 1977, 1400.

103. Ralph R. Premdas and Hugh Williams, "Tobago: The Quest for Self-Determination in the Caribbean", *Canadian Review of Studies in Nationalism* 19, nos. 1–2 (1992): 121.

Chapter 3

1. See Table 1.

2. CO 288/28: *Minutes of the Legislative Council,* 24 December 1877, 252.

3. Trinidad and Tobago, *Historical Documents of Trinidad and Tobago,* no. 3, *Tobago Hurricane of 1847* ([Port of Spain]: Government Printery, 1966.).

4. Susan Craig-James, "Milch Cow or Hard Sucking Calf: The Joining of Trinidad and Tobago and Its Aftermath, 1884–1948" (paper presented at the conference Tobago and Trinidad: One Hundred Years Together, University of the West Indies, St Augustine, Trinidad, 16–18 October 1998), 5. I am indebted to Dr Craig-James for giving me permission to cite her work.

5. Ibid., 6.

6. A casting vote is a deciding vote given by the chairman of an assembly in cases where the votes of the members are tied.

7. Craig-James, "Milch Cow", 6.

8. Ibid., 10.

9. Ibid., 7.

10. Ibid.

11. Ibid.

12. Ibid., 8.

13. Ibid. See also Holt, *Problem of Freedom,* 263–309.

14. Craig-James, "Milch Cow", 8.

15. Bridget Brereton, "Post Emancipation Protest in the Caribbean: The 'Belmanna Riots' in Tobago, 1876", *Caribbean Quarterly* 30 (1984): 115.

16. Craig-James, in "Milch Cow", 9, explains that Grenada and St Vincent were converted to wholly nominated legislatures in 1876. Like Tobago, their legislative councils came to have three nominated unofficial members, three officials and a lieutenant-governor who had sole initiative over money votes. Regarding the proposed Windward Islands federation, the Barbados confederation riots of 1876 led the 1883 Royal Commission to recommend a federation without Barbados, but the colonies in the Windward group rejected such proposals in 1884.

17. The governors were paid from two sources: the British government and the colonial government.

18. CO 288/28: Gore to Dundas, 1 November 1878, in *Mins Leg Co,* 19 June 1880, 293; C. R. Ottley, *The Story of Tobago: Robinson Crusoe's Island in the Caribbean* (London: Longman Caribbean, 1973), 90–91; C. R. Ottley, *The Complete History of the Island of Tobago in the West Indies* (Port of Spain: Guardian Commercial Printery, [1950]), 66.

19. CO 288/28: Gore to Dundas, 1 November 1878, 293.

20. CO 288/28: *Mins Leg Co,* 23 October 1879, 278b.

21. In the British West Indies the official members of the Legislative Council were those appointed to positions in the establishment, such as the colonial secretary, attorney-general, solicitor-general, auditor-general, director of public works, surgeon-general and receiver-general. They represented the government's interests on the Council. The unofficial members were nominated to the Council by the governor to represent the planting, commercial and industrial interests of the colony.

22. CO 288/28: *Mins Leg Co,* 12 June 1880, 292.

23. Ibid., 25 February 1878, 254.

24. Ibid., 16 February 1880, 281.

25. Ibid. Planters never liked to raise revenue through taxation, and did so only after they had virtually no choice.

26. Governors normally had a local salary paid by the Assembly. They also had a home salary paid from taxes taken from the colonies.

27. CO 288/28: *Mins Leg Co,* 5 March 1880, 285b. The export tax was originally imposed to provide funds for immigration. Given the "depressed state of the Sugar Market" the planters argued that the export tax threatened "total extinction" of the sugar industry. Tobago was never able to afford immigration except for a few hundred liberated Africans; some Barbadians and Grenadians also settled in Tobago in the latter part of the nineteenth century.

28. Ibid., 19 June 1880, 293b, 294.

29. Craig-James, "Milch Cow", 10.

30. CO 288/30: "Abstract of Revenue and Expenditure for the Year 1883", in *Minutes of the Proceedings of the Legislative Council of Tobago for the Half-Year Ended 30th June, 1884*, 59.

31. Eric Williams, *History of the People of Trinidad and Tobago* (London: Andre Deutsch, 1963), 136.

32. Ottley, *Story of Tobago*, 89; CO 321/99: Young to Stanhope, 29 September 1886, Tobago, Desp. 17688, Domestic. John Young, the trustee of the Gillespie firm, declared that there were "19 estates in which the firm were concerned".

33. Craig-James, "Milch Cow", 3.

34. CO 321/99: Young to Stanhope, 29 September 1886.

35. CO 288/30: *Mins Leg Co*, 25 February 1885, 78.

36. Ibid.

37. Ibid.

38. Ibid.

39. Ibid., 27 October 1886, 107b.

40. Williams, *History of the People*, 137.

41. CO 295/311: Robinson to Granville, 20 August 1886, encl. Robinson to Sendall, 20 August 1886, 162–68.

42. CO 295/311: Robinson to Granville, 162–68.

43. Craig-James, "Evolution", 485.

44. Ottley, in *Complete History*, 5, explains that in 1880, in order to reduce expenditure on the establishment, the positions of lieutenant-governor and colonial secretary were combined; the officer holding the new position was called the administrator.

45. CO 321/103: Desp. 2423, encl. Sendall to Stanhope, 20 January 1887.

46. Ibid.

47. Unofficial members of the legislature were nominated by the governor.

48. CO 288/30: *Mins Leg Co*, 19 January 1887, 113b.

49. Ibid., 113b–14.

50. Ibid.

51. Ibid.

52. Ibid.

53. Craig-James, "Evolution", 486.

54. Ottley, *Complete History*, 67.

55. CO 288/30: *Mins Leg Co*, 19 January 1887, 113b–14.

56. Craig-James, "Evolution", 489.

57. CO 321/103: Desp. 2429, 23 January 1887.

58. CO 298/43: CP 32 of 1887. See also CO 298/43: *Mins Leg Co*, 8 March and 5 April 1887.

59. CO 298/43: CP 32 of 1887.

60. Ibid.

61. Ibid.

62. CO 295/313: Desp. 6301, 18 March 1887, encl. Robinson to Holland, 18 March 1887, 404–9.

63. "Annexation", *New Era,* 11 January 1889.

64. CO 298/43: *Mins Leg Co,* 8 March 1887.

65. CO 288/30: *Mins Leg Co,* 11 May 1887, 115b.

66. CO 295/31: Desp. 6233, encl. Robinson to Holland, 9 March 1887.

67. Ibid.

68. Ottley, *Complete History,* 67.

69. Ibid.

70. CO 295/313: Desp. 4928, encl. "Draft Minutes", 23 March 1887, 244–48.

71. CO 288/30: *Mins Leg Co,* 11 May 1887, 115b. The third part of the resolution requested that the British government take the necessary steps to give effect to the union.

72. CO 289/5: *Tobago Gazette,* 15 December 1888, 209–13.

73. Ibid., 210.

74. Ibid., 209–13.

75. CO 289/5: "Government Notice No. 95", *Tobago Gazette,* 15 December 1888, 213.

Chapter 4

1. In Tobago the peasantry and the labouring class are the same, since an agro-proletariat solely dependent on wage labour did not develop after emancipation.

2. CO 295/322: Hay to colonial secretary, 23 May 1889, 454–66.

3. CO 288/30: "Remarks of the Commissioner at the First Meeting of the Financial Board", 31 May 1889, 147–47b.

4. CO 295/321: Desp. 1407, Robinson to Knutsford, 2 January 1889; also Minutes of Hales and Wingfield, 11–15.

5. CO 295/321: Desp. 1408, Robinson to Knutsford, 2 February 1889.

6. For an extended treatment of Gorrie, see Bridget Brereton, *Law, Justice and Empire: The Colonial Career of John Gorrie 1829–1892* (Kingston: University of the West Indies Press, 1997).

7. CO 295/321: Desp. 2438, Robinson to Knutsford, 11 January 1889, 79–82.

8. Ibid.

9. Ibid., encl. Gorrie to Robinson, 31 December 1888, 84–87.

10. CO 295/321: Desp. 55, 26 February 1889, encl. Hay to Colonial Secretary, 22 February 1889, 451–54.

11. Ibid., 84–87.

12. CO 295/321: Minutes of Wingfield, 22 March 1889, 450–51. A minute is a brief note or summary in writing of something to be remembered; to minute is to make a brief note or minute.

13. CO 295/321: Minutes of C. A. H. to Wingfield, 21 March 1889, 449–50.

14. Brereton, *Law, Justice and Empire,* 261. Chapter 8 deals with Gorrie's administration in Tobago from 1889 to 1892.

15. Ibid., 260.

16. These owners most likely would have come from Tobago, Trinidad and Grenada, where cocoa was already being grown successfully.

17. Brereton, *Law, Justice and Empire,* 261.

18. Ibid.

19. Ibid., 262.

20. Ibid.

21. CO 295/321: Minutes of S. Oliver, 16 March 1889, 463–65.

22. CO 295/321: Minutes of Wingfield, 16 March 1889, 465b.

23. CO 295/321: Confl, Robinson to Knutsford, 28 February 1889, 467–70.

24. Ibid.

25. Brereton, *Law, Justice and Empire,* 263. One pound sterling is made up of twenty shillings; twelve pence equal one shilling.

26. CO 295/321: Confl, Robinson to Knutsford, 28 February 1889, 467–70.

27. Ibid.

28. Robinson had spent six days in Tobago (February 9–14); Hay's letter was dated 16 February.

29. CO 295/321: Robinson to Knutsford, 28 February 1889, encl. no. 1, Hay to Robinson, private, 16 February 1889, 471–72.

30. Ibid. A puisne judge (pronounced *puny*) is a junior associate judge, one of inferior rank.

31. Ibid.

32. Ibid., encl. no. 3, Browne to Hay, 16 February 1889, 474–76.

33. CO 295/321: Robinson to Knutsford, 28 February 1889, 474–76.

34. Ibid.

35. Ibid.

36. Ibid.

37. CO 295/321: Confl desp., 28 February 1889, minutes of Oliver, 16 March 1889, 463b.

38. CO 295/321: Robinson to Knutsford, 28 February 1889, 474–76.

39. CO 295/321: Confl desp., 28 February 1889, 465.

40. Ibid.

41. Ibid.

42. CO 295/321: Robinson to Knutsford, 15 March 1889, encl. Hay to Byles, 28 February 1889, 582–84.

43. CO 295/321: Robinson to Knutsford, 15 March 1889, 577–78.

44. CO 295/321: Confl desp., 28 February 1889, minutes of Wingfield, 16 March 1889, 465b.

45. Ibid.

46. CO 295/321: Robinson to Knutsford, 15 March 1889, 582–84.

47. Ibid.

48. Ibid.

49. Ibid., 30 March 1889, encl. "Ferment in Tobago", *Public Opinion,* 20 March 1889, 794–96.

50. CO 295/321: Robinson to Knutsford, 30 March 1889, 794–96.

51. Ibid., encl. no. 4, Gorrie to Robinson, 8 March 1889, 591–94.

52. Brereton, *Law, Justice and Empire,* 263, cites the Trinidad newspaper *Public Opinion* of 4 June 1889. The paper employed a Tobago correspondent.

53. Brereton, *Law, Justice and Empire,* 264.

54. CO 295/321: Robinson to Knutsford, 591–94.

55. Ibid.

56. Ibid., 15 March 1889, 577–78.

57. CO 295/321: Desp. 87, minutes of Knutsford, 4 April 1889, 629–30; Brereton, *Law, Justice and Empire,* 265.

58. Brereton, *Law, Justice and Empire,* 265.

59. Ibid.

60. Craig-James, "Evolution", 492, shows that by this time coloureds and blacks were beginning to own estates on the island. By 1899, of the "new planters", nine were white, six were coloured, eight were black and there were eleven others. Among the "old planters", nine were white, eleven were coloured, two were black and there was one other.

61. Ibid., 491.

62. Ibid., 496

63. CO 295/321: Robinson to Knutsford, 27 March 1889, encl. Hay to Robinson, 4 March 1889, 723–26.

64. CO 295/321: Robinson to Knutsford, 27 March 1889, 720–21.

65. Ibid., 723–26.

66. Ibid.

67. CO 295/321: Desp. 96, 27 March 1889, minutes of Edward Wingfield, 25 April 1889, 722. Llewellyn was a former lieutenant-governor of Tobago who effectively managed the finances of the government, keeping it from bankruptcy.

68. CO 289/47: CP 49 of 1891, "Tobago Financial Returns" for 1890.

69. CO 295/340: Broome to Marquess of Ripon, 11 September 1892, 118–33.

70. Ibid.

71. Ibid., 118–32.

72. Ibid., 131–32.

73. CO 295/440: Minutes of C. A. H., 5 October 1892, 118.

74. CO 295/340: Minutes of Wingfield, 6, 8 and 18 October 1892, 118–19 and two unnumbered pages following; CO 295/340: Broome to Ripon, 11 September 1892, 122–33. On his visit to Tobago Broome had virtually forced Hay to resign instead of suspending him; he had found Hay very ill and "quite unfit for duty".

75. CO 295/340: Minutes of Wingfield, 6, 8 & 18 October 1892, 118–19 and two unnumbered pages.

76. CO 289/6: *Tobago Gazette,* 14 October 1892, 161.

77. Ibid., 162.

78. Ibid.

79. CO 295/346: Fowler to Ripon, 3 July 1893, encl. Low to colonial secretary, 28 December 1892, 8, 9.

80. CO 295/346: Fowler to Ripon, 3 July 1893, encl. Low to colonial secretary, 13 May 1893, 15–24.

81. CO 295/346: Fowler to Ripon, 3 July 1893, 15–24.

82. Ibid.

83. Ibid., encl. John Fanning to colonial secretary, 30 and 31 December 1892, 9–11.

84. CO 295/346: Fowler to Ripon, 3 July 1893, encl. Fowler to governor, 31 December 1892, 11–12.

85. CO 295/346: Ripon to Broome, draft, 6 October 1893, 27–28.

86. CO 298/51: *Mins Leg Co,* 4 December 1893, 108–9.

87. Craig-James, "Evolution", 507, 508.

88. Ibid., 507.

89. CO 295/348: Broome to Ripon, 11 December 1893, encl. Low to colonial secretary, 20 November 1893, 474–78.

90. CO 295/348: Broome to Ripon, 11 December 1893, encl. no. 1, "Petitioners to the Marquess of Ripon", 11 December 1893, 479–80.

91. CO 295/348: Broome to Ripon, 11 December 1893, 479–80.

92. Craig-James, "Evolution", 508.

93. CO295/348: Broome to Ripon, 11 December 1893, 474–78.

94. CO 295/348: Minutes of C. A. H. to Wingfield, 11 December 1893, 470–71.

95. CO295/348: Broome to Ripon, 11 December 1893, 474–78.

96. CO 295/348: Minutes of Wingfield, 20 January 1894, 472.

97. CO 295/348: Ripon to Broome, draft, 30 January 1894, 508–9.

98. CO 295/351: Broome to Ripon, 3 March 1894, encl. no. 1, CP 21 of 1894; Tobago, *Report of Select Committee of the Council on the Allowance to Tobago in Respect of the Loss Sustained by That Island in Customs Duties,* 369–71.

99. CO 295/351: Broome to Ripon, 3 March 1894, 369–71.

100. Ibid.

101. Ibid.

102. Ibid., encl. "Petition of Financial Board", [undated], 372–73.

103. CO 295/351 Broome to Ripon, 3 March 1894, 366–68.

104. CO 295/351: Minutes of Oliver, 23 March 1894, 363.

105. CO 295/351: Minutes of Wingfield, 31 March 1894, 363–64.

106. Ibid.

107. CO 295/351: Minutes of R. Meade, 21 April 1894, 364.

108. CO 298/53: Ripon to Broome, 19 June 1894, encl. "Minute (No. 60) from His Excellency the Governor, Laying Correspondence with the Secretary of State Relating to Compensation to Tobago for Loss of Customs Dues"; see also CO 295/351: Ripon to Broome, draft, 19 June 1894, 374–76.

109. CO 298/53: Ripon to Broome, 19 June 1894, CP 126 of 1894; see also CO 295/351: Ripon to Broome, draft, 19 June 1894, 374–76.

110. Craig-James, "Evolution", 498–99.

111. CO 298/53: Ripon to Broome, 19 June 1894, CP 126 of 1894; see also CO 295/351: Ripon to Broome, draft, 19 June 1894, 374–76.

112. CO 295/356: Broome to Ripon, 25 August 1894, 329–38.

113. Ibid.

114. Ibid.

115. CO 295/356: Marginal notes by Wingfield to minutes of Oliver, 15 October 1894, 326–27.

116. CO 295/356: Ripon to Broome, draft, 25 October 1894, 359–62.

117. CO 295/358: Broome to Ripon, 17 December 1894, encl. McEachrane, Blakely and Todd to Low, 10 December 1894, 383–84.

118. Ibid.; encl. memorial praying that union between Tobago and Trinidad be terminated and that Tobago be placed under the Windward Islands government.

119. CO 295/358: Broome to Ripon, 17 December 1894, encl. McEachrane et al.

120. Ibid.

121. Ibid.

122. Ibid.

123. Ibid.

124. CO 295/358: Broome to Ripon, 17 December 1894, encl. no. 3, Low to colonial secretary, 10 December 1894, 394–96.

125. CO 295/358: Minutes of Colonial Office officials, 14 February–26 March 1895, 373–80.

126. Ibid.

127. Ibid.

128. Ibid.

129. Ibid.

130. CO 295/358: Ripon to Broome, draft, 2 May 1895, 397–403.

131. Ibid.

132. Ibid.

133. CO 295/363: Broome to Ripon, 11 May 1895, 182–86.

134. Ibid.

135. CO 295/369: Broome to Chamberlain and various enclosures, 29 January 1896, 150–55. After a search of passenger luggage was implemented for seven months from June through December 1895, it was proved that the amount of revenue lost to Tobago was indeed negligible, only £25, or about £43 per year. The collector of customs recommended that £100 be given to Tobago as compensation, even though £50 would have been adequate.

136. CO 295/363: Ripon to Broome, draft, 17 June 1895, 199–200.

137. CO 295/365: Knollys to Chamberlain, 26 August 1895, 188–90.

138. Ibid.

139. Ibid.

140. CO 295/366: Knollys to Chamberlain, 23 October 1895, 194–96 [author's emphasis].

141. CO 295/371: Broome to Chamberlain, 9 May 1896, 40–43. Broome was also accompanied by his wife, who "entertained the society" at Government House.

142. Ibid.

Chapter 5

1. CO 295/380: Jerningham to Chamberlain, 19 August 1897, 438–42.

2. Pemberton, "Emergence of a Peasantry", 38–49; Craig-James, "Evolution". These

works show that the peasantry was extremely industrious and contributed to an enormous increase in and diversification of exports after the abandonment of sugar in the 1880s. In fact, the peasantry diversified Tobago's exports even before the 1880s.

3. Williams, *History of the People,* 149.

4. Ibid.

5. CO 295/380: Jerningham to Chamberlain, 19 August 1897, 438–42.

6. Ibid.

7. CO 295/384: Low to Jerningham, 10 December 1897, 164–66.

8. Ibid.

9. Ibid.

10. Ibid.

11. Ibid.

12. Ibid.

13. CO 295/386: Knollys to Chamberlain, 10 July 1898, 597–98.

14. Ibid., Chamberlain to Jerningham, confl draft, 1 November 1898, 614–15.

15. Ibid., Knollys to Chamberlain, 11 August 1898, 109–10.

16. CO 298/62: CP 177 of 1898, "The Secretary of State's Despatch and Royal Order in Council Constituting Tobago a Ward of Trinidad".

17. CO 295/388: Jerningham to Chamberlain, 24 November 1898, 177–82. Jerningham reported on the people's happiness at this provision during his reading of the Order in Council at Scarborough.

18. CO 298/62: CP 176 of 1898, "The Secretary of State's Despatch and Royal Instruction Re-constituting the Legislative Council".

19. *Tobago Gazette,* 16 December 1898, 201.

20. CO 295/388: Jerningham to Chamberlain, 24 October 1898, 103–7.

21. Ibid., Chamberlain to Jerningham, 30 November 1898, 108–9.

22. CO 295/391: Jerningham to Chamberlain, 7 April 1899, 657–59.

23. CO 295/392: Knollys to Chamberlain, 17 July 1899, 632–33. The actual petition is not enclosed in this document but is mentioned here.

24. Ibid., Jerningham to Chamberlain, 17 July 1899, encl. acting attorney-general to colonial secretary, 10 July 1899, 634–36.

25. Ibid. *Lis pendens* is a legal notice concerning a lawsuit over disputed title to land.

26. CO 295/396: Jerningham to secretary of state, 6 March 1900, 426–27.

27. CO 295/393: Knollys to Chamberlain, 17 August 1899, 93–94.

28. CO 295/404: Maloney to Chamberlain, 26 September 1901, encl. no. 1, Rousseau to Maloney, 30 May 1901, 537–40.

29. Ibid.

30. Ibid.

31. Governor Maloney stated that he could not find any statement by Governor Jerningham supporting Rousseau's contentions, but he thought that Rousseau's ideas came as a result of "his occupation – not originally contemplated – of Government House, which . . . [was] a mistake to have allowed".

32. CO 295/404: Maloney to Chamberlain, 26 September 1901, 537–40.

33. Ibid.

34. Ibid.

35. Ibid.

36. Ibid., encl. Wrightson to colonial secretary, 17 June 1901, 555–56.

37. Ibid.

38. Ibid., encl. Knaggs to colonial secretary, 17 June 1901, 557.

39. Ibid., Maloney to Chamberlain, 26 September 1901, encl. McCarthy to colonial secretary, 24 June 1901, 558–59.

40. Ibid., Maloney to Chamberlain, 26 September 1901, 558–59.

41. Ibid., enclosures.

42. Ibid., Chamberlain to Maloney, draft, 23 October 1901, 561.

43. CO 295/413: Knollys to Chamberlain, 16 December 1902, 211.

44. Ibid., 211–12.

45. Craig-James, "Milch Cow".

46. CO 295/413: Knollys to Chamberlain, 16 December 1902, 211–12.

47. CO 295/421: Maloney to Lyttelton, confl (1), 2 December 1903, 121–22.

48. Ibid., encl. 123–24. Between 1910 and 1913 the duties and qualifications were more detailed. In 1910 the office was simply Stipendiary Justice of the Peace and Warden, while in 1913 it was styled Commissioner-Warden. The duties and qualifications remained the same, as follows: "*Duties:* Warden – Collection of land charges and Water Rates; granting licences; inspection of Spirit shops, schools, roads, crown lands; supervision of distilleries, bush fires and preventing squatting on crown lands; opening traces, preparation of jury lists; also Supt. Registrar of Births and Deaths and Registrar of marriages. S.J.P. – To hear and decide all summary jurisdiction matters. To take the deposition in all indictable matters. To take evidence in Lunacy matters. He is also the Coroner for his district. Revise Jury list. Decide objection to all Assessments. And the duties usually required of a Police Magistrate. *Qualifications:* General knowledge of the various laws relating to the duties of the offices and ability to enforce them; force of character, tact in relation to the public and in controlling the officers of the department." See CO 295/460: Le Hunte to Harcourt, 3 December 1910, encl. no. 1 in Desp. 399, 363–69; CO 295/482: Le Hunte to Harcourt, 12 April 1913, encl. no. 1 in Desp. 147; CO 295/523: Chancellor to Milner, 13 December 1919, encl. no. 2, Desp. 564. See also CO Desp. 352978, 11 November 1924, "Notes on Duties of a Stipendiary Magistrate in Trinidad", written by Magistrate M. A. J. Clark, Victoria, Trinidad.

49. CO 295/421: Minutes of H. C. Bourne, 18 December 1903, 120.

50. CO 295/426: Maloney to Lyttelton, 10 March 1904, 699–701.

51. Ibid., Minutes of Bourne, 26 March 1904, 696.

52. Ibid., Chamberlain to Maloney, confl draft, 19 April 1904, 702–5.

53. CO 295/460: Le Hunte to Harcourt, 3 December 1910, 366–67.

54. CO 295/480: Le Hunte to secretary of state, 24 September 1912, 224.

55. Ibid.

56. Ibid., Minutes of G. Fiddes, 27 September 1912, 223.

57. CO 295/517: Chancellor to Long, 9 August 1918, 238–42.

58. CO 298/94: *Minutes of the Executive Council*, 10 October 1912, 238–40.

59. Ibid., 239.

60. CO 295/521: Biggart et al. to Milner, 2 April 1919, 164.

61. Ibid., Biggart et al. to Chancellor, 6 January 1919, 165.

62. Ibid., Milner to Chancellor, draft, 30 June 1919, 167.

63. CO 295/522: Smith to secretary, Development Committee, 4 March 1919, encl. in Desp. 426, Gordon to Milner, 25 September 1919.

64. Ibid., Short and Smith to Milner, 25 August 1919, encl. in Desp. 426, Gordon to Milner, 25 September 1919.

65. Ibid., Short and Smith to Milner, 25 August 1919.

66. Ibid. [author's emphasis].

67. Ibid., Gordon to Milner, 25 September 1919, Desp. 426.

68. Ibid.

69. CO 295/526: Chancellor to Milner, confl, 2 January 1920.

70. Ibid., Minutes by C. R. D., 6 February 1920; attached to Chancellor to Milner, confl, 2 January 1920.

71. Ibid., Chancellor to Milner, 9 January 1920.

72. Ibid.

73. Ibid. This argument was the general view of the company about its shipping business.

74. Ibid.

75. Ibid., confl, 12 February 1920.

Chapter 6

1. Williams, *History of the People*, 216. Bridget Brereton, in *A History of Modern Trinidad 1783–1962* (Oxford: Heinemann International, 1981), 148, states that the Trinidad Workingmen's Association was probably founded in 1897 by Walter Millis, a Port of Spain druggist; it "stood for reduction of taxes on food, the extension of roads, the encouragement of minor industries, the opening up of the Crown lands and (significantly) elected members in the legislative council". It was inactive between 1900 and 1906 and during World War I.

2. Williams, *History of the People*, 218. A casting vote is a deciding vote given by the chairman of an assembly in cases where the votes of the members are tied.

3. Ibid., 219–20.

4. Ibid., 219.

5. Ibid., 220.

6. Hewan Craig, *The Legislative Council of Trinidad and Tobago* (London: Faber and Faber, 1952), 40.

7. Ibid., 41.

8. CO 295/555: Byatt to Amery, 23 July 1925, Desp. 331.

9. Ibid., Maloney to Chamberlain, 9 June 1903, encl. no. 1, Biggart to secretary of state for the colonies, 9 June 1903, and other enclosures and sub-enclosures in Desp. 226.

10. Biggart eventually set up practice in Scarborough as well (interview with George E. Leacock).

11. CO 295/555: Maloney to Chamberlain, 9 June 1903, and other enclosures and sub-enclosures in Desp. 226.

12. Ibid.

13. Ibid., encl. no. 2, Prada to surgeon-general, 5 June 1903, Desp. 226.

14. CO 295/521: Biggart et al. to Chancellor, 6 January 1919, 165; Biggart et al. to Milner, 2 April 1919, 164; Milner to Chancellor, draft, 30 June 1919, 167.

15. Campbell, "Tobago and Trinidad", 21–27.

16. Campbell, in "Problems of Alignment", 25, quoted from *A Brief Account of Education in the Anglican Schools in Trinidad and Tobago from 1918 to 1930* (Trinidad: n.p., 1931), 21.

17. *Mins Leg Co,* 17 April 1925, 13.

18. Ibid., 24 April 1925, 44.

19. CP 65 of 1925: *Wardens' Administration Reports for the Year 1924.*

20. CP 53 of 1927: *Wardens' Admin. Rpts 1926.*

21. CP 58 of 1928: *Administration Report of the Director of Education for the Year 1927.*

22. *Mins Leg Co,* 21 February 1930, 3.

23. Ibid., 21 March 1930, 20.

24. Ibid., 15 October 1926, 47.

25. Ibid., 27 March 1928, 32.

26. Ibid., 11 May 1928, 39.

27. Campbell, "Problems of Alignment", 24.

28. *Mins Leg Co,* 25 July 1930, 59.

29. CO 295/555: Desp. 331, Byatt to Amery, 23 July 1925, encl. M. Short to Amery, 23 July 1925 [folios not numbered].

30. Ibid., Desp. 331, Byatt to Amery, 23 July 1925.

31. Ibid.

32. Ibid.

33. Ibid.

34. Ibid.

35. Ibid.

36. Ibid.

37. Ibid.

38. Ibid., minutes of C. R. Danley.

39. Ibid., Desp. 331. Byatt to Amery.

40. CP 74 of 1925: *Administration Report of the Director of Public Works for the Year 1924;* CP 58 of 1929: *Public Works Department Administration Reports for the Year 1928.*

41. *Mins Leg Co,* 27 February 1925, 7, 15.

42. Ibid., 3 April 1925, 7, 15, 32.

43. Ibid., 16 October 1925, 95

44. Ibid., 8 May 1925, 60.

45. Ibid., 4 November 1928, 74.

46. Ibid., 2 November 1928, 72; 22 May 1931, 362.

47. Ibid., 2 November 1928, 72; 7 December 1928, 92.

48. CP 74 of 1929: *Wardens' Admin. Rpts 1928,* 12.

49. Craig-James, "Milch Cow", 21, and the anonymous author of *Past and Present Life in Tobago* (n.p.: n.d.), 6, explain that after Tobago became a ward, the *Barima* sailed weekly between the two islands; later on two coastal steamers usually serviced the inter-island route. The first two were the *Kennet* and the *Spey,* which were replaced by two larger vessels in 1913. In 1916 one of those vessels was withdrawn for war needs, leaving the other, the *Belize,* to serve the inter-island route by itself until 1931, when it was replaced by two new steamers, the *Trinidad* and the *Tobago.*

50. *Mins Leg Co,* 6 March 1925, 14; CP 65 of 1925, *Wardens' Admin. Rpts 1924,* 13.

51. CP 23 of 1929: *Harbour Master Administration Reports for the Year 1928.*

52. *Mins Leg Co,* 13 March 1925, 20.

53. Ibid., 11 March 1927, 11.

54. Ibid., 29 April 1927, 21.

55. F. L. Casserly, "Canadian National Steamships to Call at Tobago", *Commercial Intelligence Journal* 1337 (14 September 1929): 393–95.

56. *Mins Leg Co,* 18 October 1929, 56.

57. *Debates in the Legislative Council of Trinidad and Tobago,* 10 April 1931, 238.

58. Ibid., 4 December 1931, 609.

59. *Mins Leg Co,* 27 February 1925, 7.

60. Clifford Thomas, a retired public works department foreman from Whim, Tobago, explained in a telephone conversation on 19 February 2001 that a cantonnier was a labourer in charge of maintenance of a specific portion of road approximately twenty-four miles (thirty-eight kilometres) long. This labourer was provided with tools by the government and worked alone.

61. *Mins Leg Co,* 27 March 1925, 29. The records are silent on the outcome of the issue.

62. Ibid., 30 March 1928.

63. Ibid., 1 November 1929, 68.

64. Ibid., 15 November 1929, 75.

65. Ottley, *Story of Tobago,* 112.

66. *Mins Leg Co,* 27 March 1925, 28; 17 April 1925, 38; 10 May 1929, 30; 21 March 1930, 20; 4 April 1928; 21 October 1927, 54; 4 November 1927, 74.

67. Ibid., 15 October 1926; 29 October 1926, 58.

68. Ibid., 15 March 1928.

69. Ibid., 5 April 1928, 25.

70. Ibid., 15 October 1926, 46.

71. Ibid., 29 October 1926, 64.

72. Ibid., 5 March 1926, 8.

73. CP 53 of 1927: *Wardens' Admin. Rpts 1926,* 12.

74. *Mins Leg Co,* 11 March 1927, 31; 15 March 1929, 16; 25 April 1930.

75. Ibid., 8 April 1927, 31; 15 March 1929, 25.

76. Ibid., 17 April 1925, 38.

77. Ibid., 24 April 1925, 44.

78. Ibid., 2 March 1928, 9.

79. Ibid., 16 March 1928, 15; 7 March 1930; 25 April 1930, 33.

80. Ibid., 30 March 1928, 20; 13 April 1928, 28.

81. Ibid., 19 October 1928, 60.

82. Ibid.

83. Ibid., 15 February 1929, 3.

84. Campbell, "Problems of Alignment", 24.

85. Ibid.

86. *Mins Leg Co*, 1 March 1929, 12.

87. CP 58 of 1930: *Wardens' Admin. Rpts 1929.*

88. CO 295/555: Byatt to Amery, 23 July 1925, Desp. 331.

Chapter 7

1. *Debates*, 26 February 1937, 56. In 1937 he stated that he was more than seventy years old.

2. Ibid., 5 March 1937, 104.

3. Ibid.

4. Ibid., 21 October 1932, 355.

5. Ibid., 18 November 1932, 441.

6. Ibid., 4 November 1932, 418.

7. *Debates*, 26 February 1937, 22.

8. Ibid., 24.

9. Ibid., 21 October 1932, 359, 373.

10. Ibid., 386–97.

11. Ibid., 18 November 1932, 506–7.

12. Ibid., 24 February 1933, 23.

13. See Table 2.

14. *Debates*, 10 March 1933, 52, 53.

15. Ibid., 54, 57.

16. Ibid., 24 February 1933, 22.

17. Ibid., 7 April 1932, 88.

18. Ibid., 12 April 1935, 180.

19. Ibid., 4 December 1936, 411.

20. Ibid., 10 March 1933, 48.

21. Ibid., 47.

22. Ibid., 23 April 1937, 145.

23. Ibid., 14 May 1937, 166.

24. Ibid., 21 April 1933, 131–32.

25. Ibid., 26 May 1932, 262.

26. Ibid., 5 March 1937, 71–76.

27. Ibid., 26 May 1932, 263, 264.

28. Ibid., 23 February 1934, 28, 29.

29. Ibid., 50, 51.

30. Ibid., 23 March 1934, 93, 94.

31. Ibid., 22 November 1935, 491.

32. Ibid., 6 November 1936, 348, 349.

33. Ibid., 15 January 1935, 46.

34. Ibid., 9 November 1934, 356.

35. Ibid., 366.

36. Ibid., 1 May 1936, 158.

37. Ibid., 15 May 1936, 200–201. Hope took full responsibility for the fact that he was a member of the Finance Committee.

38. Ibid., 6 November 1936, 328, 329.

39. Ibid., 23 April 1937, 145.

40. Ibid., 14 May 1937, 166

41. Ibid., 26 February 1937, 16. In 1931 two new steamers, *Trinidad* and *Tobago*, were purchased and delivered in April.

42. Ibid., 5 March 1937, 100.

43. Ibid.

44. Ibid.

45. Ibid., 101.

46. Ibid.

47. *Debates*, 12 November 1937, 447.

48. "Pinxit", "Our Portrait Gallery", *Tobagonian*, September 1938, 9, 10. This was the first issue of the magazine. A biographical sketch of de Nobriga can also be found in Anthony, *Historical Dictionary*, 182. Some of the information presented in this work differs from that of the *Tobagonian*. Anthony states that in 1903 de Nobriga started working at the electric company and then rose in the ranks to the position of chairman. There seems to be some confusion as to which firm he started working for at age seventeen.

49. "Pinxit", "Our Portrait Gallery", 9, 10.

50. "The Editor's Window", *Tobagonian*, May 1941, 26.

51. Ibid.

52. Ibid.

53. *Debates*, 18 March 1938, 79.

54. CP 3 of 1939: *Coastal Steamer Service: Report of a Committee Appointed to Advise Government Whether the Existing Coastal Steamer Service between Trinidad and Tobago Is Adequate for the Present Needs* [Nicoll Report]; Editor, *Tobagonian*, November 1938, 3. The editor expressed satisfaction with the report, noting that the island "should have a steamer capable of carrying a large number of cabin and steerage passengers comfortably and quickly" to facilitate the tourist trade.

55. Nicoll Rpt, 2.

56. Ibid.

57. Ibid., 3.

58. Ibid., 4.

59. Ibid., 5. In 1937 there were "17 miles of metalled roads, 16 miles of oiled roads, 79 miles of gravelled roads, and 120 miles of natural soil roads, a total of 232 miles".

60. Ibid., 6.

61. Ibid.

62. Ibid., 7.

63. Editor, *Tobagonian,* November 1938, 3.

64. *Tobagonian,* June 1940, 26, 27.

65. *Debates,* 18 March 1938, 79.

66. Ibid., 1 April 1938, 117.

67. Ibid., 29 November 1940, 114.

68. Ibid., 16 May 1941, 32.

69. *Tobagonian,* March 1939, 19, 20.

70. Ibid.

71. Ibid.

72. F. G. M., "The Tobago Agricultural and Livestock Exhibition 1940", *Tobagonian,* August 1940, 20–22.

73. "Editor's Window", *Tobagonian,* December 1940, 223–26.

74. "Mr. de Nobriga's Return", *Tobagonian,* April 1943, 12.

75. Editor, "Those Bus Fares", *Tobagonian,* November 1944, 3, 4; "Editor's Window", *Tobagonian,* November 1944, 17–20.

Chapter 8

1. For commentary on the elections, and especially the groups involved in Trinidad, see John Gaffar La Guerre, "The General Elections of 1946 in Trinidad and Tobago" (typescript, Main Library, University of the West Indies, St Augustine, Trinidad, n.d.).

2. Trinidad and Tobago, *Report on the Legislative Council General Election 1946* (Port of Spain: Guardian Commercial Printery, 1947), 14.

3. Editor, "The Elections", *Tobagonian,* May 1945, 3, 4.

4. *Rpt General Election 1946,* 14.

5. A pupil teacher is a graduate of an elementary school who is appointed as a teaching assistant and trained for the profession at the elementary school level. Pupil teachers take a number of exams to qualify for the position of teacher. Most were over fourteen years and were selected from the best graduates. Many later went on to secondary school and university.

6. [W. E. B. Lewis], *History of Tobago from Fifteenth Century to Present* (n.p., n.d), 1.

7. Learie Luke, "A. P. T. James and the Union between Tobago and Trinidad: 1946–1961" (paper presented at the conference Tobago and Trinidad 100 Years Together, University of the West Indies, St Augustine, Trinidad, 16–18 October 1998), 1–27.

8. *Debates,* 5 March 1948,162.

9. Ibid.

10. Ibid., 27 January 1950, 485.

11. Ibid., 15 December 1953, 415.

12. Ibid., 13 May 1955, 1425.

13. Ibid., 15 February 1957, 817, 818.

14. Ibid., 12 April 1960, 1972–75.

15. Luke, "A. P. T. James", 3, 4.

16. *Debates,* 25 March 1949, 655.

17. Luke, "A. P. T. James", 4.

18. *Debates,* 28 July 1950, 1147.

19. Ibid., 19 January 1951, 595.

20. Ibid., 9 December 1952, 338–40.

21. Ibid., 30 November 1956, 155.

22. Ibid., 146–49.

23. Ibid., 20 December 1956, 388.

24. Ibid., 17 January 1947, 131.

25. Ibid.

26. Ibid., 3 January 1947, 9.

27. Ibid., 26 January 1949, 282–83.

28. Ibid., 9 February 1951, 834.

29. Victor Wheeler (retired school supervisor), interview by author, tape recording, Scarborough, 27 January 1998.

30. *Debates,* 17 January 1947, 131, 132.

31. Ibid., 2 February 1951, 788, 790–92.

32. Ibid., 2 March 1951, 1104.

33. Ibid., 3 December 1951, 529.

34. Ibid., 5 December 1951, 702.

35. Ibid., 9 December 1952, 341–42; 7 June 1957, 1957; Wheeler, interview.

36. *Debates,* 7 June 1957, 1957; Wheeler, interview.

37. *Debates,* 7 June 1957, 1957.

38. Ibid., 6 September 1957, 2207.

39. Ibid., 22 November 1946, 20; 3 January 1947, 7. A cess is a public rate, tax or assessment.

40. Ibid., 17 January 1947, 132.

41. Ibid., 9 January 1948, 3.

42. Andre Phillips, *Governor Fargo: A Short Biography of Alphonso Philbert Theophilus James* ([Scarborough]: Tobago Printery, [1994]), 36; see also *Debates,* 7 June 1957, 1949–50.

43. "Tobago MLC Meets Mr. Creech Jones", *Trinidad Guardian,* 19 May 1948, 2.

44. Phillips, *Governor Fargo,* 37; *Debates,* 12 April 1960, 1965–66.

45. "Tobago Preliminary Survey Urged: Memorandum Tells Creech-Jones of 'Natural Wealth'", *Trinidad Guardian,* 25 June 1948, 3.

46. *Debates,* 4 November 1949, 61.

47. Ibid., 14 April 1950, 781.

48. Ibid., 783.

49. Ibid., 18 March 1949, 561.

50. Trinidad and Tobago, *District Administration Reports for the Year 1952* (Port of Spain: Government Printing Office, 1954), 58.

51. Ibid., 56.

52. *Debates,* 20 December 1956, 399.

53. Ibid., 17 January 1947, 133.

54. Ibid., 18 January 1947, 137.

55. Ibid., 16 March 1951, 1286–88.

56. Ibid.

57. Ibid., 18 January 1947, 137.

58. Ibid., 29 October 1948, 66.

59. "Tobago Preliminary Survey Urged", *Trinidad Guardian,* 25 June 1948, 3.

60. Brereton, *History of Modern Trinidad,* 166.

61. Ibid., 192.

62. *Debates,* 30 April 1948, 407.

63. CO 295/649/8: "Minority Report of the Honourable A. P. T. James", 14 November 1949, in "Constitution: Delimitation of Electoral Districts" folder, 65.

64. Ibid., "Minority Report of R. A. Joseph", 28 January 1950, in "Constitution: Delimitation of Electoral Districts" folder, 66.

65. *Debates,* 28 April 1950, 836–37. In 1956 James opposed the Legislative Council (Elections) bill (amendment no. 2), which provided for an increase of elected seats in the Council from eighteen to twenty-four without granting Tobago two seats. See ibid., 18 May 1956, 1272–78.

66. CO 295/649/8: "Resolution Passed at a General Meeting of the [County] Council held at the Office on Monday 3rd July 1950", in "Constitution: Delimitation of Electoral Districts" folder, 13.

67. Ibid., Rance to Griffiths, 28 August 1950, 12.

68. Luke, "A. P. T. James", 13.

69. *Debates,* 18 January 1947, 138.

70. Ibid., 138, 139.

71. CO 295/654/70778/1/1: "Resolution Passed at the General Meeting of the Tobago Citizens Political and Economic Party".

72. Ibid.

73. Ibid.

74. Ibid.

75. Ibid., Rance to Griffiths, 26 April 1951.

76. Ibid.

77. Ibid.

78. Ibid.

79. Ibid.

80. Ibid.

81. Ibid. Rance admitted that the figures were "not precise" on the expenditure side because it was difficult to determine the exact cost of administrative services; similarly, some of Tobago's revenue was paid in Trinidad.

82. Ibid.

83. Ibid.

84. Ibid.

85. Ibid.

86. *Debates,* 16 January 1948, 52.

87. Ibid., 68.

88. Ibid.

89. Ibid.

90. Ibid., 285.

91. CO 295/654/70778/1/1: "Memorandum from the Tobago Citizens Political and Economic Party", in "Tobago Affairs" folder.

92. Ibid.

93. Ibid.

94. Ibid.

95. Ibid.

96. Luke, "A. P. T. James", 15.

97. *Debates,* 7 June 1957, 1929.

98. Ibid., 1929–30.

99. Ibid., 1931–41.

100. Ibid., 29 January 1958, 1041, 1042.

101. Ibid., 29 December 1958, 222.

102. Ibid., 1 May 1959, 1350.

103. Ibid., 31 July 1957, 64–72.

104. Ibid., 12 April 1960, 1972.

105. Ibid., 1981–82.

106. Ibid., 13 April 1960, 1991–92.

107. "James Wants Tobago to Get Self-Rule", *Trinidad Guardian,* 18 July 1960.

108. Ibid.

109. Ibid.

110. Ibid.

111. Ibid.

112. Ibid.

113. "Disenchanted", "Tobagonians Resent Premier's Attitude", *Trinidad Guardian,* 3 October 1960.

114. Ibid.

115. Albert Gomes, "Harsh Note in the Symphony", *Trinidad Guardian,* 9 October 1960.

116. Ibid.

117. "Gomes Hit for Keeping Back Tobago", *Trinidad Guardian,* 14 October 1960.

118. Ibid.

119. Ibid. See also A. P. T. James, "Decision on Self-Government Lies with Tobagonians Alone", *Trinidad Guardian*, 2 November 1960.

120. Tobago correspondent, "James' Mess of Pottage", *Nation*, 28 October 1960, 17, 20.

121. Ibid.

122. "Background to a Case for Tobago 'Secession'", *Trinidad Guardian*, 13 December 1960.

123. "New Self-Rule Bid in Tobago Aim to Cut Down Cost of Living", *Trinidad Guardian*, 1 November 1960.

124. Ibid.

125. Ibid.

126. James, "Decision".

127. Ibid.

128. *Debates*, 4 November 1960, 335.

129. Ibid., 340.

130. Ibid.

131. "We Want More Representation in the Federal Legislature", *Nation*, 20 May 1960, 17, 20.

132. *Debates*, 4 November 1960, 341.

133. Ibid., 343.

134. Ibid.

135. Ibid., 344.

136. H. Whittaker, "Tourism, Agriculture Necessary to Tobago", *Trinidad Guardian*, 11 November 1960.

137. A. Moore, "Plebiscite to Decide Tobago Independence", *Trinidad Guardian*, 11 December 1960.

138. Ibid.

139. Lionel P. Mitchell, "Further Aspects of Tobago Independence", *Trinidad Guardian*, 22 December 1960.

140. *Debates*, 11 March 1961, 1742–43.

141. Ibid., 1744.

142. Ibid., 12 April 1961, 2308.

143. Fraser, "Independence Movement".

144. Ibid.

145. Ibid.

146. *Debates*, 12 April 1961, 2308–446. See also *Debates*, 25 April 1961, 2247–470.

147. Tobago, *Register of Deaths for the Year 1962*, 500.

148. *Debates*, 7 June 1957, 1971.

Chapter 9

1. Williams dominated leadership of the government for twenty-five years: from 1956 to 1959 he was the chief minister; from 1960 to 1961 he was premier; then from 1962, when the country gained independence, to his death in 1981 he was the prime minister.

2. Williams, *History of the People*, 242.

3. Anthony, *Historical Dictionary*, 600–601.

4. Trinidad and Tobago, County Councils Act (Act No. 22 of 1976; amended by Act 26 of 1977), in *Laws of Trinidad and Tobago*, rev. ed., vol. 5, ch. 25:04 (Port of Spain: Government Printing Office, 1980), 19–21.

5. Susan E. Craig, *Community Development in Trinidad and Tobago, 1943–1973: From Welfare to Patronage*, Working Paper no. 4 (St Augustine, Trinidad: Institute of Social and Economic Research, University of the West Indies, 1974), 90.

6. Trinidad and Tobago, Local Government Department, *Annual Administration Report 1957* (Port of Spain: Government Printing Office, 1959), 7.

7. Craig, *Community Development*, 88.

8. Trinidad and Tobago, *Report of Committee for the Re-organization of Administrative Arrangements of Tobago*, March 1957, 1.

9. *Rpt Committee for Re-organization*, 2.

10. Ibid.

11. Ibid.

12. Ibid.

13. A deK. Frampton, *Development Plan for Tobago: Report of the Team Which Visited Tobago in March/April 1957, Development and Welfare in the West Indies* (Bridgetown: Advocate Co., 1957) [Frampton Report].

14. *Debates*, 7 June 1957, 1941.

15. Frampton Rpt, 44

16. Ibid.

17. Ibid.

18. Ibid.

19. Ibid.

20. Ibid., 45.

21. Ibid., 47.

22. Ibid., 49.

23. Ibid.

24. Ibid.

25. Secretariat Circular No. 1 (Staff), March 1958, in P 9/51/2: Secretariat Circulars (Staff), 1955–57, 1958–60.

26. Secretariat Circular No. 4 (Staff) of 1957, in Secretariat Circulars (Staff), 1955–57, 1958–60.

27. Trinidad and Tobago, *Report to the Honourable the Premier by the Honourable Ulric Lee on the Reorganisation of the Public Service* (Port of Spain: Government Printing Office, 1959) [Lee Report].

28. Ibid., "Introduction".

29. Ibid., 55.

30. Ibid.

31. Williams, *History of the People*, 244.

32. Ag. accountant, Tobago, to permanent secretary, Tobago affairs, 17 August

1959, in TA 38/1/1: Ministry for Tobago Affairs – Administration: Administrative Arrangements – Tobago Affairs.

33. Nunes, "Ministry", 177; Clarence Warner (justice of the peace), interview by author, tape recording, Government House Road, 27 January 1998.

34. G. W. Gordon to permanent secretary, Ministry of Finance, Planning and Development, confl, 26 August 1959, in TA 38/1/1.

35. G. W. Gordon to permanent secretary, Ministry of Finance, 15 March 1960, in TA 38/1/1.

36. *Debates*, 12 April 1961, 2309

37. Prime Minister's Office Circular No. 1 of 1964, 30 January 1964, in Tobago Affairs Circulars docket, 1964–65.

38. PMO Circ. 1 of 1964.

39. It is not clear how long the position of commissioner lasted, but it was replaced by that of the permanent secretary.

40. PMO Circ. 1 of 1964.

41. Ministry of Tobago Affairs Circular Memorandum No. 39, 3 October 1966, in Tobago Affairs Circulars docket, 1966–70.

42. Permanent Secretary to Prime Minister Circular Memoranda docket, 1969–74.

43. Bishnu Ragoonath, *Development in Tobago: Twentieth Century Challenges* (St Augustine, Trinidad: School of Continuing Studies, University of the West Indies, 1997), 49.

44. Eutrice Thornhill (DAC member), interview by author, tape recording, Hope, Tobago, 30 January 1988.

45. Geyette to Herrera, 23 December 1976, in TA 38/1/1, vol. 2.

46. Herrera to all permanent secretaries, chief personnel officer, director of public administration, 29 December 1976, in TA 38/1/1, vol. 2.

47. Barsotti to all permanent secretaries and heads of departments, 30 December 1976, in Ministry of Finance Circular No. 17 of 1976, in TA 38/1/1, vol. 2.

48. CO 1031/1599: Confl, Beetham to secretary of state, 15 October 1955.

49. The short ton is a measure of weight commonly used in the United States and Canada, equivalent to 2,000 pounds. The British term for a similar large measure of weight is the long ton, which is equal to 2,400 pounds.

50. CO 1031/1599: Confl, "Note of a Meeting Held in the Colonial Office on 27th October, 1955".

51. Ibid.

52. PNM, *Major Party Documents*, vol. 1 (Port of Spain: PNM Publishing, 1966), 51, 52.

53. "Williams Warns: Do Not Shun Civic Duty. Post for Robinson", *Sunday Guardian*, 22 October 1961, 2.

54. *Debates*, 7 June 1957, 1923–28.

55. Ibid., 1923.

56. Ibid., 1923–28.

57. Ibid., 1727–28.

58. Ragoonath, *Development*.

59. See Figure 4; statistics taken from Trinidad and Tobago, *Five-Year Economic Programme 1956–1960: Memorandum for 1957* (Port of Spain: Government Printing Office, 1956).

60. *Debates,* 7 June 1957, 1928.

61. Ibid., 1949–50.

62. Frampton Rpt, 163.

63. Ibid., 168–69.

64. *Debates,* 7 June 1957, 1929.

65. Frampton Rpt, 171.

66. Trinidad and Tobago, *Five-Year Development Programme 1958–1962: 1958 Report* (Port of Spain: Government Printing Office, 1960).

67. Ragoonath, *Development,* 28.

68. Trinidad and Tobago, *1958 Rpt,* part 2.

69. Trinidad and Tobago, *Five-Year Development Programme 1958–1962: Report of the Premier on Development Projects for the Year 1959* ([Port of Spain]: Office of the Premier, 1961).

70. Trinidad and Tobago, *Five-Year Development Programme 1958–1962: Report of the Premier on Development Projects for the Year 1960* ([Port of Spain]: Economic and Planning Division, Office of the Premier, 1962).

71. *Rpt of Premier 1960.*

72. Not shown in Table 6; *Debates,* 12 April 1961, 2312.

73. *Debates,* 4 November 1960, 336.

74. Ibid., 336–40.

75. Ibid., 343.

76. Ragoonath, *Development,* 29.

77. Ibid., 33.

78. Trinidad and Tobago, *Report of the Tobago Planning Team* (Port of Spain: CSO Printing Unit, 1963), 34.

79. Ragoonath, *Development,* 34.

80. *Rpt of Planning Team,* 36.

81. Ibid., 109–13.

82. Ragoonath, *Development,* 37.

83. Ibid., 38.

84. Ibid.

85. Ibid.

86. Ibid., 39–51.

87. Ibid.

88. Ibid., 44.

89. Ibid., 44, 45.

90. Ibid., 43, 44.

91. Ibid., 6.

92. Ibid., 46.

93. Ibid., 47.

94. Ibid.

95. Ibid.

96. Ibid., 48.

97. Ibid.

98. Ibid.

99. "Tobago Preliminary Survey Urged: Memorandum Tells Creech-Jones of 'Natural Wealth'", *Trinidad Guardian*, 25 June 1948, 3.

Chapter 10

1. "Tobago's Position", *Evening News*, 21 May 1969.

2. "Norton Calls on Tobago to Secede", *Trinidad Guardian*, 21 May 1969.

3. Trinidad and Tobago, *Report on the Parliamentary General Elections 1966* (Port of Spain: Government Printery, 1967), 91.

4. "Tobago's Position". Norton had also charged that there was racial discrimination in Tobago.

5. Ibid.

6. Ibid.

7. Ibid.

8. " 'Secessionists' in Tobago under Fire", *Trinidad Guardian*, 30 June 1969.

9. Ibid.

10. Cyril Garcia, "Tobago Want Some Action on Their Grouses", *Express*, 3 October 1969.

11. Ibid.

12. Ibid.

13. Ibid.

14. Ibid.

15. Ingram, "Damsel".

16. Ibid.

17. Ibid.

18. Ibid.

19. "Cabinet Takes Action on Tobago Plan", *Express*, 10 October 1969.

20. "The Question Now Is: To Secede or Not to Secede", *Express*, 28 October 1969, 5.

21. Ibid.

22. Ibid.

23. "Apostle of Secession", *Express*, 3 January 1970.

24. Ibid.

25. Ibid.

26. Ibid. The article did not indicate the point from which the spur road would originate.

27. Ibid.

28. "Secession Group Sure of Success: Casino to Bring Tobago $225M", *Express*, 6 January 1970.

29. "Orlando", "Trinidad *and* Tobago: What Has the Latter Gained by Association?", *Express*, 8 January 1970

30. "Orlando", "Trinidad *and* Tobago".

31. Ibid.

32. Walling E. B. Lewis, "Tobago Sons Are Responsible", *Trinidad Guardian*, 10 January 1970.

33. "Dr Norton: Joker in the Pack", *Express*, 7 January 1970.

34. Ibid.

35. Constitution Commission of Trinidad and Tobago, *Report of the Constitution Commission* (n.p.: T&T P&P, 1974), 79.

36. Ibid., 80.

37. Ibid.

38. Ibid., 81.

39. Roach, "Why Nearby Tobago".

40. Herman L. Bennett, "The Challenge to the Post-Colonial State: A Case Study of the February Revolution in Trinidad", in *The Modern Caribbean*, eds. Franklin W. Knight and Colin Palmer (Chapel Hill: University of North Carolina Press, 1989), 141.

41. Bennett, "Challenge", 129.

42. *Hansard* (House of Representatives), 4 February 1977, 1455–58.

43. Luke, "Tobago's Struggle".

44. DAC, *Guide to Change for Trinidad and Tobago* (Barataria: DAC Publishing, 1971), 3, 4.

45. DAC, *Guide to Change*, 4.

46. Ibid., 31.

47. Ibid., 33, 34.

48. Luke, "Tobago's Struggle", 94.

49. "Residents to Be Involved in T'go Future", *Trinidad Guardian*, 9 April 1973, in "Robinson, A. N. R." newspaper clipping file.

50. Luke, "Tobago's Struggle", 94, 95.

51. Ibid., 95.

52. United Labour Front, *Trinidad and Tobago Election Manifesto 1976, United Labour Front* ([Port of Spain]: n.d.), 14.

53. DAC, *Trinidad and Tobago Manifesto: General Elections 1976* ([Port of Spain]: DAC, 1976), 6, 7.

54. Luke, "Tobago's Struggle", 96.

55. Williams's post-election speech was cited in the *Trinidad Guardian*, 27 September 1976, and quoted in Ryan, *Revolution and Reaction*, 119.

56. Selwyn Ryan, *The Politics of Succession: A Study of Parties and Politics in Trinidad and Tobago* (St Augustine, Trinidad: University of the West Indies, [1978]), 430.

57. *Hansard* (HoR), 14 January 1977, 1158–59.

Chapter 11

1. Luke, "Tobago's Struggle", 99.

2. Ibid.

3. *Hansard* (House of Representatives), 14 January 1977, 1149–1206.

4. *Hansard* (HoR), 21 January 1977, 1229–30.

5. *Hansard* (HoR), 28 January 1977, 1302.

6. *Hansard* (HoR), 28 January 1977, 1308.

7. *Hansard* (HoR), 28 January 1977, 1319.

8. *Hansard* (HoR), 28 January 1977, 1333–54.

9. Luke, "Tobago's Struggle", 102.

10. In Trinidadian parlance, tabanca is a state of depression or anger that one experiences when abandoned by a lover or rejected by the person one is trying to court.

11. *Hansard* (HoR), 28 January 1977, 1354.

12. *Hansard* (HoR), 4 February 1977, 1400.

13. *Hansard* (HoR), 4 February 1977, 1408.

14. Luke, "Tobago's Struggle", 104.

15. Ibid.

16. *Hansard* (HoR), 4 February 1977, 1423.

17. *Hansard* (HoR), 4 February 1977, 1424.

18. *Hansard* (HoR), 4 February 1977, 1427.

19. *Hansard* (HoR), 4 February 1977, 1462.

20. Luke, "Tobago's Struggle", 106, 107.

21. Ibid., 107.

22. *Hansard* (HoR), 14 January 1977, 1150–51.

23. Elvira Job (friend of A. P. T. James), interview by author, tape recording, Zion Hill, Tobago, 25 January 1998.

24. [DAC], "What Is Internal Self Government & Examples", in newpaper clippings file, EEJL.

25. Everette John to members, Regional Action Committee, DAC, 14 May 1979 (EEJL).

26. Vesta John to editor, *Trinidad Express,* 25 September 1979.

27. *Hansard,* 21 January 1977, 1281.

28. *Hansard,* 21 January 1977, 1282.

29. *Hansard,* 4 February 1977, 1401–5.

30. PNM, *Data Relating to the Question of Internal Self-Government for Tobago* (n.p.: Sultan Khan's Litho, 1977), 63–64.

31. Edgar Dove, "Open Letter to Tobago on Basic Aspects of Internal Self Government", in "Robinson, A. N. R." newspaper clipping file, Scarborough Regional Library.

32. [DAC], "Internal Self-Government Structure for Tobago", 1978, 1 (HCL).

33. Ibid., 2.

34. Ibid.

35. [DAC], "Internal Self Government", 4.

36. Ibid.

37. Ibid.

38. Luke, "Tobago's Struggle", 78.

39. Ibid., 79.

40. Carrington, "The Union of Tobago and Trinidad", 55–66.

41. PNM, *PNM Major Party Documents,* vol. 1 (Port of Spain: PNM Publishing, 1966), 52, 124, 125.

42. PNM, *Major Party Documents,* vol. 1, 52, 124, 125.

43. Pamela Nicholson (representative for Tobago West), interview by author, tape recording, Mount Pleasant, 5 August 1991.

44. [DAC], "Internal Self-Government", 5.

45. Ibid.

46. *Hansard* (HoR), 14 January 1977, 1179–82.

47. George E. Higgins, *A History of Trinidad Oil* (Port of Spain: n.p., 1996), 364–65. Wells drilled by the Phillips Petroleum company south of Tobago in 1971 – Alice No. 1 and Betty No. 1, eleven miles (17.6 kilometres) and twenty-four miles (38.4 kilometres) respectively south-east of Tobago – did not find hydrocarbons.

48. Ryan, *Politics of Succession,* 433.

49. Luke, "Tobago's Struggle", 81.

50. Susan E. Craig, *Community Development in Trinidad and Tobago 1943–1973* (St Augustine, Trinidad: Institute of Social and Economic Research, University of the West Indies, 1974), 48–52. Craig outlines a number of problems inherent in the special works programmes.

51. Luke, "Tobago's Struggle", 82.

52. Pemberton, "Emergence of a Peasantry", 38–49.

53. "Cost of Living 28.75% Higher in Sister Isle, Says Report", *Express,* 1 July 1979, 21.

54. Selwyn Ryan, "Trinidad and Tobago: The General Elections of 1976", *Caribbean Studies* 19, nos. 1–2 (April–July 1979): 19.

55. Horace Leighton-Mills, "No Gain Shipping Food to Tobago", *Express,* 22 March 1979, and "Bring the Butter with You", *Express,* 12 April 1979, 27.

56. Ryan, *Politics of Succession,* 434, 435.

57. Ryan, "Trinidad and Tobago", 21.

58. Luke, "Tobago's Struggle", 83.

59. Stanley Baird (councillor) and Hochoy Charles (leader of Assembly business, Tobago House of Assembly), interview by author, tape recording, Scarborough, 4 August 1991.

60. Baird and Charles, interview.

61. Ibid.

62. Ryan, *Politics of Succession,* 437.

63. Trinidad and Tobago Ministry of Finance (Maintenance), *Report of Ministerial Committee on Certain Problem Areas in Tobago* (June 1979), 8.

64. Trinidad and Tobago, House Paper No. 6 of 1978: *Report of the Joint Select Committee of Parliament Appointed (1) to Consider the Fourth Report of the Elections and Boundaries Commission for the Purposes of Local Government Elections and the Memorandum Thereon and (2) to Make Recommendations for Internal Self Government for Tobago in 1977,* 3.

65. Luke, "Tobago's Struggle", 111.

66. *Rpt of Joint Select Committee.*

67. Ibid.

68. Ibid., 8.

69. Ibid., 8, 9.

70. Luke, "Tobago's Struggle", 116.

71. Ryan, *Politics of Succession,* 450.

72. Seemungal to Williams (copy), 20 November 1979, attachment to original copy of "Draft Bill of the Tobago (Internal Self Government) Act", Parliament Library.

73. Citizen's Committee for the Defence of Human Rights, *Internal Self-Government for Tobago* (n.p.: Camalas Business Services, n.d.), vi; "Mass Rally Today for Internal Self Gov't", *Trinidad Guardian,* 1 May 1979, in "Robinson, A. N. R." newspaper clipping file.

74. Robinson to attorney-general, 2 May 1979, in *Hansard* (HoR), 22 June 1979, 819–20.

75. *Hansard* (HoR), 22 June 1979, 804.

76. Ibid.

77. Ibid., 815–16.

78. Ibid., 819–20.

79. Luke, "Tobago's Struggle", 119.

80. *Hansard* (HoR), 22 June 1979, 825–38.

81. J. G. Davidson, *Tobago Versus P.N.M.* (Woodbrook, Trinidad: Beacon Publishing, 1979), 181, 182.

82. *Hansard,* 27 July 1979, 1147.

83. Horace Leighton-Mills, "Tobago Team Off on Carib. Mission", *Sunday Express,* 21 October 1979, in newspaper clipping files, EEJL. See Benedict Armstrong (former DAC member and former senator), interview by author, tape recording, Carnbee, Tobago, 15 February 1998.

84. "Tobago Mission: 95% Want to Control Affairs", *Trinidad Express,* 10 October 1979, in newspaper clipping files, EEJL.

85. Baird and Charles, interview; Armstrong, interview.

86. *Hansard* (HoR), 26 February 1980, 481.

87. "The Tobago Issue", *Sunday Express,* 9 March 1980. This article reprinted, verbatim, sections of the document published by the government containing the Seemungal draft bill, the comments of the attorney-general thereon and the comments of the Cabinet.

88. "Petition of the People of Tobago, to the Secretary of Cabinet, 3 March 1980", in "Comments of the General Public on the Draft Bill for Internal Self-Government for Tobago by Trinidad and Tobago" (1980).

89. Hochoy Charles to secretary to the Cabinet, 28 March 1980, in "Comments of the General Public".

90. John to secretary to the Cabinet, 28 March 1980, in "Comments of the General Public".

91. Ibid.

92. Pamela Nicholson to secretary to the Cabinet, 27 March 1980, in "Comments of the General Public".

93. Luke, "Tobago's Struggle", 131

94. Nicholson to secretary, 27 March 1980.

95. Gibbes to secretary to the Cabinet, [March 1980], in "Comments of the General Public".

96. Moore to clerk, House of Representatives, [March 1980], in "Comments of the General Public".

97. *Hansard* (Senate), 22 July 1980, 1505, 1506.

98. Ibid., 12 September 1980, 34.

99. Ibid., 35.

100. Ibid.

101. Ibid., 37.

102. Ibid., 38.

103. Ibid., 45.

104. Bernard Romeo and Vernie Johnson (Fargo House Movement members), interviews by author, tape recordings, Bethesda, Tobago, 11 and 12 February 1998.

105. *Debates* (HoR), 12 September 1980, 47, 48.

106. "Task Ahead for A. N. R. Robinson and the D.A.C.", *People,* January 1981, 9–13.

107. Ibid.

Bibliography

Primary Sources (Unpublished)

Public Record Office, Kew (Surrey), England

CO 288, vol. 28, Tobago: *Minutes of the Legislative Council, 1877–88.*
CO 288, vol. 29, Tobago: *Minutes of the Executive Council, 1881–88.*
CO 288, vol. 30, Tobago: *Minutes of the Proceedings of the Financial Board, 1889–98.*
CO 289, vols. 5–7, *Tobago Gazette, 1887–95.*
CO 290, vols. 72–73, Tobago: Blue Books of Statistics, 1888–92.
CO 295, vols. 311–554, Trinidad and Tobago: Governors' despatches containing correspondence, etc.
CO 298, vols. 43–218, Trinidad and Tobago: Sessional Papers: *Minutes of the Proceedings of the Legislative Council* and Council Papers; *Minutes of the Executive Council, 1887–1961.*
CO 321, vols. 99 and 103, Windward Islands: Governors' despatches.
CO 1031, vols. 515, 789 and 1599, West Indies: Economic Development in Tobago; Tobago.

British Newspaper Library, Colindale, England

Nation, 1960.
New Era, 1889.
Tobago News, 1887–88.

National Archives of Trinidad and Tobago, Port of Spain, Trinidad

Tobagonian, 1938–48.

Tobago. Council Paper 195 of 1893. *Extract from Minutes of Meeting Held on 10th November 1893 of the Financial Board of Tobago Respecting the Loss to the Revenue of That Island Consequent on the Annexation of Trinidad.*

Tobago. Council Paper 21 of 1894. Tobago. *Report of Select Committee of the Council on the Allowance to Tobago in Respect of the Loss Sustained by That Island in Customs Duties.*

Trinidad (Tobago). Copy. [Despatch] 126, Secretary of state to governor, 2/5/1895, "On the Subject of Prayer of the Memorial to Dissolve the Union between Trinidad and Tobago and the Question of Local Control of Customs and Excise".

Parliament Library, Port of Spain, Trinidad

"A Guide to Differences between the Draft Bill Entitled 'The Tobago House of Assembly Act, 1980' and the Draft Bill entitled 'The Tobago (Internal Self-Government) Act, 1980' ". Legal Supplement Part C to *Trinidad and Tobago Gazette* 19, no. 291 (11 September 1980).

"Note on Self-Government Proposed for Tobago". Folder.

TBGO 31. Folder [includes correspondence from the public on internal self-government].

[Trinidad and Tobago]. "Comments of the General Public on the Draft Bill for Internal Self-Government for Tobago", 1980.

Trinidad and Tobago. House Paper 6 of 1978. *Report of the Joint Select Committee of Parliament Appointed (1) to Consider the Fourth Report of the Elections and Boundaries Commission for the Purposes of Local Government Elections and the Memorandum Thereon and (2) to Make Recommendations for Internal Self Government for Tobago in 1977.*

Registry Section, Central Administrative Services Tobago, Scarborough

LG 1/9/11, Ministry of Local Government files.

LG 1/18/1, vol. 2, Ministry of Local Government files.

Permanent Secretary to Prime Minister Circular Memoranda docket, 1969–74.

Secretariat Circulars (Staff) docket, 1955–57, 1958–60.

TA 38/1/1, Ministry for Tobago Affairs files.

TA 38/1/1, vol. 2, Ministry for Tobago Affairs files.

Tobago Affairs Circulars docket 1964–65.

Tobago Affairs Circulars docket 1966–70.

Registrar-General's Department, Scarborough

Tobago. *Register of Deaths for the Year 1962.*

Scarborough Regional Library, Scarborough

"Robinson, A. N. R.". Newspaper clipping file [contains newspaper clippings and DAC literature].

Personal Collections

Everette E. John personal library, Bacolet, Tobago [EEJL] (DAC documents; newspaper clippings file on Tobago).

Hochoy Charles personal library, Golden Lane, Tobago [HCL]:
DAC documents
Documents pertaining to internal self-government for Tobago
"Errors and Omissions in the Draft Bill: The Tobago (Internal Self-Government) Act, 1979".
Representative for Tobago East. "Joint Select Committee of Parliament, Memorandum on Internal Self-Government for Tobago – Matters Requiring Immediate Attention" (9 March 1977).
Robinson, A. N. R. "Draft Bill: An Act to Provide for a System of Internal Self-Government for Tobago and for Matters Connected Therewith and Incidental Thereto", including explanatory note to the draft bill.

Benedict Armstrong personal library, Carnbee, Tobago (DAC documents).

Interviews

Alfred, Fulton, and R. Hercules (school supervisor; clergyman). Interview by author. Tape recording. Crown Point, Tobago, 2 February 1998.

Andrews, Dalton (former member, Tobago Citizens Political and Economic Party). Interview by author. Tape recording. Belle Garden, Tobago, 25 January 1998.

Archie, Moulda (retired history teacher, Bishop's High School, Tobago). Interview by author. Tape recording. Scarborough, Tobago, 30 January 1998.

Armstrong, Benedict (former DAC member and senator). Interview by author. Tape recording. Carnbee, Tobago, 15 February 1998.

Baird, Stanley (secretary for tourism, Tobago House of Assembly). Interview by author. Tape recording. Scarborough, Tobago, 21 January 1998.

Baird, Stanley, and Hochoy Charles (councillor; leader of Assembly business, Tobago House of Assembly). Interview by author. Tape recording. Scarborough, Tobago, 4 August 1991.

Carrington, William (educator and Anglican clergyman). Unrecorded interview by author. Scarborough, Tobago, 23 January 1998.

Charles, Gonzaga (villager). Interview by author. Tape recording. Black Rock, Tobago, 19 January 1998.

Charles, Hochoy (chief secretary, Tobago House of Assembly). Interview by author. Tape recording. Scarborough, Tobago, 27 January 1998.

Cox, Simeon "Valentine" (villager). Interview by author. Tape recording. Black Rock, Tobago, 15 January 1998.

Davidson, Dr Jeff (former chairman, Tobago House of Assembly). Interview by author. Tape recording. Scarborough, Tobago, 12 July 1991.

Des Vignes, Bernadette (former assemblywoman, Tobago House of Assembly). Interview by author. Tape recording. Moriah, Tobago, 26 January 1998.

Des Vignes, Henry (close friend of A. P. T. James). Interview by author. Tape recording. Moriah, Tobago, 26 January 1998.

Dillon, Arthur (relative of A. P. T. James). Interview by author. Tape recording. Plymouth, Tobago, 11 October 1998.

Dillon, Robert Winston (high school teacher). Interview by author. Tape recording. Orange Hill, Tobago, 16 January 1998.

Frank, Jean (employee of George de Nobriga). Interview by author. Tape recording. Lowlands, Tobago, 10 February 1998.

Gift, Edrick (retired professor, University of the West Indies). Interview by author. Tape recording. St Augustine, Trinidad, 26 February 1998.

Lively, George (civil servant). Interview by author. Tape recording. Castara, Tobago, 29 January 1998.

Jack, Margaret (former assemblywoman, Tobago House of Assembly). Interview by author. Tape recording. Scarborough, Tobago, 16 February 1998.

James, Berenice Theophil M. (daughter of A. P. T. James). Interview by author. Tape recording. Shaw Park, Tobago, 19 January 1998.

James, Henry (nephew of A. P. T. James and former assemblyman, Tobago House of Assembly). Interview by author. Tape recording. Frenchfield, Tobago, 22 January 1998.

Job, Orban and Elvira (friends of A. P. T. James). Interview by author. Tape recording. Zion Hill, Tobago, 25 January 1998.

Johnson, Virnie (former member, Fargo House Movement). Interview by author. Tape recording. Bethesda, Tobago, 12 February 1998.

Keen-Dumas, Agatha (DAC member). Interview by author. Tape recording. Sargeant Cain, Tobago, 28 January 1998.

Leacock, George L. L. (amateur curator). Interview by author. Tape recording. Scarborough, Tobago, 25 January 1998.

Moore-Miggins, Deborah (legal advisor, Tobago House of Assembly). Interview by author. Tape recording. Scarborough, Tobago, 30 August 1991.

Murray, Dr Winston, and Dr Cynthia Harvey (Murray was a member of Parliament for Tobago and leader of the Fargo House Movement). Interview by author and Dr Selwyn H. H. Carrington. Tape recording. Baltimore, Maryland, 12 October 1997.

Murray-Thomas, Agnes (teacher, Bishop's High School). Interview by author. Tape recording. Mount Marie, Tobago, 26 January 1998.

Nicholson, Pamela (member of Parliament for Tobago West). Interview by author. Tape recording. Mount Pleasant, Tobago, 15 July 1991.

Parks, John (friend of A. P. T. James). Interview by author. Tape recording. Scarborough, Tobago, 29 January 1998.

Reid, Liley (close associate of A. P. T. James and mother of two of his children). Interview by author. Tape recording. Hyattsville, Maryland, 24 November 2000.

Richards, Allan (chief clerk, Tobago House of Assembly). Interview by author. Tape recording. Scarborough, Tobago, 10 February 1998.

Richards, Allan, and Vannus James (chief clerk, Tobago House of Assembly; consultant, Tobago House of Assembly). Interview by author. Tape recording. Scarborough, Tobago, 27 January 1998.

Richardson, Selwyn (former attorney-general, Trinidad and Tobago). Interview by author. Tape recording. Barataria, Trinidad, 5 August 1991.

Robinson, A. N. R. (president, Republic of Trinidad and Tobago). Interview by author. Tape recording. Port of Spain, Trinidad, 27 October 1998.

Robley, George S. C. M. (former county councillor). Interview by author. Tape recording. Goodwood, Tobago, 25 January 1998.

Romeo, Bernard (member, Fargo House Movement). Interview by author. Tape recording. Bethesda, Tobago, 11 February 1998.

Spencer, Lennox (DAC supporter). Interview by author. Tape recording. Mason Hall, Tobago, 9 February 1998.

Thornhill, Eutrice, and Caedmon Murray (DAC members). Interview by author. Tape recording. Hope, Tobago, 30 January 1998.

Warner, Clarence (justice of the peace and former head, Tobago branch, Inland Revenue Department). Interview by author. Tape recording. Government House Road, Tobago, 27 January 1998.

Wheeler, Victor (retired school supervisor). Interview by author. Scarborough, Tobago, 27 January 1998.

Yorke, Alverna (nurse and social worker). Interview by author. Tape recording. Takoma Park, Maryland, 25 January 2000.

B. Primary Sources (Published)

Legislative Council and Parliament (*Hansard*)

Trinidad and Tobago. *Debates in the Legislative Council of Trinidad and Tobago, 1931–50.*
———. *Legislative Council Debates, 1951–61.*
———. *Minutes of the Proceedings of the Legislative Council and Council Papers, 1925–30.*
———. *Parliamentary Debates (House of Representatives), 1962–80.*
———. *Parliamentary Debates (Senate), 1980.*

Legislation

Seemungal, Lionel. Draft bill of Tobago (Internal Self-Government) Act: "An Act to Make Provision for, and in Connection with the Internal Self-Government of Tobago, and All Matters Incidental Thereto, 1979". Act No. 30 of 1988.

Trinidad and Tobago. County Councils Act (Act No. 22 of 1976). Chap. 25:04, *Laws of Trinidad and Tobago*, rev. ed. Vol. 5. Port of Spain: Government Printing Office, 1980.

———. *The Laws of Trinidad and Tobago*, rev. ed. London: Eyre and Spottiswoode, 1980.

———. Order in Council 1888. Appendix, Item 3. *Laws of Trinidad and Tobago*, rev. ed. Vol. 16. Port of Spain: Government Printing Office, 1980.

————. Order in Council 1898. Appendix, Item 3. *Laws of Trinidad and Tobago,* rev. ed. Vol. 16. Port of Spain: Government Printing Office, 1980.

————. Trinidad and Tobago Act 1887. Appendix, Item 1. *Laws of Trinidad and Tobago,* rev. ed. Vol. 16. Port of Spain: Government Printing Office, 1980.

Trinidad and Tobago [Republic]. Act to Amend the Constitution of the Republic of Trinidad and Tobago. Act No. 25 of 1982.

————. Act to Amend the Constitution of the Republic of Trinidad and Tobago. Act No. 17 of 1983.

————. Act to Amend the Constitution of the Republic of Trinidad and Tobago. Act No. 8 of 1988.

————. Act to Amend the Tobago House of Assembly Act. Act No. 40 of 1980.

————. Act to Amend the Tobago House of Assembly Act. Chap. 25:03. Act No. 7 of 1988.

————. Act to Establish the Tobago House of Assembly for the Purpose of Making Better Provision for the Administration of the Island of Tobago and for Matters Connected Therewith. Act No. 37 of 1980.

————. Act to Provide for the Supplementary Appropriation for the Service of Trinidad and Tobago for the Year Ending on the 31st Day of December, 1980. Act No. 3 of 1981.

Other Published Primary Sources

Central Statistical Office (CSO). *Estimated Internal Migration Bulletin* 1. Port of Spain: CSO Printing Office, 1974.

Colonial Office. *The Colonial Office List: Comprising Historical and Statistical Information Respecting the Colonial Dependencies of Great Britain, 1875 to 1963* [between 1926 and 1935, titled *The Dominions Office and Colonial Office List*].

————. *Development and Welfare in the West Indies 1952: Report* [by Sir George Seel]. N.p.: Advocate Company, n.d.

————. *The Plan for a British Caribbean Federation, Report of the Fiscal Commissioner: Presented by the Secretary of State for the Colonies to Parliament by Command of Her Majesty, December 1955.* London: Her Majesty's Stationery Office, n.d.

Constitution Commission of Trinidad and Tobago. *Report of the Constitution Commission.* N.p.: T&T P&P, 1974.

Democratic Action Congress (DAC). *DAC Manifesto Tobago House of Assembly 1984 Elections.* La Romain, Trinidad: Rahaman Printery, n.d.

————. *Guide to Change for Trinidad and Tobago.* Barataria: DAC Publishing, 1971.

————. *Tobago Development Plan (1981–1990): An Outline Plan for Total Development, Presented to the Electors for Endorsement to the Tobago House of Assembly, Nov. 24, 1980.* San Fernando: Rahaman Printery, 1980.

————. *Trinidad and Tobago Manifesto: General Elections 1976.* N.p.: DAC, 1976.

Fargo House Movement. *A People's Manifesto for the Total Development of Tobago.* N.p., n.d.

Frampton, A. deK. *Development Plan for Tobago: Report of the Team Which Visited Tobago in March/April, 1957, Development and Welfare in the West Indies.* Bulletin no. 34. Bridgetown: Advocate Company, n.d.

Hay, L. G. *A Handbook of the Island of Tobago: Being a Brief Historical, Geographical and General Account of the Island.* Georgetown: Daily Chronicle, 1899.

Orde-Browne, G. St J. *Labour Conditions in the West Indies.* London: Her Majesty's Stationery Office, 1922.

Peoples' National Movement (PNM). *Data Relating to the Question of Internal Self-Government for Tobago.* N.p.: Sultan-Khan's Litho, 1977.

———. *Election Manifesto for the Tobago House of Assembly: Monday, November 24th, 1980.* N.p.: Sultan Khan's Litho, 1980.

———. *General Elections 1971 Manifesto.* Port of Spain: PNM, 1971.

———. *Major Party Documents.* Vol. 1. Port of Spain: PNM Publishing, 1966.

———. *Perspectives for the New Society: Peoples' Charter 1956,* revised. Peoples' National Movement Special Convention. N.p.: [1970].

———. *The Political Leader's Address to the Special Convention on the Question of Local Government with Special Emphasis on the Position of Tobago.* Presented at Chaguaramas Convention Centre, 23–24 July 1977.

———. *Trinidad and Tobago Manifesto: General Elections 1976.* N.p.: n.d.

Robinson, A. N. R. *National Emergence: The Final Round – An Address by A. N. R. Robinson to the Nation.* Port of Spain: DAC Publishing, 1972.

———. *The Politics of Transformation: Address to the Trinidad and Tobago Chamber of Industry & Commerce at the Ball Room of the Hilton Hotel on Tuesday July 2, 1985.* N.p.: n.d.

———. *Tobago Internal Self-Government: Full Text of Speech by ANR Robinson in the House of Representatives on January 14, 1977. Trinidad and Tobago.* N.p.: Superb Printers, 1977.

———. *We Have Kept the Faith: Full Text of Address to the National Congress of the DAC on Sunday 9th November 1975 at the Seamen and Waterfront Workers Trade Union Hall at Wrightson Road, Port of Spain and Broadcast to the Nation.* Barataria: DAC Publishing, n.d.

Trinidad and Tobago. *Administration Report of the Director of Education for the Year 1927.* Council Paper 58 of 1928.

———. *Administration Report of the Director of Public Works for the Year 1924.* Council Paper 74 of 1925.

———. *Administration Reports of the Wardens for the Year 1914–1915.* Council Paper 14 of 1916.

———. *Annual Report, Colony of Trinidad and Tobago, 1948.* Port of Spain: Government Printing Office, 1949.

———. *Annual Report, Colony of Trinidad and Tobago, 1951.* Port of Spain: Government Printing Office, 1952.

———. *Annual Report of Trinidad and Tobago for the Year 1955.* Port of Spain: Government Printing Office, 1958.

———. *Annual Reports of Wardens for 1907–1908.* Council Paper 144 of 1908.

———. *Census 1931.* Port of Spain: Government Printing Office, 1933.

———. *Census 1946.* Port of Spain: Government Printing Office, 1948.

———. *Coastal Steamer Service: Report of a Committee Appointed "To Advise Government Whether the Existing Coastal Steamer Service between Trinidad and Tobago Is Adequate for the Present Needs"* [Nicoll Report]. Council Paper 3 of 1939.

————. *District Administration Reports for the Year 1932*. Council Paper 55 of 1933.

————. *District Administration Reports for the Year 1933*. Council Paper 83 of 1934.

————. *District Administration Reports for the Year 1934*. Council Paper 76 of 1935.

————. *District Administration Reports for the Year 1935*. Council Paper 54 of 1936.

————. *District Administration Reports for the Year 1936*. Council Paper 78 of 1937.

————. *District Administration Reports for the Year 1937*. Council Paper 82 of 1938.

————. *District Administration Reports for the Year 1950*. Port of Spain: Government Printer, 1951.

————. *District Administration Reports for the Year 1951*. Port of Spain: Government Printing Office, 1952.

————. *District Administration Reports for the Year 1952*. Port of Spain: Government Printing Office, 1954.

————. *Draft Second Five-Year Plan 1964–1968*. [Port of Spain]: National Planning Commission, n.d.

————. *Economic Survey 1958*. Port of Spain: Yuille's Printerie, 1959.

————. *Education 1800–1962: Trinidad and Tobago Independence Exhibition*. Port of Spain: Government Printing Office, 1962.

————. *Five-Year Development Programme 1958–1962*. Port of Spain: Government Printing Office, 1958.

————. *Five-Year Development Programme 1958–1962: 1958 Report*. Port of Spain: Government Printing Office, 1960.

————. *Five-Year Development Programme 1958–1962: Projects for 1959*. [Port of Spain]: Economic Planning and Development Department, 1958.

————. *Five-Year Development Programme 1958–1962: Projects for 1960*. [Port of Spain]: Economic and Planning Division, Office of the Premier, 1960.

————. *Five-Year Development Programme 1958–1962: Projects for 1961*. Port of Spain: Government Printing Office, 1961.

————. *Five-Year Development Programme 1958–1962: Projects for 1962*. Port of Spain: Government Printing Office, 1962.

————. *Five-Year Development Programme 1958–1962: Report of the Premier on Development Projects for the Year 1959*. [Port of Spain]: Office of the Premier, 1961.

————. *Five-Year Development Programme 1958–1962: Report of the Premier on Development Projects for the Year 1960*. [Port of Spain]: Office of the Premier, 1962.

————. *Five-Year Economic Programme [1950] Parts I–V*. Vol. I. N.p.: n.d.

————. *Five-Year Economic Programme 1956–60: Memorandum for 1957 Showing Progress of Work on the Course of Execution and Work Proposed for 1957*. Port of Spain: Government Printing Office, 1956.

————. *Handbook of Trinidad and Tobago*. Port of Spain: Government Printing Office, 1934.

————. *Harbour Master Administration Reports for the Year 1928*. Council Paper 23 of 1929.

————. *Historical Development of Education in Trinidad and Tobago* [1800–62]. Port of Spain: Government Printing Office, 1962.

————. *Historical Documents of Trinidad and Tobago*. No. 3, *Tobago Hurricane of 1847*. Port of Spain: Government Printing Office, 1966.

————. *Memorandum Showing Progress of Certain Development Schemes in the Colony of Trinidad and Tobago* [up to 1946]. Port of Spain: Government Printing Office, 1947.

————. *Memorandum Showing Progress of Certain Development Schemes in the Colony of Trinidad and Tobago up to 1947.* Port of Spain: Government Printing Office, 1948.

————. *Memorandum Showing Progress of Certain Development Schemes in the Colony of Trinidad and Tobago up to 1948.* Port of Spain: Government Printing Office, 1949.

————. *Memorandum Showing Progress of Certain Development Schemes in the Colony of Trinidad and Tobago up to 1949 and Work Proposed for the Year 1950.* Port of Spain: Government Printing Office, 1949.

————. *Public Works Department Administration Reports for the Year 1928.* Council Paper 58 of 1929.

————. *Register of Business Establishments Employing 10 or More Persons as at November 1970.* Port of Spain: CSO, 1973.

————. *Report of Committee for the Re-organization of the Administrative Arrangements of Tobago.* March 1957.

————. *Report of the Committee Appointed to Enquire into the Medical and Health Policy of the Colony* (Part 1). *Memorandum on the Above Report* (Part 2). Council Paper 65 of 1944.

————. *Report of the Director of Medical Services for the Year 1938.* Council Paper 95 of 1939.

————. *Report of the Tobago Planning Team.* Port of Spain: CSO Printing Unit, 1963.

————. *Report on the Election of Members to the Federal House of Representatives from the Territory of Trinidad and Tobago.* Port of Spain: Government Printing Office, 1960.

————. *Report on the Legislative Council General Election 1946.* Port of Spain: Guardian Commercial Printery, 1947.

————. *Report on the Legislative Council General Elections 1950.* Port of Spain: Government Printing Office, 1954.

————. *Report on the Parliamentary General Elections 1961.* Port of Spain: Government Printing Office, 1962.

————. *Report on the Parliamentary General Elections 1966.* Port of Spain: Government Printery, 1967.

————. *Report on the Parliamentary General Elections 1971.* Port of Spain: Elections and Boundaries Printing Section, 1972.

————. *Report on the Parliamentary General Elections 1976.* Port of Spain: Elections and Boundaries Commission Printing Section, 1977.

————. *Reports of the District Administration for the Year 1947.* Port of Spain: Government Printing Office, 1948.

————. *Reports of the District Administration for the Year 1948.* Port of Spain: Government Printing Office, 1949.

————. *Reports of the District Administration for the Year 1949.* Port of Spain: Government Printing Office, 1950.

————. *Reports of the Wardens for the Year 1906–1907.* Council Paper 149 of 1907.

————. *Reports of the Wardens for the Year 1908–1909.* Council Paper 147 of 1909.

————. *Reports of the Wardens for the Year 1909–1910.* Council Paper 140 of 1910.

————. *Reports of the Wardens for the Year 1910–1911.* Council Paper 194 of 1911.

————. *Reports of the Wardens for the Year 1911–1912.* Council Paper 184 of 1912.

————. *Reports of the Wardens for the Year 1912–1913.* Council Paper 18 of 1914.

————. *Report to the Honourable the Premier by the Honourable Ulric Lee on the Reorganisation of the Public Service.* Port of Spain: Government Printing Office, 1959.

————. *Second Five-Year Plan 1964–1968: Modifications to Draft Plan, as Approved by Parliament in November, 1963.* N.p.: n.d.

————. *Ten-Year Development Scheme.* Port of Spain: Government Printing Office, 1946.

————. *Third Five-Year Plan 1969–1973: As Approved by Parliament.* N.p., n.d.

————. *Tobago Producers' Association Limited: Report of an Inquiry by the Treasurer into the Constitution, Working and Financial Condition of the Association.* Council Paper 22 of 1938.

————. *Wardens' Reports for 1904–5.* Council Paper 135 of 1905.

————. *Wardens' Reports for 1905–6.* Council Paper 144 of 1906.

————. *Wardens' Reports for the Year 1916.* Council Paper 92 of 1917.

————. *Wardens' Administration Reports for the Year 1917.* Council Paper 103 of 1918.

————. *Wardens' Administration Reports for the Year 1918.* Council Paper 103 of 1919.

————. *Wardens' Administration Reports for the Year 1919.* Council Paper 115 of 1920.

————. *Wardens' Administration Reports for the Year 1920.* Council Paper 116 of 1921.

————. *Wardens' Administration Reports for the Year 1921.* Council Paper 73 of 1922.

————. *Wardens' Administration Reports for the Year 1922.* Council Paper 59 of 1923.

————. *Wardens' Administration Reports for the Year 1923.* Council Paper 66 of 1924.

————. *Wardens' Administration Reports for the Year 1924.* Council Paper 65 of 1925.

————. *Wardens' Administration Reports for the Year 1925.* Council Paper 66 of 1926.

————. *Wardens' Administration Reports for the Year 1926.* Council Paper 53 of 1927.

————. *Wardens' Administration Reports for the Year 1927.* Council Paper 82 of 1928.

————. *Wardens' Administration Reports for the Year 1928.* Council Paper 74 of 1929.

————. *Wardens' Administration Reports for the Year 1929.* Council Paper 58 of 1930.

————. *Wardens' Administration Reports for the Year 1930.* Council Paper 50 of 1931.

————. *Wardens' Administration Reports for the Year 1931.* Council Paper 54 of 1932.

Trinidad and Tobago, CSO. *An Analysis of Government Revenue and Expenditure 1966–1971.* Port of Spain: CSO Printing Unit, 1974.

————. *1970 Population Census: Bulletin No. 1.* Port of Spain: CSO Printing Unit, 1971.

Trinidad and Tobago, Local Government Department. *Annual Administration Report 1957.* Port of Spain: Government Printing Office, 1959.

————. *Annual Administration Report 1958.* Port of Spain: Government Printing Office, 1960.

————. *1970 Population Census: Bulletin No. 1A.* Port of Spain: CSO Printing Unit, 1974.

Trinidad and Tobago [Republic]. *Accounting for the Petrodollar 1973–1983.* Trinidad: Government Printery, 1984.

Trinidad and Tobago [Republic], CSO. *1980 Population and Housing Census.* Bulletin no. 1. Port of Spain: CSO Printing Unit, 1981.

————. *1990 Population and Housing Census.* Vol. 1, Part 1, *Administrative Report.* Port of Spain: Office of the Prime Minister, CSO, 1993.

————. *1990 Population and Housing Census.* Vol. 2, *Demographic Report.* Port of Spain: Office of the Prime Minister, CSO, 1993.

————. *Statistics at a Glance 1996.* Port of Spain: CSO Printing Unit, 1997.

Trinidad and Tobago [Republic], Ministry of Finance (Maintenance). *Report of Ministerial Committee on Certain Problem Areas in Tobago,* June 1979.

Trinidad and Tobago Industrial Development Corporation. *Special Incentives for the Promotion of Light Manufacturing Industries in Tobago, with Emphasis on Small Business and Co-operatives.* Port of Spain: The Corp., 1977.

United Labour Front. *Trinidad and Tobago Election Manifesto 1976, United Labour Front.* N.p.: n.d.

Wood, E. F. L. *Report by the Honourable E. F. L. Wood, MP (Parliamentary Under-Secretary of State for the Colonies), on His Visit to the West Indies and British Guiana, Dec. 1921–Feb. 1922.* London: His Majesty's Stationery Office, 1922.

Newspapers and Magazines

Evening News, 1969

Express, 1969–79

Gleaner, 1961

People, 1981

Sunday Express, 1980

Sunday Guardian, 1961–72

Sunday Mirror, 1964

Nation, 1960

New Era, 1889

Tobago Gazette, 1888–98

Tobagonian, 1938–48

Trinidad Guardian, 1948–73

Weekend Express, 1969

C. Secondary Sources

Abrahams, Roger D. "Public Drama and Common Values in Two Caribbean Islands". Offprint no. 82, Institute of Latin American Studies, University of Texas at Austin. Reprinted from *Trans-action* (July–August 1968), 62–71.

Action Committee of Dedicated Citizens. *The Road to Freedom.* San Fernando, CA: Vanguard Publishing, 1970.

Anthony, Michael. *Historical Dictionary of Trinidad and Tobago.* Lanham, MD: Scarecrow Press, 1997.

————. *Towns and Villages of Trinidad and Tobago.* Port of Spain: Circle Press, 1988.

Archibald, Douglas. *Tobago "Melancholy Isle".* Vol. 1, *1498–1771.* Port of Spain: Westindiana, 1987.

Bennett, Herman L. "The Challenge to the Post-Colonial State: A Case Study of the February Revolution in Trinidad". In *The Modern Caribbean,* edited by Franklin W. Knight and Colin Palmer, 129–46. Chapel Hill: University of North Carolina Press, 1989.

Blackette, C. R. "The Len Han: Tobago's Traditional Fold Co-operative". In *Conference on Culture and the Cultural Heritage*. Scarborough, Tobago: n.p., 1984.

Bobb-Lewis, Verlene. "Proverbs". In *Conference on Culture and the Cultural Heritage*. Scarborough, Tobago: n.p., 1984.

Brereton, Bridget. *A History of Modern Trinidad 1783–1962*. Oxford: Heinemann International, 1981.

———. *Law, Justice and Empire: The Colonial Career of John Gorrie 1829–1892*. Kingston: University of the West Indies Press, 1997.

———. "Post Emancipation Protest in the Caribbean: The 'Belmanna Riots' in Tobago, 1876". *Caribbean Quarterly* 30 (1984): 110–23.

Campbell, Carl. "Tobago and Trinidad: Problems of Alignment of Their Education Systems at Union: 1889–1931". *Antilia* 1, no. 3 (April 1987): 21–27.

Carmichael, Gertrude. *The History of the West Indian Islands of Trinidad and Tobago 1498–1900*. London: Alvin Redman, 1961.

Carrington, Selwyn H. H. "The Union of Tobago and Trinidad: The Emergence of Underdevelopment and Dependency". In *Forging a New Democracy*, edited by Ralph Sebastien, 55–66. Freeport, Trinidad: HEM Printers, 1985.

Casserly, F. L. "Canadian National Steamships to Call at Tobago". *Commercial Intelligence Journal* 1337 (14 September 1929), 393–95.

Citizens' Committee for the Defence of Human Rights. *Internal Self-Government for Tobago*. N.p.: Camalas Business Services, n.d.

Conference on Culture and the Cultural Heritage. Scarborough, Tobago: n.p., 1984.

Constitution Commission of Trinidad and Tobago. *Addresses of Members of the Commission Delivered at the National Convention* (presented at Chaguaramas Convention Centre, March–May 1973).

Craig, Hewan. *The Legislative Council of Trinidad and Tobago*. London: Faber & Faber, 1952.

Craig, Susan E. *Community Development in Trinidad and Tobago, 1943–1973: From Welfare to Patronage*. Working Paper no. 4. St Augustine, Trinidad: Institute of Social and Economic Research, University of the West Indies, 1974.

Davidson, J. G. *Tobago Versus P.N.M.* Woodbrook, Trinidad: Beacon Publishing, 1979.

Dowdy, Frank A. *Supplement to the Report on Some Observations of Tobago's Economic Progress*. [Port of Spain]: n.p., 1966.

Elder, J. D. "The Dependence Syndrome: Tobago as a Special Case with Reference to the Areas of Politics and Economics". In *Forging a New Democracy*, edited by Ralph Sebastien, 67–71. Freeport, Trinidad: HEM Printers, 1985.

———. "Tobago Folk Songs". In *Conference on Culture and the Cultural Heritage*. Scarborough, Tobago: 1984.

———. "The Tobago Reel Dance". In *Conference on Culture and the Cultural Heritage*. Scarborough, Tobago: 1984.

———. "Tobago's Peculiar Culture". In *Conference on Culture and the Cultural Heritage*. Scarborough, Tobago: 1984.

Gellner, Ernest. *Nations and Nationalism*. Ithaca, NY: Cornell University Press, 1983.

Harewood, Jack. "Estimates of Internal Migration and of Current Population Distribution in Trinidad and Tobago". *CSO Research Papers* no. 3 (June 1967): 45–75.

Higgins, George E. *A History of Trinidad Oil*. Port of Spain: n.p., 1996.

Holt, Thomas C. *The Problem of Freedom: Race, Labor, and Politics in Jamaica and Britain, 1832–1938*. Baltimore: Johns Hopkins University Press, 1992.

Hroch, Miroslav. *Social Preconditions of National Revival in Europe: A Comparative Analysis of the Social Composition of Patriotic Groups Among the Smaller European Nations*. Translated by Ben Fowkes. London: Cambridge University Press, 1985.

James, Winford. "Tobagonian Dialectology: Form and Character". In *Conference on Culture and the Cultural Heritage*. Scarborough, Tobago: 1984.

Kingsbury, Robert C. *Commercial Geography of Trinidad and Tobago*. Technical report no. 4. Bloomington: Department of Geography, Indiana University, 1960.

Laurence, K. O. *Tobago in Wartime 1792–1815*. Kingston: University of the West Indies Press, 1995.

Levitt, Kari, and Lloyd Best. "Character of Caribbean Economy". In *Caribbean Economy: Dependence and Backwardness*, edited by George L. Beckford, 34–60. Kingston: Institute of Social and Economic Research, University of the West Indies, 1975.

[Lewis, W. E. B.]. *History of Tobago from Fifteenth Century to Present*. N.p.: n.d.

London, Clement B. G. "Forging a Cultural Identity: Leadership and Development in Mass Education in a Developing Caribbean Country". *Journal of Black Studies* 21, no. 2 (December 1990): 251–67.

Meditz, Sandra W., et al. *Islands of the Commonwealth Caribbean: A Regional Study*. Washington, DC: US Government Printing Office, 1989.

Meikle, H. B. "Tobago Villagers in the Mirror of Dialect". *Caribbean Quarterly* 4, no. 2 (December 1995): 154–60.

Microsoft Encarta 2000. "Trinidad and Tobago".

Niddrie, David L. "Kaye Dowland's Book: A Record of Mid-Nineteenth Century Tobago". *Caribbean Quarterly* 9, no. 4 (1963): 44–51.

———. *Land Use and Population in Tobago: An Environmental Study*. N.p.: Geographical Publications, 1961.

———. *Tobago*. Middleton: Litho Press, 1980.

Nunes, F. E. "A Ministry and Its Community: Tobago – A Case Study in Participation". *Social and Economic Studies* 23, no. 2 (June 1974):176–85.

Ottley, C. R. *The Complete History of the Island of Tobago in the West Indies*. Port of Spain: Guardian Commercial Printery, [1950].

———. "How They Dance the Reel in Tobago". *Tobagonian*, June 1941, 19–22.

———. *The Story of Tobago: Robinson Crusoe's Island in the Caribbean*. Trinidad: Longman Caribbean, 1973.

———. *Tobago Legends and West Indian Lore*. Georgetown: *Daily Chronicle*, 1950.

———. *Tobago: Robinson Crusoe's Island in the West Indies*. [Port of Spain]: PNM Publishing, 1969.

Pantin, Raoul. "The Man From Castara, Tobago: A Moses Leading His People to the Promised Land?" *Caribbean Affairs* 1, no. 1 (1988): 161–71.

Past and Present in Tobago. N.p.: n.d.

Pemberton, Rita. "The Emergence of a Peasantry in Tobago and Its Impact on the

Colony of Trinidad and Tobago 1838–1950". *Antilia* 1, no. 3 (April 1987): 38–49.

Phillips, Andre. *Governor Fargo: A Short Biography of Alphonso Philbert Theophilus James.* [Scarborough]: Tobago Printery, [1994].

Premdas, Ralph R. "The Caribbean: Ethnic and Cultural Diversity and a Typology of Identities". In *Identity, Ethnicity and Culture in the Caribbean*, edited by Ralph R. Premdas, 3–12. St Augustine, Trinidad: School of Continuing Studies, University of the West Indies, [1999].

————. "Ethnic Conflict and Levels of Identity in the Caribbean: Deconstructing a Myth". In *Ethnicity, Race and Nationality in the Caribbean*, edited by Juan Manuel Carrion, 11–36. San Juan, PR: Institute of Caribbean Studies, 1997.

————. "Identity and Secession in Nevis". In *Identity, Ethnicity and Culture in the Caribbean*, edited by Ralph R. Premdas, 447–84. St Augustine, Trinidad: School of Continuing Studies, University of the West Indies, [1999].

————. "Public Policy and Ethnic Conflict". *Management of Social Transformations (MOST)*. Discussion paper series no. 12. UNESCO, 1997.

————. *Secession and Self-Determination in the Caribbean: Nevis and Tobago.* St Augustine, Trinidad: School of Continuing Studies, University of the West Indies, 1998.

Premdas, Ralph R., and Hugh Williams. "Tobago: The Quest for Self-Determination in the Caribbean". *Canadian Review of Studies in Nationalism* 19, nos. 1–2 (1992): 117–27.

Ragoonath, Bishnu. *Development in Tobago: Twentieth Century Challenges.* St Augustine, Trinidad: School of Continuing Studies, University of the West Indies, 1997.

Richardson, Bonham C. *Economy and Environment in the Caribbean: Barbados and the Windwards in the Late 1800s.* Kingston: University of the West Indies Press, 1997.

Robinson, A. N. R. *The Mechanics of Independence: Patterns of Political and Economic Transformation in Trinidad and Tobago.* Cambridge, MA: MIT Press, 1971.

————. *The Politics of Transformation: Address to the Trinidad and Tobago Chamber of Industry & Commerce at the Ball Room of the Hilton Hotel on Tuesday July 2, 1985.* N.p.: n.d.

————. "Unity and Change in the Caribbean Region". In *Forging a New Democracy*, edited by Raphael Sebastien, 33–54. Freeport, Trinidad: HEM Printers, 1985.

Ryan, Selwyn. *The Disillusioned Electorate.* Port of Spain: Inprint, 1975.

————. *The Politics of Succession: A Study of Parties and Politics in Trinidad and Tobago.* St Augustine, Trinidad: University of the West Indies, [1978].

————. *Race and Nationalism in Trinidad and Tobago.* Toronto: University of Toronto Press, 1972.

————. *Revolution and Reaction: Parties and Politics in Trinidad and Tobago 1970–1981.* St Augustine, Trinidad: Institute of Social and Economic Research, University of the West Indies, 1989.

————. "Tobago's Quest for Autonomy: From Colony to Ward to . . .". *Caribbean Review* 14, no. 2 (1985): 7–9, 38–39.

————. "Trinidad and Tobago: The General Elections of 1976". *Caribbean Studies* 19, nos. 1–2 (April–July 1979): 5–32.

Ryan, Selwyn, et al. *The Confused Electorate: A Study of Political Attitudes and Opinions in Trinidad and Tobago.* St Augustine, Trinidad: Institute of Social and Economic Research, University of the West Indies, 1979.

Samaroo, Brinsley. "Towards a New System of Popular Government: Proposals for the Devolution of the Political and Administrative Systems of Trinidad and Tobago". In *Forging a New Democracy,* edited by Ralph Sebastien, 158–69. Freeport, Trinidad: HEM Printers, 1985.

Scruton, Roger. *A Dictionary of Political Thought.* New York: Harper and Row, 1982.

Shaw, Gregory, ed. *A. N. R. Robinson, Caribbean Man: Selected Speeches from a Political Career 1960–1986.* Port of Spain: Inprint, 1986.

Smith, Anthony D. "The Myth of the 'Modern Nation' and the Myths of Nations". *Ethnic and Racial Studies* 11, no. 1 (January 1988).

———. "Nationalism: A Trend Report and Bibliography". *Current Sociology* 21, no. 3 (1973).

———. "The Origins of Nations". *Ethnic and Racial Studies* 12, no. 3 (July 1989): 341–67.

Tobago Educational Review (1972).

Tobago Improvement Corporation. *An Outline for the Improvement of Tobago, W. I. in Twelve Main Departments.* London: [by the author], 1969.

Will, H. A. "Colonial Policy and Economic Development in the British West Indies, 1895–1903". *Economic History Review* 23 (April 1970): 129–47.

Williams, Eric. *Forged from the Love of Liberty: Selected Speeches of Dr Eric Williams.* Trinidad: Longman Caribbean, 1981

———. *History of the People of Trinidad and Tobago.* London: Andre Deutsch, 1963.

Woodcock, Henry Isles. *A History of Tobago.* Ayr: Smith and Grant, 1867. Reprint, London: Frank Cass, 1971.

Yelvington, Kevin A. "Vote Dem Out: The Demise of the PNM in Trinidad and Tobago". *Caribbean Review* 15, no. 4 (Spring 1987): 8–14.

Zabaida, Sami. "Nations: Old and New, Comments on Anthony D. Smith's 'The Myth of the "Modern Nation" and the Myths of Nations'". *Ethnic and Racial Studies* 12, no. 3 (July 1989).

Unpublished Papers, Theses and Dissertations

Craig-James, Susan. "The Evolution of Society in Tobago: 1838 to 1900". PhD diss., London School of Economics and Political Science, University of London, 1995.

———. "Milch Cow or Hard Sucking Calf: The Joining of Trinidad and Tobago and Its Aftermath, 1884–1948". Paper presented at the conference Tobago and Trinidad: One Hundred Years Together, University of the West Indies, St Augustine, Trinidad. 16–18 October 1998.

Douglin, Monica Yula Dolores. "A History of Tobago: 1815–1854". MA thesis, University of the West Indies, St Augustine, 1986.

Dylan, Antoine. "A History of the Tobago House of Assembly". Caribbean Studies Project, University of the West Indies, St Augustine, 1989–90.

George, Jean. "The Effectiveness of Development Administration Within the Constitutional Framework of the Tobago House of Assembly". University of the West Indies, St Augustine.

La Guerre, John Gaffar. "The General Elections of 1946 in Trinidad and Tobago".

Laurence, K. O. "Council, Assembly and Taxation in Tobago, 1793–1815". Paper presented at the Association of Caribbean Historians conference, University of the West Indies, St Augustine, Trinidad, 1–6 April 1990.

Luke, Learie B. "A. P. T. James and the Union between Tobago and Trinidad: 1946–1961". Paper presented at the conference Tobago and Trinidad: One Hundred Years Together, University of the West Indies, St Augustine, Trinidad. 16–18 October 1998.

———. "Tobago's Struggle for Internal Self-Government 1970–1980". MA thesis, Morgan State University, 1992.

Ottley, C. R. "Constitutional Changes in Tobago from House of Assembly 1770 to House of Assembly 1980". 1980.

Premdas, Ralph R. "Ethnic Identity in the Caribbean: Decentering a Myth". Keynote address to Association for the Study of Ethnicity and Nationalism, London School of Economics and Political Science, 21 March 1995.

———. "Nevis: Ethno-Regional Identity and Secession in the Caribbean". Monograph.

Pyde, Peter. "Livelihoods, Inequality and Collective Identity in Tobago, West Indies". PhD diss., University of Toronto, 1995.

Index

Murray, Winston: break with DAC, 43; criticisms of THA bill, 275; and elections, 247; and motion for internal self-government, 251, 253; radical views of, 44; and secession, 267; as separatist parliamentarian, 38

Nathan, N., 107
Nation, 195
National Emergency Relief Organization, 218
National Joint Action Congress (NJAC), 244
Nicholson, Pamela, 272
Nicoll, J. F., 159
Nicoll Report. *See* Sea Communications Committee Report
Niddrie, David, 13, 24
Nock, W. C., 114–15
Norton, Rhodil, 39, 200, 233, 233–43 passim, 276, 281n30
Nylon Pool, 29

Ogieste, James Ivan, 276
old representative system, 48, 51, 93
Oliver, S., 76, 90, 96
Orde Brown, Granville St John, 36
Orde, T. L. M., 122–23
Order in Council: of 1763, 4; of 1885, 7, 56; of 1888 uniting Tobago and Trinidad, 64–65, 69–70, 81, 97; of 1898 making Tobago a ward, 106–7, 154
Ordinance to provide for the receipt in Tobago . . . of deeds, 109
Orlando, 241
Owen, A. Douglass, 112

Padmore, Overand, 253, 257
Panday, Basdeo, 268
Paris, Treaty of, 3, 4, 6
Parlatuvier, 120, 142, 170, 262
Parliament, 247–76 passim
Patience Hill, 168
peasantry: access to Trinidad market, 68; affected by disruption of steamer

service, 139; and economic activity, 3, 14, 26; formation of, 35; industry of, 36, 292; status of, 26
People's National Movement (PNM): and A. P. T. James, 187–200 passim; colonial mentality of, 195; convention in 1970; government of, 37–38; defeat in Tobago, 222; and development of Tobago, 187, 201–33 passim; interest in Tobago, 221; and internal self-government, 243–76 passim; and promises to Tobago, 43
permanent secretary for Tobago affairs, 209–18 passim
Peters, Louis A., 174, 180
petition: to accept Seemungal Draft Bill, 271; for druggist exam in Tobago, 128; by Mercantile Firms and others, 60; to re-establish office of clerk of the peace, 118–19; by residents of Tobago in 1899 regarding land deeds, 107–9;
Pigeon Peak, 2
Pitt, Benjamin L. Basil, 235–37, 241,
Plagemann, C. L., 87, 92–93
Planning and Housing Commission, 165
Plymouth, 138
Port of Spain: concentration of power in, 64; creole population, 25; government bureaucracy in, 263; harbour of, 155; jetty of, 139, 160; seat of government, 101; travel to 143–44
Premdas, Ralph R., 9, 10, 278n10
Prescott, Joseph, 75
Public Opinion, 77
Public Service Commission, 217

Queen's Royal College, 27, 132–33, 158

Radcliffe, Joe, 22
Ragoonath, Bishnu, 229
Rance, Hubert, 178, 181–83
Rapsey, John Alfred, 158
Rawson, Rawson William, 49–50

Red Cross Society: Tobago branch of, 268
reel dance, 34
Report of Committee for the Re-Organization of the Administrative Arrangements of Tobago, 204–7, 209, 219
Report of the Tobago Planning Team, 229, 231
resolution to secretary of state for the colonies: by Tobago Planters Association, 134–35
Richardson, Selwyn, 257, 267
Ripon, Lord, 88, 98
Roach, Eric, 25–28, 243
road(s): appeal to improve, 170; Arnos Vale, 151; Charlotteville-Speyside main, 137; conditions of, 69, 137, 154, 230, 264; construction/extension/repair of, 138; Culloden, 151; Des Vignes, 151; lack of proper, 186; from Moriah to Charlotteville, 176; from Parlatuvier to Charlotteville, 152; North Coast, 170, 189, 196, 202, 226; Northside main, 137; to provide access to beaches, 238; provision of adequate, 224; Windward main, 137–38
Roberts, S. E., 180
Robinson, A. N. R.: advocacy by, 129; cabinet positions of, 202; and devolution of power, 10; and federal legislature, 195; and general elections in 1961, 199; as integrationist, 202; and internal self-government, 39–40, 243–76; as minister of state, 238; and petroleum offshore Tobago, 40; and PNM manifesto, 221, 260; and representation in national institutions, 43; resignation from PNM, 216, 241; and right to self-determination, 38–39; on Trinidadians' view of Tobago
Robinson, Lionel M., 241, 254
Robinson, William, 55, 57–58, 62, 70–79
Rogers, P., 220–21
Rousseau, James T.: and administrative

impact of union, 111; advocacy for greater powers, 109–13; appointed warden, 107, 115–16; claims made by, 134; commendation of, 109; sentiments of, 206; and Tobago identity, 110
Rowbottom, R. S., 115
Roxborough: cargo facilities, 119; construction of district hospital, 119, 123; health facilities, 231; magistrate's travel to, 119; main road of, 120; market in, 141; riot, 6, 51; steamer service to, 159; typhoid outbreak in, 149
Royal Commission. *See* West Indian Royal Commission; Commissioner Crossman
Royal Mail Steam Packet Company (steamers), 57, 79, 87, 121–23
Ryan, Selwyn, 24, 25, 280n29

Sandy Point, 117–18
Scarborough: as alternative port, 62; breakwater of, 162; cargo facilities of, 119; Colonial Hospital of, 141, 154, 231; commercial class, 142; Customs House of, 143; development of harbour, 190; distance from Charlotteville, 137; District Hospital, 153, 171–72; fire station of, 141; jetty of, 153, 161; Legislative Council meeting, 58; phone calls to, 164; Poor House, 12; port of call, 161; public latrine in, 117–18; water supply of, 123; wharf of, 220; wireless station in, 142
Scarborough Development Plan, 263
Scarlet Ibis (steamer), 170, 190, 227
schools: built, 202, 231–32; Delaford R. C., 163; dilapidated, 172; elementary at Bon Accord and Montgomery, 173; Franklyn Methodist, 163; James's Foundation, 173; Mason Hall Government, 163; Patience Hill Roman Catholic, 163; recommendation for a trade; 173; request to build in Roxborough, 172; types of, 278n5

supply for, 120; image of, 171; industrial development of, 173–74; Legislative Assembly of, 5; Legislative Council of, 4, 6,53, 55–58, 63; legislature of, 55–56; local government of, 4; location and size of, 2; migration from, 283n81; need to separate from Trinidad, 190; official view of, 170; oil deposits of, 261; parishes of, 4; population of, 220; pride of, 146; problems of class and race in, 68; relationship with Trinidad, 1; religious diversity of, 280n29; school crisis of 1930, 144–45; seats in legislature of, 177, 198; social stratification of, 24; tourism of, 23, 27, 43, 175, 188, 196, 230, 239, 240, 260; uneven development of, 223; villages of, 31; white population of, 5, 31, 283n81

Tobago Advisory Board, 206
Tobago Affairs Committee, 238
Tobago Banking Services Limited, 261
Tobago Chamber of Commerce, 165, 180, 191, 196, 235, 268
Tobago Christian Council of Churches, 268
Tobago Citizens and Economic Party (TCPEP), 174–87 passim, 208
Tobago Committee for the Defence of Human Rights, 268–69
Tobago County Council, 178–80; 206, 238, 264, 272
Tobago Development Company, 164,
Tobago Development Programme, 188, 199, 206, 223
Tobago District Agricultural Society, 165, 180
Tobago Emancipation Action Committee, 239–40
Tobago Garment Factory, 261
Tobago Gazette, 58
Tobago Government Farm, 155, 164;
Tobago House of Assembly: Act of, 275; bill of, 272–74; and dominant class, 5; elections of, 275; re-establishment

of, 9, 250; relations with central government, 276; resolution to dissolve union, 178; and self-government, 4
Tobago Independence Movement (TIM), 191–99
Tobago Island Council, 4, 265–66, 269–70, 272
Tobago Lime Growers Association, 141
Tobago Metal Fabricating Company Limited, 261
Tobago News, 73, 77
Tobago Peasant Proprietors Association, 163
Tobago Planters Association (TPA), 117–24, 134–37
Tobago Producers Co-operative Association, 153
Tobago Sea Communications Committee, 140
Tobago Women's League, 268
Tobago Youth Council, 268
Tobagonian, 157, 167, 168
Tobagonian(s): African descent of, 29; arts of, 34; and birth certificates, 263, 265, 267; complaints of, 10, 11, 19, 31; cooperative work of, 33; crafts of, 34; cultural values of, 29–31; dialect of, 20; endogamy in, 32; and East Indians, 24, 44, 74, 253, 263; family of, 30; grievances of, 40–44; home ownership of, 35; and independence, 192; and land, 23; landownership of, 35–36; manhood of, 35; neglection complex of, 182–83; and religions, 14; representation on Executive Council, 134, 179; representation on Legislative Council, 70, 126; representation on policy-making committees/boards/ institutions, 130; representation in union, 186; seen as minority group, 180–81; support of PNM, 221–22; treated as second class citizens, 234, 237; view of Trinidadians, 9, 21–23, 27